Music in the Classical World

Music in the Classical World: Genre, Culture, and History provides a broad sociocultural and historical perspective of the music of the Classical Period as it relates to the world in which it was created. It establishes a background on the time span—1725 to 1815—offering a context for the music made during one of the more vibrant periods of achievement in history. Outlining how music interacted with society, politics, and the arts of that time, this kaleidoscopic approach presents an overview of how the various genres expanded during the period, not just in the major musical centers but also around the globe. Contemporaneous treatises and commentary documenting these changes are integrated into the narrative.

Features include the following:

- A complete course with musical scores on the companion website, plus links to recordings—and no need to purchase a separate anthology
- The development of style and genres within a broader historical framework
- Extensive musical examples from a wide range of composers, considered in context of the genre
- A thorough collection of illustrations, iconography, and art relevant to the music of the age
- Source documents translated by the author
- Valuable student learning aids throughout, including a timeline, a register of people and dates, sidebars of political importance, and a selected reading list arranged by chapter and topic
- A companion website featuring scores of all music discussed in the text, recordings of most musical examples, and tips for listening

Music in the Classical World: Genre, Culture, and History tells the story of classical music through eighteenth-century eyes, exposing readers to the wealth of music and musical styles of the time and providing a glimpse into that vibrant and active world of the Classical Period.

Bertil van Boer is Professor of Musicology-Theory and former Dean of the College of the Fine and Performing Arts at Western Washington University, USA.

Music in the Classical World
Genre, Culture, and History

Bertil van Boer

First published 2019
by Routledge
52 Vanderbilt Avenue, New York, NY 10017

and by Routledge
2 Park Square, Milton Park, Abingdon, Oxon, OX14 4RN

Routledge is an imprint of the Taylor & Francis Group, an informa business

© 2019 Taylor & Francis

The right of Bertil van Boer to be identified as author of this work has been asserted by him in accordance with sections 77 and 78 of the Copyright, Designs and Patents Act 1988.

All rights reserved. No part of this book may be reprinted or reproduced or utilised in any form or by any electronic, mechanical, or other means, now known or hereafter invented, including photocopying and recording, or in any information storage or retrieval system, without permission in writing from the publishers.

Trademark notice: Product or corporate names may be trademarks or registered trademarks, and are used only for identification and explanation without intent to infringe.

Library of Congress Cataloging-in-Publication Data
Names: Van Boer, Bertil H., author.
Title: Music in the classical world : genre, culture, and history / Bertil van Boer.
Description: New York ; London : Routledge, 2019. | Includes bibliographical references and index.
Identifiers: LCCN 2018045676 (print) | LCCN 2018048602 (ebook) |
 ISBN 9781315145570 (ebook) | ISBN 9781138503830 (hardback) |
 ISBN 9781138503847 (pbk.)
Subjects: LCSH: Music—18th century—History and criticism.
Classification: LCC ML196 (ebook) | LCC ML196 .V35 2019 (print) |
 DDC 780.9/033—dc23
LC record available at https://lccn.loc.gov/2018045676

ISBN: 978-1-138-50383-0 (hbk)
ISBN: 978-1-138-50384-7 (pbk)
ISBN: 978-1-315-14557-0 (ebk)

Typeset in Sabon
by Apex CoVantage, LLC

Visit the companion website: www.routledge.com/cw/vanboer

Timeline of Important Works, Composers, and World Events

1720   Benedetto Marcello publishes *Il Teatro alla moda*.
           The Duke of Savoy, Victorio Amadeo, trades Austrian Naples and Sicily for Sardinia.
1722   Jean-Philippe Rameau publishes his *Traité de l'harmonie*.
1725   The Concerts Spirituels established in Paris.
           Johann Adolph Hasse's serenata *Antonio et Cleopatra* premieres in Naples.
           Peter the Great dies in Russia.
1727   George II becomes King of the United Kingdom to Handel's *Coronation Anthems*.
1728   John Gay's *The Beggar's Opera* premieres in London.
           Benedetto Marcello publishes his cantata *Cassandra* in Venice as an example of music drama.
1730   The Riddarhus public concerts are established in Stockholm by Johan Helmich Roman.
           Pietro Metastasio becomes court poet in Vienna.
1731   Laura Bassi is appointed as Professor of Anatomy at the University of Bologna as the first woman to hold academic rank in Europe.
1732   Joseph Haydn is born in Austria.
1733   War of the Polish Succession begins, with Austria and Russia opposing France and Spain.
           Giovanni Pergolesi's intermezzo *La serva padrona* premieres in Naples.
1734   Fire destroys the music archives at the Capilla Real in Madrid.
1735   Charles of Bourbon drives out the Austrians from Naples and reestablishes musical ties to Spain.
           Peace treaty with Austria results in Louis XV obtaining Alsace and Spain Naples and the Two Sicilies.
           First ballad opera is performed in Charleston in the Carolina colony of North America.
1736   Pergolesi dies suddenly near Naples from tuberculosis.
           Pope Clement XII publishes an encyclical against freemasonry.
1737   The Vitterhetsakademie (Academy of Sciences) is established in Stockholm.
           Rameau's opera *Castor et Pollux* premieres in Paris.
           Title of the Duke of Tuscany passes to the Austrian crown after the death of Gian Gastone de Medici.
           Teatro San Carlo opens in Naples as the principal opera house.
1738   Domenico Scarlatti publishes his *30 Essercizi*.
           The Hamburg opera goes bankrupt and closes.
1739   German composer Reinhard Keiser dies in Hamburg.
1740   Maria Theresia becomes Holy Roman Empress in Vienna (though without coronation).
           Frederick II (the Great) crowned King of Prussia in Berlin and invades Silesia to begin the War of the Austrian Succession.
           Viceroyalty of New Granada is formed from the northern portions of the Viceroyalty of Peru.
           The Berlin School is inaugurated with Carl Philipp Emanuel Bach, Johann and Carl Graun, and others brought to the German capital by Frederick.

1741	Christoph Willibald von Gluck's opera *Artaserse* premieres in Milan.
	John Immyns establishes the Madrigal Society in London.
	Antonio Vivald and Johann Joseph Fux die in Vienna.
1742	George Frédéric Handel's oratorio *Messiah* premieres in Dublin.
	The German Singspiel is inaugurated in Berlin and Hamburg with a translated version of the ballad opera *The Devil to Pay*.
	Opera houses open in Berlin and Mannheim.
	Public outdoors concerts are established during the summer at Ranleigh Gardens in London.
1744	Franz Xaver Richter publishes his *12 Grands Symphonies* in Paris.
1745	Elector Carl Theodor in Mannheim hires Johann Stamitz as concertmaster.
	Rameau's *Platée* premieres in Paris.
1746	Frederick builds the palace of Sans Souci in Potsdam.
	Gluck visits London and competes with Handel.
	Bonnie Prince Charlie's attempt to overthrow English rule in Scotland fails at Culloden.
1747	Handel's *Judas Maccabeus* premieres in London.
	Johann Sebastian Bach composes the *Musical Offering* for Frederick in Berlin.
	The pasticcio *Syrinx* is performed as the first Swedish language opera in Stockholm.
1748	War of the Austrian Succession ends with the Treaty of Aix-la-Chapelle.
	The Holywell Rooms open in Oxford, England, as a public concert venue
	Samuel Richardson's novel *Clarissa* published in London.
1750	Johann Sebastian Bach dies in Leipzig.
	Denis Diderot and Jean le Rond d'Alembert begin their work on the monumental *Encyclopédie*.
	India, Britain, and China all compete as centers of goods manufacturing.
1751	Francesco Geminiani publishes his *Art of Playing the Violin*.
	Voltaire publishes his *Age of Louis XIV* and moves to Berlin at the invitation of Frederick II.
1752	Beginning of the *Querelle des Bouffons* in Paris on the merits of Italian versus French opera.
	Johann Joachim Quantz publishes his seminal treatise *Versuch einer Anweisung die Flöte zu spielen*.
	A performance of Christian Felix Weisse's *Der Teufel ist los* sparks the Comic War in Leipzig.
	A troupe of comedians writing ballad opera is in residence in Williamsburg, Virginia.
	The Gregorian calendar is adopted in Britain and its colonies.
1753	Carl Philipp Emanuel Bach publishes his *Versuch über die wahre Art das Clavier zu spielen*.
	Jean-Jacques Rousseau publishes his *Lettre sur la musique française* in Paris.
1754	French and Indian War begins in North America.
	Johann Stamitz creates a sensation for his symphonies in Paris at the Concerts Spirtuels.
	Niccolo Jommelli becomes *Kapellmeister* in Stuttgart.
1755	Massive earthquake destroys much of Lisbon including musical archives.
	Carl Heinrich Graun publishes his oratorio *Der Tod Jesu* in Berlin.
	Samuel Johnson publishes his *Dictionary of the English Language*.
	William Boyce is appointed Master of the King's Music in London.
	Francesco Araja composes his *Cephal et Procris* as the first Russian-language opera.
1756	Wolfgang Mozart is born in Salzburg shortly before his father, Leopold, publishes his treatise *Versuch einer gründlichen Violinschule*.
	The Seven Years' War, pitting Britain and Prussia against France and Austria, begins.
	Charles Simon Favart imports exotic costumes for his comic opera *Soliman II*.
1757	Domenico Scarlatti dies in Madrid, and Johann Stamitz dies in Mannheim.
	John Palma presents the first public concerts in Philadelphia.
	British East India Company wins political suzerainty in Bengal.
1759	Jesuits are expelled from Portugal; the monastic composers migrate to Brazil.
	Haydn becomes *Kapellmeister* to Count Morzin.
	Handel dies in London.

1760	George III becomes King of the United Kingdom.
	The earliest collection of Psalmody *Urania* is published in Philadelphia.
	Breitkopf in Leipzig publishes his first music catalogue.
	Jean Georges Noverre becomes balletmaster in Stuttgart.
1761	Haydn becomes *Vice-Kapellmeister* at Eisenstadt to the Esterházy family.
	Opera buffa becomes popular in London with the music of Baldassare Galuppi.
	The Nobleman and Gentleman's Catch Club begins in London.
	Gluck's ballet *Don Juan* premieres in Vienna.
1762	Catherine II (the Great) becomes Empress of Russia.
	Gluck's opera *Orfeo ed Euridice* premieres in Vienna.
	Johann Christian Bach moves to London to compose opera seria.
1763	The Treaty of Paris ends the Seven Years' War.
1764	Rameau dies in Paris.
	A French city named St. Louis is founded on the Mississippi River in North America.
1765	The Bach–Abel public concerts begin in London.
	André-Danican Philidor premieres his *Tom Jones*.
	The Diderot–d'Alembert *Encyclopédie* is completed.
1766	Haydn becomes *Kapellmeister* at Eisenstadt and the new palace called Esterház.
	The Stamp Act causes rebellion in England's North American colonies.
1767	Georg Philipp Telemann dies in Hamburg.
	Gluck's *Alceste* premieres in Vienna.
	Samuel Wallis inaugurates diplomatic relations with the Kingdom of Tahiti.
1769	The first zarzuelas featuring folk elements are composed in Spain by Antonio de Hita.
	Luigi Boccherini becomes court cellist in Madrid.
	C. P. E. Bach becomes Telemann's successor in Hamburg.
	Father Junipero Serra begins to establish missions in Alta California, beginning with San Diego de Acala.
1770	The *Liebhaber* concerts are established in Berlin and the Concerts des Amateurs in Paris.
	Padre Sojo founds the Chacao School in Caracas, Venezuela.
	Giuseppe Tartini dies in Padua; Ludwig van Beethoven born in Bonn.
1771	The Royal Academy of Music is founded in Stockholm.
	Charles Burney publishes his *The Present State of Music in France and Italy*.
	Hasse's last opera, *Ruggiero*, fails in Milan.
1772	Gustav III becomes King of Sweden in a coup d'état.
	The Tonkünstlersozietät is founded in Vienna.
1773	Anton Schweitzer and Christoph Wieland produce *Alzeste* for Weimar.
	The Royal Swedish Opera is inaugurated with Francesco Uttini's *Thetis och Pelée*.
	Burney publishes *The Present State of Music in German, the Netherlands, and United Provinces*.
	Haydn's *L'infedetà delusa* premieres at Esterház.
1774	Johann Friedrich Reichardt becomes *Kapellmeister* in Berlin.
	Johann Wolfgang von Goethe publishes his *Die Leiden des jungen Werthers*.
	Antonio Salieri becomes *Kapellmeister* in Vienna.
	Gluck arrives in Paris to produce his *Iphigénie en Aulide*.
	The Boston Tea Party incites rebellion against taxation on tea by the British in America.
1775	The War of Independence in America begins.
	Georg Benda composes his melodrama *Ariadne auf Naxos* in Gotha.
	The Hanover Square Concerts begin in London.
1776	Burney publishes the first volume of *The General History of Music*.
	The Ancient Concerts sponsored by the Academy of Ancient Music begin in London.
	A Declaration of Independence is signed in Philadelphia at the Continental Congress.
	Wolfgang Mozart seeks his fortune in Mannheim and Paris, composes the Paris Symphony.

1777 The Accademia de'Cavalieri concerts begin in Naples.
Ignaz Holzbauer's *Günther von Schwarzburg* premieres in Mannheim.
France enters the American revolution on a "voluntary" basis.

1778 Elector Carl Theodor moves his court from Mannheim to Munich after skirmishes of the War of the Bavarian Succession.
The Teatro a la Scala opens in Milan.
Joseph II, co-ruler with Maria Theresia, inaugurates the German Singspiel in Vienna.
Abbé Georg Joseph Vogler publishes his *Betrachtungen einer Mannheimer Tonschule*.

1779 The opera house at Esterház burns.
The Gluck–Piccinni feud reaches its height in Paris.
Captain Cook is killed in Hawaii, while the Dutch expand their territory in South Africa.

1780 Mozart composes *Idomeneo* for Munich.

1781 Mozart moves to Vienna.
Haydn publishes his Op. 33 string quartets.
The Loge Olympique concerts are inaugurated in Paris.
Johann Adam Hiller becomes the first conductor of the Gewandhaus Orchestra in Leipzig.
Tupac Amaru II begins a revolt against the Spanish in Peru.
Lord Cornwallis surrenders to George Washington at Yorktown.
Joseph Martin Kraus is appointed Vice-Kapellmeister in Stockholm.

1782 Giovanni Paisiello's *Il barbiere di Siviglia* premieres in St. Petersburg.
Mozart's *Die Entführung aus dem Serail* premieres in Vienna.
The first volume of Heinrich Koch's treatise *Versuch einer Anleitung zur Composition* is published in Leipzig.
Metastasio dies in Vienna, Johann Christian Bach dies in London, and castrato Farinelli dies in Bologna.

1783 The Treaty of Paris concludes the American War of Independence.
Benjamin Franklin and Thomas Jefferson import French music into the United States.
The National Opera in Prague opens.
Archbishop Colloredo of Salzburg promotes his reforms throughout the Austrian empire.

1784 The Handel Centennial celebration begins in London.
Padre Giovanni Battista Martini dies in Bologna.
André Grétry's rescue opera *Richard Coeur de Lion* premieres in Paris.
The Continental Congress ratifies the Treaty of Paris.
Icelandic volcano Laki's eruption prevents European crops from harvest.

1785 Napoleon Bonaparte is appointed as a lieutenant in the French military.
The Caecilian Society of London is founded.

1786 Johann Peter Salomon creates a concert series in London.
Mozart's *Le nozze di Figaro* and Vicente Martín y Soler's *Una cosa rara* premiere in Vienna.
Haydn's symphonies are performed at the Loge Olympique in Paris.
Frederick II dies in Berlin and is succeeded by Friedrich Wilhelm, himself a cellist.

1787 The new United States proposes a constitution to replace the Articles of Confederation.
Mozart's *Don Giovanni* premieres in Prague.
Gluck dies in Vienna.
A prohibition against the theatre is lifted in Philadelphia.

1788 Paris riots when Louis XVI overturns the French assembly.
The Catch and Glee Club is formed in London.
C. P. E. Bach dies in Hamburg.
The Felix Meritis concerts begin in Amsterdam.
British undesirables are shipped off to a new colony called Botany Bay (Australia).

1789	The New French Assembly advocates for human rights; the Bastille is stormed on July 14, inaugurating the French Revolution.
	Daniel Gottlob Türk publishes his *Clavierschule*.
	The Berlin Opera is made a public venture.
1790	The Concerts Spirituels close in Paris.
	Joseph Quesnel produces operas in Montreal, Canada.
	Prince Nicolas Esterházy dies, and Haydn is pensioned.
	Mozart's *Così fan tutte* premieres in Vienna.
	Joseph II dies in Vienna.
1791	Haydn goes to London as part of the Salomon concerts.
	Mozart dies in Vienna shortly after the premieres of *Die Zauberflöte* and *La clemenza di Tito*.
	Leopold II is crowned Holy Roman Emperor.
	Revolution on the Caribbean island of Hispaniola results in the independence of Haiti.
1792	Gustav III is assassinated in Stockholm at a masked ball.
	Ludwig van Beethoven moves to Vienna as a student of Haydn.
	Domenico Cimarosa's opera *Il matrimonio segreto* premieres in Vienna.
	Carl Friedrich Zelter establishes the Singakademie in Berlin.
	The Teatro La Fenice is reborn in Venice.
	The Théâtre de la Rue opens in New Orleans, Louisiana.
	The French declare war on Austria and Britain.
1793	Louis XVI and Marie Antoinette are guillotined in Paris as part of the Reign of Terror.
1794	Haydn visits London for the second time.
	The Chestnut Street Theatre opens in Philadelphia with Samuel Arnold's *The Castle of Andalusia*.
	Russia crushes revolution in Poland.
1795	The Reign of Terror ends, replaced by the Directorate.
	The Conservatoire de Paris is established.
	The third partition of Poland is done between Russia, Germany, and Austria.
	The opera society Nytt och Nöje founded in Stockholm.
1796	Gustav IV Adolf crowned King of Sweden.
	Haydn is recalled as *Kapellmeister* at Eisenstadt.
	William Shield's opera *The Poor Soldier* is performed in Botany Bay, Australia.
1797	All conservatories in Naples are closed due to the revolution.
	Luigi Cherubini's *Medée* premieres in Paris.
	The Treaty of Tripoli is signed between the North African states and the United States.
1798	Haydn's *Die Schöpfung* premieres in Vienna.
	The French forces of Napoleon conquer Italy.
	Cimarosa is imprisoned for revolutionary activities.
	Napoleon invades Egypt but retreats after Lord Nelson defeats the French fleet at Aboukir.
1799	Napoleon becomes dictator in France.
	George Washington dies at Mt. Vernon.
	Beethoven becomes a major musical celebrity in Vienna.
1800	François Boieldieu's opera *Le Calife de Baghdad* premieres in Paris.
	France regains Louisiana from Spain in a secret treaty.
	Beethoven's first symphony premieres in Vienna.

Contents

Preface	xvii

PART I
Music and Style in the Classical Period — 1

  1 Defining the Classical Period — 3

  2 The Emergence of the New Styles of Classical Period Music — 24

PART II
New Developments, Convergences, and Genres in the Classical Period — 49

  3 The Expansion of the Orchestra and the Development of the Instruments — 51

  4 Genre as the Core of Musical Development: Orchestral Works — 74

  5 Genre as the Core of Musical Development: Chamber Music — 99

PART III
Opera! The Development of Popular, Nationalist, and Exotic Entertainment — 123

  6 The Structure and Meaning of Italian Opera in the Classical Period — 125

  7 Opera in France, Germany, and Elsewhere: Escaping the Past for an Exotic Future — 144

  8 Sacred Music in the Era of Secularism — 170

PART IV
Capitals and Centers of Music-Making in the Classical Period — 199

  9 Urban Musical Centers and Their Musical Establishments — 201

xii *Contents*

10 Cities and Courts on the Periphery 225

11 From Universal Composer to Icon: Joseph Haydn and Wolfgang Amadeus Mozart 248

PART V
Music for the People: Music as a Social Phenomenon in the Classical Period 275

12 The Folk and Their Music 277

Register of Names 297
Selected Reading 307
Glossary 310
Index 314

Detailed Contents

Preface — xvii

PART I
Music and Style in the Classical Period — 1

1 Defining the Classical Period — 3

What's in a Name? 9
The Chronological Conundrum 10
Parallels of the Late Baroque and Early Classical Periods 12
Definitions and the Rise of Theory, Aesthetics, and Musical Pedagogy 15

2 The Emergence of the New Styles of Classical Period Music — 24

National Styles 26
  The Italian Style 26
  The French Style 28
  The German Style 30
Style Trends: Galant and Empfindsamkeit 34
Sturm und Drang: *The Passionate Musical-Dramatic Embrace* 41
High Classicism 42

PART II
New Developments, Convergences, and Genres in the Classical Period — 49

3 The Expansion of the Orchestra and the Development of the Instruments — 51

Development of Instruments and Performance Techniques 53
The Strings 53
The Woodwinds 57
Brass and Percussion 59
Keyboard Instruments 62
The Voice 64
The Expansion of the Orchestra 66
Performance Practice 67

4 Genre as the Core of Musical Development: Orchestral Works … 74

The Concerto and Sinfonia Concertante 74
The Symphony and Its Offspring 79
The Symphony: Social Context 80
The Symphony: Types and Formats 82
Structures and Instrumentation 85
The Symphony Emerges, 1730–1750 87
The Symphony in Full Bloom, 1750–1780 89
The Symphony of the Future, 1780–1800 91
The Symphony's Relatives 92

5 Genre as the Core of Musical Development: Chamber Music … 99

Music for Professionals and Amateurs: The Rise of Chamber Genres 99
"Sonata, What Do You Want from Me?" 103
The Major Instrumental Chamber Genres: Duos, Trios, Quartets, Quintets, and Beyond 107
The Chamber Vocal Genres: The Rise of the Lied 115

PART III
Opera! The Development of Popular, Nationalist, and Exotic Entertainment … 123

6 The Structure and Meaning of Italian Opera in the Classical Period … 125

Popular Opera as Musical Business and Taste 125
Baroque Opera Versus Classical Opera: The Battle of the Genres 132
Opera in Italy: Old Versus New, Local Versus International 136

7 Opera in France, Germany, and Elsewhere: Escaping the Past for an Exotic Future … 144

Opera in France: From Lully to Gluck and Beyond: Crisis, Controversy, and Social Commentary 144
Opera in Germany: Defining Nationalism Without a Nation 152
Opera Goes Global: The Importance of National Cultural Definition 157
   "Turkish" Opera 157
   Opera in England 158
   Opera in Scandinavia 160
   Opera in Russia 162
   Opera in Iberia 165
   Opera in the Americas 166

8 Sacred Music in the Era of Secularism … 170

Church Music for Secular Glory or Devout Worship 170
Catholic Church Genres: Liturgical and Nonliturgical Music 174
Music in the Monasteries and Elsewhere: Serving God and the Flock 184
The Protestant Church Genres: The Fall of the Cantata and Rise of the Secular 186

Church Music of Other Realms: Between the Orthodox and Paradox 189
Conclusion 194

PART IV
Capitals and Centers of Music-Making in the Classical Period   199

9 Urban Musical Centers and Their Musical Establishments   201

The Proud Hubs: Vienna, Paris, Berlin, London 201
  Vienna 201
  Paris 204
  Berlin 207
  London 209
The Italian Rivals: Naples, Venice, Rome 212
  Naples 212
  Venice 213
  Rome 216
The Musical Centers of the Holy Roman Empire: Dresden, Prague, Mannheim/Munich 217
  Dresden 217
  Prague 218
  Mannheim/Munich 219

10 Cities and Courts on the Periphery   225

The Northern Rivals: The Netherlands, Scandinavia, Russia 226
  Amsterdam/The Hague 226
  Copenhagen 227
  Stockholm 229
  St. Petersburg 232
Some Exemplary Courts: Esterház, Regensburg, Oettingen-Wallerstein, Salzburg 233
  Esterház 234
  Regensburg 235
  Oettingen-Wallerstein 235
  Salzburg 236
Music on the Periphery: The Mediterranean Sphere 238
  Iberia 238
  Malta 239
Music on the Periphery: Music Outside Europe 240
  New Spain 241
  Brazil 243
  New France and English North America (the United States) 244

11 From Universal Composer to Icon: Joseph Haydn and Wolfgang Amadeus Mozart   248

Haydn 249
Mozart 261

xvi *Detailed Contents*

PART V
Music for the People: Music as a Social Phenomenon in the Classical Period   275

12 The Folk and Their Music   277

Folk Music as a Source and Repository of Popular Cultures 277
Music in the Service of the State: Politics and Revolution 284
The Rise of the Popular Music Business 290

Register of Names   297
Selected Reading   307
Glossary   310
Index   314

Preface

This text, *Music in the Classical World: Genre, Culture, and History*, is intended to provide an in-depth and kaleidoscopic overview of one of the most vibrant and brilliant periods of music history, with an emphasis upon the social and cultural history of music in relationship to the development of style and genre. The Classical Period is one of the most difficult ones in the history of music to encompass in a comprehensive manner. Less than a century long, it marked a seismic shift in worldviews known as the Enlightenment, but the effects of this change affected virtually every aspect of culture, from politics to the arts. Moreover, the boundaries of the period are indistinct, with new trends and ideas bubbling up for several decades during the late Baroque of the 1720s and 1730s, as noted by musicologist Carl Dahlhaus, while the later decades of the eighteenth century witnessed revolution, the overthrow of the feudal order, and the beginning of scientific thought that has led to our world today. There is literally no avenue left untouched by the trends and movements of the period, and yet to comprehend it from the cultural point of view of music, let alone everything else that was going on, in the form of a textbook would seem as Herculean a task as one could imagine. No other period in music history has had such an impact on our culture, and during the Classical Period more music was composed by more composers throughout the world than at any other era. And yet, it lasted less than a century, merging logically and imperceptibly into that nineteenth-century era we call Romantic.

In order to comprehend the scope of the Classical Period, between 1725 and 1805 musicologist Jan LaRue documented more than fourteen thousand symphonies being composed (current research has increased that figure considerably to twenty thousand or more), with similar numbers of works in genres such as opera, string quartets, trios, sonatas, and so forth. Music was ever present as family pastimes (with most families musically literate, even quite well trained by today's standards), entertainments for the myriad of courts, towns, and cities; pedagogical tools for even the smallest of towns; and for liturgical use in churches and monasteries. Music was an integral part of the social and cultural structure, whether at the farthest reaches of European settlement in Asia, Oceania, and the Americas or closer to its home continent.

Approach

Given the breadth of the topic, it would seem difficult if not impossible to encompass it within a single text.[1] Therefore, most focus on the music of two iconic composers, Joseph Haydn and Wolfgang Amadeus Mozart. Some have even occasionally extended this to include Ludwig van Beethoven. They do not by themselves represent the vitality of the entire period, however, nor ought they to be considered completely out of context. Viewed through an eighteenth-century lens, all were certainly considered among the top composers of their time, but there are others whose stature was equally as important, either due to their progressive style or their influence on a particular genre. This text takes a different approach, one that contextualizes the period without being forced to view it piecemeal.

The approach in writing this text is to lead the reader by **shifting the topics from individuals to music**, its meaning, and its cultural significance for the age. In order to understand the brilliance of the period, I felt it necessary to see it through the eyes of those who lived during the time and, therefore, read how they saw their own age. For example, how did the Classical style emerge, and why? What were composers trying to do to appeal to an ever-increasing appetite for new music, and how did they react to changes in attitudes or fashion? How did the reception of and opportunities for musicians change over the short span of time? These discussions are interwoven into a fabric that ranges from the development of style and genre to an overview of select places where music gained a global reach and concludes with some brief nod to areas not normally explored in general histories: music of the people, music of politics, and the rise of music business that was based on economics.

Features

- A systematic approach that includes the development of style and genres within a broader historical context
- Illustrations that show both documents and art that is relevant to the music of the age
- Extensive musical examples that are discussed in context of the development of the genres
- An online, downloadable set of scores found in the text and a website devoted to outlining the music and drawn from original sources (edited by the author)
- A comprehensive perspective that includes global reaches of the music of the period
- Extensive student learning aids, including a timeline, glossary, register of people and dates, sidebars of political importance, and a bibliography arranged by chapter and topic
- Performances linked to the musical examples available on demand

Organization

The main organizational principle of this text is to lead the reader through the period by **focusing on the genres**, placing them in context with their chronological development, their social and cultural history, and by geographical location. The first two chapters are meant to engage the reader in defining both the time in an interdisciplinary manner but also to give an idea of both style and education of musicians. The core questions of what constitutes the Classical Period and how it was perceived by those who lived within it are discussed. The third chapter introduces the development of instruments, the evolution of the orchestra, and some performance practice considerations that will help in the understanding of how the music was done. Thereafter, the next chapters discuss the development of the major genres: instrumental music (orchestral and chamber), vocal music, opera, and sacred music. Two chapters then give examples of the important centers in Europe and globally and of how the music fit into the lives of those living there. A biographical chapter on the two iconic composers, Mozart and Haydn, follow, and the book concludes with a brief exploration of several features that are often overlooked in our view of the Classical Period, ranging from music publishing to folk music and how it was perceived.

Music in the Classical World: Genre, Culture, and History is meant to tell **the story of the period through eighteenth-century eyes**, locating the music that continues to be revived within both a social and historical context. You will notice some differences with this text.

1. I have chosen to eliminate the usual birth and death dates in the body of the text; these will be found in a Register at the end.
2. The text is intended to be read as a narrative at a level that will encourage readers to ask questions about what they read and to serve as a springboard for further in-depth exploration. By limiting the purely historical narrative, or subsuming it into the context of the overall story, it reveals the various sorts of music and musical activity that made this period so brilliant.
3. This volume has only the barest minimum of musical analysis. As noted, the number of works written is gargantuan, and the temptation is always to limit musical examples to the better-known works, namely, Mozart and Haydn. While I do use some from these two icons, I have deliberately chosen **examples**

from a broad range of composers, which, in turn, I hope gives the reader an idea of the wealth of music and musical styles that existed. This will finally put to rest the hierarchy where many talented composers who worked globally have been relegated to second-class musical citizenship. The purpose is to give the reader a glimpse into that vibrant and active world that is the music of this time.

Ancillaries

Source Documents

The documents chosen are all drawn from sources from the period, in many cases from original publications and documents that have been translated by the author. The idea is to provide pertinent commentary on the text through eighteenth-century views rather than rely on the lens of modern research. In that way it is hoped that the reader will gain an understanding of the minds and thoughts of those who lived during this period.

Online Resources

www.routledge.com/cw/vanboer

This companion website is a vital part of *Music in the Classical World*. It contains full scores (in downloadable PDF form) for all of the music of the text, some in new editions that have been created from the original sources. Recordings are also provided for the majority and reflect the latest performances of historical groups. Tips for listening to the music (also appropriate for other periods) are included.

Acknowledgments

Each chapter has been read and commented on by actual students who used it in the course of their normal study. These ideas and comments have been incorporated into the work based on their often-keen observations of the story and how it unfolds. I would like to thank Cori Holquinn, Robert Fredriksen, Mieke Doezema, Samantha Estrada, Steven Pontius, David Mills, Derek Stephenson, Namarea Randolph-Yosea, Gabe Taylor-Uding, Alex Kocsis, Gabriel Sadzewicz, Erin Martin, and Ajaleigh Irons for their extensive and extremely thoughtful and helpful comments. A special vote of thanks goes to Chloe Hovind, who helped immeasurably by looking over the chapters.

My sincerest appreciation goes to many people at Routledge who helped shepherd this work through a stage where few have ventured to tread. First and foremost, the Music Acquisitions Editor Constance Ditzel guided me through the process, providing fine commentary, and is a wonderful sounding board for a work that took longer to complete than anticipated, as well as Peter Sheehy for his patience and perseverance in helping with the various technical details.

Note

1 As an example, musicologist Daniel Heartz published his excellent history between 1995 and 2003 in three volumes, each of which consists of eight hundred to a thousand pages, and he still omitted music in several places for because of a lack of space (Scandinavia, for instance).

Part I

Music and Style in the Classical Period

1 Defining the Classical Period

There is perhaps no other period in music history that has fired the imagination more than the Classical Period. It was a time when much of our modern thought was formulated and developed, when scientific achievement finally began to break loose from the fetters of religion that had dictated its concordance with doctrine, when political rearrangements spelled the demise of the feudal order and fostered the creation of nations defined by their language and culture, and when the focus in social life, philosophy, and the arts began to revolve around the human element. There was, for the first time, belief in a progressive future for humankind, expressed in the epithet *ad astra per aspera* (to the stars through difficulties or challenges), indicating that human beings were to achieve a future by themselves, no matter what the cost. This, in turn, meant that the rigid class structures that had been in existence for over a millennium began to break down, aided and abetted by a renewed interest in a global perspective as another wave of exploration began to bring Europe into contact with other cultures around the world, stimulating new thoughts and concepts.

At the beginning of the eighteenth century, Europe still adhered to the style known as Baroque. The style of Louis XIV, with its complete authoritarian rule by the monarch and rigidly stratified social structure, was epitomized by the resplendent court at Versailles, and culture itself was based on extravagance and opulence. The political divisions were like the arts, ornate, shifting, and subject to intricate divisions of *chiaroscuro* (light and shadow). Empires were either monolithic, like France and England, or kaleidoscopic like the Holy Roman Empire and Italy, with alliances and noble families shifting constantly. For example, when Spanish king Carlos II, a member of the Habsburg family, died in 1700, it was his intent to pass the crown on to Philippe of Anjou, the grandson of Louis and a Bourbon. This led to the War of the Spanish Succession that lasted for a decade and a half, brought to a conclusion only because the Habsburg emperor himself passed away in 1711. A realignment of political power was deemed important to maintain balance among the realms and thus to avoid the general destruction similar to that which had marred the seventeenth century's Thirty Years' War. By 1740, further political changes, such as the changeover in the United Kingdom from the House of Orange to the Hanoverians in 1717, had occurred, thus weakening the power of the courts and allowing for social and political changes to happen. During the Classical Period, these changes manifested themselves in ways unimaginable in earlier times, from the American War of Independence beginning in 1776 to the chaotic French Revolution of 1789 to the rise of a popular dictator (and, later, emperor) Napoleon Bonaparte, almost a decade later. Such a political ferment has led to this being called the Age of Revolution.

The Classical Period was not, however, solely determined by political events. Rather, the concept of revolution spread across all aspects of cultural life, even as the power and prestige of the courts and church waned. The same era has been called the Age of Enlightenment due to the shift in focus away from doctrine and dogma toward a more liberal (in the literal sense of the term) attitude that encouraged new philosophical precepts, a wider range of intellectual thought, and freedom of expression. One only needs to look at the views of French philosopher Voltaire, who said, "Dare to think for yourself," or Jean-Jacques Rousseau, who noted that "[m]an was born free, and he is everywhere in chains; those who think themselves the masters of others are indeed greater slaves than they" to understand the seismic shift in perception during this time. This, in turn, led to more humanistic philosophies by such men as Immanuel Kant, who proclaimed,

4 Music and Style in the Classical Period

"*Sapere aude*! 'Have courage to use your own reason!'—that is the motto of enlightenment" in his *Kritik der reinen Vernunft* (*Criticism of Pure Reason*) of 1781, as well as the blunt statement of Johann Gottfried Herder: "The people need a master only as long as they have no understanding of their own."[1]

One can find the same sort of intellectual creativity in the arts during this time. The often voluptuous and extravagant art forms of the Baroque shifted to more humanist subjects. In painting, the pictures of Jean-Antoine Watteau were harbingers of this new, more realistic age by depicting convivial domestic scenes, such as his painting *The Pleasures of Love* from 1716 (Figure 1.1). Portraits of people and places replace the penchant for allegorical and religious-inspired works. French artist Élisabeth Vigée Le Brun depicted her subjects with an eye toward fashion and elegance, while her British colleagues, Thomas Gainsborough and Sir Joshua Reynolds, both sought to portray their portraits with a human intimacy. Elsewhere, Italian artists such as Canaletto (Giovanni Antonio Canal) broadened their scope to depict conventional scenes of places; he, in particular, painted the city of Venice enumerable times from different perspectives so that one almost seems to view the places as if one were actually there (Figure 1.2). In architecture, a renewed study of the works of ancient Rome and Greece provided a foundation for the creation of structures that were without the gaudiness and opulence of palaces like Versailles, opting instead for Classical symmetry and beauty. For example, this sketch of the famed Pantheon in Rome by Giovanni Battista Piranesi is precise and without fantasy (Figure 1.3). Not all artists of the Classical Period were stuck on realistic portrayals, however. Swiss artist Henry Fuseli explored the darker side of humanity, producing nightmarish pictures that blended humans and supernatural beings, such as *The Nightmare*, in which a demon squats on top of a supine woman, a vision that is both horrific and erotic at the same time (Figure 1.4).

In the literature of the Classical Period, developments in style paralleled those in music. The range and depth of the works in all fields, from drama (which often contained incidental music) to novels, was

Figure 1.1 Jean-Antoine Watteau, *The Pleasures of Love* (1719)

Source: bpk Bildagentur/Gemäldegalerie Alte Meister—Staatliche Kunstsammlungen Dresden/Art Resource, NY.

Figure 1.2 Canaletto (Giovanni Antonio Canal), *Piazza San Marco Venezia* (ca. 1723–1724)
Source: Used by permission from the Museo Nacional Thyssen-Bornemisza, Madrid.

significant. One could find raw and satirical works, such as Jonathan Swift's *Gulliver's Travels* of 1720 (or his rather more pointed pamphlet "A Modest Proposal" of 1729 in which he advocates cannibalism of the Irish), or more refined comedies, such as *La putta onorata* (*The Honorable Maiden*) by Italian playwright Carlo Goldoni, many of which derive from the time-honored commedia dell'arte. Both Voltaire and Rousseau wrote plays, and both tragedy and comedy were continuously written, published, and performed in eighteenth-century France. One of the more controversial playwrights was Pierre Auguste Caron de Beaumarchais, whose trilogy *Le Barbier de Séville*, *Le Mariage de Figaro*, and *La Mère coupable* (*The Barber of Seville, The Marriage of Figaro, The Guilty Mother*, respectively) was censored as insulting to the nobility. Yet, the first two works were transformed into popular operas, the first by Giovanni Paisiello and the second by Wolfgang Amadeus Mozart. The closest parallel to the development of musical style, however, could be seen in German-speaking lands. The so-called Enlightenment style of Johann Christoph Gottsched, a professor at Leipzig University and a literary power, featured static plots and was often an adaptation of French Baroque models. He also produced theoretical works on German poetry (1730) and drama (1740–1745), which he intended would be seen as the models for a national literature. Unfortunately, he was seen as overly pedantic, and by 1748, with the emergence of his student Gotthold Ephraim Lessing, a more emotional and dramatic style of literature known as *Empfindsamkeit*, his style of literature quickly vanished.[2] Lessing's most important works began with the play *Miss Sara Sampson* in 1755, which was regarded as a bourgeois tragedy by his contemporaries. His colleague in Hamburg, Friedrich Gottlieb Klopstock, took the style further by promoting the plays of William Shakespeare in translation and producing his own epic *Messias* (1748–1773) in imitation of John Milton's epic *Paradise Lost*. Here, the musical

6 *Music and Style in the Classical Period*

Figure 1.3 Giovanni Battista Piranesi, *Interior Sketch of the Pantheon in Rome* (1790)

connection was more direct; Klopstock was a friend of composer Carl Philipp Emanuel Bach in Hamburg and often collaborated with him.

Perhaps the most radical change in literature came in 1774 with the publication of the novel *Die Leiden des jungen Werthers* (*The Sorrows of the Young Werther*) by Johann Wolfgang von Goethe, in which a young psychotic man is completely ruled by his own passions and forms a fatal attachment to a married woman (Figure 1.5). This heralded the introduction of a new style of literature, known as *Sturm und Drang* (Storm and Stress), in which extreme passions predominate. This style, whose name was taken from a turgid tragedy by Maximilian Klinger by the same name,[3] featured unrestrained human emotions, extremes of temperament, dark imagery, and hopeless disaster. As with *Empfindsamkeit*, the models were the works of Shakespeare and an alleged "Celtic bard" named Ossian, the content of which featured dark and brooding nature and violent primitive emotions of the characters.[4] Although the literary *Sturm und Drang* was short-lived—the final work by Friedrich von Schiller was the 1784 *Die Räuber* (*The Robbers*)—it nonetheless set the stage for the Gothic horrors and supernatural literature of the Romantic Period of the nineteenth century. The most representative work by Goethe, however, was his play *Faust* that was begun about the same time as *Werther* but not published in its final version until 1808. The story, which fascinated Romantics throughout the nineteenth century, involves a professor who sells his soul to the devil (Mephistopheles) in order to regain his youth for a time. It is a clear representative of the more modern and expansive drama that both Goethe and Schiller embraced in the middle of the 1780s, known as Weimar Classicism. Here, authors sought to merge the various eighteenth-century literary styles into a more humanistic form,

Figure 1.4 Henry Fuseli (Johann Heinrich Fussli) *The Nightmare* (oil on canvas, 1781)
Source: Produced by permission from the Detroit Institute of Arts, USA/Founders Society Purchase with funds from Mr. and Mrs. Bert L. Smokler and Mr. and Mrs. Lawrence A. Fleischmanf/Bridgeman Images.

incorporating the human emotions (and occasional passion) of the *Empfindsamkeit* and *Sturm und Drang* with the higher poetic speech of the Enlightenment. Goethe himself noted that it owed much to what can be termed "neoclassicism," that is, the reinvention of the dramaturgy of classical Rome and Greece but with the addition of modern aesthetics, structure, and content. Other authors who adhered to this movement included Christoph Martin Wieland, who as will be shown was one of the major figures in the development of Classical Period German dramatic opera.

Finally, a word needs to be said about the Classical Period as the age of discovery. With the focus on human creativity and humanism came a renewed interest in scientific achievement. From 1730 to 1800 Europe was in the throes of a wave of scientific advances, once the restrictions on it were lifted. A few should be mentioned here. First, there were a number of attempts at flight, the first since the radical ideas of Leonardo da Vinci several centuries earlier. While the airplane (and glider) lay in the future, the concept of lighter-than-air belonged to the Montgolfiére brothers Joseph-Michel and Jacques-Étienne. While at work as paper manufacturers, they noticed that heat made the paper rise and, by 1783, had flown a balloon in Paris for almost ten kilometers (Figure 1.6). Second, in 1781 Scottish inventor James

Figure 1.5 Johann Wolfgang von Goethe, title page of *Die Leiden des jungen Werthers* (1774)

Watt created the first reliable steam engine, producing power to operate machinery and functioning as the precursor to the Industrial Revolution of the following century. Third, Edward Jenner discovered in 1797 that an inoculation could prevent one of the scourges of Europe, smallpox, beginning the path toward disease vaccines. Finally, astronomer and scientist Frederick William Herschel discovered the planet Uranus in 1781, the first outside the six known in antiquity, by building an improved telescope with which he probed the skies in Bath, England. Here, too, there is a direct connection to music, for Herschel not only led a public concert series in that city; he was one of the most prolific composers of symphonies in the United Kingdom.

More could be said about this vibrant and brilliant age, especially in terms of scientific discoveries (the advances in knowledge of electricity, for example), but it can also be said that it was one where a revolution in thought and idea led to the fostering of creativity, expressed in the arts and other fields through progressive experimentation and development. In terms of music, such an introduction may seem too broad, but given that music was often associated with these various trends and styles in other disciplines, it is crucial to understanding its role in the Classical Period. Music and musical style were crucial and far-reaching components of culture, for within this art form not only were social and cultural foundations forged, but the impact of the development of political thought and action, of the creation of forms, styles, and genres, and of the role of the musician in society were also momentous in terms of the progress of music that carried on into the centuries that followed.

Figure 1.6 Engraving of a Montgolfier balloon (1782)

What's in a Name?

Although we have already used the term *Classical Period*, it is so generic that a precise definition is often hard to find. Indeed, a number of terms or labels exist that have been used to give some sort of historical boundaries or styles that are representative of the period. These include the following:

> **Rococo.** This architectural term developed in eighteenth-century France and came to include mainly ornamentation in the arts, as well. It is usually described as defining the style of the *ancien régime*

of Louis XV and Louis XVI, being replaced following the revolution in 1795 or so with the term *neoclassical*. In music, it sometimes describes a more indistinct period that is often synonymous with the *galant* and was used during the eighteenth century in France as the "*style rocaille* [shell-like or curvaceous ornaments]" and by the French musicologist Leonel de La Laurencie around the turn of the twentieth century to describe the French violin school of Jean-Marie Leclair.

Pre-Classical. From the German (*Vorklassik*), it generally was used in Germany to describe anything that came from the operatic style of Giovanni Pergolesi forward to the music of Mozart and Joseph Haydn. It seems to have been used more broadly to discuss the music of composers apart from these two, often with a pejorative undertone defining such music as the work of *Kleinmeister*, a term defined invidiously as "masters of lesser light." It contains neither historical nor teleological substance.

Viennese Classicism. Also from German (*Wiener Klassik*), this term is used to compare late eighteenth-century works to those of Mozart and Haydn. Vienna, however, was not the only musical center in Europe during this period. While it was a prominent capital to which musicians migrated from across the continent (and elsewhere), it did not dictate musical style across countries and regions, even though composers resident there did achieve international reputations for their music.

Galant. The *galant* can be defined specifically as early as the Baroque Period as being polite and adhering to the rules of high society. Voltaire noted that "being *galant* . . . means seeking to please." In other words, it was an attitude, characterized by good taste (*bon goût*) and intellectual nuance that theorists of the eighteenth century used specifically to indicate the courtly French style of music. Indeed, it is a definitive style that emerges from the Baroque, as we shall see later, but this narrow definition precludes it from being a metaphor for the entire Classical Period, despite the fact that later theorists, such as Heinrich Christoph Koch, allude to it in this manner.[5]

Each of these definitions is often used in lieu of the general term *Classical Period*, sometimes without realizing their inadequacy to encompass the period and its musical development as a whole. Yet, they continue to appear with regularity as determinants of what constitutes the music of this age. Indeed, the other lesser-used labels such as *Empfindsamkeit*, *Sturm und Drang*, Gothic, neoclassicism, and so on, are all too limited in the description of the overall systemic changes that appear in the various humanistic fields: art, literature, philosophy, theatre, and, most important, music. To find a label apart from the generic, one finds the definition of the complexity of the period, both historically and subjectively, too vague. This being said, there can be no doubt that the concept of the period itself was a product of the eighteenth century, yet even here a precise definition seems problematic.

The Chronological Conundrum

The use of the birth or death dates of important composers is often used as a means of defining periods of music history chronologically; for example, the death of Johann Sebastian Bach in 1750 is said to mark the end of the Baroque, and subsequently, the death of Haydn in 1809 heralds the end of the Classical Period. Alternatively, one finds that the Classical Period began with the emergence of a new musical style in Italy around 1740 and merged into the Romantic Period in the 1820s or so with the music of composers like Franz Schubert.[6] This led musicologist Friedrich Blume to postulate a combined Classical–Romantic Period, which demonstrated both the continuity and evolution of musical style across the nineteenth-century divide.[7] Moreover, there are a plethora of various time spans and, on occasion, arguments for a continuum of musical development from the Renaissance to the modern age for those who avoid assigning chronological boundaries at all.

Despite this debate, it can be said that a new style of music emerged from a more traditional one we now call the high Baroque during the decade between 1720 and 1730. It emphasized a simpler and lighter texture, more attention to longer and more lyrical melody lines, and homophonic harmonies. The structures and forms were also simplified, with contrasting sections, increased use of dynamics, and a less improvisatory performance practice. This contrasted to the Baroque, with its emphasis on static lines expanded by spinning out motives in sequences, complex counterpoint, instrumental doubling of lines, and a high florid style that required expansion and intricate ornamentation to be improvised.

This beginning was not one of abrupt change, but rather the transition was more gradual over the next decade or so, and there was considerable overlap between the styles of the two periods. Baroque composers such as Johann Sebastian Bach, Jan Dismas Zelenka, George Frédéric Handel, and Antonio Vivaldi were all active well into the period. For example, it is instructive to note that when Handel died in 1759, Mozart was already three years old and would, within a year or so, begin composing music, and when Georg Philipp Telemann passed away in 1767, Mozart was already eleven and shortly to write his first opera. The elder generation of composers may or may not have chosen to delve completely into the new style, but they were certainly cognizant of it; one is reminded here of Handel's rather off-handed remark that Classical opera composer Christoph Willibald von Gluck knew no more about counterpoint than his cook.

A timespan for the ending of the Classical Period is likewise difficult to determine. Neither 1791 nor 1809, the death dates of the quintessential musical icons, Mozart and Haydn, can be considered since others continued to write in the same style for decades afterward. Moreover, ending it in 1800 has no musical justification whatsoever. As with the beginning, there is considerable overlap between conservative and progressive composers. Up to 1820 Ludwig van Beethoven may have been experimenting with a new musical style, but both Schubert and Carl Maria von Weber adhered to a traditional musical style, though the latter's music contained typical nineteenth-century nationalist elements. Even popular Italian opera composers such as Gioachino Rossini knew of a newly emerging Romantic compositional style but preferred to write in a manner reflecting the old in his early works.

These various beginning and end points based on the lives of the principal composers may seem all too debatable, and so more recently the trend has been to create an amorphous time span, labeled the "long" eighteenth century that includes the entire hundred-year span and sometimes beyond, and a "short" eighteenth century, wherein more specific dates, such as events, for example, the Napoleonic wars or the French Revolution or dates of important rulers or composers, are determined to be significant markers.

Musicologist Neal Zaslaw has described the Classical Period "a natural watershed, in political, social and cultural history alike," which defines the character of the period and yet avoids the issue of defined chronology.[8] Yet, such a designation could be seen as too amorphous, offering no real definition beyond arbitrary dates that either are chosen for specific purposes or simply a gross time span. This makes a chronological definition all the more difficult.

If labels and chronology are inadequate, the period uses stylistic development, in which form, structure, and genre are correlated in an attempt to demonstrate some sort of a linear evolutionary trend. This has formed the core of important scholarship, such as Leonard Ratner's *Classical Music: Expression, Form and Style* and Charles Rosen's *The Classical Style*, which, although focused on the development of style, nonetheless seek to determine a historical progress at the foundation of their analytical work. Such work has been important in defining matters of style, but the focus on the triumvirate of composers and their works, not to mention the lack of parallels that occurred throughout Europe (and elsewhere) during this period gives only a partial picture, which leaves other parameters, extra-musical but both cultural, political, and social, as the best means of defining the Classical Period.

There can be no doubt that an almost infinite variety of possibilities for the creation and performance of music existed during the Classical Period. Virtually all the modern traditional genres were either developed or perfected during the era, and there was an ample creative spark that led to new genres, styles, or variations thereof. The flexibility even during this period led to important experimentation and redefinition on the road to conventionality. For example, a sonata could be virtually anything, from what we might consider a "standard" three-movement work for a single instrument generally with keyboard accompaniment to a larger piece such as a piano trio or a work for a single instrument. A symphony may have been normally either in three or four movements, but there are symphonies that range from a single movement with a slow introduction to perhaps as many as nine movements, and they may even have picturesque titles. A concerto may exist as a standard three-movement format, but if embedded within or extracted from a larger work such as a serenade, it could range from two movements to several more, and the soloists could be expanded beyond one to as many as half a dozen. Vocal music could range from simple songs meant for performance in intimate salon settings to monumental operas that required substantial stage effects. Finally, sacred music could be expansive and celebratory with large-scale orchestra accompaniment or restricted to simple hymns or *a cappella* choruses. In short, the question of form and genre varies so considerably that all one can deduce is that this period was a time of rapid stylistic and structural change. This, in turn, allows for the Classical Period to be defined as a combination of musical developments in form, structure, and style, coupled with those responsible throughout Europe at courts and cities for their creation and progressive development, with finally an eye toward the more meaningful historical factors—social, political, and economic—that provide us with the data to begin to set some of the chronological limits of the period.

The solution to this periodization is to use a variety of means to show how music developed during a span of about eighty or ninety years beginning early in the eighteenth century and moving into the first part of the nineteenth. Although arbitrary or subject to debate, such a time span and generic description allow us to view the changes, some evolutionary and some revolutionary, that occurred. At the same time, it allows flexibility to view these changes from a number of points of view: stylistic, technical, political, sociological, and historical. Thus, it seems clear that one must approach the music and those who wrote it from several perspectives in defining the chronology of the Classical Period. This chronology is used, although it will be represented through the various streams of those elements that define it. The end point will be the important changes that occur during the first decade and a half of the nineteenth century, but in order to arrive there, it is first necessary to begin with the more ambiguous parallels that resulted in the changeover from the music of the later Baroque to the early Classical Period, a time when the latter emerged as a new and more progressive direction.

Parallels of the Late Baroque and Early Classical Periods

The musical styles of the Baroque Period coexisted with the emergence of the new Classical style about 1725. At this time, the French style was widely imitated throughout Europe. When Louis XIV passed away in 1715, he had already established his court and his palace at Versailles as the epitome of civilization and taste, elegant and opulent, reflecting both social and political power (Figure 1.7). The buildings were highly decorated and grand in layout and structure, the gardens reflected careful aesthetics in the design meant to bring nature under the control of the king, and the court itself was ruled by a strict set of etiquette that required formal interaction and obeisance at all levels. The society was complex and rigid, a state of affairs that was reflected in the arts. Here, the fluid ornamentation, defined in the architectural term *rococo* was meant to dazzle both the court and visitors alike, and when combined with vibrant colors and the reflection of gold and silver, glass and porcelain, in the furnishings, the effect was brilliant, and yet the complexity revealed a stasis whereby the beauty was meant to be admired, even imitated, but not changed. The churches and estates or palaces throughout the rest of Europe subsequently repeated this aesthetic.

Such opulence, however, began to be replaced after Louis's death by a simpler, more modest and less ostentatious approach, and the result of the changes in political events that marked a beginning in the decline of absolutism. This was not just a French phenomenon, although a period known as the Regency from 1715 to 1723 when France was governed by Philippe Duc d'Orleans did begin to change trends and attitudes away from the style of Louis XIV. Elsewhere in Europe the same sort of issues of royal succession created new opportunities as the new rulers struggled to adapt to the changing times. In England, the death of Queen Anne in 1717 ended the House of Orange, and the crown was passed to the Elector of Hannover, named George I in England, who was not greeted with overwhelming joy by the citizens. In the Holy Roman Empire, the death of Charles VI in 1740 without a male heir brought on a period of instability when his daughter, Maria Theresia, was not allowed to become Holy Roman Empress (though she retained the title as queen of her hereditary domains of Austria, Hungary, and elsewhere to the

Defining the Classical Period 13

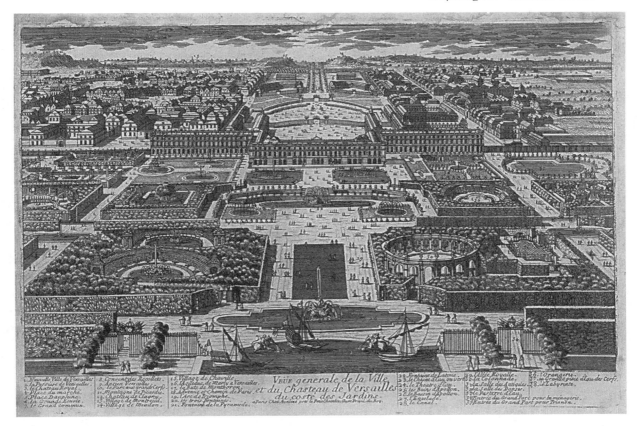

Figure 1.7 Engraving of the City and Palace of Versailles (*ca.* 1715)

east), leading to a brief War of the Austrian Succession. While she was able to get her husband, Franz I, crowned Holy Roman Emperor in 1745, the war disrupted the normal smooth transition of power. In Russia, there was a power struggle between the children of Peter I and Ivan V that lasted from 1725 until the ascension to the throne by Elizabeth in 1740, with the rivalry exacerbated by illness and death, leading to instability in the ruling classes. The same sort of turmoil afflicted the courts in the Netherlands, Denmark, Sweden, and the various principalities in Italy. As a consequence, the tight control over all aspects of the arts and aesthetic values relaxed and the chance for reform and a more cosmopolitan humanist approach was possible.

Aesthetics in this new approach could be seen in the simple bucolic scenes of Watteau's paintings, the growing popularity for rustic and entertaining comedies featuring common people, and a simpler style of dress. This, in turn, led to a distinctive contrast in virtually all aspects of life and, subsequently, with the retreat of the dominance of French taste and rise of more local or national idioms. While much can be seen as creating momentary fads, the notion that there were two parallel paths in society became ingrained, with simultaneous coexistence becoming the norm.

In music, one finds that the high Baroque style was being contrasted with a new and potentially revolutionary new one that began to emerge during the period from 1725 to 1730. The contrasts were often striking, both technically and aesthetically. One good example of this is the *Beggar's Opera*, which premiered on January 28, 1728, at Lincoln's Inn Fields Theatre in London. At that time, opera in the English capital was dominated by Italian opera seria at the King's Theatre at the Haymarket, where Handel was the chief

Figure 1.8 Caricature of *The Beggar's Opera* (etching, 1729) showing singers and an orchestra of low-caste instruments (a dulcimer, bagpipe, harmonica, and tromba marina)

composer and which was the home to the Royal Academy of Music. Here the traditional Baroque opera, replete with its gods and heroes, provided a higher class of entertainment in a style that was conventional spectacle. The *Beggar's Opera*, however, had a plot written by John Gay that focused on the common lowlife folk of London, with central characters that included thieves, prostitutes, rakes, and other assorted criminals (Figure 1.8). Although the overture by violinist Johann Pepusch was Baroque in style, the common human element manifested itself in simple tunes and diatonic harmonies that were accessible, memorable, and the antithesis of the serious opera. Public reaction was immediate and positive, with the satire proving to be both popular and controversial, as a note in the newspaper *The Craftsman* from February 17, 1728 shows: "We hear that the British Opera, commonly called *The Beggar's Opera*, continues to be acted, at the Theatre in Lincoln's-Inn Fields with general Applause, to the great Mortification of the Performers and Admirers of the Outlandish Opera in the Haymarket." While it might be a stretch to consider this work part of the Classical Period, it nonetheless had a different aesthetic that foreshadowed the musical changes that were on the horizon, for it began a genre called ballad opera that both competed with and eventually overwhelmed the Baroque spectacle over the next decade.

The attention to homophony, long lyrical melodies, and simple formal structure offered the most obvious counterbalance to the static melodies, extensive use of counterpoint, and polyphony of the Baroque during this period of coexistence. Often, the latter was characterized as the "learned" (*gelehrte*) style. Johann Joachim Quantz, writing in his *Versuch einer Anweisung die Flöte traversiere zu spielen* (*Essay of a Method for Playing the Transverse Flute*) in 1752, noted the parallels that were in existence during the emergence of the new style. He comments:

> Old musicians complain of the melodic extravagances of the young, and the young mock the dryness of the old . . . they either choose for their practice very difficult pieces for which they are not yet prepared . . . or in the wish to be *galant*, they lapse into pieces which are so easy that their only advantage is that of flattering the ear.[9]

For Quantz, the existence of parallel styles of music composition was a means of educating the prospective musician into the advantages and difficulties of each, causing them to weigh various styles in an equal manner that reflects not only the aesthetical taste but also the circumstances under which a compositional style is to be chosen. This he labels "musical discernment" and further states that "anyone who only cares to devote himself to music haphazardly, as to a trade rather than an art, will remain a lifelong bungler." Given that this theorist was well-traveled, having toured from Italy to France during between 1724 and 1728 and witnessed the emergence of the new Classical style along with the heyday of the high Baroque, his opinions were based on his own experiences dealing with colleagues in the places he visited. Such sentiments that he expressed were echoed by others such as his Dresden colleague Johann David Heinichen or Johann Adolf Scheibe, but the consensus was that the new style was both moribund and static, while the new *galant* style was more progressive but lacked depth. It is therefore not surprising that two streams of thought emerged: first, that it was not just a case of old versus new but, rather, the adaptability of various styles to the genres and, second, a competent composer needed to be educated enough in both so that he (or she) could navigate between the old and new styles. Moreover, the educational process as outlined by Quantz and others incorporated an understanding of the eighteenth-century musical world, with not only an eye toward mastery but also the ability to synthesize and adapt to a cultural world that was rapidly changing.

Definitions and the Rise of Theory, Aesthetics, and Musical Pedagogy

Composers during the Classical Period were expected not only to be masters of their craft at whatever level they expected to attain but to also be aware both of how music was changing over time and the various stylistic trends that were emerging. Moreover, they were to have been well educated and focused, and in so doing were likewise expected to pass their knowledge on to students, either formally or informally. Music education, however, did not always depend upon a specific academic curriculum or specialized private instruction, but rather encompassed a wide variety of sources through which they honed their professional abilities.

These can be defined as follows: (1) foundational works in the form of treatises and pedagogical exercises, (2) general historical overviews of music and its components, (3) critical writings on music, and (4) encyclopedias or lexicons that provide specific definitions. Not all of these were used as part of the educational process, and it was expected that prospective composers would familiarize themselves with all styles and genres, as they could anticipate the need to write in that style on commission or at the behest of their employers or patrons.

During most of the Classical Period, music as an educational subject was common, but there was a division between those deemed knowledgeable, labeled *connoisseurs* (in German, *Kenner*), and those for whom music was deemed of secondary interest, *amateurs* (in German, *Liebhaber*). These rubrics applied equally to composers and their audiences, but the dividing line was not clear or unambiguous. A *connoisseur* could range from being a professional composer or musician to an educated member of the audience. An *amateur* was someone who either involved him- or herself in music as a pastime or who regarded music from the perspective of another field. In the eighteenth century, this distinction was perhaps sharper than it

Figure 1.9 Title page of Johann Joseph Fux, *Gradus ad Parnassum* (1725)

appears, for although both connoisseurs and amateurs could be well trained in music, those who made it their profession as musicians (which includes both composers and performers, most of which were one and the same) were obliged to undergo a rather rigorous training.

At the foundation of almost all musical learning was counterpoint, also deemed the "learned" or strict style (and here *style* is used in the broadest sense of the term).[10] This was defined at the time principally in terms of fugue or imitation (see Document 1) and was mainly employed in sacred music, though it was also a metaphor for Baroque compositions in general. Perhaps the most important text for composers of the period was *Gradus ad Parnassum* (*Steps to Parnassus*) by Austrian composer Johann Joseph Fux (Figure 1.9). Fux, *Kapellmeister* to the Imperial court in Vienna, published his work in Latin in 1725, and within a few short years it became the most celebrated tutorial in Europe, influencing composers from Johann Sebastian Bach to Ludwig van Beethoven over the course of the century. Fux himself regarded it both as the foundation of the study of polyphony and as a means of providing future students with the ability to learn and understand counterpoint in a step-by-step process.[11] Fux's *Gradus* was based on the historical strict style of Palestrina to such an extent that the main "teacher" in the Socratic work named Aloysius is directly referred to as the Renaissance composer himself.

Thereafter, students were taught the rules of harmony, another watchword for music composition. Here, the educational focus differed as the student became more specialized. In Italy, both private study and educational institutions existed. The latter came in the form of conservatories, many of which were attached to churches or monasteries. In Venice, for example, the *ospedale* was a charitable institution that catered mainly to young women. Originally an orphanage, throughout the eighteenth century it became more open so that both foundlings (*figlie di coro*) and daughters of more well-to-do families (*figlie di spese*) could attend. Here, such teachers as Antonio Vivaldi and Baldassare Galuppi trained them in music. In Naples, four conservatories (*Santa Maria di Loreto*, *Pietà dei Turchini*, *Sant'Onofrio a Capuana*, and *I Poveri di Gesù Cristo*) catered to students from throughout the Mediterranean region. Students came from as far away as Spain or Malta to study with the teachers there. While travelers like Charles Burney noted that the living conditions for the students were sometimes primitive, he was surprised by the vibrant atmosphere in which musicians were constantly practicing. Here, leading composers of the day, such as Nicola Porpora and Francesco Durante, turned out a steady stream of composers who became international successes, such as Paisiello, Niccolò Jommelli, and Pergolesi; Porpora later became the teacher of Joseph Haydn, using the same educational methods as in Naples. The chief musical tool for teaching harmony involved the *partimento*, the realization of both melody and harmony from a simple upper voice and bass line. Though its use of the tool resulted in predictable musical devices—voice-leading patterns, phrase structure, motivic sequences, cadential structures—it served to define the Italian compositional style throughout the century throughout Europe. One of the more important texts, which in many ways comes close to also being a lexicon, is the *Elementi teorico-pratico di musica* (*Theoretical-Practical Elements of Music*) by Francesco Galeazzi from 1791, in which the musical education of Italian composers is described in a series of articles. In France the main instructional tool for harmony were the treatises, the chief one of which was the *Génération harmonique, ou Traité de musique théorique et pratique* (*Harmonic Generation, or Treatise on Theoretical and Practical Music*) by Jean-Philippe Rameau published in Paris in 1737, based largely on his 1722 *Traité de l'harmonie réduite à ses principes naturels* (*Treatise of Harmony Reduced to its Natural Principles*) and the 1726 *Nouveau système de musique théorique* (*New System of Music Theory*). Although conceived as a pedagogical exercise based on historical forebears, it nonetheless provided rules and methods for musical composition based on practical applications. As Jean-Benjamin de Laborde, a pupil of Rameau noted, "[m]usic since the revival of arts was abandoned to the ear, caprice, and conjecture of composers, and was equally in want of unerring rules in theory and practice—Rameau appeared, and chaos was no more."[12]

In Germany, the widely read book *Der vollkommene Kapellmeister* (*The Consummate Musical Director*) published in 1739 by theorist Johann Mattheson was often used as a means of education for composers (Figure 1.10). This was especially pertinent since this work contains commentary on both the French and Austrian handbooks noted earlier. Within a few years, theorists such as Friedrich Wilhelm Marpurg and Scheibe began publishing treatises that were regarded as pedagogical tools in an ever-increasing number. Perhaps the best known and perhaps most controversial of these were the two handbooks written by Abbé Georg Joseph Vogler entitled *Tonwissenschaft und Tonsetzkunst* (*The Science of Notes and Art of Composition*) and *Stimmbildungskunst* (*The Art of Voice Leading*) and published in 1778 and 1776, respectively. Both expand the rules of harmony and composition, the last for the voice, by creating a new system of analytical signs; these still exist as defining tonal centers by Roman numerals.

Pedagogical treatises for individual instruments also began to be published beginning about 1730. These not only contained technical information on the instruments themselves, including range, limitations, and ornaments; they often also included exercises to increase proficiency and develop skills for performers. Composers also saw them as relevant, for this information was invaluable in terms of writing for the instruments. Moreover, they often provided other information on, placement within the ensemble, types of music, and even audiences. We have already noted Quantz's work on playing the flute, but some of the earliest works of this type come from the Baroque Period in works on playing the keyboard by François Couperin[13] and others. As the keyboard was at the foundation of music pedagogy, since learning figured bass (called thoroughbass at the time) was an important tool in both harmony and voice leading, many of these taught both improvisation and accompanying as part of the continuo practice, as well as practical methods of performing on keyboard instruments, most prominently the harpsichord, the clavichord, the organ, and fortepiano (see Chapter 3). Perhaps the most influential of these works was the *Versuch über die wahre Art das Clavier zu spielen* (*Essay on the True Art of Playing the Keyboard*) published in 1753 by Carl Philipp Emanuel Bach. The second-eldest son of Johann Sebastian Bach, C. P. E. (as he is known), achieved a reputation as a progressive innovator of both technique and compositional style, with special attention to improvisation and the expression of emotion in music through technical elements. He was one of the chief composers of the *Empfindsamkeit* musical style and was admired by successive generations of composers, including Mozart, Haydn, and Beethoven. He states directly: "No piece can be well performed without some form of keyboard accompaniment . . . [and] in order to become a skilled performer of thorough bass, due time must first be given to the playing of good solos."[14] Its equivalent for the violin was published in 1756 by Leopold Mozart and titled *Versuch einer gründlichen Violinschule* (*A Treatise on the Fundamental Principles of Violin Playing*), itself based partly on an Italian treatise *Trattato di musica secondo la vera scienza dell'armonia* (*Treatise on Music along with the True Science of Harmony*) from 1754 by Giuseppe Tartini. Other such pedagogical tools—for example, Valentin Roeser's 1764 work on the clarinet and horn or Johann Ernst Altenburg's 1795 treatise on trumpets and timpani[15]—became abundant by the middle of

Figure 1.10 Title page of Johann Mattheson, *Der vollkommene Kapellmeister* (1739)

the period. Indeed, one notes that such a variety existed that, with the founding of the Paris Conservatoire in 1795 under Bernard Sarette, a concerted effort was made to provide primers to teach all of the instruments, music theory, and composition by the instructors there. These treatises are discussed further in a later chapter on the instruments.

Along with the increasing number of pedagogical works came a renewed interest in music history. Two of the best-known works in English were Charles Burney's *A General History of Music* published in 1789 in two volumes, which is a reaction to *A General History of the Science and Practice of Music* in five volumes from 1776. Both were the result of extensive travels by both authors but were, in turn, based on works from the countries they visited. In Italy, for example, a Baroque history written by Giovanni Bontempi in 1695 was supplanted by the *Storia della Musica* (*History of Music*) published in 1757 (with further editions in

1770 and 1781) by Padre Giovanni Battista Martini, himself a composer and collector of a vast library of more than seventeen thousand books. In France, Charles-Henri de Blainville published a more accurate *Histoire générale, critique et philologique de la musique* (*General, Critical, and Philological History of Music*) in 1767, while in Germany Marpurg wrote his *Kritische Einleitung in die Geschichte und Lehrsatze der alten und neuen Musik* (*Critical Introduction to the History and Methodology of Old and New Music*) in 1759 while at the court of Frederick the Great. All these histories, whether based on documents, anecdotes, or unsupported assumptions, were read by a great many musicians during the Classical Period, which can be said to have been the first time professionals and amateurs became aware of their place in the larger historical context and, as such, provided them both the excuse to retain an older style or the prod for further progressive development.

The third educational area was in the realm of critical writings on music. Beginning with the widely read treatises of Mattheson, such as the *Vollkommene Kapellmeister* already mentioned or the 1722 *Critica Musica*, and Scheibe, whose *Critische Musikus* in 1745 reflected the state of music of the time; music criticism and aesthetics formed an important educational tool for prospective musicians during the Classical Period. Most treatises on the various instruments, such as that by Quantz, include large sections on how music should be heard and received by both performers and audiences, which styles were the most appropriate and for what occasions, and how to avoid complacency. He states specifically,

> He who wishes to excel in music must feel in himself a perpetual and untiring love for it, a willingness and eagerness to spare neither industry nor pains, and to bear steadfastly all the difficulties that present themselves in this mode of life . . . changes of taste, the weakening of bodily powers, vanishing youth, the loss of a patron—upon whom the entire fortune of many a musician depends—are all capable of hindering the progress of music.[16]

Beginning in 1750, Marpurg wrote no fewer than fifteen treatises, but his views on the aesthetics of music can be found in two works: *Der critische Musicus an der Spree* (1750) and the *Kritische Briefe über die Tonkunst* (*Critical Letters on Composition*, 1759–1763). Both of these contain descriptions of contemporary music and performance, criticizing both the aesthetics and practices, sometimes with musical examples appended. Philosophy is also noted in such works as *Etwas von und über Musik fürs Jahr 1777* (*Something on and about Music for the Year 1777*) by then–university student Joseph Martin Kraus, in which rules of musical passion are given alongside detailed critiques of German operas, or in the *Musikalisch kritische Bibliothek* (*Musical Critical Library*, Gotha, 1778) by Johann Nikolas Forkel (who also wrote a history of music). Journals were also widely produced, many of which contained information on music drawn from throughout Europe. One of the most widely read of these was the *Wöchentliche Nachrichten* (*Weekly News*) published by Johann Adam Hiller that included commentary on style, criticism of works, and news of musical events for several years beginning in 1766. In Paris, such commentary was delivered either in the form of pamphlets or in newspapers such as the *Mércure de France* or *Chronique de Paris*, and in Vienna the *Wiener Diarium* often contained articles of interest on the latest trends in music. Musicians were well aware of the aesthetics of the time, and even if direct criticism was often buried among broader philosophical musings, the educational value was important in that it provided a direction for their own stylistic development.

One of the most useful tools available for educational purposes was the encyclopedia or lexicon. These were an outgrowth of Enlightenment thought that began in Paris, where savants like Jean-Jacques Rousseau sought to create reference resources. His *Dictionnaire de Musique* from 1768 was widely available throughout Europe and translated into several languages. Extensive definitions of music and musical terms could also be found in the voluminous *Encyclopédie* published between 1757 and 1770 by Denis Diderot (Figure 1.11). These inspired similar efforts by Johann Georg Sulzer, whose *Allgemeine Theorie der Schönen Künste* (*General Theory of the Fine Arts*), which appeared in 1771, was widely used throughout Germany; other important lexicons include Heinrich Koch's *Musikalische Lexikon* (1802) and the two-volume *Historisch-biographisches Lexikon der Tonkünstler* (*Historical-biographical Lexicon of Composers*) by

Figure 1.11 Title page of a volume of Denis Diderot's *Encyclopédie* (1770)

Ernst Ludwig Gerber, published in 1790–1791, with an expanded second edition published between 1812 and 1814. These reference works were not only a good educational resource for musicians; they also encouraged the compiling of similar books in various regions outside of central Europe.[17]

Finally, one of the most important educational opportunities for professional musicians was the Grand Tour. While there was no set itinerary for such travel, going to musical centers was both enlightened and brought people into direct contact with whatever musical style existed in that place. Grand Tours were not limited to novice or aspiring composers but, rather, could be undertaken at different stages of their careers, each with the idea of reinvigorating and reinventing themselves by absorbing what they learned as they traveled. The musical establishments were not the only reason for going abroad; composers were also offered the opportunity to meet and interact with acknowledged masters in the field, if they so chose. The results were often felt not only in terms of musical style; they could also inspire further critical and historical works, as well.

The best examples of the Grand Tour can be seen in the published diaries of travels in both northern and southern Europe by Burney. By getting to know the chief personalities in the various courts and towns, he was not only able to give a valuable contemporaneous description of people and places; he also collected data that formed the foundation of his history of music. Another well-documented set of travels is that of the young Wolfgang Mozart, who as a child prodigy traveled to France and England, as a youth to Italy, and as a mature composer to France, Germany, and Bohemia. He performed and was educated during the first, and achieved a solid reputation as a young composer in the second, becoming a member of Padre Martini's Accademia Filarmonia and a Knight of the Golden Spur in Rome. Although success eluded him when he traveled to Paris via Mannheim, intending to make his fortune, his later journeys to Bohemia to produce operas and Germany—seeking potential employment in Dresden, Leipzig, and Berlin or supporting the coronation of Leopold II in Frankfurt am Main—were experiential.

The opportunities for education in music were legion, from personal study with more established composers or musicians to influences that could be had from reading treatises ranging from specific methodology in counterpoint, harmony, and so on to more esoteric ones that discussed the purpose and philosophy behind musical style. The creation of comprehensive histories and musical dictionaries provided definitions that could be used to become knowledgeable about the overall world of music, while direct experience could be had if one was willing to travel and learn. All these contributed to the well-constructed musical tool chest of a composer who continued to develop professionally as they kept up with the information presented. But musical education was, by itself, not limited to opportunity, but rather, it was intricately bound up with the actual musical-stylistic trends that define the Classical Period.

Documents

Document 1. From Heinrich Christoph Koch, *Musikalisches Lexikon* (1802), col. 1453 *Style or Manner of Writing* (translation by the author).

The rubric of the strict manner of writing has been partially retained, therefore, because in order to compose in this fashion stricter rules must be observed that now and again have been especially pointed out in the articles included herein, and partially also because the fugue, as the most prominent product of this manner of writing, is supported by a stricter form than the other artistic products. The common compositions done in this way are:

1. The two main types of fugue, namely the canon and the common fugue, as well as
2. All of those sorts of movements that are worked out without being cast in the normal form of the fugue; that is, in which a principal theme is carried out in the aforementioned sequence of notes, or replaced and imitated in the various parts, without conforming to a specific form through this development or imitation. To this belongs the fugal choruses of motets, contrapuntal chorales, etc.

The free or nonconforming manner of writing, that one also calls the galant style, differentiates itself from the foregoing

1. Through a copious ornamentation of the melody and the dismembering of the main notes of the melody through more prominent diversions and insertions, through more changes in the rhythmic portions of the same, and especially through the conjoining of such melodic parts that do not always exist in close proximity to each other, etc.
2. Through a less confusing harmony, and
3. Subsequently, so that the remaining parts serve simply as an accompaniment to the main voice, and as accompanying parts have for the most part no completely obvious participation in the expression of the emotion, etc.

All types of individual movements of the larger vocal pieces, such as arias, choruses, and so forth; all types of ballet or dance music, as well as all of the introductory pieces, concertos, and types of sonatas that are not contrapuntal, can be counted among the compositions in the free manner of writing.

Document 2. From Johann Joachim Quantz, *On Playing the Flute* (1752), translated by Edward Reilly (2nd edition, New York: Schirmer Books, 1985), 22–23.

None must imagine, however, that I demand that every piece must be composed in accordance with the rigid rules of double counterpoint, that is, in accordance with the rules that prescribe how to adjust the parts to that they are inverted, exchanged, and transposed in an harmonious manner. This would be a reprehensible kind of pedantry. I maintain only that it is the duty of every composer to know such rules; that he should seek to use the artifices only at places where good melody permits, so no rupture is felt either in the beauty of the melody or in its good effect; and that listeners should perceive no laborious industry, but nature alone shining forth everywhere. The word counterpoint usually makes a disagreeable impression upon the majority of those who propose to follow only their innate ability; they consider it bookish pedantry. The reason is that they know only the name, and not the nature of the subject and its benefits. Had they acquired only a little understanding of it, the word would sound less frightful. I do not wish to play the part of panegyrist for all kinds of double counterpoint, although each, employed in a certain manner and at a suitable time, many have its uses. I cannot, however, refrain from rendering justice to counterpoint *all'ottava*, and strongly recommending exact knowledge of it as an indispensable matter for every young composer, since this form of counterpoint is not only most necessary in fugues and other artful pieces, but is also of excellent service in many *galant* imitations and exchanges of parts . . . if then, all teachers of music were at the same time connoisseurs of it; if they knew how to impart proper notions of artful music to their pupils; if they had their pupils play pieces that are skillfully worked out enough and explained their contents to them; then amateurs not only would gradually accustom themselves to music of this kind, but would also acquire greater insight into music in general, and find more pleasure in it. In consequence, music would be more highly esteemed than at present, and true musicians would earn more thanks for their labors. Since, however, the majority of amateurs only learn music mechanically, these benefits are suppressed; and since we lack both good masters and willing students, the state of music remains very imperfect.

Notes

1. An even more revolutionary statement was inserted into a play *Julius von Tarant* by author Johann Anton Leisewitz: "The state kills freedom."
2. This term is difficult to translate into English with any precision, given that it has many nuances. Generally, it means "sensibility" or "sensitivity," but the meaning is closer to emotionalism.
3. The original name of the drama was *Wirrwarr* (*Confusion*) when it was produced in 1776.
4. Ossian was a fictitious creation of Scottish author James Macpherson, who published the series of poems in 1760. Nonetheless, it had an immediate and powerful effect on European culture, eventually being translated into most languages.
5. See Document 1.
6. Neal Zaslaw, ed. *Man and Music: The Classical Era: From the 1740s to the End of the 18th Century* (Englewood Cliffs, NJ: Prentice Hall, 1989), 1–2. Zaslaw notes: "Such limits chime naturally—which may not be wholly coincidental—with the traditional periodization of musical history . . . such beginning and ending points in music history represent perceived disjunctions in the evolution of musical styles—disjunctions that must be taken into account even by those historians who might prefer to treat the whole of the eighteenth century as a more-or-less coherent unit."
7. See Friedrich Blume, *Renaissance and Baroque Music* (New York: Norton, 1967) and *Classic and Romantic Music* (New York: Norton, 1970).
8. Zaslaw, ed. *Man and Music*, 1. The quotation occurs within a larger context, where he defines the musical period as being between about 1740 and the death of Haydn in 1809, give or take a year. Zaslaw, however, argues convincingly for the fluidity and subjectivity of such boundaries.
9. Johann Joachim Quantz, *On Playing the Flute*, trans. Edward Reilly (New York: Schirmer Books, 1985), 21.
10. See Chapter 2.
11. Johann Joseph Fux, *Gradus ad Parnassum*, trans. Alfred Mann (New York: Norton, 1965). Translations into various European languages began almost immediately after the work was first published in 1725.
12. Quoted in Charles Burney, *A General History of Music* (London, 1776–1789; reprint New York: Dover, 1957), II: 969.
13. *L'art de toucher le clavecin* (*The Art of Playing the Harpsichord*) published in Paris in 1716.
14. See Carl Philipp Emanuel Bach, *Essay on the True Art of Playing Keyboard Instruments*, trans. William Mitchell (New York: Norton, 1949), 173. Mitchell interprets Bach's original "Klavier" as multiple instruments, which is technically correct, but can be translated (as here) by the generic term *keyboard*.
15. Valentin Roeser, *Essai d'instruction à l'usage de ceux qui composent pour la clarinette et le cor* (*Essay for the Instruction and Use of Those Who Composer for the Clarinet and Horn*; Paris, 1764); Johann Ernst Altenburg, *Versuch einer Anleitung zur heroisch-musikalischen Trompeter-und Paukerkunst* (*An Essay on the Development of the Heroic and Musical Art of the Trumpeters and Kettledrummers*; Halle, 1795). See Chapter 3.
16. Quantz, *On Playing the Flute*, 15.
17. See, for example, Carl Envallsson, *Musikalisk Lexikon* (Stockholm, 1802).

2 The Emergence of the New Styles of Classical Period Music

In his book *The Classical Style: Haydn, Mozart, Beethoven*, musicologist Charles Rosen noted that the "Classical Style" was a difficult concept to define.[1] The general term *style* itself was even more tenuous, particularly in the eighteenth century, for no one single definition seems to have been commonly agreed upon. Rosen mainly equates it with the musical language of the period as expressed through the form and structure of the compositions themselves (with a focal point on the three composers noted in his title). He does, however, acknowledge that "style" had other meanings, ranging from a commonality of the music in all of its aspects, called the "coherence of the musical language," to how the various audiences for whom this music was written defined style on their terms, whether in public or private performance. The former seeks cohesiveness in defining such particular things as sonata form, harmonic modulations, thematic contrast or development (called in German *thematische Arbeit*), and so on. The latter surrounds the matter of *taste* (in French *goût*), which was extremely variable with respect to time and place. For example, the musical tastes could vary between places such as Berlin and Vienna, manifesting themselves as different styles of music being in vogue, and consequently the expectations of both resident composers and audiences that the pieces being written and performed would conform to these local preferences. Moreover, "style" could also be a means of defining how composers were to write for both the voice and instruments. Neal Zaslaw, in his introduction to *Man & Music: The Classical Era*, notes that general notions of style during this period are based on "stylistic innovations . . . brought to fruition by great 'masters,'" further stating that a broader approach based upon various developments in both music and society would be "revelatory."[2] This view is a good starting point for realizing that "style" should be discerned on several levels during this time, each fostered by time and circumstances.

In approaching this topic, it is instructive to note that the Classical style overall can first be defined as broadly as possible, but it should also be noted that the levels of definition of musical language ("style" at its most concise interpretation) can have more nuanced meanings. Specifically, one can find the concept of style in various guises, ranging from a narrow personal definition to encompassing broader trends that evolved over the course of the eighteenth century. For the sake of clarity, we note the following: first, every composer was usually credited with a *personal style*, which was defined by his or her musical creativity. Second, the term is used broadly to divide instrumental and vocal music, each category of which requires a different type of music to be written. These are the *generic styles* that are linked to specific genres, such as the symphony, concerto, sacred music, opera, and so on. Third, there are the so-called *national styles* that are depicted as representing a musical language seen during the time as endemic to a place or culture. Finally, and most important, there are the broader *style trends* manifested across the entire musical spectrum as defined by various specific musical trademarks or compositional devices. These trademarks are often used to define the new style of Classical Period music; for our purposes we can call them **Galant, Empfindsamkeit, Sturm und Drang,** and **High Classicism**. Their chronological boundaries are indistinct, and they do not represent a sequential development but, rather, coexisted more or less simultaneously and incorporated both the generic and national concepts of style. Each also displays a sense of stylistic evolution over course of the eighteenth century. Before discussing these further, it is necessary briefly to discuss the more common definitions of style.

The broadest generic notion of a Classical style is a stereotype. Meant to evoke the elegance and grace of all the arts during the so-called Classical civilizations of ancient Greece and Rome, in music it is generally defined by the notion of structural and formal symmetry (often expressed in terms of the sonata form but also including elements of texture, rhythm, and musical development on a smaller scale), elegance and moderation (in terms of emotional expression and lyrical beauty), and logical compositional development using restrained emotion (precise and logical modulatory patterns, contrasting main and secondary themes, thematic lyricism, controlled dynamics and articulations, reduced improvisatory moments and select ornamentation). This was done in an attempt to appeal to a broader section of the musical audiences, many of which regarded music as an intellectual pursuit, as they did the other creative arts. For them, the Classical style acted as an overarching, all-encompassing definition, purposely vague yet providing a perception of the music of this age that mirrored its role in society. Today, it still persists whenever the historical period is discussed, yet it does not lend itself to the complexity inherent within such a broad definition.

The concept of *personal* style is often used during this period as a metaphor for individual genius or originality. For instance, in 1783 a visit by Swedish *Kapellmeister* Joseph Martin Kraus to well-known opera composer Christoph Willibald von Gluck in Vienna elicited the enthusiastic declaration: "This man has a great style, the like of which I have never seen in any other composer."[3] This comment makes the matter of "style" synonymous with originality, at least in the eyes of the elder composer. On the other hand, Charles Burney, visiting Braunschweig during his travels, commented on composer Friedrich Gottlob Fleischer: "M[r] Fleischer is another Brunswic [sic] composer of great merit, whose church music, comic operas, and harpsichord lessons are all written in an elegant and pleasing style."[4] Here, *style* is relegated more to the music and its reception, with the composer being praised for his music's accessibility rather than any specific musical trademarks. Finally, the term *style* can refer to the imitation by others. Perhaps the best example of this during the period can be found in the international reputation of Joseph Haydn, whereby his personal style was so popular that it was imitated by numerous others. Cellist Luigi Boccherini was even later labeled "the wife of Haydn," an epithet coined by violinist Giuseppe Puppo to note the imitative personal style of that composer.[5] In these cases, the term *style* as a personal musical attribute can mean a number of different things and defies a single definition at this level, even though it was commonly acknowledged and used.

The eighteenth century, however, usually divided the generic definition of style into two broad categories: vocal and instrumental. These, in turn, were subdivided into other appropriate "styles" meant to be used for each genre within these categories. Quantz notes in his treatise:

> Music is either vocal or instrumental: only a few pieces, however, are intended for voice alone; instrumental music usually has a part in and is combined with the majority of vocal pieces. Yet these two kinds of music differ greatly from one another not only broadly, in purpose and therefore in organization, but also in their subdivisions, each of which has its own particular laws and requires its particular style of composition.[6]

For vocal music, the concept differentiated further between the sacred and secular styles, specifically between music meant for church and employing learned or strict counterpoint and that meant for venues ranging from the opera house to the salon, requiring a more lyrical and less complex musical style. Instrumental music appears to have been regarded as secondary to vocal music in the eyes of many theorists. Johann Mattheson in 1739 called vocal music "the mother" and instrumental music "the daughter," while Johann Adolph Scheibe notes a year or so later in his *Critische Musikus* that "soon one finds theatrical music, and among it a sacred movement so that everything is so mixed up that one cannot find an overarching style at all."[7] In other words, even the theorists of the time who were aware of the division between vocal and instrumental work, as well as the styles needed to compose them, knew that this concept was quite vague and that boundaries of the styles were often crossed.

If a personal style was linked too closely to an individual composer (or style of playing or singing to a musician) and there was a feeling in the Classical Period that the clear division between vocal or instrumental genres was often blurred, the concept of style as reflected in the various geographical regions was better understood.

National Styles

A more widely known definition concerns the so-called *national* styles.[8] Quantz (Figure 2.1) notes that "the *diversity of style* manifest in different nations that fancy the fine arts, although less related to the essentials than to the incidentals of music, has the greatest influence upon musical judgment."[9] This being said, the principal three that appeared during the Baroque Period were defined as the Italian, French, and German styles, each of which had specific musical characteristics associated with them and were most often a reference to vocal music, principally opera. They were considered common knowledge among the various writers on music, and composers themselves were aware of them whenever they composed music.

The Italian Style

Perhaps the most widely known of these was the Italian style. There were musical characteristics that define it over the course of the Classical Period. First and foremost, the Italian language, with its plethora of long vowels, both hard and soft consonants, and a natural poetic linguistic rhythm, was deemed ideal for vocal music, particularly since the accentuation is regular and predictable. As a result, the musical emphasis lies in flowing and flexible melodic lines that have graceful contours and are able to be expanded or contracted according to internal lyricism. Second, the rhythmic structures are often clearly defined, with a preference for symmetrical and regular duple, triple, or complex meters that derived from the graceful dances of the Baroque Period. Third, harmonies tend toward a regular modulatory pattern, often straying little from the closer related keys of I, IV, V, or vi, and the progressions, coupled with contrasting longer thematic phrases, seem to be done according to a standard pattern, thus making any abrupt or unusual chords or harmonies seem jarring or out of place. Finally, textures tend to be on the thinner side, with emphasis on the clarity of the melodic line, a rhythmic foundation, often an ostinato drum pattern in the bass, an accompaniment that is either an ostinato or makes use of the so-called Alberti figuration, sustained or lightly orchestrated winds and brass that provide a harmonic foundation, and thematic reinforcement through doubling or parallel

Figure 2.1 Portrait of Johann Joachim Quantz by Francesco Solimena (*ca.* 1725)

Source: © Kulturstiftung des Hauses Hessen, owner of the picture. The painting is reproduced by kind permission of Kulturstiftung des Hauses Hessen, Museum Schloss Fasanerie, Eichenzell near Fulda.

The Emergence of the New Styles 27

thirds or sixths. In terms of periodicity, the Italian style tended toward regular phrases, generally of a 3+3 or 4+4 pattern sometimes doubled in antecedent–consequent format.

The Italian style did evolve over the course of the century in both vocal and instrumental music. At the beginning, a new vocal style was exemplified by operatic works such as Pergolesi's *La serva padrona*, an intermezzo composed in 1733 as the comic work in between the acts of his *Il prigionier superbo*. The comic plot by Gennaro Antonia Federico involves the machinations of the maid Serpina to win over her master, the gullible Uberto. In Serpina's second aria, "Stizzoso, mio stizzoso," the simplicity of the lyrical theme and structure can be seen in the opening bars. The first phrase is a repeated 3+3 bar pattern, where the first violins in unison double the vocal line and violas fill in the inner texture. The second phrase is a repeated consequent of 4+4 that modulates, as expected to E major, the dominant of the main key of the aria (Example 2.1). From a harmonic standpoint, the entire A section stays within these closely related keys, while a brief B section (before a da capo) is a brief modulatory sequence from D major (IV) back to the tonic (I) without changing either texture or main theme. It is this simplicity and accessibility that epitomizes the lyrical Italian style as the Classical Period began. Of course, the virtuosity contained in the coloratura of the late Baroque is not lacking, as the example from the cantata *L'amor prigioniero* by German composer Johann Adolph Hasse, who worked in both Italy and Germany, demonstrates (Example 2.2). Here one can

Example 2.1 Giovanni Pergolesi, *La serva padrona*, No. 4 Aria "Stizzoso, mio stizzoso," mm. 1–14

Example 2.2 Johann Adolph Hasse, *L'amor prigioniero*, Aria "Se tutto il mondo," mm. 65–78, vocal line only

see the technical challenges faced by singers, as well as the clear ease with which such coloratura was able to be accomplished in a musically fluid fashion, enhancing the melodic line and providing it with an extensive musical contour even while maintaining a harmonic simplicity.

By the middle of the century, the Italian style had begun to become more stereotyped and less novel as it dominated much of Europe (and elsewhere) thanks to the spread of Italian music and musicians. For example, traveling troupes such as that led by Pietro Mingotti, whose musical directors Gluck, Giuseppe Sarti, and Francesco Antonio Baldassare Uttini wrote music in the style that was performed throughout Scandinavia and Russia. In the latter, Empress Catherine the Great continued a practice of her predecessor, Empress Elisabeth, of importing Italian composers to write for her court. England, of course, had long been a goal of Italian composers, and even though the Italian opera seria had varied fortunes there since George Frederick Handel's company went bankrupt in 1728, subsequent companies such as the King's Theatre required Italian singers, and opera seria continued to be performed through the middle of the century. For example, castrato Giusto Fernando Tenducci, also called "Senesino," composed music for the public concerts in Great Britain up until 1789, and Johann Christian Bach wrote Italianate works for both his Bach-Abel concerts and the King's Theatre. Even as far away as Mexico in New Spain, Italian-born Ignacio de Jerusalem, among others, brought the style an intercontinental dimension. Finally, even in Paris Italian composers dominated musical life, particularly in the opera.

Antoine-Chrysostome Quatremère de Quincy, an architectural historian and savant, noted the dominance of the Italian style as represented by both composer and performer:

> All agree that in music, Italy is richer than all of the other nations combined. She has produced, out of proportion, more great masters than all the rest of Europe has ever produced. She owes this advantage to the harmonious idiom, sonorous and malleable, in which the simple prosody somehow becomes the principal element of the melody; to the nature of the soft and luxurious climate, which lulls the senses, excites the passions, embellishes the language, and provides the imagination with forceful strokes of nature; to all those institutions favorable to the execution of music; and finally to the excellence of the schools thus established for the cultivation of this art.

If the Italian style was considered dominant during the Classical Period, it was certainly not without rivals, particularly in France.

The French Style

The French style was considered to be more rigid and regulated than the Italian and was often described as its antithesis. It was an outgrowth of the control exercised over music during the Baroque Period during the *ancien régime* under Louis XIV and Louis XV. It was mainly intended either as court entertainment or for the pleasure of connoisseurs, and thus, music as an art was both highly intellectual and conservative at the beginning of the Classical Period. While the Italian style featured mood and feeling, the French style was concerned with the expression of detailed nuances, reasoned and precise in terms of articulation and more restrained in terms of stirring passionate feelings.

When discussing the French style, most eighteenth-century authors noted that the melodies were fairly compact, often triadic, and rhythmically angular, so that the lyrical fluidity of the Italian melodies is rare or lacking altogether. In the vocal music, the texts were set mostly syllabically, with little or no opportunity for virtuoso display, all improvisatory nuances being generally restricted to precise and intricate ornamentation. There is an increased emphasis on complex harmony, with modulations that are sometimes quite abrupt and unprepared, and often-harsh dissonances occur. In terms of texture, the French retained the irregular patterns of the Baroque *style brisé* (broken style), which manifested itself in a lack of regular textural patterns, arpeggiated dislocation of the chord and rhythmic displacement of the notes, and irregular phrase lengths that avoid repetition. Rhythmic structures were generally derived from the penchant for the French to imitate ballet or stylized court dances, which in Paris and elsewhere were considered the epitome of high culture and exported throughout Europe. This, in turn, made most of the movements rather short and more succinct than in the Italian style, with less contrast and more emphasis on detailed performance practices. And yet, given that France was regarded as the model of civilized society, the musical trademarks of the style were often imitated, particularly the use of various dotted (or double-dotted) rhythmic motives and sometimes tortuous harmonic development.

Given the conservative nature of the French style, it is not surprising that musical aesthetics and treatises were more widely produced by French authors than elsewhere, perhaps with the exception of Germany. These came in the form of musical dictionaries, such as the *Dictionnaire de Musique* by Rousseau from 1768 or the entries in the *Encyclopédie, ou dictionnaire raisonné des sciences, des arts et des métiers* (*Encyclopedia, or a Systematic Dictionary of the Sciences, Arts, and Crafts*) published between 1754 and 1772 by Diderot and Jean d'Alembert, to specific treatises such as the *Démonstration du principe de l'harmonie* (*Demonstration of the Principles of Harmony*) by Rameau, an expansion on his seminal 1722 work on harmony, or Denis Ballière's 1764 *Théorie de la Musique*. The number of theoretical works elicited the admiration of musicians throughout Europe, even though the general view was that they reduced the creative art form to quantifiable sets of principles and rules. Burney quotes the four-volume *Essai sur la Musique ancienne et modern* (*Essay on Ancient and Modern Music*) published in 1780 by Jean-Benjamin de La Borde: "We will allow that the Italians are superior to us in *melody*; but they in return must grant that with respect to *harmony* we write in a manner superior to them in correctness, purity, and elegance." Quantz, however, notes, "For just as the Italians are almost too changeable in music, the French are too constant and slavish in it. . . . The French proceed very scrupulously in composition."[10] Here, the German theorist comments that both of these styles oppose each other but that the French style, conservative and static, has an element of consistency that is lacking in the Italian.

It is instructive to take a look at two examples of the French style. The first is the "Air des Sauvages" from Rameau's *Les Indies galantes* first performed in Paris in 1735. This forms the foundation of the fourth *entrée* or section in which natives of North America are featured. The opening dance of this air is a rondeau in the key of G minor. It is harmonically static, with a decisive rhythmic structure that is perfect for the dance, with a clear, angular harmonic contour, yet lively string textures and voice leading (Example 2.3). The piece is elegant and balanced, and although it purports to depict an exotic scene, the harmonic and melodic stability marks it as clearly French in style, conforming to the emerging homophonic and texturally rich style of early Classicism. This is all the more interesting considering that it dates from several years earlier, yet similar movements in the same style continue for several decades thereafter. The second example comes from the opera *Zémire et Azor* written in 1771 by Belgian-French composer André-Ernest-Modest Grétry, which has virtually the same plot as *Beauty and the Beast* (here with a nod to William Shakespeare's *Tempest* thrown in). The short arietta "Les esprits dont on nous fait peur" sung by the servant Ali in the first act shows how the French style evolved and yet stayed stable over the course of several decades. The

30 *Music and Style in the Classical Period*

Example 2.3 Jean-Philippe Rameau, *Les Indes galantes*, "Air des Sauvages," mm. 1–8

Example 2.4 André-Ernest-Modest Grétry, *Zemire et Azor*, "Les esprits dont on nous fait peur," mm. 1–8

short, even perfunctory, instrumental introduction is static harmonically in F major, with only a brief statement of the main theme. The broken figuration of the accompaniment, first in the second violins and then in the violas as the seconds join in reinforcing the first violins, provides a reinforcement of the regular duple rhythms in the melody and bass. All too soon, the voice enters with the same angular rhythms, and at the end of his first phrases, the *forte* dotted cadential colophon reemphasizes a French rhythmic motive. The vocal line is quite syllabic, with no extra notes other than a brief appoggiatura passing tone in the third measure (there only to support the F-major tonality). As simple as this example is, it, too, demonstrates both harmonic and melodic stability that characterizes the earlier French style, even though it is from a work worlds apart from the staid grand opera (Example 2.4). Although both of these examples differ widely in style, they conform to the views on what constitutes the French style during the Classical Period.

The German Style

The German style is likewise a concept that was continued from the Baroque Period. It was commonly believed that German composers created their own particular style by blending the best of both the Italian and French styles. As Quantz states,

> [i]f one has the necessary discernment to choose the best from the styles of different countries, a *mixed style* results that, without overstepping the bounds of modesty, could well be called *the German style*, not only because the Germans came upon it first, but because it has already been established at different places in Germany for many years, flourishes still, and displeases in neither Italy nor France, nor in other lands.[11]

He admonishes composers and musicians alike to retain the best of both major styles along with absorbing the older learned style, then he proposes that a "good style that is universal" will be the result. Later in the century, the concept of a purely German style shifted to become a more defined style rooted in a decisive and heavier type of performance practice, as noted by Daniel Gottlob Türk in his 1789 *Klavierschule* (Document 2). One might be tempted to conclude that a distinctive German style was composed only of the best elements of the two leading ones, taking a good sense of fluid melody from the Italians, the harmonic and rhythmic foundations from the French, and combining them with a nod to old-fashioned counterpoint. This is indeed what Scheibe says in his *Critische Musikus*: "In music we have come so far that we no longer find outsiders necessary for the composition of our pieces and that we have seen that the beauties of Italian and French music are practiced by our own countrymen with better intuition, substance, and experience."[12]

Combining the French and Italian styles and calling them German is problematic. As Leonard Ratner states: "Germany's contribution to eighteenth-century music was the talent of its composers, rather than a distinctive national idiom."[13] This mirrors the view expressed by Quantz, who wrote,

> Even if it cannot be said that the Germans have produced an individual style entirely different from that of other nations, they are all the more capable in taking whatever they like from another style, and they know how to make use of the good things in all types of foreign music.[14]

Many German theorists devoted large portions of their descriptive aesthetical commentary to the matter of a German style, but for the most part their sometimes nationalist-cultural notions are either devoted to equating it with specific major composers (Haydn or Carl Philipp Emanuel Bach) or reflecting on how it was in danger of being corrupted by elements of either the French or Italian styles. This is not, however, how others in Europe perceived the German style. Rousseau noted that the German style equates to a more powerful type of music, implying a thicker texture, brightness, and contrast. This generally took on the view that it consisted of a modern blend alongside the contrapuntal or learned style. While this may have been vague in their eyes, whenever it appeared in places such as Paris in the form of mainly instrumental works, the German style was considered progressive, an outgrowth of the performance practices in German realms.

For example, in March, 1758 the newspaper *Mércure de France* reviewed a set of symphonies by Mannheim composer Johann Stamitz:

> Mr. Johann Stamitz has presented us with six fine symphonies in the German style, which were composed for the famous orchestra in Mannheim. One cannot doubt the beauty and grace of these works with clarinets and hunting horns, which have heretofore not been known in Paris.

This followed on the publication in 1755 of another set of six under the rubric *La melodia Germanica* (Op. 11), of which the first by Stamitz can be seen as a good example of what the French considered the progressive German style (Figure 2.2). The decisive unison Mannheim hammer stroke offset by a softer two-bar answer in the violins and violas is doubled and immediately followed by a chain of rising tremolos supported by the oboes and horns. This, in turn, leads to a powerful second theme ending in a unison descending triad (Example 2.5). The effect is robust and powerful, replete with contrasts in texture, articulation, and dynamics, all things that characterize the German style in eighteenth-century eyes.

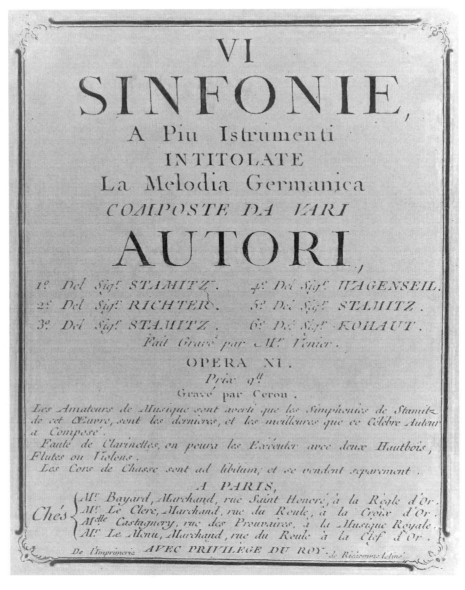

Figure 2.2 Title page of the *La melodia Germanica* symphonies printed by Bayard, Le Clerc, Castagnery, and Le Menu (1758)

If notions of what constituted national styles were commonplace during the eighteenth century, the actual musical definitions are very broad for determining the concept of the Classical style. Given that, as Rousseau notes in his *Dictionnaire* (Document 1), there were many, often conflicting definitions during the period, perhaps it is time to rethink how one should approach style with regards to actual musical-compositional trends. Indeed, one can find that certain style trends existed that crossed regional, cultural, and chronological boundaries, coexisting and yet each developing over the course of the entire period. As noted, these *general styles* are marked by specific musical trademarks that are discernible in a variety of places and contexts, and among a broad number of composers.

Example 2.5 Johann Stamitz, Symphony in D major, *La melodia Germanica*, Movement I, mm. 1–17

Style Trends: Galant and *Empfindsamkeit*

It should be noted that the designation of the four style trends found in the Classical Period requires both a revision and broadening of their original meaning. As noted earlier, all four coexisted simultaneously and overlapped chronologically to some degree. All are marked by particular compositional-stylistic trademarks that identify them, and all coincide to some degree with other definitions, such as the national styles. If one is attempting to define style in the Classical Period, however, these four style trends can be useful in placing composers, their music, and their affiliations in context.

The first of these has already been seen to have a number of definitions already. During the eighteenth century, the term **galant** was used frequently as a means of contrasting modern music with the more learned or contrapuntal style. This broad and all-encompassing identifier has lasted until the present day in monumental historical-analytical works such as musicologist Daniel Heartz's 2003 *Music in European Capitals: The Galant Style 1720–1780* or Roberg Gjerdingen's groundbreaking study *Music in the Galant Style* from 2007. The former uses the term as a metaphor for music outside such centers as Vienna and by composers other than Haydn or Mozart, while the latter discusses it quite intuitively as denoting compositional method developed through schemata present in the partimento. Both of these general definitions should be acknowledged first as having eighteenth-century antecedents, and second as demonstrating an educational practice derived from the Italian style and practiced by composers over a wide area and timespan. However, it is perhaps useful to redefine the term *galant* in a narrower context as a metaphor for the style of music that arose as an early reaction to that of the High Baroque.

The term itself stems from Old French and originally meant something that gave pleasure or enjoyment. It is an outgrowth of Enlightenment thought that characterized humans as rational, logical creatures whose tastes were formed by civilized mannerisms and intellectual interactions. It consisted of a negation of impulsive emotions and reveled in intricate nuances. In music, it meant homophonic simplicity occasionally spiced with elaborate ornamentation. The themes were generally monothematic, with room for improvisation by the performer (as a means of showing skill), limited use of counterpoint save when it was required, such as in sacred music, continued use of motivic sequencing (*Fortspinnung*), rigid diatonicism (but with the insertion of some dissonant and non-sequitur harmonies), and formal stability. Many of these same stylistic devices were also common to the Baroque, and thus our definition of *galant* could well be termed the post-Baroque style.

In terms of genres, *galant* music still adhered to the older types of works, such as the trio sonata or sinfonia. The musical expectation was that it would create pleasure, incite intellectual discussion, and reflect civilized society at its most rational. It is also an attempt at making the rather dry and static style of the Baroque more modern through drum or Alberti basses, parallel consonant and lyrical melodies, and contrasting forms while retaining some of the elements of the older style. Early composers include Quantz and Rameau, not coincidentally also theorists, but others can be found across the geographical spectrum, from Sweden (Johan Helmich Roman) to Spain (Domenico Scarlatti). Of course, each place had its own take on the *galant* style. In Italy, for example, one finds a more energetic sample in the early symphonies of Giovanni Battista Sammartini, such as the opening of the first movement to the Symphony in C major, JC 7. The imitative octave openings in the violins have a Baroque pattern one finds often in Antonio Vivaldi, yet the textures in the accompanying violas and bass give the work a thickness, with the second section being driven along by the viola ostinato, even as it supports imitative suspensions in the violins (Example 2.6). The work is still in ritornello form, but the parallel harmonies and rhythmic drive all point to a more modern direction in the music.

The *galant* style, of course, soon was considered too sterile and not progressive enough. When writing about listening to some works by Quantz, diarist Charles Burney diplomatically noted in 1773: "His music is simple and natural; his taste is that of forty years ago."[15] This indicates that it was old-fashioned and regarded already at that time as being completely replaced by a newer style.

Because, in the words of Burney, composers found this transitional *galant* style "insipid and vapid," they sought the means of introducing more emotion into their works. This was called in Germany the

Example 2.6 Giovanni Battista Sammartini, Symphony in C major, JC 7, Movement I, mm. 1–12

empfindsamer Stil. The term *empfindsam* is difficult to define precisely; it is usually translated as "sensitive" or "sentimental," though it goes beyond what ordinarily might be thought of either sensitive or sentimental; perhaps the phrase "acutely expressive" might be closer to the mark, but the gist of it is that composers (and performers) must imbue their works with a sense of feeling or emotion. Carl Philipp Emanuel Bach remarked on this in his treatise on playing the keyboard:

> A musician cannot move others unless he too is moved; he must of necessity feel all of the effects that he hopes to arouse in his audience, for the revealing of his own humor will stimulate a like humor in the listener. In languishing, sad passages, the performer must languish and grow sad. Thus will the expression of the piece be more clearly perceived by the audience. . . . Similarly in lively, joyous passages, the executant must again put himself into the appropriate mood. And thus, constantly varying the passions, he will quiet one before he rouses another.[16]

While Bach is referring to performance practice, his description is also valid for music composition. Here, though, it might be more appropriate to speak of the style as **Empfindsamkeit**, a term taken from German literature of the period that provided a wide range of emotional expression in contrast to the staid dramas of the Enlightenment (*Aufklärung*) movement.[17] *Empfindsamkeit* rejects the stereotypes and static nature of the *galant*, requiring a composition to be fluid and expressive, in turn inciting a variety of emotions in the

36 *Music and Style in the Classical Period*

listener. Specific stylistic devices express these: the use of contrasting themes or motives; the unexpected and momentary insertion of the minor mode; contrasting rhythms such as duple versus triple, dotted rhythms, and ostinatos; alternating dynamic levels from *ppp* to *fff*; increasing instrumental virtuosity; tightly controlled ornamentation; and fluid harmony and melodic lines. One of the specific trademarks is the unisons that occur at cadential endings or codas of the sections. There is a tendency to use binary form more frequently but to contrast the themes in the A sections often with a turn toward the parallel minor (in major key movements). Counterpoint is often limited to suspensions, but the motives that sometimes compose the main themes are sequenced through several pitch levels.

There seems to have been five separate streams that compose *Empfindsamkeit*: an early development derived from Italy and Italian opera, a mainstream variant noticeable especially in Germany, a freer form found in the works of C. P. E. Bach and imitated widely, a more intensely emotional one that led to more passionate expression, and a characteristic variety found in central Europe that depicted local events. All display the same musical devices, with composers moving freely between them as location and circumstances required.

The early development comes both out of the need for expression in Italian music, especially opera, and the instrumental musical developments in Germany that rely on sudden and rapidly changing thematic or motivic contrasts. One example of this trend can be found in the works of Antonio Brioschi, a composer about whom very little is known, even though his music, especially his symphonies, was widespread throughout Europe. An example of this early stylistic development can be seen in the Symphony in E-flat major, composed about 1740 to 1745. The opening theme of the first movement consists of dotted rhythms outlining the triad in sequence in the violins, which by the third bar begins to expand both rhythmically and texturally as the violins divide. In measure seven, there is a contrasting triplet motive before the cadence, followed by a couple of bars of varied triadic ascents in the violins and a push in the violas and basses to modulate to the V/V (F major). The homophonic nature of the accompaniment, the use of unison, the inclusion of the triplet versus the steady duple rhythm, and the steady modulatory sequence are all elements of the new trend, and later on in the movement at the end of this rounded binary, the strings all collapse into the trademark unison cadence, this time in the mediant minor (G minor). The essential elements of *Empfindsamkeit* are present, but there still remains the old-fashioned thematic sequences of Baroque practice (Example 2.7).

The second variant comprises the bulk of music written during the period from 1735 to 1760, coinciding with the rise of instrumental genres, especially in Germany. This was a common enough trend that examples abound, but two composers in particular can be said to exemplify it. The first is Franz Xaver Richter. Trained in Bohemia and Vienna, Richter had a varied career that took him from being a Vice-Kapellmeister for the Benedictine Prince-Elector of Kempten, a provincial town in Bavaria, to being employed as a singer

Example 2.7 Antonio Brioschi, Symphony in E-flat major, Movement I, mm. 1–8

Example 2.8 Franz Xaver Richter, Symphony in B-flat major, Boer 59, Movement I, mm. 1–8

at the court of the Elector of Mannheim to being *Kapellmeister* in the city of Strasbourg in France in 1769. He was one of the early mainstream composers of the new style, found especially in his early symphonies. In 1744 he published two volumes of symphonies in Paris under the title *Six Grands Simphonies*. Richter's method of composing in this style is to divide his principal and secondary themes by suspensions. This technique appears as early as this set of symphonies, such as the Symphony in B-flat major. Here Richter uses simple suspensions and textures between the main theme statements, keeping the more complex ones for moving into the secondary theme (Example 2.8).

Charles Burney commented that this particular format was not successful in his eyes: "His detail and manner of treating them is frequently dry and sterile, and he spins and repeats passages in different keys without end."[18] This judgment aside, Richter turned out to be one of the most popular composers of symphonies throughout the Classical Period, expanding by never deviating from his mixed style; even Mozart noted that his music was "charmingly written."

The bulk of the mainstream of *Empfindsamkeit* makes good use of the aforementioned stylistic devices, even as it seeks to broaden its emotional appeal. Quantz noted in particular: "He who wishes to devote himself to composition must have a lively and fiery spirit, united with a soul capable of tender feeling; a good mixture without too much melancholy."[19] This restrained, yet changeable music was particularly evident in Berlin at the court of Frederick the Great. Here, the stable of composers refined and expanded this style so that it achieved widespread recognition. An example can be seen in the overture to *Adriano in Sciro* by Frederick's main opera composer, Carl Heinrich Graun, in which there is a rhythmic vitality in

Example 2.9 Carl Heinrich Graun, *Adriano in Sciro*, Overture, mm. 1–4

the violins atop a steadily moving bass, all accompanied by florid horn parts (Example 2.9). The opening flourishes and discrete ornaments are also contrasted by a repetition of the main theme *piano*.

The main purveyor of *Empfindsamkeit*, however, was Carl Philipp Emanuel Bach, whose works demonstrate a more intense and varied style. Bach was the main developer of the Classical free fantasy, a work for keyboard that he frequently composed without bar lines. This was intended to allow the performer considerable latitude to vary the speed and emphasis of the work, depending on his own temperament, and the result was intended to convey to audiences the power and emotion it contained (Figure 2.3). In his more conventional works, Bach displayed a more mainstream *Empfindsamkeit* tendency, although he frequently used shorter motives and often abrupt modulations into remote keys. For example, in his ode *Morgengesang*, Wq 239, the opening of the duet is light, airy, and joyous, with the ostinato bass driving the rhythmic motion, with small, controlled ornaments and triplet flourishes in the flutes and sopranos (Example 2.10). The text "Hallelujah, do you see the beaming immortal approach" unfolds with simplicity and emotion, demonstrating that this style's adeptness at both supporting and underlying the words.

Empfindsamkeit composers also showed a preference for minor keys, often using the various musical devices to emphasize these. This heightened the emotional content of music by using tension-filled devices, such as tremolo strings, florid and penetrating woodwinds, and both rhythmic and dynamic variation. Indeed, the impression can be as intense as with the following *Sturm und Drang* style, though it still relies on the musical trademarks to define it. One good example of this is the Flute Concerto in E minor by Franz Benda. Here at the conclusion of the exposition, the violins have the jagged melody above the tremolo strings, creating a tension-filled moment that collapses into the cadential unison. When the flute enters, however, it begins with an emotional sustained *mezza di voce*, allowing the main theme to be carried by the first violins (Example 2.11).

Finally, in central Europe a variety of *Empfindsamkeit* developed that in its most characteristic mode actually incorporated nontraditional or pictorial music that depicted special events. This *musica concreta* or "actual music" can be found in the occasional works by composers such as Leopold Mozart, who enjoyed writing works that depicted local events and traditions in Salzburg. These include a serenade about a musical sleigh ride, a hunting symphony replete with actual horn calls, a peasant wedding, and other works that included instruments such as alphorns, sleigh bells, shotguns, and toy instruments. While this was a more or less localized style, it nonetheless was written using the same musical devices as found in the mainstream.

Although widespread and crossing the boundaries of the national styles, *Empfindsamkeit* proved to be relatively limited in terms of actual expression. Emotions were at the foundation of it, but by the middle of the century a new concept of drama emphasizing human passions and emotional extremes began to

Figure 2.3 Autograph score of the Keyboard Fantasia in F major by Carl Philipp Emanuel Bach, Wq 59/5 (1782)

Example 2.10 Carl Philipp Emanuel Bach, *Morgengesang am Schöpfungsfeste*, Wq 239, No. 5 Duet, mm. 1–8

Example 2.11 Franz Benda, Flute Concerto in E minor, Movement I, mm. 30–37

appear. In literature, this has been termed the *Sturm und Drang* (Storm and Stress) movement in which these extremes often border on the psychotic, but in music it came to represent the next logical step beyond *Empfindsamkeit*.

Sturm und Drang: The Passionate Musical-Dramatic Embrace

The difficulty in defining *Sturm und Drang* in music comes because the manifestation in music does not coincide with its appearance in German literature. It can be said that in the literary world, *Sturm und Drang* was a short-lived phenomenon, with its first real appearance in 1774 with the publication of the novel *Die Leiden des jungen Werthers* (*The Sorrows of Young Werther*) by Johann Wolfgang von Goethe, as noted in the previous chapter. Its protagonist falls in love with a married woman, carrying his infatuation to obsessive extremes of emotion and finally committing suicide. Werther lives entirely by his own emotions, casting aside the rules of society in favor of immediate passion. It caused a phenomenon known as "Werther fever," in which young men began to imitate the character in dress, mood swings, emotional excess, and occasionally even suicide. It was, however, not the only literary manifestation of the movement, for a group of poets at the University of Göttingen also took on the often dark and foreboding naturalism in their poetic works, as did other dramatists such as Maximilian Klinger (after whose play the movement is named), Jakob Reinhold Lenz, and especially Friedrich von Schiller, whose play *Die Räuber* (*The Robbers*) is said to have concluded it when produced in 1784. The adulation of nature, the rejection of social norms in favor of immediate emotional extremes, the honoring of Shakespeare and Ossian as models, and the use of dark and foreboding imagery in word and art all point toward the Romanticism of the nineteenth century, having an effect far beyond the limited timespan of the movement itself.

In music, there can be no doubt that a similar trend or style began to emerge, though it makes its appearance almost a decade earlier. One of the prototypes can be found in the novel ballet *Don Juan* by Christoph Willibald von Gluck, which premiered in Vienna at the Kärntnertor Theatre on October 17, 1761. The story of the womanizer Don Juan was the brainchild of choreographer Gasparo Angiolini, who created a ballet in which the dancers would be required to pantomime a dramatic story, in this case the sins of Don Juan and his ultimate fate being dragged off to hell by demons. Angiolini and Gluck began with the notion that the music and dance were separate, but that the passions found in the music had to be expressed by the dancers in order for the drama to unfold. Its success demonstrated that music could lead to a dramatic climax that did not have to depend upon stereotypical dances but, rather, could be directly connected to the action. As an independent instrumental work, it was regarded as an important forerunner of a new dramatic style, which depicted the demise of the main character in a powerful finale that began with menacing wide vibrato and dissonance as the statue of Don Juan's victim invites him to a fatal feast and concluded with swirling strings and tremolos as the Don is dragged off to hell. The harmonies contain harsh dissonances, the modulations fluid above a D minor foundation, and at the end there is a soft benediction, a sudden turn to the parallel D major.

This dramatic, passionate style consists of jarring syncopations, a preference for minor and unconventional keys, continued use of tremolos, rapidly changing dynamics and accentuation, restless ostinatos, expansive mournful and poignant themes in the slow movements, brilliant but austere orchestration, wildly fluctuating registers and wide leaps of motivic material, a renewed interest in intricate counterpoint (but not conventional fugues or imitation), harsh dissonances, and abrupt modulations often into remote keys. Underlying these devices or trademarks is a sense of passion that endows the music with a tension-filled quality. For the most part, it represents a darker, even more Romantic (or, more properly, proto-Romantic) side to music, differentiating itself from *Empfindsamkeit* through its wilder, more emphatic content.

Musicologists have attempted to explain the *Sturm und Drang* as a well-defined period, but few composers wrote exclusively in the style for any length of time. Moreover, it has been almost exclusively associated with the sudden interest in minor keys, especially by the mainstream composers such as Haydn or Mozart in Vienna, even though the literary trend was more of a north or central German phenomenon. This discrepancy has led some scholars, such as Théodore de Wyzewa or H. C. Robbins Landon, to postulate some sort of *crise romantique* (Romantic crisis) that infected composers in the 1770s. Even though composers such as Wolfgang Amadeus Mozart (Symphony in G minor, KV 183), Haydn (a number of works including the Symphony in G minor, Hob. I:39; Symphony in D minor, Hob. I:26, *Lamentatione*; or the Symphony in F minor, Hob.I:49, *La Passione*), or Johann Baptist Vanhal (numerous minor-key symphonies) began to explore minor-key symphonies about 1768, musicologist Matthew Riley has recently noted that "*Sturm und Drang* as a discrete period in the history of compositional style has likewise fallen into disrepute, even if restricted to minor-key works."[20] He goes on further to state that "*Sturm und Drang* is a useful label for individual movements by various composers, for a set of recurrent characteristics . . . and for a conventional 'topic' that could be invoked in almost any piece, but not for an historical period."[21] While this statement alleviates the need to define *Sturm und Drang* as a subperiod within the larger Classical Period, it does not adequately define the appearance or conscious use of the musical trademarks, which can best be described as a style trend, one not limited to Viennese musical circles. As an example, one can note the dark and moody Symphony in G minor Op. 6 No. 6 by Johann Christian Bach, published in London in 1769. Imitative triadic ascents in the second violins and bass ending in a powerful accent and answer in the oboes, all above a driving ostinato in the violas and an austere tension-filled octave tremolo in the firsts. This leads into a soft mincing sequence in the violins followed by a forte cadence, and finally a unison that suddenly dies away without definitive resolution (Example 2.12). Here one finds the sort of abrupt and powerful musical content that epitomizes the *Sturm und Drang*: energetic, restless, intense, and gripping.

Thus, the notion of endowing music with a more passionate mood beyond the emotions expressed in *Empfindsamkeit* seems to have blossomed in between 1765 and 1775 and then been absorbed into the overall set of compositional tools thereafter. Whether one ascribes to a *Sturm und Drang* period, there can be no doubt that aesthetic parallels between music and literature in terms of extreme passion and drama do exist within the Classical Period and, moreover, that they provided composers with a means of new expressiveness that was meant to stir the passions, sometimes over the course of complete works and at others in the occasional movement. The effects, whether in literature, music, or art, are jarring and unsettling, and their continued use and redefinition throughout the century mark an acceptance of this trend and its musical devices as a means of expanded the musical language, regardless of geographical location.

High Classicism

Toward the last quarter of the century, composers also sought a broader representational style that both incorporated the trends mentioned so far and expanded the musical language to accommodate the ongoing development of musical style and changing audience tastes. This can be labeled the **High Classicism**. Sometimes known as the "Viennese Classical Style," though it was widespread throughout Europe and beyond, it is characterized by formal symmetry (the chiasm of the sonata principal, the return of a melody throughout the rondo, etc), logical structural design, expansive orchestration, and a more fluid sense of harmonic, rhythmic, and thematic contrast. In this trend, one finds genres that have now been well-defined in terms of overall format and structure, and they contain one or more characteristics of the other style trends. Music was meant to be both emotional and, where appropriate, expressive of drama or passion but integrated through the use of expanded orchestration, a wide range of dynamic variation, contrasting themes laid out in formal patterns such as the sonata or rondo, and accessibility for audiences. Expectations included enough variation in terms of ornamentation and articulation to enhance the music, and a design that was both familiar and yet offered a degree of novelty. Koch notes in his *Lexikon*: "This material must distinguish itself through inner strength and emphasis, and the feeling must carry all before it."[22] Regular phrase structures and periods were to be emphasized, and musical material was to be expanded, developed, or varied as the composer wished. The compositional devices drawn from the earlier trends were refined and reconfigured for clarity and usefulness. These were then distinguished as high, middle, and low styles, with the first devoted to a serious and expressive type of music, the second to music that was merely pleasing and less intricate, and the final more popular and simple. High Classicism allows for all three to exist at the same time, with composers altering their works according to the circumstances such as performance,

Example 2.12 Johann Christian Bach, Symphony in G minor, Op. 6 No. 6, a) Movement I, mm. 1–10; b) Movement III, mm. 72–82

Example 2.12 (Continued)

Example 2.12 (Continued)

publication, local use or dissemination abroad, performance practices, or, more increasingly, personal preferences. The last led to an increased importance of a work's originality.

Virtually all music composed after about 1780 conforms to this "style," which flows directly into the early Romantic Period during the first decade or so of the nineteenth century. Perhaps the best examples are the late symphonies of Haydn composed for London during the last decade of the century. Here one finds the symmetrical forms expanded laterally to extensive length in the first and final movements, all the while taking advantage of the fuller orchestral textures, the contrasting thematic structures, and expressive use of dynamics and rhythms that underscore the longer lyrical. This is not just a high point of musical development in terms of style, it points the way toward its evolution during the first years of the nineteenth century.[23]

The number of musical examples in this chapter may seem overly large, but they are necessary to give a glimpse into the variety of style present during the Classical Period. It should be said, however, that no matter how much styles differed or how they were exploited by the composers of the time, they were still dependent upon other factors. These include the creation or re-creation of genres, influences of popular tastes, and appropriateness of use for various occasions. They were also dependent on geographical locations beyond the cultural borders of the Italian, French, or German styles, for each evolved nuances in the various musical centers throughout Europe and its colonies around the world. In each of these places, stylistic adaptations often went hand in hand with the development of instruments and musical ensembles, eventually creating both reputations and opportunities for composers and musicians that furthered musical development in the period.

Documents

Document 1. Excerpt from the *A Complete Dictionary of Music* by Jean-Jacques Rousseau, English edition translated by William Waring, London, 1779, p. 384.

STYLE. The distinctive character of composition or execution. This character varies greatly, according to the countries, the taste of the people, the genius of the authors, etc. according to matter, place, subject, expression, etc.

We say, in France, the style of Lully, or Rameau, or Modonville, etc. In Germany, the style of Hasse, of Gluck, of Graun. In Italy, the style of Leo, Pergolesi, of Jommelli, or Buranello. They style of church music is not the same as that of the theatre or a private room. The style of German compositions is lively, divided, but harmonious. That of the French composition is flat, rough, ill-cadenced, and monotonous. That of the Italian compositions flourishing, pleasing, energetic.

The dramatic or imitative style is proper for painting the passions. The style of the church is serious, majestic, grave. The style of the motet, where the artist affects to shew himself as such, is more classic and ingenious than energetic and affecting. The hyporchematic style is peculiar to joy, pleasure, dancing, filled with lively movements, gay and well-expressed. The symphonic or instrumental style: as every instrument has its touch, its fingering, its character peculiar to it, it also has its style. The melismatic or natural style, which is first present to persons who have not yet studied. The style of fantasy, little united, filled with ideas, free from every constraint. The choratic or dancing style, which is divided into as many different branches as there are characters dancing. The ancients also had their different styles.

Document 2. Excerpt from Friedrich Gottlob Türk, *Klavierschule, oder Anweisung zum Klavierspielen für Lehrer und Lernende, mit kritische Anmerkungen*, Leipzig, 1789, pp. 361–364, 404–405.

The Italian style is pleasant, lyrical, thick ([and] often overblown), brilliant, varied, and quite expressive. At least it has heretofore been characterized. Now one finds much that is aimless, often stale, unimportant, shallow, etc. in the works of various Italian composers; yet, they must still be credited with melody that has a captivating flexibility.

The French style would be, according to the opinion of Rousseau, "insipid, flat, hard, poorly articulated, and monotonous." This is a judgment that is certainly too hard and betrays that writer's preference for the Italian style. Apart from the fact that French composers sometimes write in a somewhat empty and dry manner, or that they neglect harmony a bit, one nevertheless must give [them] more credit for their taste. There is no doubt, however, that they have long had an eminent position as composers for the keyboard and with this consideration deserve greater preference than the Italians.

Rousseau does not consider the German style in a favorable light. It is flighty, choppy, and yet harmonic, as he says. If this had been the case formerly in keyboard works, it is certainly no longer true today. I believe that our style expresses itself through careful development, comprehensiveness, and a powerful harmony. Moreover, we have absorbed much from the French and Italians, and perhaps not always the worst of them. Too, we can match foreigners with many of our own musical masters in instrumental, as well as vocal music. . . . A piece composed according to the *Italian* taste is generally performed in a moderate style (somewhere between heavy and light), though there are many exceptions. *French* music requires a lighter style. On the other hand, *German* music calls for a heavier, more powerful style, generally.

Document 3. Excerpt from the *European Magazine and London Review*, October 1784.

It must be understood, that for the sake of pleasant melody, and sweet air, our author has neglected and laid aside that part of music that constitutes the great master, namely *imitation* and *fugue*. With those strokes of art all his capital music abounds. From his hands they neither appear pedantic nor heavy, being continually relieved by pleasant touches of fancy, and luxuriant flights of endless variety.

Notes

1. Charles Rosen, *The Classical Style* (New York: Norton, 1972)-in particular his chapter entitled "The Origins of the Style," pp. 43–53.
2. Neal Zaslaw, ed. *Man and Music*, 3.
3. Fredrik Silverstolpe, *Biografi öfver Kraus* (Stockholm, 1833), 132; translated by the author. Gluck's pupil and successor, Antonio Salieri, reported the comment. This mirrors the comment by Joseph Haydn on the composer: "I remember Kraus. What profound thoughts, what a Classical talent."
4. See Burney, *A General History of Music*, II: 323.
5. Musicologist H. C. Robbins Landon calls these stylistic imitators *seguaci* or followers, noting that more works were attributed to Haydn by publishers during his lifetime than he actually wrote.
6. Quantz, *On Playing the Flute*, 105.
7. See Johann Adolph Scheibe, *Critische Musikus* (Hamburg, 1740), III: 108.
8. Of course, during the eighteenth century, the modern concept of a nation was still in the future, but here "nation" can best be described as language and culture, not a political entity.
9. Quantz, *On Playing the Flute*, 320.
10. Quantz, *On Playing the Flute*, 328–329.
11. Quantz, *On Playing the Flute*, 341.
12. Scheibe, *Critische Musikus*, I: 122.
13. Leonard Ratner, *Classic Music: Expression, Form and Style* (New York: Schirmer Books, 1980), 355.
14. Quantz, *On Playing the Flute*, 338.
15. Charles Burney, *The Present State of Music in German, the Netherlands and United Provinces* (London, 1775), II: 157.
16. Bach, *Essay on the True Art of Playing Keyboard Instruments*, 152.
17. See, for example, the didactic plays of Leipzig professor Johann Christoph Gottsched as opposed to those by Gotthold Ephraim Lessing, such as his *Emilia Galotti*, in which human emotions are emphasized.
18. See Burney, *A General History of Music*, II: 329.
19. Quantz, *On Playing the Flute*, 13.
20. Matthew Riley, *The Viennese Minor Key Symphony in the Age of Haydn and Mozart* (New York: Oxford University Press, 2016), 24.
21. Riley, *The Viennese Minor-Key Symphony*, 25–26.
22. Heinrich Christoph Koch, *Musikalisches Lexikon* (Frankfurt am Main, 1802), col. 1450–1451.
23. Musical examples from this High Classical style will be found throughout this text.

Part II

New Developments, Convergences, and Genres in the Classical Period

3 The Expansion of the Orchestra and the Development of the Instruments

The Classical Period was a time during which both instruments and instrumentation changed radically. At the beginning during the 1730s, Baroque standards were commonplace. The core of the orchestra was a three- or four-part group of string instruments, all supported by or subordinate to a continuo group. This was based on an Italian model wherein the upper two voices were played by two violin lines, often in counterpoint, while the continuo consisted of whatever supportive bass instruments could be mustered to enhance a keyboard. Inner harmonies were given by the latter in the form of figured chords, and the technique for creating them was called **thoroughbass** in English. To give works some inner texture, a viola and sometimes a viola da gamba were included. Music thus was pushed to the melody and bass, and whatever other instruments that were included provided textural or aural contrasts without undue disruption of this standard. French models of the time included numerous extra subdivisions of the string group, often arranged according to a specific range and notated with a variety of clefs (see Figure 3.1).

The choices of instruments in the Baroque were often limited due to technical or textural limitations, and by the requirements for displaying **Affekt**, described by theorists as a **Doctrine of Affections** (*Affektenlehre*). In terms of the woodwinds, for instance, flutes were regarded as pastoral instruments, with G major as the principal key, largely on the basis that they were too soft to compete with a larger string group and had *d′* as their lowest note. Both oboes and bassoons were louder and could be better integrated into the violins and continuo, occasionally emerging for solos that were used by composers such as Handel to provide textural variety. All three of these woodwinds had one or no key, limiting the number of notes and ranges. Trumpets consisted of two types, the long trumpet and the hunting trumpet, the first of which still retains its basic shape today and the second looks like French horn, as the famous portrait of Gottfried Reiche shows (Figure 3.2). Both were cylindrically bored tubes, and the most common pitches were F, D, and C. The sound, invariably accompanied by timpani, made the music martial or brilliant, though the lower ranges were called simply *tromba* and the upper *clarino*, by which was meant that the first should be more accompaniment and the second used for solo work. By 1700, the solo brass section was augmented by the hunting horn, which likewise came in two versions; the coiled single-pitched *Jagdhorn* still used in the hunt and the *Orchesterhorn* that was a conically bored tube in a single pitch to which a series of sequential tubes could be added at the mouthpiece, each of which lowered the standard pitch by an interval. As theorist Johann Mattheson noted in 1713, the standard pitches for the horn were in high C (C *alto*) and F, the same "*ambitus*" (or ranges) as trumpet, stating that their sound was mellower than the "brilliant and shrieking clarini." Both instruments were nontransposable and dependent on the partials found in the harmonic series (Example 3.1).

In the Baroque, keyboards used for ensemble work were invariably harpsichords; the clavichord, under various names such as spinet, virginal, and so forth, was too soft to be used with other instruments. The exception was the organ, which still functioned in sacred music as a powerful continuo instrument. Other instruments did exist but were either in their infancy, such as the clarinet predecessor known as the *chalumeau*, or were being used more infrequently as having limited means of further development, such

Figure 3.1 Manuscript score of Jean-Philippe Rameau, *Les Sauvages* (1750); note the clef placement on the staff

Figure 3.2 Elias Haussmann, Portrait of Gottfried Reiche with a coiled trumpet (1726)
Source: Courtesy of the Bach Archiv, Leipzig.

Example 3.1 The Natural Harmonic Series (used for trumpets and horns during the Classical Period). The partials that are not in tune are indicated by quarter notes, with + or –, whether sharp or flat.

as the recorder or members of the viol family such as the gamba, or had a function that often precluded anything more than vocal support (the cornetto and trombone/sackbut quartet). To be sure, other odd instruments did exist and popped up on the rare occasion in the music of the period, such as the single-string *tromba marina*, but by and large, these were quirks, used by composers such as Vivaldi for special aural effects.

Beginning in the early parts of the Classical Period, however, the more diverse and progressive styles of music required both the technical development of the standard instruments and the standardization of the orchestral ensemble. As new genres emerged, and older ones such as the sonata and concerto, were revisited and reenergized through new and bolder harmonies, textures, contrast, and use, the ensembles had to cope with changing tastes, performance practices, and other evolutionary musical developments. It is this evolution that created the foundation for a new soundscape, one that led directly into the modern age. Much of the technical developments for instruments during the period was the result of the need for experimentation, but each new step that was successful was accepted and refined alongside the evolution of the musical styles. Moreover, such refinements meant that methodologies, often published in specialized treatises, were written to facilitate the new techniques and improvements.

Development of Instruments and Performance Techniques

In the eighteenth century, all instruments were codified and characterized by their timbre, facility of playing technique, and their ability to function either as solo instruments or as accompaniment, generally as part of an ensemble or orchestra. Initially, the main group of instrumentalists were the strings (still known during the period as the *ripieno*), though more increasingly the more virtuoso players were sought out to perform solos (the *concertante* parts) in both chamber and instrumental genres, as will be seen in the next chapters. Because of these functions, improvements in the instruments themselves, either in the form of technical progress or playing techniques, occurred during the Classical Period. This led to more virtuoso displays by soloists, the expanded use of obbligato parts within genres such as the symphony, and eventually to a new breed of composer-performers, who were able to make a living off their talent. During the early part of the eighteenth century, both the *galant* and *Empfindsamkeit* styles reflected the awakening of the possibilities of instrumental techniques through increasingly difficult concertos and more opportunities for public appearances, whether at localized courts or public concerts. One of the most proficient performers, if the sources are to be believed, was Frederick the Great. His concertmaster, Franz Benda, noted that he accompanied the king in ten thousand concertos, even as he himself perfected his own playing technique on the violin (Document 1).[1]

The Strings

The thickening of orchestral textures during this period meant a redefinition of the main ensemble. As in the Baroque Period, the main group consisted of four parts, most commonly a pair of violins, viola, and a foundational bass instrument. Through much of the eighteenth century, the violin was considered as the main instrument playing the melody, and the viola was intended to fill in the harmonic gap between it and

Figure 3.3 Etching of Leopold Mozart, frontispiece to his *Violinschule* (1756)

the bass. The foundation (in Italian, *Fondamento*, also known as *Basso* or *Basso continuo*) consisted of several string instruments playing the bass line in unison; initially these were not specified, but generally they included the violoncello and either a contrabasso or violone. The former was a bass instrument of the violin family, while the latter was a bass viol, though the terms were used interchangeably, as was the term *double bass*.

The violin was perhaps the ubiquitous instrument of the Classical Period and the one most commonly used for solo work. In the courts, it was the core of the musical ensemble, and in chamber music, it often was often the instrument of choice in genres such as solo sonatas. Violinists of the time produced a wide variety of manuals on how to play the instrument, but perhaps none was as important and widely read as the *Violinschule* of Leopold Mozart (Figure 3.3), first published in 1756. This treatise included chapters on types of instruments,[2] history, functions, bowings, positions (Figure 3.4), and other elements that were of use to both performers and composers writing for it. As a how-to manual, it proved invaluable to prospective musicians, but though it contains precise details of the instrument's musical capabilities, it does not provide information on the professional uses of the violin.

The position of the viola in the ensemble was initially equivocal. In the Classical Period it was not always required to double the bass instruments at the octave, nor was it simply a redundant filler for the inner harmonies, and yet the viola initially did not achieve stature until after about 1760. Quantz notes:

> The viola is commonly regarded as of little importance in the musical establishment. The reason may well be that it is often played by persons who are either still beginners in the ensemble or have no particular gifts with which to distinguish themselves on the violin, or that the instrument yields all too few advantages to its players, so that able persons are not easily persuaded to take it up.[3]

He goes on further to dissuade violists from adding "embellishments" and cautions that the instrument is capable of overpowering the violins is played too strongly. For solo work, the viola, often the favorite personal instrument of composers, could employ *scordatura*, or retuning of the strings higher to achieve a brighter sound. For example, for Wolfgang Mozart's *Sinfonia concertante* for Violin, Viola, and Orchestra, KV 364, the work is in E-flat major, but the viola is written in D major, with the instructions to tune the instrument a half tone higher.

The violoncello, however, formed the main instrument of the bass line, having a resonant, solid tone. Quantz, however, suggests that two instruments are to be used, one with thin strings and a bow with white

The Expansion of the Orchestra 55

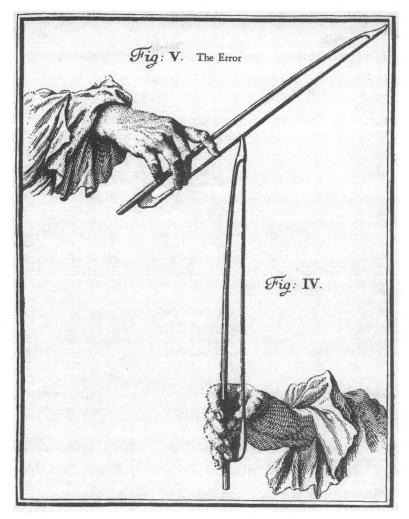

Figure 3.4 Drawing from Leopold Mozart's *Violinschule* (1756) showing correct bowing position

hairs while the other is to have thicker strings and a bow with black hair. Otherwise, in his view, a solo cello would be useless as an orchestral instrument. He states:

> Since the violoncello has the sharpest tone of all the basses . . . its player is in an advantageous position to help the other parts in the expression of light and shadow, and can give vigor to the entire piece.[4]

One of the earliest manuals is Michel Corette's *Méthode, thèorique et pratique pour apprendre en peu de temps le violoncelle dans sa perfection* (*Theoretical and Practical Method for Learning the Violoncello Perfectly in a Short Time*) published in Paris in 1741 (Figure 3.5). Although he explores the technical extremes of the instrument, he also is careful to note that it is required to provide a cautious and firm foundation as the most versatile and sonorous of the continuo instruments. He notes specifically, "The cello holds the reins of the concert, making itself heard better than any other bass instrument because it is the most harmonious."[5] Other treatises by François Cupis (1772) and Joseph Tillière (1774) supplemented Corette's by providing additional practical information, as well as studies and short pieces to demonstrate the facility of

Figure 3.5 Front illustration from Michel Corette, *Méthode* for the cello (1741)

students on the instrument. Corette also published a manual for the contrabass in 1781, in which he stated that the instrument, most commonly known as a means of strengthening the bass line an octave below the cello and having four strings, once had six strings and was used during the Baroque as a solo instrument; he also provides duets for cello and bass as a means of demonstrating its efficacy (Example 3.2).

Example 3.2 Duet for 2 violoncellos or violoncello and contrabass by Michel Corette (1781), Movement III, mm. 1–8

The Woodwinds

During the Classical Period, the most common woodwind instruments found in chamber music and in the orchestra were the transverse flutes and oboes. During the Baroque Period, it was more common to have at least three sorts that could be described as families: recorders, flutes, and oboes. The former ranged from the shrill *flautino* or *ottavino* to the bass recorder, while the oboes ranged from the traditional instrument downwards to include the tenor range *oboe d'amore* and baritone *oboe da caccia*. Both the recorder and oboe families were used extensively throughout the Baroque, and one should remember that the instrument designated *flauto* referred almost exclusively to the recorder. But by the beginning of the Classical Period, the sound limitations of the recorders and the raw timbre of the lower oboes made them less effective in the newly expanded orchestra.[6] The traditional transverse flute and oboe, on the other hand, blended well with the violin sections, strengthening them when a full *tutti* was required but offering color alternatives as they had more or less the same ranges as the violins. Quantz, who published the main treatise on flute in 1752, was both a master performer and innovator for the flute. During his early years he had become acquainted in Paris with leading French performers such as Michel Blavet and Jacques-Christoph Naudot, and noting the difficulties in tuning the instrument to the various prevailing pitches, he was responsible for adding a second key and interchangeable central portions of the instrument (see Figure 3.6). Quantz's treatise was probably the most thorough work on the instrument during the period and often referred to by composers and theorists not only for its exhaustive coverage of the instrument and its capabilities but also for its explanation of the orchestra in general.

For the oboe (in French, *hautbois*), however, the Baroque descriptions found in the 1719 revision of a treatise by Jean-Jacques Hotteterre, *Principes de la Flute Traversiere, ou Flute d'Allemagne. De la Flute A Bec, ou Flute Douce, et du Haut-Bois, Divisez part Traitez* (*Basics of the Flute, the Recorder, and the Oboe, in Three Parts*) seem to have been an important pedagogical source throughout the Classical Period, even though the instrument itself underwent a development that included the addition of a foot joint (to extend the range down to c' and to add the $c\#'$), expansion of the number of keys to as many as eight, and a narrower conical bore. All of these features produced an instrument that had both great sustaining power and versatility, making it the ideal woodwind for the standard Classical orchestra. Quantz noted that it was on the same level as the flute and bassoon in terms of usage, but warned that players needed to maintain a "good posture" in order to sustain the tone.[7] Oboists of note include Johann Christian Fischer and Carlo Besozzi, both of whom were lauded by Charles Burney for their abilities. About the latter in particular he noted:

> His taste and ear are exceedingly delicate and refined, and he seems to possess a happy and peculiar faculty of tempering a continued tone to different bases . . . on the whole his performance is so capital that a hearer must be extremely fastidious not to receive from it a great degree of pleasure.[8]

Figure 3.6 Title page to Johann Joachim Quantz, *Anweisungen zur Flötenspielen* (1752)

The bassoon, like the oboe and flute, was considered an essential part of the instruments playing the bass line during the period, although increasingly it was used for its softer and more refined tone in the upper registers. Provided with a fifth key (later increased to seven), it was equally as versatile as it provided the supportive depth for the bass string instruments. In practice, ensembles varied the number of bassoons, from a single continuo instrument to as many as four, such as in the famed Mannheim orchestra: two to perform obbligato roles and one or two to support the bass lines. Generally, however, the foundational support was considered optional during the period, with separate parts only occasionally being written out. In his treatise *Méthode Nouvelle et Raisonnée pour le Basson* (Paris, 1803), Étienne Ozi, principal bassoon at the Conservatoire in Paris, discussed range, playing position, embouchure, and tone quality of the Classical Period instrument.

The newcomer in the Classical orchestra was the clarinet, a development from the Baroque single-reed chalumeau by the addition of a register key sometime around 1700. Even though it produced a suitable sound and was more flexible than the chalumeau, its use was limited for the early portion of the Classical Period. The name (*clarinetto* or little clarino) indicates that it was generally used as a less expensive substitute for the brass trumpet (*clarino*), whose performance was in the hands of various guilds during the 1730s. Since woodwind performers were often generic, performing on all of the reed instruments, the clarinet player could be drawn from the regular *Kapelle* without worrying about special permissions or payment. Initially, these instruments were pitched in the keys of C and D, the same as the more common trumpet keys, and they were more versatile due to their ability to produce chromatic notes. It was especially common in Germany, where *Empfindsamkeit* composers such as Christoph Graupner and Johann Melchior Molter wrote concertos that ventured into the higher ranges of the instrument.

In 1754, the Mannheim orchestra introduced the clarinet as a permanent part of the woodwind section thanks to Johann Stamitz, who wrote possibly the first concerto that explored the lower, or chalumeau register on the instrument. This work was for a new, improved instrument in B♭ that had several new keys to make it more flexible, especially in the deeper tones. About the same time, a longer instrument pitched in A was introduced, with these two keys becoming the standard for the remainder of the Classical Period. In 1764 Valentin Roeser published his treatise *Essai d'instruction a l'usage de ceux qui composent pour la clarinetto et le cor* in Paris, noting the ranges and registers (Figure 3.7). He also states, "Since this instrument is inflexible and cannot be treated like an oboe or transverse flute, it is necessary to have several types to play in different tones."[9] By 1770, the clarinet had begun to become a regular part of the woodwind section in the larger orchestras, with players who specialized on the instrument being hired, rather than relying upon it to be performed generically. Yet, a few years earlier Roeser thought it new enough to gloss over some of the more technical details: "I could have many other things to say about this instrument, but I merely gave the most necessary rules, afraid of making this little book too obscure and confusing for the reader."[10]

By the end of the century, there were two other woodwind instruments whose use was comparatively rarer. These were the *cor anglais* and the basset horn. Both were pitched in F, had the same chromatic compass as the mainstream instruments, but were used relatively infrequently, probably due to their focus on the deeper and less flexible registration. Called today the English horn, the first is neither from England nor a horn, but rather, it was the successor to the oboe d'amore of the Baroque Period. The origins of the word are obscure, but it seems to have developed around 1740 as a more versatile instrument than the lower-pitched members of the oboe family.[11] Although it appears occasionally in works such as Joseph Haydn's Symphony No. 22 (subtitled "The Philosopher") and operas by Nicolò Jommelli, Joseph Martin Kraus, Christoph von Gluck, and others, as well as a concerto by oboist Josef Fiala, its use was limited in the period. The basset horn, however, became a predecessor of the bass clarinet. It was a longer version of the basset clarinet, an instrument favored by clarinetist Anton Stadler for whom Mozart wrote his Clarinet Concerto, KV 622, for which an additional section was added to provide for an extended downward range. Pitched in either G or F, it was already known by Carl Stamitz in the 1770s, and although its use was more widespread during the period than the cor anglais, the limitations in its upper register made it less suitable for the orchestra. It was, however, considered more appropriate as a member of the *Harmonie* wind band, where it would blend better with the other woodwinds and horns.

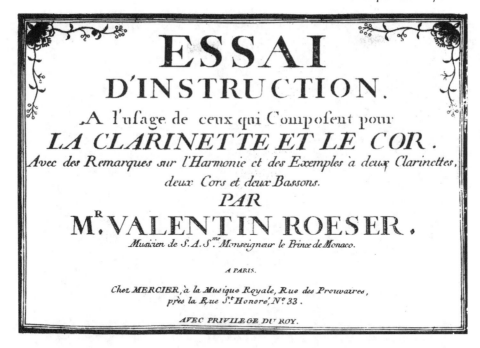

Figure 3.7 Title page of Valentin Roeser's *Essai d'instruction a l'usage de ceus qui composent pour la clarinette et le cor* (Paris, 1764)

Brass and Percussion

The brass instruments of the Classical Period were both the conically bored French horn and the cylindrically bored trumpet. Both instruments entered the orchestra during the Baroque Period, the first as an outgrowth of its main purpose of providing signals for the hunt and the second as a military instrument.

The Baroque horn has already been described by theorist Mattheson as being softer and rounder in tone than the trumpet, even if one of the two pitched instruments was in the same register. Horns in the Baroque Period were either a single-pitched spiral tube (called a *Jagdhorn* or *Corno da caccia* or hunting horn) or a fixed pitched tube to which crooks could be added. Each of the basic instruments (in high C and F) could play in different lower keys by inserting a succession of crooks; for example, if one adds one crook to the F horn, the pitch is lowered to E, two crooks to E-flat, and so on. This caused considerable strain on the instrument when playing, particularly since engravings of the time show the playing position to have been bell up at times. Finally, intonation problems with this sequential crook arrangement were legion. By 1750, however, improvements in the instrument were undertaken by a collaboration between Johann Georg Werner, a maker, and Dresden performer Anton Hampel. The latter experimented with a new position that allowed for notes not in the harmonic series to be played by stopping the bell with the hand, thus increasing the lower register and allowing for some chromaticism. The collaborative experiments resulted in the so-called Inventionshorn, where the terminal crooks were replaced by a series of internal tubes that allowed for all keys from B-flat to low C to be played. In addition, a tuning slide was incorporated so that various instruments could tune to each other and to the orchestra as a whole.

From a musical standpoint, this made it possible for the horn, with its often-powerful harmonic foundation and excellent tonal blend, to enter the orchestra on a permanent basis. The expansion of the playable notes through the hand-stopping technique further allowed from solo works to be performed that used the more mellow lower register of the instrument. A final development occurred about a decade later when Viennese horn maker Anton Kerner produced his *Orchesterhorn*, an instrument pitched in high C with a

60 New Developments, Convergences, and Genres

Figure 3.8 An *Orchesterhorn* with all of the crooks

Source: Photo courtesy of The Horn Guys.

series of crooks that lowered the key down an octave, to which a coupler to extend it further down to low B-flat was added. The internal tubing was modified to become the tuning slide, and in this guise the Classical Period horn attained its final form (Figure 3.8).

Horn players were often paid significantly more than ordinary musicians were, probably because the instrument itself was difficult to master. Roeser notes in his treatise,

> The hunting horn is even more inflexible than the clarinet, due to the diatonic series, as we will see in its range; It is also for this reason that we have up to eight types, [all of] which are indispensability required.[12]

Given that by the 1770s the horn was used almost constantly, it was necessary for some specialization to occur. This had already been developed in the Mannheim orchestra, possibly as early as 1745, by employing four horns, two to play in the keys from F up to high C and two from F down to low C. This gave a greater sonority and breadth to a composition by allowing the instruments to play full chords, as well as be used in the tonic and dominant (or tonic and relative major for minor keys).

Like the French horn, the trumpet was also an important brass instrument for composers of the period, due mainly to its brilliant and martial tone. It, too, was largely relegated to the harmonic series, with lower register (called *tromba* or *principale*, though the first was also the generic name for the instrument itself) dependent on notes of the triad, while the upper register (*clarino*) allowed for a more melodic function. The Baroque Period had been the heyday of this instrument, when clarino players were able to perform solo works that extended into their uppermost registers. There were two types of trumpets in the early part of the period: the so-called hunting trumpet (*tromba da caccia*), which looked like a tightly wound horn (Figure 3.9a), and the regular trumpet, which was elongated (Figure 3.9b). The latter sometimes had added at

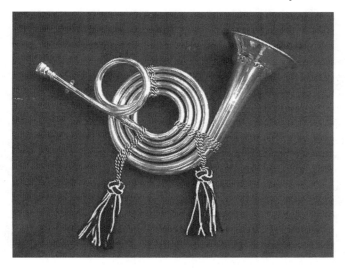

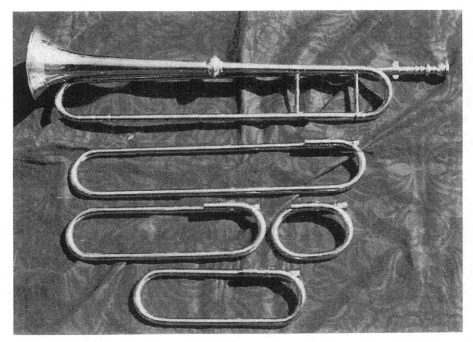

Figure 3.9 (a) Photo of a Baroque *Jagdtrompette*; (b) Photo of a regular Baroque natural trumpet with all of the crooks
Source: Photo courtesy of *The Boston Musical Intelligencer*.

the mouthpiece a short tuning slide, or a hole was bored into the tubing and covered by a leather sleeve; this not only allowed for some tuning but also made the indistinct partials of *f-sharp"* or *f-natural"* and *a-flat"* become clear. Given the military origins of the instrument, the principal keys were D major and C major, though others did exist.[13] In many instances, the trumpeters and timpanists often associated with them were assigned to special regimental units or were part of guilds (*Stadtpfeifer* or City Pipers in northern Germany, whose job it was to use trumpets for civic purposes, such as watch signals). This meant that the numbers available for orchestras were often exaggerated, though in most cases only a pair were needed. Given the festive occasions both a court and in churches, the trumpets provided the appropriate ambience to celebrate events, from the mundane to the extraordinary.

The main treatise of trumpet performance was Johann Ernst Altenburg's *Versuch einer Anleitung zur heroisch-musikalischen Trompeter-und Paukerkunst* (*An Essay on the Introduction to Heroic and Musical Trumpeters' and Kettledrummers' Art*; Halle, 1795, but advertised as early as 1770). He outlines the usage of the instruments, dividing it into celebrations and military signals and allows for the special status trumpet players held. He states: "According to the Imperial privilege, proficient trumpeters and timpanists should play their instruments only in public celebrations, but never in the company of the unlearned, under penalty of punishment." He goes on to say: "This prohibition extends even to churches . . . but to perform with other instruments in company is always possible on every occasion."[14] In his description of the instruments, he notes that, like the horn, smaller crooks were used to lower the tone, however, cautioning that for the key of B-flat, the wear and tear on the trumpet and the player would be mitigated by the use of a so-called "long" trumpet.

The range of the trumpet he expected was up to and beyond written g''', indicating that even at the end of the eighteenth century these specialized performers were expected to be able to negotiate the extremes of the register, although he also cautions the routine performances with other instruments to be discrete and blend in with the orchestra.

Around 1790 Viennese court trumpeter Anton Weidinger and trumpet player Lorenz Merckl from Stockholm invented simultaneously a keyed trumpet. The latter performed a solo in 1783 on his *Inventionstrumpet*, but this instrument has not survived. Weidinger, however, was able to get composers such as Haydn and Leopold Kozeluch to write solo works for his five-key instrument pitched in E or E-flat. The sound was not as clear in tone as the natural trumpet, but nonetheless, it was able to produce a chromatic scale, which made it a more useful and versatile instrument, later replaced in the nineteenth century by the valved modern version.

Keyboard Instruments

Keyboard instruments were key to the music of the Classical Period, having an important and often crucial function in both orchestral and chamber genres. As we will see, it served to provide a harmonic foundation as a continuo instrument, as well as an important part of such genres as the duo sonata. It also served as a solo instrument in concertos, even to the point of being occasionally both ritornello and solo all in one.

Three basic keyboard instruments of this period are members of the chordophone family; the clavichord, the harpsichord, and the fortepiano. To this can be added as an indispensable part of sacred music the organ, which although having a keyboard, was actually an aerophone with a different set of mechanical requirements than the others. The generic term for the three instruments during the Classical Period was *Clavier* in German, though what might be thought of as equivalents in French (*Clavecin*) or Italian (*Clavicembalo*) mostly meant the harpsichord. Like the violin, pedagogical treatises on keyboard instruments abounded during the eighteenth century, but perhaps the most influential was the *Versuch über die wahre Art das Clavier zu spielen* (*Essay on the True Art of Playing the Keyboard*) by Carl Philipp Emanuel Bach, published in 1753 (Figure 3.10). Like the Quantz treatise, it was the result of work at the Prussian court in Berlin, but its approach is quite different in that it focuses almost entirely on the technical and pedagogical aspects of all the instruments. Bach stated in his preface that it was the most versatile instrument, capable of playing full harmony and bass lines that required several others to do correctly. He also stated,

> Apart from this, it is required that he be able to improvise fantasias in all styles, to work through by extemporization any requested composition according to the strictest rules of harmony and melody; perform easily in all keys and transpose instantly without mistakes from one to the next; play everything at sight and without music, whether or not it is meant for his instrument; to have a comprehensive

knowledge of figured bass which he must play with full force, knowing the difference of playing sometimes in many parts, sometimes in few; sometimes with strict harmony and sometimes in the galant style, sometimes extensive and insufficient figures or unfigured and incorrectly figured basses, extracting from full scores . . . and reinforcing the ensemble.[15]

In short, the keyboardist was expected to be musically indispensable during the middle of the century, following on to the Baroque practice of continuo playing, as well as more contemporary solo work. Bach notes that the clavichord is performed by itself, while the harpsichord is generally meant to accompany ensembles, further stating that "the more recent fortepiano . . . sounds good by itself and in small ensembles." In the second part of the treatise, Bach adds the organ to the instruments, noting that it is "indispensable in church music with its counterpoint, large choruses, and sustained style; it provides splendor and maintains order."[16]

By the 1780s, the fortepiano began to attain ascendancy over the harpsichord, particularly since keyboard instruments began to vanish as part of the bass. The range and depth of this instrument provided the fullness of sound lacking in the clavichord and the facility and dynamic range lacking in the harpsichord. Improvements in the mechanism by Johann Andreas Stein and Anton Walther in Vienna, John Broadwood in London, and composer Ignaz Pleyel later in Paris enhanced the sound, eventually developing it into the modern piano. Bohemian composer Jan Ladislav Dussek was particularly important in his work with Broadwood in expanding the range of the keyboard about 1790. As steady as these advancements were, however, the first edition of Beethoven's *Pathetique Sonata* still offered the harpsichord as a possible performance instrument, despite the idiomatic music for the fortepiano (Figure 3.11).

Figure 3.10 Title page of Carl Philipp Emanuel Bach, *Versuch über die wahre Art das Clavier zu spielen* (1753)

Figure 3.11 Titlepage of the first edition of Ludwig van Beethoven, Sonata in C minor Op. 13 "Pathetique" indicating the instruments

The Voice

The voice was an important component in music performed by both amateurs and professionals during the Classical Period. Proficiency and voice types were delineated during the period as the need for singers increased. As the development of singers was critical for a wide variety of genres, both sacred and secular, individual instruction was often done in the context of institutions. The conservatories in Naples, according to Charles Burney, had two *maestri di cappella*, part of whose position involved the teaching of singing to the young, exclusively male pupils.[17] During his visit in 1772, he inquired about the creation of *castrati*, males whose abilities as young prepubescent children were recognized and encouraged to undergo the removal of the testicles to preserve the voice against the inevitable changes that normally occur as they went through puberty. He notes that the operation was generally prohibited throughout Italy (and especially elsewhere) but that it still occurred in private. Given that there was a need for this voice type, described as powerful and lyrical, for both opera and in the church, such operations were unofficially sanctioned, even though technically against the law.

Throughout the Classical Period, the need for castrati declined as more and more women took to the stage, and tenors and occasionally basses filled the heroic roles. Nonetheless, the public often regarded castrati as the epitome of singing, with a number achieving international recognition for their talent. Farinelli (real name, Carlo Broschi), Senesino (Francesco Bernardi and Giusto Tenducci), Caffarelli (Gaetano Morjano), and Venanzio Rauzzini were all active from the late Baroque, when both Farinelli and Bernardi were rivals in London, into the late century. Tenducci and Rauzzini were also noted composers. Given that word *castrato* was used in a pejorative manner, the normal name for these singers was *musico*, as Burney notes: "The word *musico* in Italy seems now wholly appropriate to a singer with a *soprano* or *contralto* voice, which has been preserved by art."[18] The number of prospective castrati declined throughout the period, with the operation itself being gauged as secretive even in Italy (Document 2). By the middle of the century the male soprano or alto had largely been replaced by women, save in the churches where they were still used up into the nineteenth century, though they were a rarity. It was not unusual for secondary male roles with the upper voice types to be performed by women dressed as men, such as that of Cherubino in Mozart's *Marriage of Figaro*.

Naples was not the only place where voice training was taught systematically. Schools of Singing were some of the earliest to be created, forming the core for providing singers for the regional and national operas or concerts. Italian composer Paolo Scalabrini established an institution in Copenhagen as early as 1755, while in Germany Johann Adam Hiller formed his in Leipzig in 1760. Hiller, whose school not only trained singers but also trained choral conductors and *Kapellmeisters*, wrote two significant treatises on singing: *Anweisung zur Singekunst in der deutschen und italienischen Sprache* (*Manual in the Art of Singing in German and Italian Language*), published in 1773, and the popular *Anweisung zum musikalisch-richtigen Gesange* (*Manual for Musically Correct Singing*) a year later. Both of these works went through a number of editions and were used throughout Germany and the Holy Roman Empire. In 1783, the *École royale du chant* was established in Paris with Niccolò Piccinni as its first director. This institution served as one of the founding organizations of the Conservatoire in 1795.

Musical training in voice was more than a matter of simply practice and exercises (vocalizes) but, rather, a comprehensive course of study that required both stamina and facility. Here, the Italians were regarded as superior to all others. Hiller notes in the second of these treatises above: "In singing, the Germans are far behind the Italians, not least because the number of good singers [is] so nowhere as large as among them."[19] He then states: "There are mainly two items that define singing, competence and eloquence." His intent was to build on a small handbook by theorist Friedrich Wilhelm Marpurg titled *Anleitung zur Musik überhaupt und zur Singkunst besonders* (*The Instruction of Music Overall, and Especially of Singing*), published a few years earlier in Berlin. His criteria for a singer are fourfold: (1) they must possess a good voice with clear and unambiguous declamation, (2) they must be able to sing on pitch all the notes and intervals, (3) they must be able to sustain each note for a specific length of time without variance, and (4) they must be able to express to the listener all of the eloquence that is contained within the music. This set of criteria can still be seen today in the need for aural skills training. Moreover, the trained voice must be flexible and precise, able to encompass numerous styles and moods. For Hiller, this was the only way that a potential singer could master music, become proficient, and be able to achieve the necessary reputation that would guide them in their professional careers. An anonymous English manual, *The Convivial Songster* from 1782, notes that good singers declaim the text with a full sound (and never making a consonant sound like a vowel); never sing too loudly (which produces a "dissonant bawling"); avoid singing nasally; should sing from the chest and diaphragm, not from the throat; and must sing without affectation of any kind (avoiding unnecessary improvisation or ornaments).[20]

Two of Hiller's protégées, Gertrude Elisabeth Mara (Figure 3.12) and Corona Schröter, became international successes both as singers with powerful soprano voices, but also as teachers. As a result of Hiller and others who imitated his methodology, voice training became more pedagogical during the Classical Period and formed the basis for the nineteenth century German *Fach* system of vocal classification.

The development of musical instruments and playing technique advanced continually throughout the eighteenth century, with both pedagogy and art music being developed in tandem. As Pierre-Louis Ginguené

Figure 3.12 Engraving of Gertrude Elisabeth Mara (after a painting by Louise Élisabeth Vigée LeBrun, 1785)

noted in his 1791 *Enclyclopédie méthodique*, "[i]nstrumental performance has now reached so advanced a state of perfection that there is no instrument that cannot claim to shine in a concert."[21] This rapid evolution was not only for solo instruments, but rather affected the growth of the ensemble or orchestra as well (Document 3). As the voice was more directed toward genres such as opera, other developmental criteria were used in the pedagogy, as is explained in Chapter 6.

The Expansion of the Orchestra

The expansion of the orchestra during the Classical Period was steady though uneven, as there were no real standards for either size or constituent instruments. The earliest works from before 1740 commonly require a conventional four-part string orchestra, with the bass line being performed by a continuo with keyboard and a variety of instruments such as the cello, bass, and bassoon.[22] Although in places woodwinds and brass instruments were available, their participation was not taken for granted. If present, the oboes often doubled the violins as in Baroque practice, with the bassoons added to the continuo as reinforcement of the timbre, and horns occasionally made an appearance. In the keys of D and C, one could occasionally find trumpets and timpani, as well. This might be called the *Early Classical Orchestra*. By 1745, however, a pair of oboes and/or flutes,[23] as well as horns, became more commonplace, and as a result, the textures available to an orchestra became thicker, with the melodic line being enhanced, and the latter having a function of harmonic support. Most ensembles of the period would have at least this instrumentation, and this might be called the *Standard Classical Orchestra*. The woodwinds would have most likely been played by the same performers on either instrument, and the continuo instruments were retained, though occasionally the use of figuration of the bass line was omitted.

With the advent of Johann Stamitz and the Mannheim orchestra around 1745, new colors emerged as larger woodwind sections were added, so that flutes, oboes, and bassoons could fill and reinforce the main themes. With the addition of clarinets about 1755, the entire range and sound quality of the woodwinds could be used, allowing for a large diversity in texture and contrast. This also required performers to begin specializing on their primary instrument. While woodwind players could still perform on a variety of instruments, the need for such coloristic textures led to an increase in their numbers within a single ensemble. About this time, the bassoons emerged from their continuo function, and at least a pair were often used to provide a foundation for the woodwind texture; a third bassoon was often added to support the bass line. The use of four horns in many orchestras about the same time now allowed them to play several keys, mainly tonic and dominant, thus strengthening the harmony considerably. By 1780 in Paris, a trombone was sometimes added to the ensemble at the Concerts Spirituels as additional tonal reinforcement, and with the fad for the so-called Turkish or military music that emerged from opera, full percussion sections were occasionally inserted as well. Austrian composer Georg Druschetzky often incorporated complex percussion, but the best-known example is the Symphony in G Major, Hob. I:100, by Haydn, often called the "Military" due to the sudden appearance of the percussion in an otherwise conventional second movement. Exotic instruments also made their appearance on occasion. Leopold Mozart, for instance, requires an alphorn in at least one symphony, and in the far north at Trondheim, Norway, Johan Daniel Berlin used a solo cornetto in his first symphony (Example 3.3).

By the end of the eighteenth century, most orchestras were of substantial size, what today would be considered the instrumentation of a large modern chamber orchestra. This followed the pattern developed by the Mannheim orchestra, providing a foundation against which other non-orchestral instruments such as the fortepiano could be matched. As the power and depth of the orchestra increased, however, the continuo keyboard fell out of fashion as it was deemed useless as an instrument to fill out the harmony and keep the ensemble together. In opera, of course, it was necessary to accompany the recitative sections, but the sound was simply subsumed into the thicker orchestral textures during the arias and ensembles; in instrumental works it became redundant, and therefore, it began to disappear about 1780. It did not entirely vanish, however, for even up to the end of the century conductors were still led to the keyboard to direct the concerts. For example, during his visits to England Joseph Haydn was seated at a keyboard, even though he

Example 3.3 Johan Daniel Berlin, Symphony in D major, Movement III, mm. 1–8

thought it absurd for the overall balance of Johann Peter Salomon's ensemble; in the final movement of his Symphony in B-flat major, Hob. I:98, he reduces the orchestration to just the "continuo" and solo violin, demonstrating that his contribution was nothing more than a series of bland arpeggiated figures.

Of course, places such as Mannheim, Paris, or Vienna were the exceptions to the standards from early on, but in the smaller courts and cities, the growth of the orchestra was slower and more deliberate. How these ensembles sounded, however, depended on the proficiency of the players and their cohesiveness as a unit.

Performance Practice

The study of how music was performed during the Classical Period is called generally **performance practice**. Of course, every period and every place has its own set of practices that give insight not only how music was played at any given time; it also informs us of the various aspects of music, ranging from composition to tuning, from articulation to ornamentation. Much was dependent on individual factors, and given such a broad definition, a movement that began in the 1960s to define how the music of the eighteenth century was performed has evolved into what can be called **Historically Informed Performance, or HIP** for short. In a time when most modern audiences are aware that a performance of any work by a modern orchestra is sometimes more interpretive than authentic, given the differences that have occurred over the course of almost three centuries since it was written, the trend has been to reconstruct the eighteenth century sound world through the use of replicas of period instruments, performance techniques, and accurate articulation or ornamentation. This, in turn, has led to a number of institutions wherein the focus is on re-creating the music of the Classical Period in an innovative and sometimes subjective manner. This has borne fruit in a wave of groups dedicated to this study who, in turn, have often led the revival of music that lies outside the traditional concert canon; that is, relying on Mozart, Haydn, and Beethoven as the sole representative composers of the period.

HIP is an evolving movement, in which new facets and variability make it less about a specific standard practice but, rather, encourages the same sort of experimentation done during the eighteenth century within our knowledge of the historical parameters. One recalls the early arguments of the 1960s during the movement's infancy regarding the practice of the dot or double-dot articulation by Robert Donnington[24] or whether modern instruments such as the piano are appropriate for more delicate textures required for the expression of that time. Virtually every aspect of how music was performed during the Classical Period is subject to debate or a variety of interpretations, but in understanding how music appealed to or was received by audiences of the time, some examples are instructive.

The first is still a controversial one today, and that is whether a work written for a specific place was intended to be performed one on a part (OOAP) or by a larger group. For today's performers, the practice is often determined by the economies of the ensemble; it is cheaper to pay five or six performers than an entire orchestra. The Classical Period, however, had a more pragmatic attitude toward numbers of performers. Moreover, the composer's intended or desired orchestration of a work such as a symphony or the accompanying ensemble for a concerto was certainly dependent on the circumstances. One document is a letter from a Benedictine monk concerning a domestic performance of "several beautiful, brilliant, and large" symphonies by Swedish composer Kraus, in which he states, "They are performed in his parents' house only as a quartet, because we didn't have the necessary people."[25] On the other hand, Charles Avison notes that an ensemble performing a concerto should consist of a larger complement of ten violins, possibly three violas, four cellos, and doubling the contrabasses alongside the keyboard continuo instrument. He specifically states,

> A lesser number of Instruments, near the same Proportion, will also have a proper Effect, and may answer the Composer's Intention: but more would probably destroy the just Contrast, which should always be kept up between the Chorus and Solo.[26]

This creates an ambiguity that a smaller ensemble can be justified but that a larger one than suggested would "destroy" the music by being too thick in terms of sound. Indeed, an engraving from about 1760 shows a private concert with one on a part accompanying a singer (Figure 3.13), which would verify Avison's appropriate texture for a chamber group in terms of "just contrast." Musicologist Neal Zaslaw has noted that there was little consistency on how this was applied across the board, but the treatises of the time attempt to provide clues as to what good arrangements might be.[27]

In terms of numbers, Quantz recommends that only single lower strings be used when there are only four or six violins, though the last one should add a bassoon for balance. Doubling the lower strings should occur when there are eight or ten violins; here, he suggests adding woodwinds and an additional cello. With twelve violins, the complement rises yet again with additional violas, cellos, contrabasses, and woodwinds.[28] He concludes: "Since the success of a composition depends as much on an arrangement of the instruments in the proper proportions as upon good execution, foresight in this matter is particularly important."[29] The balance issue seems to have been addressed in other treatises by Francesco Galeazzi, Heinrich Koch, and others, and while there are differences, the view is always the same; proportional balance is the goal to be achieved in any ensemble.

Figure 3.13 Engraving of a small orchestral ensemble rehearsal in Germany (*ca.* 1760)

Figure 3.14 Woodcut of Vauxhall Gardens about 1765 showing the orchestra and singer on the second story of the pavilion

A "proper" distribution of a larger group was necessary to provide the right aural combination for the listeners. Arrangements, however, were highly dependent on the venue, which meant that it varied considerably depending on the space available, as well as the purpose for which the orchestra was used. For example, a concert out of doors could have the instruments spread out depending on whether it was in a public space, such as the Vauxhall Gardens in London, or a private courtyard. In the former, pavilions were arranged for the performers above the audience, while in the latter, they were set around the periphery of the space on a level with the audience (Figure 3.14). In opera houses, the setting was rather different since the orchestra pit was often more constricted, and the instruments were often situated in rows with various arrangements of instruments.

Quantz noted that the placement of these larger groups should be left up to the concertmaster:

> The leader must know how to distribute, place and arrange the instrumentalists in an ensemble. Much depends upon the good distribution and placement of the instruments, and upon their combination in the proper ratio.[30]

He then goes on to note that, in opera houses, there were sometimes two harpsichords, the primary one of which ought to be put in the center, with the keyboard facing the audience, and both contrabasses and cellos just behind it. If a second harpsichord is required, this should also be on the left side with its own smaller continuo group, including a theorbo, behind (Figure 3.15). He recommends that the violas sit with their backs to the stage on one side, with bassoons on the other. Violins should be to the right of the harpsichord, firsts with their backs to the audience in front of the seconds. To the left would be the woodwinds, with oboes and horns likewise with their backs to the audience and flutes in a diagonal, or if space permits in a line.

70 New Developments, Convergences, and Genres

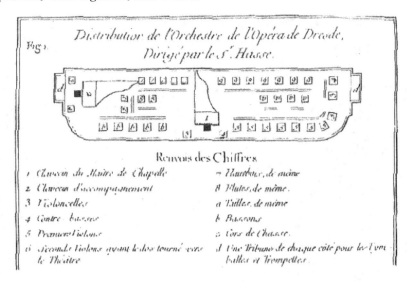

Figure 3.15 Engraving of the disposition of the orchestra in Dresden during the time of Johann Adolph Hasse (*ca.* 1750)

This is not the only configuration recommended by Quantz, for he also notes that in concert halls, the keyboard is to be turned 180 degrees, and the flutes, "on account of the weakness of their tone," should be front and center. In smaller chamber ensembles, the keyboard is on the right, and the instruments lined up in rows on the left. This configuration appears to conform to the numerous diagrams and prints from the period.

Toward the last part of the century when orchestras required for public concerts increased in size, the placement became more normalized than impromptu as Quantz noted. For example, one Parisian orchestra in 1778 could have been standard for the period:

> The disposition of the orchestra is accountable, and one ought to observe the following rules, namely, place the second violins opposite and not alongside the firsts; put the bass instruments as close as possible to the first violins, for the bass is an essential part of the chords in the harmony; finally, gather the winds—such as oboes, flutes, horns, etc.—and complete it with the violas.[31]

The evolution in the size and types of instruments in the orchestra required a parallel development of genres that would define them. One such genre was the concerto, which demonstrated the range and versatility of the instruments themselves, while ensemble works such as the symphony rose to parallel the development of the orchestra.

Documents

Document 1. From Carl Friedrich Zelter, *Karl Friedrich Christian Fasch* (Berlin, 1801), p. 11.

In the year 1751 the Royal Prussian Concertmaster Franz Benda came to visit Strelitz and was asked to play before the court. Benda responded with a solo. Good old [Georg Friedrich] Linke was at that time the keyboardist at the Strelitz court, and, although he was a capable man, he did not now trust himself to play in the style of Benda, which was new at that time. Benda preferred to play his own violin sonatas, to which he set very lively and difficult continuo parts that required a very strong left hand and vivacious accompaniment. Young Fasch was the only one in Strelitz who could accompany the master properly. He found therein such complete pleasure in the difficulties of the Benda continuo line and to the satisfaction of this great violinist he delved into the accompaniment for a long time, thereby developing a very deft left hand, an ability still found in his late years, for without exception he was able to bring out clearly and naturally all of the ornaments, articulations, and displacements with one hand, as well as the other.

Document 2. From Charles Burney, *The Present State of Music in France and Italy* (London, 1775), pp. 310–311.

The number of scholars in the first conservatory is about ninety, in the second a hundred and twenty, and in the other, two hundred. Each of them has two principal *Maestri di Capella*, the first of whom superintends and corrects the compositions of the students; the second the singing and gives lessons. That there are assistant masters, who are called *Maestri Secolari*; one for the violin, one for the voloncello, one for the harpsichord, one for the hautbois, one for the French-horn, an so for the other instruments. . . . The boys are admitted from eight or ten to twenty years of age; when they are taken in young they are bound for eight years; but, when more advanced, their admission is difficult, except they have made a considerable progress in the study and practice of music. After boys have been in the Conservatorio for some years, if no genius is discovered, they are dismissed to make way for others. . . . I enquired throughout Italy at what place boys were chiefly qualified for singing by castration, but could get no certain intelligence. I was told at Milan that it was at Venice; at Venice that it was at Bologna, but at Bologna the fact was denied, and I was referred to Florence; from Florence to Rome, and from Rome I was sent to Naples. The operation was certainly against the law in all of these places, as well as against nature; and all the Italians are so much ashamed of it, that in every province they transfer it to some other.

Document 3. Pierre-Louis Ginguené, "Concerto" from the *Encyclopédie méthodique* (Paris, 1791), p. 301.

Instrumental performance has now reach so advanced a state of perfection that there is no instrument that cannot claim to shine in a concert. The character of the work is now fixed, and perhaps cannot be changed without loss. I speak not only of concertos for the violin, because they have been the first and for long were the only ones, those that were then composed for other instruments were based entirely on the same model. The construction of the instruments has improved so much, that all can maintain the pretense of shining forth in a concerto. The harpsichord formerly had this privilege, and rightly so, but now rather it has been passed on to the fortepiano. The flute, the oboe, and the clarinet have long had their concertos. Even the horn has concertos, and the sad bassoon has not foregone that advantage. I have heard the nephew of the great Stamitz play concertos for the viola;[32] concertos for the violoncello have made the reputation of more than one famous artist, and concertos have now been composed for the contrabass.

Notes

1. See Franz Benda, *A Musician at Court: An Autobiography of Franz Benda*, trans. Douglas Lee (Warren, MI: Harmonie Park Press, 1998), 40–41. The *Autobiography* was completed in 1763, but only three years later, the number had soared to forty thousand, and by 1784 the total was fifty thousand. Given Benda's longevity at the Berlin court, the numbers are not beyond the bounds of reason.
2. In the introduction, Mozart notes that the violin differs from the "fiddle," showing that the instruments of the violin family were wide ranging during the time, from "pocket violins" used to accompany dance lessons to the "Great Bass," a sort of variable contrabass. These include things like "bassoon fiddles" or "half fiddles" (*violino piccolo*), the viola da gamba, and even the *tromba marina*, a sort of one-stringed monochord). See Leopold Mozart, *A Treatis on the Fundamental Principles of Violin Playing*, trans. Editha Knocker (London: Oxford University Press, 1951), 12–13.
3. Quantz, *On Playing the Flute*, 237.
4. Quantz, *On Playing the Flute*, 244.
5. Michel Corette's *Méthode, thèorique et pratique pour apprendre en peu de temps le violoncelle dans sa perfection* (Paris, 1741), 46. Corette also wrote treatises on the harp, violin, and flute.
6. The transverse flutes were also a family, as Quantz (34) notes. The instruments include a low *Quartflöte*, the *flauto d'amore*, and the little *Quartflöte*, with the equivalents being an alto flute, tenor flute, and piccolo in modern parlance. He liked the tone of the *amore* but noted, "none approaches the regular transverse flute in trueness and beauty of tone." These family instruments likewise disappeared in the Classical Period.
7. Quantz, *On Playing the Flute*, 85–86. He states specifically: "In an orchestra, the oboist must hold his instrument up as much as possible."
8. Burney, *A General History of Music*, II: 46. Regarding Fischer, he states, "Fischer seems to me the most natural, pleasing, and original writer of the two for this instrument."
9. Roeser, *Essai d'instruction*, 2. He also notes that there are, in all, seven different clarinets; these are built in the keys of G, A, B-flat, C, D, E, and F, with the first and last three rarely used as of that date.
10. Roeser, *Essai d'Instruction*, 12.
11. Since it has a bend in the middle to accommodate the length, it has been suggested that the name is a misreading of *cor anglé* (or angled horn). The Italian *corno inglese* came into use almost a decade after its invention, probably as a translation of the French *cor anglais*. A recent suggestion is that it was reminiscent of the medieval instruments in various manuscripts, and that the German original was *Engellische Horn*, or Angelic horn, which was bowdlerized in the French translation.
12. Roeser, *Essai d'instruction*, 13. Roeser than goes on to outline the eight "types" as horns (or crooks) ranging from high C (C *alto*, called the "most sonorous and painful to play") down to low C (C *basso*, defined as the "most sweet but of lesser sound, but easier to play the higher partials and more difficult to play in the lower.")
13. These include the keys of G (a so-called English trumpet), F, E, E-flat, and, after about 1780, a coupler lowering the pitch to B-flat and even A. In France, a high A trumpet also existed, though almost never used.
14. Johann Ernst Altenburg, *Versuch einer Anleitungzur heroisch-musikalisch Trompeter und Paukerkunst* (Halle, 1795), 23.
15. Carl Philipp Emanuel Bach, *Versuch über die wahre Art das Clavier zu Spielen* (Berlin, 1753), 2–3.
16. Bach, *Versuch*, 143.
17. See Charles Burney, *The Present State of Music in France and Italy* (London, 1773), 311.
18. Charles Burney, *The Present State of Music in France and Italy*, 314.
19. Johann Adam Hiller, *Anweisung zum musikalisch-richtigen Gesange* (Leipzig, 1774), 5.
20. See *The Convivial Songster, being a Select Collection of the Best Songs in the English Language* (London, 1782), vi.
21. Pierre-Louis Ginguené, *Enclyclopédie méthodique* (Paris, 1791), 301.
22. Early instrument ensembles sometimes also add a theorbo, though this seems optional.
23. At this stage, the flutes were transverse flutes, forebears of the modern instruments; the term *flauto* generally referred to the recorder in the early part of the century, but these were too soft to find a place in the emerging Classical orchestra.
24. Robert Donnington, *The Intrepetation of Early Music* (New York: Norton, 1989).
25. See Bertil van Boer, *The Musical Life of Joseph Martin Kraus* (Bloomington, IN: Indiana University Press, 2014), 341. The monk is Pater Romanus Hoffstetter (1742–1815), also the probable author of the Op. 3 string quartets once attributed to Joseph Haydn; see Chapter 11.
26. Charles Avison, *An Essay on Musical Expression* (London, 1752), 113.
27. See Neal Zaslaw, *Mozart's Symphonies: Context, Performance Practice, Reception* (Oxford: Clarendon Press, 1989), 445–509. Zaslaw reviews that various points with respect to Mozart's orchestras in the context of the general views of the eighteenth-century practices. He notes specifically that there is no actual standard period orchestra, but rather, it depended upon various "traditions and practices" in each individual place.

28 Quantz, *On Playing the Flute*, 214. With twelve violins, he recommends three violas, four cellos, three bassoons, and four each of flutes and oboes. He also notes that horns can be added "depending upon the nature of the piece."
29 Quantz, *On Playing the Flute*, 214.
30 Quantz, *On Playing the Flute*, 211.
31 Jean Olivier de Meude-Monpas, *Dictionnarie de musique* (Paris, 1787), 132–133. He is describing the Concert des Amateurs, the rival group to the Concerts Spirituels.
32 Ginguené actually means either Carl or Anton Stamitz, both sons (and not nephews) of Johann Stamitz.

4 Genre as the Core of Musical Development
Orchestral Works

The rise of orchestral music during the Classical Period paralleled the development of the orchestra itself. By the early part of the eighteenth century, as already noted, the size of the ensembles grew both in terms of numbers and instruments, and with it the need for music to reflect this growth likewise expanded. The main focal point of the majority of cities and courts remained the opera or theatre, but increasingly the larger orchestras were involved in performances wherein instrumental music began to dominate. Indeed, we will see that these larger ensembles were a source of pride and reputation for major centers such as Paris, Vienna, Stockholm, or London, and in courts such as Mannheim, Ludwigsburg, Oettingen-Wallerstein, and Esterháza, the well-disciplined orchestras achieved international recognition for their innovations and excellence. This was achieved largely through their performances of orchestral works designed both to show off the abilities of the performers and to expand the scope of the music they played. These required a more progressive development than was available in the main instrumental genres of the Baroque Period, the suite and concerto grosso.

Because the concerts described in the previous chapter had a wide variety of works in several different genres, vocal and instrumental, using larger or smaller numbers of performers, they required some sense of continuity to satisfy the expectations of the audiences. Moreover, with the rise of the virtuoso, works that displayed their talents were also necessary. Both requirements led to the development of genres that could fulfill these new requirements, one derived from the late Baroque when the virtuoso began to appear on an international scale and the other that emerged mainly from the theatre as an independent type of work: the concerto and the symphony.

The Concerto and Sinfonia Concertante

Rousseau defines the concerto during the Classical Period as "a work done for some particular instrument which plays alone from time to time with a simple accompaniment following an opening by a large orchestra." It then "always continues in the same alternation between the same instrument *recitant* and the orchestra in chorus."[1] Koch elaborates further on the genre:

> The word *concerto* designates a special type of composition within which an individual musician is allowed to be heard on his instrument with the accompaniment of an orchestra. One divides this type of artistic product in two formats . . . the second of which the performer carries the main portion of the composition by himself, separated through interjections of the entire orchestra.[2]

These and other theorists of the period note that the genre continued from Baroque practice, only now the substance of the work placed more of an emphasis on the interaction between the soloist and accompanying orchestra so that both presented textural and formal contrast and yet were integrated in terms of musical content. Moreover, Koch also notes that more than one solo instrument could be required, noting that the term for this was "duo-concerto" (*Doppelkonzert*), further stating, "the concerto is especially an imitation of a solo vocal work with full-voiced accompaniment."[3] As the instrumental version of the aria, Koch states, it should "express a specific emotion according to its particular manner of expression." All too often, performers and composers make it a point to exceed the simpler displays in favor of extreme virtuosity. Koch reminds us that this sort of performance, all too common as the century advanced, began to focus all the attention on what he calls "mechanical" virtuoso display at the expense of the broader purpose of the concerto (see Document 1):

> Performers who have placed mechanical ability as the highest and only goal of their performance are not satisfied with the difficulties that are contained within the accessible concertos for their instrument, but rather go one step further to complete the depredation of their art.[4]

Calling this sort of sterile display "hocus pocus," Koch rails against display only for the sake of display, requiring both concertos and those who perform them to exercise both virtuosity and emotional depth in their performances, playing "from the heart," as he states.

While the eighteenth century did see the rise of the importance of the traveling virtuoso, the bulk of the concertos were composed to reveal the abilities of individual players who were also members of the ensembles in which they were employed. Quantz is particularly clear about the need for soloists to be drawn from the orchestras themselves and for them to be able to perform concertos on a regular basis:

> The brilliance of an orchestra will also be greatly enhanced if it contains good solo players on various instruments. Hence, the leader must seek to encourage good solo players. To this end he must give those equipped to play alone frequent opportunities to distinguish themselves, not only privately, but also in public concerts.[5]

Quantz thus conflates both composer and the performer, for concertos were often written either by the performers themselves or for colleagues, with a second step being a more general distribution of the music through publication.

The late Baroque concerto came of age with the works of Georg Philipp Telemann and Antonio Vivaldi, both of whom composed music that pushed the limits of instrumental virtuosity and display. Vivaldi, himself a violinist, began his career writing for the young women of the Ospedale di San Pietà in Venice, where at the beginning of the eighteenth century his charges were notable for their precociousness and ability "to play the most difficult concertos," as a visitor reported. The Italian violin school had already created opportunities for virtuosos such as Pietro Locatelli and Giuseppe Tartini, both of whose abilities had been demonstrated to audiences throughout Europe. In their wake appeared the occasional performer on other instruments, such as oboist Giuseppe Sammartini. These virtuosos sometimes made their home abroad; Locatelli in Amsterdam and Sammartini in London, for example. For Telemann, however, virtuoso display focused on a particular soloist was not the impulse for his concertos, and while Vivaldi wrote numerous works for various combinations of solo instruments, his work like that of Telemann seemed more like a series of experiments in orchestral color or expansions on the traditional concerto grosso. That is not to say that Vivaldi, for example, did not pay attention to technical display, but the musical content was often predictable and consisted of the spinning out of smaller nonthematic motivic units in a three-movement format.

As the *Empfindsamkeit* composers began to write for the abilities of their own ensembles beginning in the 1740s, however, a renewed focus on the concerto began to emerge. This was coupled with the improvements in instrumental technique and design, resulting in works that not only required the utmost proficiency by the soloist but also pushed the limits of the instruments themselves. Moreover, there was a sense of experimentation that included nontraditional instruments to see if composers could write music for their limited ranges or versatility. As an example of the former, the virtuoso sections of a trumpet concerto by Franz Xavier Richter from the 1750s demonstrate a degree of difficulty that even Baroque players would have seen as challenging (Example 4.1). The concertos for exotic or unusual instruments seemed most prominent in central Europe, and the limitations were accommodated in interesting ways. For instance,

76 *New Developments, Convergences, and Genres*

Example 4.1 Franz Xaver Richter, Trumpet Concerto in D major, Movement I, mm. 50–56

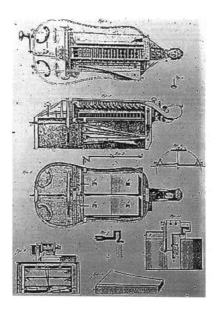

Figure 4.1 Schematic of a lyra organizzata

Austrian composer Georg Druschenzky wrote concertos for multiple timpani and orchestra, while Johann Georg Albrechtsberger wrote six concertos for Jaw Harp and Mandora (a sort of large lute, also known as a *gallichone*); perhaps the best example is the six concertos by Joseph Haydn for the lira organizzata, a hybrid instrument cross between a hurdy-gurdy and organ (Figure 4.1).[6]

Even as extreme virtuosity was practiced, lyrical moments were also encouraged so that both brilliance and sensitivity could be displayed. The final movement was often a stylized dance, perhaps even a minuet, in which the main section would be static, with solo display in the trios. As Quantz noted, this allowed a soloist to demonstrate technical skill, emotion or sensitivity, and a playfulness that could combine various elements.

The ability to perform concertos required both skill and taste, yet performers were often limited to playing with the ensembles in which they were employed, meaning that the genre was localized. Violinist Franz Benda, as noted, claimed in his autobiography that during his career he had performed solos in more than twelve thousand concertos, but few if any were done on tour. At the court of Frederick the Great, pictures of the period show the King performing concertos on the flute with a small chamber ensemble, and his teacher, Quantz, composed about three hundred flute concertos (and several others for two flutes, as well as with other instruments), many of which were intended to be played by Frederick at his evening concerts. These works for the king, a solid, "respectable" performer who was known to take liberties with tempos in the faster movements, were for select audiences only (Figure 4.2).

Figure 4.2 Nineteenth-century painting by Adolph Menzel of a concert with Frederick the Great (1852)
Source: Alte Nationalgalerie, Staatliche Museen zu Berlin.

By the middle of the century, the concerto became more visible as public concerts, such as the Parisian Concerts Spirituels, offered opportunities for both composers and performers to display their talent to larger audiences. This, in turn, provided players the possibility of achieving a reputation while on tour. For the genre itself, this meant that more standardization had to occur. The solo lines began to avoid extreme virtuosity in favor of more integration with the now-larger accompanying orchestra, and exotic instrumentation for solos became a rarity. In terms of structure, the opening ritornellos were expanded, the instrumentation fuller, and the themes more developed. There needed to be a balance between the virtuoso opening movement and the finale, which expanded by using a rondo form. The solo became rather a *primus inter pares* (or first among equals) with the orchestra, meaning that it was up to the soloist to distinguish himself without destroying the balance. Reputations were built on solid technical playing with just just enough flash to demonstrate ability, and sometimes soloists gained their notoriety in another manner. For example, the French Caribbean violinist Joseph Boulogne de Saint Georges was notorious as both a violinist, a composer, and a swordsman, one of a number of performers who achieved a celebrity status for both their music and other things (Figure 4.3; see also Figure 9.4). As the number of possible venues increased, so did the ability of touring virtuosos to travel broadly, thereby enhancing their own reputations. Vocal soloists also began to tour as concertizing artists, as well, about this time. A form of vocal concerto called the concert aria, generally with texts drawn from well-known operas of the period, developed especially for the concert hall. This can be called a **rondò** (distinct from the rondo form), which musicologist Daniel Heartz calls a "fashionable showpiece aria." The structure of this was usually an accompanied recitative, followed by a slow section, and concluding with a section in a faster tempo that is usually in some sort of binary form and sometimes with a gavotte rhythm. Not infrequently, composers would also employ obbligato instruments to accompany the voice. Johann Christian Bach's "Ebben si vada," written for the castrato Giusto Tenducci (known as Senesino) in 1774, uses a solo oboe and keyboard.

78 New Developments, Convergences, and Genres

Figure 4.3 Colored drawing of the Chevalier de Saint-Georges (1785)

By the last two decades of the eighteenth century, the concerto had achieved its maturity. Koch notes that the soloist and orchestra were now juxtaposed with each other in an integrated interaction that mimicked a play:

> In short, the concerto has much similarity with the tragedies of the ancients, where the actor expresses his emotions not to the audience, but rather to the chorus, and this therefore interacts to the greatest extent with the story and at the same time is capable of eliciting the most emotional expression.[7]

The theorist Sulzer states similarly, "The form of a concerto appears to have the intent of giving a talented performer the opportunity to be heard accompanied by many instruments, as if being used to divide the passions."[8] This corresponds to the rise of instruments that can complement the orchestral accompaniment, such as the fortepiano, whose versatility was recognized by both performers and composers alike. A composer such as Mozart could write works that displayed the talents of himself and his students on the fortepiano, expanding the structure of the works to include such features as interpolated and expressive introductions between the opening orchestra ritornello and the second exposition (for example, the D minor concerto, KV 466; see Example 4.2). The violin and violoncello were also favored in the late Classical Period concerto, and solo works for other instruments became fewer and fewer as the concertos for them took on a more pedagogical role. This, in turn, set the stage for the expanded forms of the Romantic Period, as well as the role of the virtuoso, paving the way for the celebrity status embodied by Nicolo Paganini in the early years of the nineteenth century.

Single instrument solos were not the only means of defining the concerto. Larger works, sometimes labeled *concertone*, were developed in Italy about 1750, as was the smaller version, the *concertino*. The

Example 4.2 Wolfgang Amadeus Mozart, Piano Concerto in D minor, KV 466, Movement 1, mm. 77–84

former could employ both soloists and orchestral obbligato performers, while the latter were defined as shorter than a regular concerto, often in only one or two movements. Both rubrics, however, were vague; a "concertone" could also mean a large concert, while there is an overlap between the second in that it also defined the solo group in a concerto grosso. By 1765, there was a distinct need to differentiate concertos for several solo instruments from both solo concertos and the symphony, which had begun to expand in terms of form and structure. The result was the *sinfonia concertante*, which can be defined generally as a symphonic composition in two or more movements that is simultaneously a concerto for two or more instruments. The exact origins of the term are not known, but it rose quickly to prominence as a vehicle both for composers interested in providing contrasts between instruments and for performers in varied groups who sought solo works to perform together. The earliest of these appear in both London and Paris, where in the latter city they became a staple of the public concerts. One composer, Giuseppe Cambini, wrote eighty-five of them for various combinations of solo instruments, many in two movements (leaving out the slow movement). The record for most solo instruments during the Classical Period was probably Carl Ditters von Dittersdorf's "Grosses Konzert" from about 1766, with eleven soloists, though the bulk of the sinfonia concertantes were generally for pairs of strings: two violins, violin and viola, or violin and cello. Major contributors to this genre include Carl Stamitz, J. C. Bach, and Ignaz Pleyel.

The solo concerto was not the only venue for talented performers to demonstrate their skill. Concertante or obbligato parts in symphonies took on the role of the soloist that came directly from the orchestra personnel, those being integrated into the larger generic context of the symphony, which can be considered as *the* major instrumental work of the Classical Period.

The Symphony and Its Offspring

One of, if not *the*, most important and popular genres of the Classical Period was the **symphony**. Although the genre had developed in the middle of the Baroque Period,[9] in 1713, theorist Johann Mattheson acknowledged that it had begun to appear in a variety of venues, ranging from the conventional introductions to operas or other stage works to the church and chamber concerts. Modern opinion seems to show that he may have been talking more about appropriate venues and styles of composition rather than a distinct and emerging genre.[10] By 1739, however, he had solidified his view, implying that this was a new genre that had a particular purpose in the music of the period (Document 2). Theorist Scheibe defined them in his *Critische Musikus*: "Symphonies comprise a threefold genre: they are namely used for church services, for stage and other vocal pieces, and finally and particularly only as instrumental pieces that have no connection to any vocal genres."[11] This was paraphrased and expanded by an anonymously published entry in a multifaceted theoretical work from about forty years later attributed to composer Johann Abraham Peter Schulz, in which the genre and its recent historical development were noted (Document 3). In 1768, Rousseau noted in his *Dictionnaire de Musique* that in France, at least, the term *symphony* was not as clear as perhaps elsewhere, confusing title with texture or instrumentation (Document 4). Koch furnished the final important definition of the symphony in 1802, noting that the symphony had achieved a stature as one of the pillars of the concert hall, an evolution that early lexicographers and theorists had not foreseen (Document 5).

Given this rapid evolutionary development, it is not surprising that the symphony can be considered one of the most popular genres of the Classical Period, with virtually every composer who lived during this time participating in its composition and development. Musicologist Jan LaRue compiled a thematic database of roughly seventeen thousand symphonies written during this period.[12] A number of composers, such as Joseph Haydn, Johann Melchior Molter, Dittersdorf, and Ignaz Holzbauer, wrote more than one hundred symphonies during their careers, and others approached that number.[13] In view of this vast repertory and its importance to the Classical Period, it is worthwhile exploring it from several viewpoints: types and formats, structures, and instrumentation, history, and subgenres.

The Symphony: Social Context

It is difficult to define the symphony's place in the musical life of the period, save to say that it was ubiquitous. There were two main objectives for the composition of symphonies from a social perspective: first, as works for performance, either in public or private, and, second, publication. In the first, performances often occurred in public venues that varied according to location. The bulk of the works were intended to be played at court, where the need for musical entertainment was constant, and the wealth and status were often on display. Not only was the cultural reputation in places like at Mannheim or Esterház built on the strength and proficiency of their ensembles; it was also dependent on the works that were created for them, either operas or symphonies. While not entirely public, the concerts given sometimes on a daily basis were heard by both resident courtiers and the frequent visitors, whose opinions were crucial to the spread of the court's reputation abroad.

A sit-down concert by the ensemble was not always done, but rather, performances were often done within the context of a larger social gathering. In Mannheim, the absolute discipline of the famed orchestra noted by Burney was subject to broader social interaction, as was noted in an anonymous description by a visitor:

> The court was to assemble after six o'clock . . . around and to the right of the windows card tables had been set up and to the left was the space for the orchestra, raised somewhat off the floor and encircled with a railing. After six o'clock the court entered, the Elector and Electress, the dowager Electress of Bavaria, and the ladies-in-waiting and cavaliers. Then the music began, and at the same time, everyone began to play cards. . . . The elector stood up every now and then and went from table to table with a cheerful laugh.[14]

Court instrumental concerts often served as background music, though many of the musically literate noblemen and their families may not have been quite so cavalier about such evening soirées. A number even composed their own symphonies, even though they may not have had their own court in which to perform them.

The more common concerts were those held in public venues. These could be of various types. For example, the quote above labels the gathering an "Academy," a term generally used for impromptu concerts created either as social or musical events and often arranged by composers themselves. Elsewhere, however, public concert series provided venues for the commissioning and performance of symphonies. Most major and a fair number of minor centers maintained public concerts, often managed professionally (though not always profitably). Here, the symphony, which often began and concluded the concert, was a mainstay. In the city of Bath, a fashionable spa in England, composer William Herschel wrote twenty-four symphonies for his series, while in London a series organized by J. C. Bach and Karl Friedrich Abel in 1764 supplemented a long tradition of summer concerts at outdoor venues such as Ranleigh and Vauxhall Gardens. Other organizations, such as the Academy of Ancient Music and Philharmonic Society, active as early as the 1720s in various tavern halls, were supplemented by the completion of the Pantheon in 1772, where public events could be held. Smaller buildings such as the Hanover Square Rooms were home to a series, such as the Professional Concerts of Johann Peter Salomon, for which Joseph Haydn composed his final twelve "London" symphonies. In Paris, the Concerts Spirituels spawned numerous imitations in other European capitals, as well as rivals at home, such as the Loge Olympique or Concerts des Amateurs.

Figure 4.4 Title page of a set of parts of six symphonies by Joseph Schmitt published by Hummel in Berlin and Amsterdam (1766)

Printed editions served this clientele with a stream of symphonies, usually published as sets of parts (Figure 4.4). Given the lack of copyright and publisher oversight, it is not surprising that issues of authenticity arose as both pirated editions and spuriously attributed works were offered for sale. The most notorious city for this was Paris, but many Parisian editions were pirated in London, where a booming market for works existed. The most egregious example is Haydn, whose 108 authentic symphonies were eclipsed by his name being attached to more than 150 works he did not compose. This means that his name and reputation carried considerable weight among the purchasers, and in at least one remarkable instance, Chilean composer José de Campderrós ordered the latest editions of Haydn's Paris symphonies for use in the cathedral in Santiago de Chile in 1794, with them arriving there within a few months of their publication. The social market also included amateur music-making, when families who were musically inclined would play through symphonies for their own enjoyment, even though they did not usually have the necessary forces. These were often manuscript parts or scores produced by copy shops such as Breitkopf in Leipzig and Traeg in Vienna, precisely with both professional and amateur buyers in mind. Since the supply seemed continual, it may be assumed that the symphony served as social cohesion for both types of clientele, even if the original reason for a work's composition was more specific or occasional.

The Symphony: Types and Formats

Most composers were aware of three purposes for the Classical Period symphony: as an introduction to dramatic music (generally opera or oratorio), in church, and for secular occasions such as concerts both public and chamber. The first purpose needs little introduction, since it was identical to the Baroque Period, where it was known in Italy as a *Sinfonia* or in France as an *Ouverture*. Today, these would be called simply *overtures*, and it was not unknown even during the period for composers to label such pieces with a generic title of "Overtura," as Mozart did for the opening to the opera *Don Giovanni*. To this should be added the additional terms *Introduzzione* (Italian) or *Einleitung* (German), both of which translate simply to "introduction." Many were akin to the French Overture, generally a single movement that could be either contrapuntal or an expanded sonata principle but were prefaced by a slow introduction featuring powerful dotted rhythms. As the century wore on, these evolved into generally a single movement that sometimes even contained music from within the opera or oratorio itself. Although overtures were sometimes excerpted as concert pieces from the vocal works to which they were attached, they properly remain theatre pieces and thus are not true symphonies.

The church symphony, the *sinfonia da chiesa*, is a genre that has remained difficult to define despite its being mentioned in contemporary documents. It is clear that eighteenth-century theorists regarded it as a particular genre as early as Mattheson (Document 1). Musicologist Neal Zaslaw noted in 1982 that it reflected a separate genre based on his review of these contemporary sources, though this has been far from accepted as universal.[15] Haydn scholar H. C. Robbins Landon avoided the issue by renaming some early Haydn symphonies that began with a slow movement or used paraphrases of plainchant as "sonata da chiesa" works. Based on the format of the church sonatas of Archangelo Corelli, which reversed the fast–slow order of movements, he described certain symphonies of Haydn as being composed with this use in mind. Here, too, the ambiguity of terminology can be seen, for example, in his Symphony in D Minor, Hob. I:26, where the slow first movement is based on a segment of Gregorian chant, giving rise to its nickname "Lamentation" (Example 4.3).[16]

The term *da chiesa* itself refers to two separate uses; symphonies that were used in churches, particularly in Catholic countries, but which were not composed for that purpose originally, and a single-movement genre, akin to or derived from the Baroque French Overture that was specifically intended as part of the worship service. The purposes were the same; the symphony was intended to bridge the obvious gaps in the worship service. In most churches of the period, Catholic and Protestant, there was a distance between the altar and the pulpit that had to be covered, and there was no traditional liturgical music that covered the time it generally took to move from one place to the next. In addition, there could be periods meant for congregational reflection that also did not have music traditional to the liturgy. In Protestant countries, this was often left up to the organist to improvise, but in Catholic countries, the *sinfonia da chiesa* may have been one way to address this.[17]

Regarding the regular formats of the symphony, the number of movements was quite variable, from two up to ten, reflecting its origins in Baroque genres such as the suite. There were, however, two that predominated: the three-movement form, often called after its Italian operatic predecessor a *Sinfonia*, consisting of an arrangement of a fast–slow–triple-meter dance (generally a minuet), and the four-movement form that adds a fast movement to the end, usually a rondo or sonata principle, in order to create a symmetry to the work. In these compositions, the placement of the minuet and slow movement could be variable. For example, the earliest four-movement symphonies in the modern format from the Mannheim School from

Example 4.3 Joseph Haydn, Symphony in D minor, *Lamentation*, Hob. I:26, Movement 2, mm. 1–13

about 1750 seem to have the minuet as the third movement, indicating that a finale was added on to the end. This is one of the trademarks found in the set *La melodia Germania* by Johann Stamitz, one of the first that includes this arrangement. In Vienna, however, the four-movement format probably came about as the result of removing one of the minuets from the five-movement divertimento. This means that the fast finale was already in place, but the arrangement of the two internal movements was variable as to the placement of the minuet. The Italian three-movement format seems to have been preferred at least up through about 1770 and beyond throughout Europe, but it was soon replaced by the more conventional four-movement model from Mannheim, possibly due to the popularity of Mannheim's *Kapellmeister* Holzbauer, who was employed originally in Vienna and whose works were often performed there.

In the Classical Period one finds works that have specific titles that evoke a certain image or mood. Titling symphonies was a means of advertising a work, but it left much to the imagination of audiences and many of the titles did not originate with the composers themselves. There was, however, a separate subgenre called the *sinfonia characteristica* (in French *charactéristique*) developed around 1750 or possibly shortly before.[18] In the beginning, it was a sort of *musica verità* in which the traditional movements were crafted around a specific theme, often using specialized instruments to set the mood. One of the best examples of this is the Hunting Symphony (*Jagdsinfonie*) in G major by Leopold Mozart. In this three-movement work, one Viennese source requires a shotgun, and the composer himself noted that the four horns should be played "as roughly and loudly as possible," accompanied by huntsmen who cry, "Ho, Ho!" and a few

84 *New Developments, Convergences, and Genres*

Example 4.4 Leopold Mozart, Sinfonia da caccia, Movement 1, mm. 11–15

"hounds" bellowing if in unison (Example 4.4). Other works of his include hurdy-gurdies and alphorns. By the 1770s, this had become more refined, with characteristic symphonies being created surrounding a central theme or subject, with each individual movement subtitled accordingly. One of the best examples of this are the 12 Symphonies on Ovid's *Metamorphosis* composed by Dittersdorf in 1783, of which six survive. Although each has a conventional four-movement format, each of the movements has a programmatic function. For example, in Symphony No. 6 in A Major, the Lycian peasants are turned into frogs, replete with musical croaking in the final movement (Example 4.5).

One composer, Heinrich Justinius Knecht, from the city of Stuttgart, specialized in this subgenre, composing four symphonies, including a "Portrait Musical de la Nature," or Pastoral Symphony, in 1785 consisting of five movements that anticipates Beethoven's Sixth Symphony two decades later.

Finally, composers sometimes attempted to link thematic material throughout a symphony, resulting in what has been termed the *Symphonie périodique* (Periodical Symphony). This appears to have been a

Example 4.5 Carl Ditters von Dittersdorf, Symphony in A major, Movement 4, mm. 214–219

favorite subgenre in Paris, where composers such as François Gossec, composer of forty-eight symphonies, and Pleyel, who wrote more than forty symphonies, were significant contributors. The best-known example, Haydn's Symphony in B Major, Hob. I:46, is not known by that title, but it brings back excerpts from the previous three movements in the finale. Not all symphonies published as *périodique* adhere to this definition, however.

Structures and Instrumentation

The symphony in the Classical Period is difficult to characterize from a structural point of view. The early works have first movements generally in either ritornello or a binary form, often with the main themes or motives sequenced through various key centers. Initially, these were limited to tonic and dominant, with an occasional foray into the relative minor in central portions. Second movements were more lyrical and often either in simple binary or through-composed in a contrasting but related key, such as the parallel minor or subdominant. Final movements could be either a stylized dance or an *Alla breve* fugue. These were generally quite fast, and one can discern the remnants of the gigue that often-concluded Baroque suites or minuets (many in 3/8 time) if no counterpoint was done. By the middle of the century, however, the first movements had begun to expand. These often had contrasting themes in a first section, followed by a brief development in the relative minor and a return of the main themes focused on the tonic key, a rounded binary that developed rapidly into a formal chiasm known today as the sonata principle (formerly, sonata form). Second movements also expanded laterally with internal variation and fluid lyrical lines, while the third movement minuets often became more conventional, with one or two trios contrasting texturally and harmonically with the main section. In four-movement formats, the finale developed variously so that rondos, a chiastic or arch form in which a main theme returns in the tonic key a number of times, a fugue, or other forms of the first movement that acted as a bookend of the symphony all were options. By 1760, brief harmonically diverse slow introductions could be appended to the first movements at the discretion of the composer.

Minor-key symphonies did not automatically signify the drama of the *Sturm und Drang*, particularly since many were written prior to this style emerging. The use of the minor key in Vienna, for instance,

86 *New Developments, Convergences, and Genres*

was extensively explored by musicologist Matthew Riley, who noted that composers such as Vanhal, composer of seventy-six symphonies, Haydn, Florian Gassmann (who wrote forty-eight symphonies), Dittersdorf, and Carl von Ordonez, author of seventy-three symphonies, often used the more variable modulations in minor keys to increase the harmonic language of their works rather than provide dramatic episodes.[19]

As the Classical Period progressed, symphonic movements became longer and more complex by means of internal thematic development (in German *thematische Arbeit*), an addition of a third theme in the closing portions of the exposition, more extensive development that introduced new thematic material, new harmonic centers, as well as more expansive dialogue between the instruments, and extended codas. For second movements, this lengthening was also notable, and the finales were more complex. In the finale of Mozart's C Major Symphony, KV 551, known as the *Jupiter*, he uses as a *stretto* all four of his contrapuntal themes at the same time in a highly original juxtaposition (see Example 11.10). Even the conventional minuet was not immune to such invention. In the Symphony in G Major, Hob. I:47, by Haydn and in Kraus's symphony in the rare key of C-sharp minor (Example 4.6), both composers use a musical palindrome,

Example 4.6 Joseph Martin Kraus, Symphony in C-sharp minor, VB 140, Movement 3, mm. 1–10; to be read backward for the complete minuet

called *al roverso* or *rovescio*, in which the second section of the minuet is the first performed backward. As curious or progressive as this development was, the overall criteria for a successful symphony remained, as was noted in a commentary of 1766 in the *Wiener Diarium*, a composition that had "beauty, order, clarity, [and] a fine and noble expression."[20]

The history of the symphony during the Classical Period as a separate genre was one of both evolution and revolution, with several stages defining its creation.

The Symphony Emerges, 1730–1750

It is not known when the first Classical Period symphony was written. Tradition has it that it evolved about 1720 to 1735 in Italy, where an early group of composers, such as Giovanni Battista Sammartini and Antonio Brioschi from Lombardy, appear to have pioneered the form. The earliest identifiable published set of symphonies was by Andrea Zani, who titled his works from the Op. 2 as *Sinfonie da camera*, or chamber symphonies, an example of the type noted by Mattheson (Document 2). It has been suggested that these were part of an emerging tradition that was drawn from the opera *Sinfonia* as the model. The instrumentation, however, seems closer to the trio sonata, with a pair of violins and continuo (noted as *a 3*) being used. There is no indication whether these were to be performed by single musicians or by a group, and even by 1733 when the four-part string setting began to emerge, the distinction between a minimum of performers and more than one on a part was not clarified (see Chapter 3). Brioschi's symphonies reflect both energy and lightness, as well as expanding the binary form to create musical contrast in the first movements. This new style can be seen in the opening of the Symphony in G major, probably composed about 1735, where the contrasting motives and subsequent contrapuntal consequences demonstrate the newer homophonic style (Example 4.7).

Another antecedent was the Italian Ripieno Concerto, a work that developed as early as 1721 with twelve works published by Pietro Locatelli as his Op. 1. Although these works conform stylistically to the Baroque, their form and structure anticipate the development of the early symphony. Throughout the 1730s this form was cultivated throughout Italy, and music by Neapolitan composers such Francesco Durante reflect its popularity outside of Lombardy. Durante, who composed at least nine of these "concerti a quattro," still adhered to the ritornello form, but the lack of more than brief solo episodes, always for the first violin, shows a structural relationship with the Milanese symphony.

Not surprisingly, Italian composers who took up residence outside of the country or foreigners who visited Italy during the 1730s brought this new genre north. Music patron Pierre de Blancheton obtained a vast collection of early Italian symphonies of both types (now known as the *Fonds Blancheton*), which served to popularize the new genre in France. In 1732 Fortunato Chelleri, *Kapellmeister* to the court of Friedrich I of Hesse-Kassel, who had also become King of Sweden, allowed Chelleri's early symphonies to be circulated to the far north. This, in turn, influenced Johan Helmich Roman to travel south to Italy, and on his return, he began to devote himself to developing the new genre, blending Italian lyricism with northern styles. The result was by 1738 that he had begun a new trend, later further developed by his colleague Johan Agrell, who had become *Kapellmeister* in Nuremberg in 1746 and who probably studied under Chelleri while a musician in Kassel during the 1730s. Other Chelleri students from the north include Arvid Niklas von Höpken, whose early compositions also include stylistically mixed symphonies featuring extensive counterpoint and lyrical style.

In 1738, the genre had come so much to the public's attention outside of Italy that Dutch composer and organist Jan Ulhoorn created a unique concert to celebrate the centennial of the Schouwburg Theatre in Amsterdam, consisting of ten new symphonies representing a compendium of the then-current styles. It was to have been led by Vivaldi, but although he did not appear, he did send a large work that included oboes, horns (performed in Amsterdam by trumpets), timpani, and strings of the ripieno concerto variety. Other composers who were invited to contribute included Bernhard Hupfeld, Agrell, local Dutch composer Willem De Fesch, and a number of Italians including Sammartini and Andrea Temanza. These works are, except for Vivaldi, all for strings alone, but they do demonstrate the full emergence of the string symphony

88 New Developments, Convergences, and Genres

Example 4.7 Antonio Brioschi, Symphony in G major, Movement 1, mm. 1–16

into the public spotlight. Indeed, only a couple of years later, symphonies began to be inserted into the Concerts Spirituels in Paris and Riddarhuskonserter in Stockholm.

By 1745, it became clear that the symphony had emerged a major instrumental genre, with the publication of works, particularly in Amsterdam and Paris, in sets of six or twelve. One of the first of these popular editions was the *Six [sic] Grandes Symphonies* by Richter published in 1744 in Paris consisting of two volumes of a total of twelve works, followed within the next three years by further sets. This first was for strings alone, but Richter soon enlarged this orchestra to include horns and woodwinds. The style was progressive, with strong main themes in contrasting sections linked by an inventive use of the suspension, of which Richter was a master, often repeating primary thematic material in various keys. Indeed, composer John Marsh regarded Richter as the inventor of the modern symphony, though not especially the father of its popularity.[21] His earliest works from this collection, however, gained widespread distribution throughout Europe, and his adaptable music ranged from the dotted rhythms of the French style to smoother and more Italian lyrical themes.

During this decade, the symphony also progressed rapidly in centers such as Mannheim and Vienna, with cross-fertilization for the genre occurring in both places. In 1745 Elector Carl Theodor began to build up what was generally considered to be the finest orchestra in Europe. His concertmaster, Johann Stamitz, composed a series of string symphonies or orchestral trios. These are all in a recognizable binary form, with some thematic development occurring in central sections.

Elsewhere in Germany, the early symphony was developed in the major courts such as Dresden, Darmstadt, Berlin, and other centers. For example, in Darmstadt court of Landgrave Ernst, composers Christoph Graupner and Johann Samuel Endler began to cultivate the genre during the 1730s. Graupner, in particular, was at the forefront of the development of the new genre with 113 works, although he also continued to compose suites in the Baroque manner on through the 1750s. By 1747, he had expanded the symphony in Darmstadt in scope by adding additional instrumentation including horns and trumpets. Endler, who rose to prominence at the Darmstadt court under Ernst Ludwig's successor, Landgrave Ludwig VIII, expanded the texture even further in his twenty-nine works, including some almost impossible parts on high trumpets. In Berlin, the symphony came of age with the reign of Frederick the Great, who as crown prince in 1732 secretly began gathering around himself a group of composers at his court in Rheinsberg; he was himself a composer who wrote his first symphony about 1734. When he ascended the throne in 1740, he was finally able to develop his so-called Berlin School, and the Berlin *Kapelle* was expanded to support both the opera and public concerts under the direction of composer Johann Gottlieb Janitsch. The Berlin School composers were crucial in creating the powerful ostinatos, driving rhythms, and unisons that characterized the style of *Empfindsamkeit* in their works.

The symphony had reached a crucial stage of development by 1750. The Italianate works that began its emergence from its musical forebears—simple, harmonious, and tasteful—were being rapidly replaced by more progressive works. In France and Holland, new markets for printed sets of symphonies were beginning to appear as their appeal became commonplace. Further experimentation in style in Germany and in some of the more isolated regions of Europe, as well as expanded formal structures in Austria and throughout the Holy Roman Empire emphasized thematic contrast and development, and the genre began to become one of the most popular during the next several decades.

The Symphony in Full Bloom, 1750–1780

Around the middle of the eighteenth century, the symphony began to be produced in quantity, and in virtually every court, city, monastery, and church could be found ensembles of greater or lesser numbers of musicians who were called on to perform them in a variety of circumstances. As noted, the more prestigious the ensemble or court, the more prolific the composition of symphonies. By 1755, for example, the Mannheim court of Elector Carl Theodor boasted a highly disciplined orchestra, as noted by Burney as "an army of generals, equally fit to plan a battle as to fight it."[22] Their fame was due principally to the cohesiveness of the ensemble, which, in turn, emphasized a number of orchestral effects, such as the layered crescendo (the so-called Mannheim Steamroller), the driving ostinato (drum bass), the weak-beat appoggiatura (Mannheim sigh), the powerful opening of three chords (Mannheim hammer stroke), and running up the scale or triad (Mannheim rocket). As musicologist Eugene Wolf has pointed out, none of these effects was invented in Mannheim, most having Italian origins, but it was the Mannheim orchestra under Johann Stamitz that made the best use of them. Stamitz enhanced his reputation by a visit to Paris in 1754 at the request of merchant and impresario Alexandre del la Pouplinière, one of the few people in the French capital to maintain his own private orchestra. Stamitz's first symphonies were instant popular successes, thereby securing the reputation of not only the Mannheim orchestra for which they were written but also Stamitz's own, as well as his German colleagues. This set of six symphonies became a best seller and was widely disseminated throughout Europe, becoming in essence models for both his colleagues and others. This, in turn, encouraged Stamitz's colleagues and successors to make their own reputations in Paris, including Anton Fils, who Christian Daniel Schubart called "the greatest composer of symphonies who ever lived,"[23] and Christian Cannabich, whose output may have totaled as many as ninety works. While these works were orchestrationally colorful, pieces such as Fils's Symphony in A major often dispensed with lyricism in favor of the mannerisms, raising the effects into the realm of cliché (Example 4.8).

In 1753 one of the most prolific symphonists of the Classical Period, Holzbauer, arrived in Mannheim, bringing with him a direct connection with the Viennese symphony pioneered by Christoph Wagenseil and Georg Matthias Monn; the former expanded the instrumentation, while the latter developed formal

Example 4.8 Anton Fils, Symphony in A major, Movement 1, mm. 1–14

structures. Holzbauer's contributions included evening out the often-overt clichés through longer lyrical themes and more extensive solo passages for the woodwinds.[24] These sometimes include lengthy fugal finales. Along with Richter, he continued to experiment with both orchestration and formal structures. The second generation of Mannheim composers solidified their symphonic styles. For example, Johann Stamitz's two sons, Carl and Anton, both made Paris their home around 1770, where the former, in particular, became a regular composer for the Concerts Spirituels. His fifty symphonies are noted for their accessible themes, good ensemble, and formal clarity.

By 1770, the symphony had become ubiquitous among the competing court orchestras so that the genre became a point of pride in terms of its innovation and progress. Issues of form and structure had largely been stabilized, instrumentation was generally solidified into pairs of either flutes or oboes and horns along with the strings, although at the larger and better-supported courts such as Esterház and Regensburg had larger ensembles at their disposal. As a result, the symphony flourished.

While virtually all composers during this thirty-year period composed symphonies, a few composers gained wide reputations for the quality of their works. Chief among these was Joseph Haydn, who composed the bulk of his 108 symphonies during this time. The primary reasons for his innovative works were twofold: first, he had at his disposal at the Esterházy court a well-disciplined and cohesive ensemble, and second, he was allowed to experiment by his patron, Prince Nicholas II. As he noted himself,

> [m]y Prince was content with all my works, I received approval, and I could, as head of an orchestra, make experiments, observe what enhanced an effect, and what weakened it, thus improving, addition cutting away, and running risks. I was set apart from the world, there was nobody in my vicinity to confuse and annoy me in my course, and so I had to be original.[25]

This originality manifested itself in the structural and formal developments, and it also gave Haydn's symphonies an international reputation. He employed portions of plainchant, local folk tunes and rhythms, as well as often-brilliant orchestration to enhance his symphonies.

Other examples of the stylistic innovations of the mature symphony of this time can be seen in the Bach brothers, C. P. E., J. C., and Johann Christoph Friedrich. Each approached the genre in an original way, though the music of the last named is difficult to study due to the loss of most of his symphonies from these years. What does remain shows a style that is smooth and polished, with good lyrical themes and development. C. P. E expanded the often-complex harmonic style of his Berlin years once he had moved to Hamburg in 1769, writing a trio of symphonies that link each movement through sudden and unexpected cadences. The orchestration is often brilliant and his penchant for musical surprise appears throughout. For Johann Christian, his set of six symphonies, Op. 6, published in 1769 includes one of the most dramatic works of the period, which has an unusual 12/8 finale that is powerful and emotional, with driving rhythms and spare, effective orchestration, as noted earlier. At the court of Oettingen-Wallerstein Antonio Rosetti used his experience as an instrumentalist to expand the use of solo instruments within his symphonies, often using the thicker string textures of divided violas to provide a darker and richer tone, and his woodwind writing is especially challenging.

Rapid development also made itself felt in court cities. In Salzburg, for instance, Wolfgang Amadeus Mozart embarked on a progressive evolution of a more modern lyrical style that saw him develop as a prolific composer of the genre. The bulk of his symphonies date from this period and include the dramatic G minor symphony, KV 183, as well as the Symphony in A major, KV 201, with its humorous finale. During his visit to Paris in 1778, he was commissioned to compose a work for the Concert Spirituels, which his father cautioned needed to cater to popular tastes. Mozart wrote back that although he included the clichéd *coup d'archet*, a device that often had the strings doing arpeggios or scales in unison, he saw little reason for it: "What a fuss the oxen make of this trick! The Devil take me if I can see any difference: they all begin together, just as they do other places."[26] His colleague Michael Haydn also devoted considerable effort toward the symphony during this period, often incorporating what musicologist Michael Ruhling calls "dramatic variety" by using his instrumentation to create distinctive contrast, as well as longer, more fluid second movements.[27] In Vienna, a major figure was Johann Baptist Vanhal, who devoted many years to developing a style of symphonic composition that featured a progressive internal thematic development in all movements; in the minor-key works, he often changed to the parallel major at the last portion of the finale in order to diffuse any dramatic tension created.

As this thirty-year period drew to a close and the symphony became commonplace, the symphony became more geared toward longer and more expressive works as the international reputations of composers such as Haydn provided directions toward which the symphony should evolve.

The Symphony of the Future, 1780–1800

The final two decades of the eighteenth century (and the first of the nineteenth) saw the symphony expand in size and instrumentation, mirroring the further expansion of the orchestra throughout Europe. The symphony became the centerpiece of most public concerts around the globe as private courts diminished in importance; their musical ensembles no longer had either the personnel or the resources to support a plethora of new works. This left the public concerts as the primary venues for symphonies, and it is telling that the final twelve works by Haydn were commissioned especially for the Salomon concerts in London. Patrons now were more frequently intellectuals and impresarios, rather than the nobility, and in order to appeal to audiences, the size and scope had to be expanded. The trend in the composition of symphonies was toward larger and more self-contained works. These often had extensive, slow introductions and long sonata principle first movements in which three separate themes or more could be found, as well as extensive development sections, and often-substantial codas. The second movements were equally as expansive, often with considerable internal variation, while the minuet and trio third movements became faster and eventually replaced by the scherzo. Finales were the bookends to the work, often likewise in the form of the sonata principle and likewise of substantial length. The instrumentation also expanded as the size of the orchestra increased. Finally, with the dissolution of many of the courts during the Napoleonic wars, the main performance venue was transferred entirely to the public concert hall, which meant a changeover from patronage to public support, which meant that financial and critical considerations became fundamental to music's success. With such a trajectory, it was not unusual that during the waning years of the Classical Period, 1800 to 1815, composers were loath to expend too much time composing a raft of symphonies. What is more, those that were written cost them a great deal of effort. Finally, critics in journals such as the *Allgemeine musikalische Zeitung* expected each new work to be original and innovative, moving music into the future.

The main composer who was most important for later generations in its development was Ludwig van Beethoven, whose nine symphonies were considered the epitome of the genre. He and his contemporaries were even more progressive in their evolution of the genre, building on Classical forms and structure, altering them as new styles and trends appeared.

Although the dominant orchestral genre of the Classical Period, the symphony was not the only one to exist. Other related genres provided contrast and filled in the gaps for which the symphony was not suited. These relatives were also conspicuous through their unusual forms and structures, as well as their use in everyday concert life.

The Symphony's Relatives

Since the main purpose of the symphony was for entertainment, it is not surprising that different related genres evolved over time. They went under a variety of names, though generic identification had considerable crossover. These include serenade, divertimento, cassation, parthie (in Document 3 regarded as an alternate name for the symphony as a whole), orchestral quartet/trio, quodlibet or medley, versos, and various independent nongeneric pieces such as series of dances or entr'actes to spoken plays. There even specialized works, such as *Servizio di Tavola* (literally "dinner music") from Imperial Vienna or "*Divertissement*," a French term for a series of instrumental movements, mainly dances, were performed at the conclusion of large operas but that also were suitable for the concert hall. Instrumentation was variable, ranging from the common four-part string ensemble to a full orchestra to a wind band, the *Harmonie*, popularized by military bands.

The largest of these related genres was the **serenade**, a multimovement work intended solely for entertainment. Though serenades can be found throughout Europe, they appear to have been concentrated in the Holy Roman Empire, where they were particularly popular. The format was not entirely consistent, but many conform to a certain pattern. This begins with a fast sonata principle Allegro (often with an Adagio introduction), followed by a minuet, a slow movement, a second minuet, and a fast-paced finale in either sonata or rondo form. To this could be added one or more additional minuets, an introductory march, and a concerto-like section (*concertante*) consisting of a slow movement followed by an Allegro with one or more solo instruments. Thus, the usual five-movement pattern could be stretched out to as many as a dozen with additions. In terms of orchestration, apart from the usual there could be added some specialized instrument

Example 4.9 Wolfgang Amadeus Mozart, Serenade in D major, KV 320, "Posthorn," Movement 6, mm. 24–32

to provide an exotic color. For example, Wolfgang Amadeus Mozart, who composed seven serenades of this larger sort, added a post horn, a small instrument used to announce the arrival of the mail in central Europe, as a soloist in the trio of the second minuet of his Serenade in D major, KV 320 (Example 4.9).

The concertante movements were often extracted from the serenades as independent concertos and could be of extreme difficulty. For example, Michael Haydn, who composed 21 serenades of substantial length, inserted a trumpet concerto into his Serenade in D major, in which the soloist is required to ascent to the very top of his register (g''').

The smaller version of the serenade was known as the **divertimento** or **cassation**, an Austrian term that apparently derives from the word for street (*gasse*). If the instrumentation was for a small ensemble of wind instruments, it was generally called a *parthie* (also known as *partita*). It was arranged like the serenade into five movements, including two minuets. The movements are a sonata principle Allegro, a binary form Andante or Adagio, and a final rondo or sonata principle movement as a finale, in addition to the minuets. The difference is that the music is often shorter and less complex than the serenade, and there are usually no additional added movements. The earliest divertimentos date from the Baroque, but they seem to have been increasingly popular as occasional pieces during the Classical, enough so that at least one has achieved a sort of iconic character. This is Wolfgang Mozart's *Eine kleine Nachtmusik*, KV 525, which has served as "Classical" music for countless motion picture soundtracks. The work, one of about twenty-five that the composer wrote, represents a purity in form in each of the four movements (one of the original minuets has been lost).

The distinction between the cassation and either serenade or divertimento is vague, given that these works often had the same number of movements. The same can be said for the **parthie**, which generally is meant for the *Harmonie*, a group consisting, at minimum, of pairs of oboes, clarinets, bassoons, and horns. Both these relatives of the symphony were intended to be performed out of doors, thus the titles (the parthie was often labeled a *Feldparthie* or Outdoors Divertimento). This genre was particularly favored in central Europe, especially Vienna, which had a tradition of roving street musicians (*Gassenmusikanten*), as noted by Burney. The *Harmonie*, however, developed mainly in courtly military circles, where the performers were soldiers. They were available for various ceremonial marches and displays, and during the latter half of the period many noblemen maintained exclusive groups for their entertainment outside the barracks. Indeed, it became more of a civil chamber ensemble (Figure 4.5), while larger bands were created for traditional functions. Examples of the music of these equal genres abound, with works composed by most central European composers, including Mozart, the two Haydns, Rosetti, Joseph Fiala, and Druschetzky, who composed more than 150 parthies and wind serenades. As one might expect, given the technical limitations of the performers and instruments, particularly the winds, the musical substance tends toward the triadic, homophonic, and simple.

The orchestral trio (for three string instruments, generally two violins and bass) and quartet (adding a viola) appear to have been created as offshoots of the early symphony in Mannheim, probably beginning about 1740. These works were chamber symphonies, usually in three or four movements, following the usual symphonic structure of the time, but less expansive, often with simple themes and a rounded binary format in the faster movements. The differences with the symphony were that the orchestral trio/quartet was meant to be performed by a smaller group of instrumentalists, more than a single one on a part but less than an entire ensemble. The best examples are the ten orchestral trios composed by Johann Stamitz (Op. 1), which demonstrate solid form, often an ostinato drum bass accompaniment, and good thematic contrast.

One of the more interesting relatives of the symphony was the **Quodlibet** or **Medley** (sometimes also called a potpourri), where a series of well-known tunes are strung together and orchestrated by a composer, whose own creative role was mostly limited to transitional portions between the tunes. Since these were often derived from popular songs, the harmonic motion tends to be static, with little modulation or counterpoint. It thus relies on the main themes to convey the musical character of the work. This form of symphonic music was mostly in a single through-composed movement, called a Medley Overture, and was extremely popular beginning about 1765 in Great Britain, but also in France, where they were known as *Recueils*. These works were also published in chamber transcriptions, mainly for keyboard, often with another accompanying instrument. With little alterations being done to the original tunes, this genre contained a purer rendition of folk melodies and dances than would ordinarily be found in conventional symphonies. Composers in English colonies also made use of this genre, such as Alexander Reinagle, whose *Medley Overture* from around 1798 opens with a section of the Overture from the opera *Le Deserteur* by Pierre-Alexandre Monsigny and concludes with an orchestrated version of the popular song *Yankee Doodle*. Another example is the young Wolfgang Mozart's *Galimathias musicumi*, KV 32, containing a quodlibet of Dutch tunes.

What began as two short five-bar transitions between choral Psalms in Hispanic realms grew by the middle of the Classical Period into sometimes lengthy and independent orchestral movements known as ***versos***. Originally written as simple organ interludes, cathedrals in Iberia and New Spain soon began to require substantial works that allowed for contemplative thought during Matins or Vespers of Holy Week and other feast days. Examples of this particular genre can be found in Mexico in the music of José Aldana and other colonial composers, but perhaps the most famous of these is Haydn's *The Seven Last Words*, Hob. XX:1, commissioned by the bishop of Cádiz in 1786. Performed on Good Friday, it consisted of seven Adagios, followed by a musical rendition of an earthquake. For Haydn, who had no knowledge of the *verso* tradition, this was an undertaking that was particularly difficult, but it was published and widely disseminated; meanwhile, Haydn also adapted versions with chorus, for string quartet, and in keyboard arrangement. Each sonata was carefully conceived on broad formal planes, with a sort of internal variation based upon a monothematic structure.

Incidental music for plays usually consisted of a series of movements that were placed between the acts of spoken plays, and sometimes prefaced by an overture. The instrumental portions could be extracted and performed as orchestral music outside of the play to which it belonged. For example, Haydn's Symphony No. 60 in C major, Hob. I:60 was created as entr'actes for the comedy *Le Distrait* (*The Absent-minded One*) by Jean François Regnard, but later the six movements were performed as a symphony apart from the play. Like the *verso*, these various movements often had a direct musical allusion to the action of the drama, although when performed alone, it was not necessary to know the play to appreciate the powerful or comic content.

There are other genres related to the symphony during this time and most derive from occasional use. For example, the Redoubtensaal in Vienna was home to public access dances and balls, for which resident composers wrote chains of various dances, mainly contredances or minuets. These were written in groups of as many as a dozen by the composers resident in the city, including Haydn, Mozart, and many others. While musically superficial, they did serve as important entertainment, and many had some colorful orchestration.

As this trend developed, composers either focused on the progressive development of the symphony or, more or less, avoided it. Other genres, such as the divertimento and serenade, became moribund, and few works were written after the close of the eighteenth century. In Italy, a few church symphonies continued to be written by people such as Niccolò Zingarelli, but these had only limited circulation, and the medley was subsumed into the so-called battle symphony, losing much of its folk origins in the process in favor of musico-pictorial imagery and political overtones (see Chapter 12). This, in turn, began to develop into the program symphony and tone poems of the Romantic Period.

Documents

Document 1. From Heinrich Koch, *Musikalisches Lexikon* (Frankfurt am Main, 1802). Translated by the author.

The form of this composition [the concerto] consists in brief of the following; that the execution of the solo part is preceded by a ritornello as an introduction, in which the audience is made aware of the content of the solo, and within which the main parts of the melody of the entire movement are presented altogether in a sequential or closely related connection to each other that is to be done when the solo voice enters thereafter. . . . The concert performer who has placed mechanical ability as the sole and highest goal of his career is not content with the difficulties that are inherent in the accessible concertos for his instrument, but rather one proceeds one step further to complete the denigration of his art. Each one portrays in his organization an especially suitable hocus-pocus and attempts to absorb it without the necessary melodic and harmonic knowledge, to publish it. . . . Now entire pages filled with passages hunt each other, each more neck-breaking than the next.

Document 2. From Johann Mattheson, *Der vollkommene Capellmeister* (Hamburg, 1739). Translated by the author.

The *Sinfonia* (Symphony); *da Chiesa* (in church), *da Camera* (in the chamber), *del Drama* (in opera), which, although they require a rather substantial complement of string and wind instruments all at the same time, ought not to be therefore so fancy and extravagant as the grand concerto. For, with the exception of the symphonies that serve to opening of the most fashionable *Singspiele* [operas], as well as the introductions of those more unimportant, they nonetheless contain nothing quite as full-bodied in their content. In churches, they must become even more modestly conceived than in theatres and in the chamber. Their main purpose consists in giving a short idea and, in introductions, a brief impression of what is to come. One can therefore easily conclude that the expression of the *Affects* in such a symphony must be directed towards those passions that must emerge from the work itself.

Document 3. From "Symphonie," in Johann Georg Sulzer, *Allgemeine Theorie der schönen Künste* (Leipzig, 1771–1774), II:1121–1122. Published anonymously but attributed to Johann Abraham Peter Schulz (1747–1800).

Symphony. A multi-part instrumental piece that has been used instead of the obsolete overtures [e.g. suites]. The difficulty executing an overture well and the even greater difficulty of creating a good overture has led to the simpler form of the symphony, which in the beginning was made up of one or several contrapuntal movements, alternating with dance movements of various types, and was thus called generally a *Parthie*. The overture nonetheless remains prior to great church works and operas, and one uses the *Parthies* only in chamber music; one soon tired of these independent dance movements that were without dancing, and finally replaced them with one or two contrapuntal or non-contrapuntal Allegros, alternating with a slower Andante or Largo. These genres were called symphonies, and were introduced in chamber music, as well as prior to operas and church music, as is now the custom. The instruments used for the symphonies are violins, violas, and bass instruments; each part to be strongly reinforced. To complement or to strengthen these can be added horns, oboes, and flutes. The symphony is particularly apt for the expression of the great, the solemn, and the noble. Its ultimate goal is to prepare the listener for an important music, or in a chamber concert to summon all of the brilliance of instrumental music. If this ultimate goal is to achieve a perfect pleasure, and if one is to become an integral part of the opera or church music that it precedes, then it yet must have apart from the expression of the mighty and solemn a character that places the listener in the frame of mind that is required by the succeeding piece as a whole, and thus through the manner of style differentiates itself as for the church or the stage.

Document 4. From Jean-Jacques Rousseau, *Dictionnaire de Musique* (Paris, 1768).

At present, the word *symphony* is applied to all instrumental music, as well as for pieces which are destined only for instruments, such as sonatas and concertos, as well as for those where the instruments are found blended with the voice, as in our operas and in several [other] sorts of music. We distinguish vocal music as music without symphony (when it has no other accompaniment than the basso continuo), and music with symphony, which has at least a treble of instruments: violins, flutes, or oboes. We say of a piece that it is in *grand symphony* when, besides the bass and treble, it also has two other instrumental parts, i.e. a tenor and a fifth of the violin [i.e. viola and second violin].

Document 5. From Heinrich Christoph Koch, *Musikalisches Lexikon* (Leipzig, 1802), col. 1385–1386. Translation by the present author.

Sinfonie or *Symphonie*. A full-bodied and expansive instrumental piece for an entire orchestra, which was originally intended to serve as the introduction to a large vocal work, or a chamber [work], or concert music, but at the present time is used on other occasions, for example, at the conclusion of a concert or between the acts of a comedy, etc. Because instrumental music is nothing less than the imitation of singing, the symphony substitutes especially for the chorus and thus, just like the choir, has the expression of emotion in all its variety as its purpose; thus through the performance of it one is accustomed to absorbing each of the four main voices, namely the first and second violins, the viola, and the bass. Older symphonies were either performed simply with these four main parts, or one made use of only a few wind instruments: now, however, one is used to set this genre of composition with all of the wind instruments belonging to a complete orchestra in a full-voice form, and therewith to make the entirety all the more powerful and full-bodied. One differentiates the symphony according to the special type of music that it serves to introduce; the opera, church, and chamber symphony.

Notes

1. Jean-Jacques Rousseau, *Dictionnaire de Musique*, I: 178.
2. Heinrich Christoph Koch, *Musikalisches Lexikon* (Frankfurt am Main, 1802), 351–352.
3. Koch, *Musikalisches Lexikon*, 352.
4. Koch, *Musikalisches Lexikon*, 351.
5. Quantz, *On playing the Flute*, 211. He also cautions against allowing performers too much leeway, for doing such will lead to "false conceit," bringing things in line with Koch's admonitions.
6. Haydn, realizing that this would have limited appeal in the music of 1788, rearranged the solo parts for flute and oboe (Hob. VIIh: 1–6). Five of the six concertos have survived, as have eight of nine notturnos for the instrument.
7. Koch, *Musikalisches Lexikon*, 354.
8. Johann Georg Sulzer, *Allgemeine Theorie der schönen Künste* (Leipzig, 1771–1774), s.v. "Concert."
9. His father, Giovanni Maria Bononcini, may have been the first actually to apply the term to an independent instrumental genre. In 1671 he published in Bologna a set of works titled *Sinfonia, allemande, correnti, e Sarabande aggiunta d'una sinfonia a quattro, che si può suonare ancora al contrario*, which was, like earlier Italian instrumental works, more or less an early form of the Baroque suite, though compiled under a single rubric that absorbed the earlier designation of *sinfonia* to mean merely a brief instrumental interlude, often of only a few bars, within an opera.
10. See Johann Mattheson, *Das neu-eröffnete Orchestre* (Hamburg, 1713), 171–172. For example, musicologist Stefan Kunze notes that at this stage Mattheson was more intent on a systematic categorization of styles and venues than actual genres. See Stefan Kunze, *Die Sinfonie im 18. Jahrhundert: Von der Opernsinfonie zur Konzertsinfonie* (Laaber: Laaber Verlag, 1993), 144. In 1706, however, Friedrich Erhardt Niedt noted in his *Musicalische Handleitung*

98 *New Developments, Convergences, and Genres*

that "a symphony is used instead of a sonata and written only for instruments," implying a larger ensemble genre, though his subsequent explanation in 1721 links it to the Baroque suite.
11 See Scheibe, *Critische Musikus*, 304. Translation by the present author.
12 Jan LaRue, *A Catalogue of Eighteenth Century Symphonies: Volume I Thematic Identifier* (Bloomington, IN: Indiana University Press, 1988). There are actually about twelve thousand works in this volume, but others were added by LaRue as more sources became available, such as *RISM*. Unfortunately, this was the first in a three-volume set, the second and third volumes of which were never published. Since LaRue's death, further expansion of the number of symphonies written has occurred, and the number may eventually reach in the neighborhood of twenty-two thousand.
13 Mary Sue Morrow and Bathia Churgin, *The Symphonic Repertoire: Volume 1 The Eighteenth Century* (Bloomington, IN: Indiana University Press, 2012). This work includes generally essays, overviews arranged geographically, and specific analyses of the works of individual composers by twenty-two scholars.
14 Quoted in Eugene Wolf, "The Mannheim Court," in *The Classical Era: From the 1740s to the End of the 18th Century* (Englewood Cliffs, NJ: Prentice Hall, 1989), 226–227. The identity of the visitor is not known, but he published his views in a collection titled *Lustreise in die Rheingegenden* in 1791.
15 Otto Biba, for example, dismisses the notion that it is a separate genre altogether but, rather, notes that these theorists are merely speaking about usage. See Kunze, *Die Sinfonie*, 144.
16 See H. C. Robbins Landon, *Haydn Chronicle and Works, Volume I: The Early Years* (Bloomington, IN: Indiana University Press, 1980), 105. He says specifically, "The church tradition also included the old *sonata da chiesa* of Corellian fame, which began with a whole slow movement and continued with a fugal allegro, the whole then being repeated . . . to make the customary slow-fast-slow-fast pattern."
17 Mozart and other composers such as his Salzburg colleagues Michael Haydn and Anton Cajetan Adlgasser wrote single-movement sonatas for organ with orchestral accompaniment called Epistle sonatas to cover this gap. This specialized genre was also popular in the various Benedictine monasteries throughout the central European region; for example, Einsiedeln composer Pater Marianus Müller composed for as many as four organs all at once; only six works of his have survived.
18 For further information, see Richard Will, *The Characteristic Symphony in the Age of Haydn and Beethoven* (Cambridge: Cambridge University Press, 2002), which lists more than 225 of these works from the Classical Period up through Beethoven's Sixth Symphony.
19 See Matthew Riley, *The Viennese Minor-Key Symphony in the Age of Haydn and Mozart* (New York: Oxford University Press, 2014).
20 See H. C. Robbins Landon, *Haydn Chronicle and Works* (Bloomington, IN: Indiana University Press, 1978), II: 130. The reference is particularly to the music of Haydn.
21 See Charles Cuthworth, "An Essay by John Marsh," *Music and Letters* 36 (1955), 161. Marsh states: "The first inventor of the style of the modern symphony is said to be Richter, whose compositions being more scientific than those of the generality of his immediate successors, (the last strains of many of them being short fugues) are therefore more pleasing to connoisseurs. Music, however, is capable of being so constructed, as to give pleasure to people in general. Perhaps the proper test of excellence in this art should not be that it affords pleasure to professors and connoisseurs only, but to the greatest number of amateurs indiscriminately taken. As we are therefore obliged to Richter for the invention of this style, so we are, perhaps, much obliged to others for the improvement of it."
22 Charles Burney, *Dr. Burney's Musical Tours*, ed. Percy Scholes (London: Oxford University Press, 1959), II: 35. Christian Daniel Schubart, who wrote in his 1784 work *Ideen zu einer Ästhetik der Tonkunst* (Vienna, 1806) that "no orchestra in the world has ever surpassed that of Mannheim in performance," mirrored this.
23 Schubart, *Ideen zu einer Ästhetik*, 141.
24 In 1782, Holzbauer noted that he had written 205 symphonies during his career, though only about 60 have actually come to light. See Sterling Murray, "The Symphony in South Germany," in *The Symphonic Repertoire*, I: 304.
25 As quoted by his biographer Georg August Griesinger in Vernon Gotwals, *Haydn: Two Contemporary Portraits* (Madison, WI: University of Wisconsin Press, 1968), 17. The translation is by Vernon Gotwals.
26 Letter to his father dated June 12, 1778, quoted in Alfred Einstein, *Mozart, His Character, His Work* (New York: Oxford University Press, 1945), 227.
27 Michael Ruhling, "Johann Michael Haydn," in *The Symphonic Repertoire*, I: 502–503.

5 Genre as the Core of Musical Development
Chamber Music

Chamber music played an increasingly important role during the Classical Period as music-making was viewed as an important part of entertainment. Given that a large portion of the population was musically literate—that is, they not only were knowledgeable about the art but also practiced it in some form or another—it is not surprising that it developed rapidly throughout the eighteenth century. This, in turn, led to the creation of genres that were suitable for performance in both more intimate settings, such as in a salon, at home, or at court, and public venues, where the smaller groups were often used to offset larger orchestral and vocal works. Here, the division between the professional and amateur, between those knowledgeable about music and those who merely dabbled in it, was manifest, for chamber music was an integral part of polite society, and the performance of the chamber genres was frequent both by members of the court musical ensembles and their employers. Moreover, these were the most liable to be published, as there was a flourishing market for all manner of works. As Chapter 12 shows, some of the publications were done as collections or compendiums, but in many cases individual genres, sometimes printed in sets of four, six, or eight works, were meant to appeal to (and be purchased by) both amateurs and professionals alike, with varying degrees of difficulty. For publishers, this meant that works could be produced for a variety of musicians and audiences for their own enjoyment, as well as being at times demonstrations of both compositional and practical skill. As orchestras and soloists attained reputations in public for their skill and ability, so, too, did smaller groups of musicians require pieces that reflected both the needs of a knowledgeable (and sometimes critical) society and a means of demonstrating their cultural status. Chamber music fulfilled this niche.

Music for Professionals and Amateurs: The Rise of Chamber Genres

During the Baroque Period, chamber music or *musica da camera* was common, with sets of works being published as practical pieces suitable for use in virtually any court or household. Musicality was commonplace throughout Europe, and chamber genres fulfilled a need at the most fundamental level of entertainment for most of the nobility and middle classes. Levels of difficulty were variable, and little if any of these smaller works were intended as concert pieces in the modern sense. Rather, they were occasional, meant to be performed in private or smaller venues for intimate audiences. In 1746 Pater Meinrad Spieß noted that it "takes its name from the rooms and salons of the nobility, where it is usually performed."[1] This implies that it could also be used as a sort of background music. This mirrors the description by theorist Heinrich Koch in 1802, who noted,

> Chamber music, in the actual sense of the word, is music that is normally used at court, and, because it is merely organized for the private entertainment of the rulers, no one is allowed entrance as an audience member without special permission. But in the various courts this is designated through the expression of so-called Court Concerts, which includes more or less only the court and those attached to it, but in which other persons are able to participate as listeners, though isolated from the court in another room.[2]

100 *New Developments, Convergences, and Genres*

In 1744, author Johann Heinrich Zedler defined the general use of one variety, table music (in German, *Taffelmusik*), that also seems to define chamber music as solely for entertainment:

> Table Music: This is heard daily at the noble courts, as long as no major mourning occurs, when the court and chamber musicians at noon and in the evening await in a neighboring room to the dining room to play the most pleasant symphonies and concertos for the enjoyment of the nobly born on all sorts of instruments. The same table music can also be heard at public weddings, baptisms of children, and other celebrations that are held by well-to-do citizens.[3]

Here, the social purpose of music, in this case, meant specifically for a chamber, is to provide an accompaniment for mealtimes of the higher classes, but it also seems to have had importance for regular citizens who require music for special circumstances. The genres mentioned (symphony, concerto) seem to imply a larger ensemble, yet the implication is that the performance practice was for something more limited, probably only a few musicians. Quantz reinforces this with a brief description of what he calls "chamber concertos," depicting it as a class where the soloist is accompanied by a smaller group: "Anyone who knows how to write a concerto of this kind [larger works with orchestra] will find it simple to compose a jocular and playful *little chamber concerto*."[4] While he is dismissive of the smaller group, his statement implies that such exist. Finally, chamber symphonies are mentioned by early theorists Mattheson (1739), Scheibe (1745), and Schulz (1774), all of whom describe it as a third type of work meant to be performed in smaller settings with smaller groups.[5]

This blurs the definition of chamber genres for instruments by making them accessible to a variety of groups, and the theorists concentrate on how they are formulated, not their components or functions. For example, any symphony and some concertos can be considered a "chamber" genre if performed by smaller ensembles, and conversely, genres such as the orchestral quartet or trio can also be performed by either large or small groups, with the titles indicating only the number of parts, not the number of musicians required. Specific chamber genres, however, were recognized as continuations from the Baroque Period. First and foremost among these was the trio sonata, a genre consisting of two melody instruments (generally a pair of violins) and continuo that were classified into two types (see Figure 5.1): *da camera*

Figure 5.1 Silhouette of an early Classical Period trio sonata showing two violins and a continuo group

(or for the chamber) and *da chiesa* (for the church). The most famous sets of these were the Op. 1 through 4 by Archangelo Corelli, published between 1681 and 1694. All were in a four-movement format, with the chamber works consisting of stylized dances and the church works of contrapuntal movements. These works were used as models, especially in Italy up through the 1730s, spawning numerous imitations throughout Europe. The second-most common type was the duo sonata, consisting of a single melody instrument accompanied by the continuo. These were likewise commonplace throughout the Baroque Period. Quantz is quite dismissive about the large number of works composed and published:

> Writing a solo today is no longer considered an art. Nearly every instrumentalist tries his hand at it. If he has no inventiveness of his own, he helps himself to borrowed ideas. If he lacks knowledge of the rules of composition, he has someone else write the thorough bass. As a result, instead of good models, a considerable number of monstrosities appear.[6]

Here, too, one can find a Corellian model in his violin sonatas Op. 5. To this can be added solo sonatas for a single instrument (violin being the most favored, as well as the keyboard and transverse flute), as well as the occasional quartet, defined during the Baroque as three instruments and continuo. In all these cases, the structure follows the suite, with a succession of stylized dances alternating fast and slow.

The market for chamber music was enormous during the eighteenth century, given that virtually any household or court had a need for pieces that could be played regularly and by whatever instruments were available. For example, English publisher John Walsh offered an edition of "solos" or duo sonatas by George Frederick Handel around 1742, which the title page makes clear could be performed by either an oboe, flute, or violin as the melody instrument (Figure 5.2). This conforms to stereotyped Baroque models requiring continuo and generic melody instrumentation. These publications were common and meant good profits for the publishers of the time.

By about 1730, however, a newer sort of chamber music based upon the Baroque models began to appear, coinciding with the latest formal structures found in the Italian sinfonia. Instead of four dance-derived movements, these reduced the number to three: an Allegro first movement with contrasting themes and longer melodic phrases, a contrasting slow movement, and a triple meter finale, often a stylized minuet. Harmonies were expanded and the use of counterpoint limited. One of the main contributors to this change was Georg Philipp Telemann, whose prolific output made him one of the most important German composers of the Baroque Period. As he began to alter his style toward the *galant*, he experimented with introducing a new chamber form in Paris during his visit in 1737, the quartet. Although he had composed part of his set of "Parisian" quartets as early as 1730, these works created a sensation when published. The composer himself noted in his autobiography that these works, created for four solo instruments without continuo, were highly regarded (see Document 1). These quartets remained in the Parisian repertory for over a decade, and they were purchased by courts throughout Europe.

The term *sonata* itself had, by the beginning of the Classical Period, become relatively well-defined, even though it could be used both specifically and generically. The most common solo sonatas were for keyboard alone, while the duo sonata came to be considered the means of highlighting individual instruments against an accompaniment of a continuo, often figured but perhaps only meant for the keyboard instead of a full continuo group. There were other terms, as well, as William Newman points out in his monumental study *The Sonata in the Classical Era*. For instance, "lessons" were published in England, though these were identical to what we would term as a sonata. *Solo* did not necessarily mean only one instrument but, rather, could be used to designate a duo sonata, with the keyboard accompaniment implied. *Pièces* could substitute for the title in France, while in central Germany "divertimento" was also a known rubric. Finally, terms such as *overture* or *partita* could be used, even if only for the keyboard. When it came to content, often composers and publishers (more the latter) would designate the level of difficulty, such as easy or short (employing further other labels such as "sonatina"). Despite this

102 *New Developments, Convergences, and Genres*

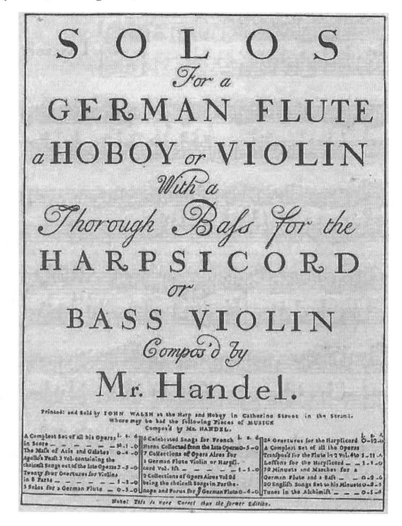

Figure 5.2 Title page of the Walsh Edition of George Frédéric Handel's Sonatas, Op. 1 (1742)

insecurity in the name, most eighteenth-century musicians and audiences knew precisely what a sonata was and how it was to be both performed and heard. As the early period progressed, the subject of novelty and style were more important than the title.

As Charles Burney noted when discussing the sonatas published as works of Pergolesi many years later, "[t]hey are composed in a style that was worn out when Pergolesi began to write; at which time another was forming . . . which has been since polished, refined, and enriched with new melodies, harmonies, modulation, and effects."[7] To this, one may add that chamber music in the Classical Period now evolved into a number of distinctive genres based upon the numbers of individual performers that could serve the markets of both professional musicians and amateurs for a variety of purposes. While the common duo sonata was not displaced by the development of the other chamber genres, it found itself in need of evolution as the variety of combinations of instruments and types emerged. The definition of the sonata, therefore, became more restrictive as the eighteenth century progressed and the social venues for which it was created expanded to include all levels of society.

"Sonata, What Do You Want from Me?"

The Classical Period duo sonata can be defined as one, if not the most important instrumental chamber work that evolved from the Baroque Period. In smaller salons, it was ideal given that it required only a minimal amount of room, and it could function as an easy means of entertainment that demonstrated the performer's skill, along with that of the keyboard accompanist, but also allowed for the latest works to be heard. While many of the theorists of the Classical Period were not entirely unified in what constituted a "sonata" on the whole, it being used as a generic title for various numbers of instruments in a chamber work—*à solo, à due, à tre, à quatre*, as at least one defined it in general terms (see Document 3)—the duo sonata (in German, *Doppelsonate*) was certainly considered the most common. The exception was that intended for a solo keyboard. Türk notes in his *Klavierschule* that "the sonata belongs in the first position—and rightly so—among the compositions designed for the keyboard."[8] The duo sonata, on the other hand, was more adept at a dual function, the display of the performer demonstrating virtuosity and the transmitting of musical emotion to the listeners, many of whom were knowledgeable about both technique and aesthetics.

While the Classical sonata was considered as the ideal means of musical expressivity, its beginnings in the middle of the century were hardly auspicious, as the Baroque sonata had evolved into the sort of mechanical display deplored by Quantz. Rousseau also commented on it in his musical dictionary, noting that it was largely a virtuoso work meant to integrate both music and performer. He states: "One seizes upon whatever is the most favorable for showing off the chosen instrument, whether the contour of the lines, the selections of the tones that best suit this sort of instrument, or the boldness of the execution."[9] The moribund state of the sonata during this portion of the eighteenth century can be summarized in a well-known statement attributed to French philosopher Bernard le Bovier de Fontenelle: "Sonata, what do you want from me?"[10] As Document 2 shows, this exasperated remark shows that there was a concern over the lack of expression in instrumental music and that these works proliferated as a sort of meaningless exercise.

It is clear that a change needed to occur, and the first change was the function and purpose of the sonata from being solely a means of instrumental display to conveying a variety of emotions; in other words, becoming more *empfindsam*. Rather than simply being an "exercise," as many early theorists viewed it, the sonata became a vehicle for intimate inclusion of both performer and audience into the music. In 1775, Schulz noted,

> Clearly, in no form of instrumental music is there a better opportunity than in the sonata to depict feelings without words . . . there remains only the form of the sonata, which assumes all characters and every expression. Through the sonata, the composer can hope to produce a monologue by way of notes of melancholy, grief, sorrow, tenderness, or delight and joy: or sustain a sensitive dialogue solely through passionate tones or similar or various qualities; or simply depict violent, impetuous, and contrasted, or light, gentle, fluid, and pleasing emotions.[11]

This required both the composer and performer to imbue their work with emotional intensity, to work in tandem to absorb the audience. C. P. E. Bach states simply, "Play from the soul, not like a trained bird!" Additionally, he noted, "A musician cannot move others unless he himself is moved."[12] A famous print of opera composer Christoph Willibald von Gluck shows the sort of emotional performance at the keyboard implied in the performance practices of the sonata (Figure 5.3). Charles Burney gave a description of C. P. E. Bach performing on his clavichord, one of the three keyboard instruments he preferred for chamber concerts: "He grew so animated and possessed, that he not only played, but looked like one inspired; his eyes were fixed, his under lip fell, and drops of effervescence distilled from his countenance."[13] Performers of sonatas were expected to communicate explicitly between composer and audiences, thus providing an integrated experience. As Schulz noted, "[a]fter vocal pieces they hold first place in chamber music, and, since they require only one player to a part, they can be performed in the smallest music society without much ceremony."[14]

Figure 5.3 Joseph Duplessis, Christoph Willibald von Gluck at the Spinet (1775)
Source: Used with permission from the Kunsthistorisches Museum, Vienna.

The sonata itself had to be reformulated to accommodate this purpose. By 1760, it had settled into a three-movement format that was seen as a standard. The opening movement was intended as a faster display piece that showed off various contrasting themes, while the second was more lyrical and even passionate. The third concluded with a Presto or Allegro, a sort of bookend to the first. In 1785, the French savant Lacépède noted,

> Its works are similar in substance to those airs destined for the voice, or, rather, symphony, about which we have just spoken; these are evenly divided into three movements of different characters. It is presented in as dramatic a manner possible, with all of its charms. We recognize within the progression of the passions, and through an interesting action we note a beginning, center, and end, in which can be found a development, a bit of intrigue, and a conclusion. Or, to put it better, those who execute it can follow all the parts of a drama in which they will be the actors.[15]

German theorist Koch too noted that this format was the expected one a few years later in 1793 in his *Anweisungen*. The reason for this lies in the need for musical and emotional contrast. As French composer Grétry pointed out, the first movement was required to be majestic or pompous, a major tour de force for the players, while the second was to plumb the emotions or provide a contrasting character, with the third returning to a lighter and more playful mood. Bach biographer Johann Nikolas Forkel even likened the sonata to the state of a person progressing from optimism to melancholy and then finally to happiness.[16]

The creation of the salon society, particularly in cities such as Berlin, where Frederick the Great held evening soirees dedicated to instrumental music in which he himself performed frequently, provided the perfect venue for the sonata, as did any venue for private music-making, as a painting by Philip Mercier illustrates (Figure 5.4). Because of the prevalence of the genre, musical structures were developed to provide stability in terms of form. These include in the Allegro opening movement contrasting themes, usually in the tonic and dominant keys, linked by modulatory transitions and a concluding section in the first part (the exposition), development of the melodic material from the first part that modulated through various harmonies until reaching a return of the opening section, this time in the main key (development and recapitulation). This set of thematic and harmonic contrasts, a complex binary rounded binary form, became known as the *sonata form* or *sonata principle*, so named because of its common use in the sonata. The other movements, while just a contrasting, usually had differing structures, ranging from theme and variations to expanded dances (such as the minuet) to light and jocular rondos, wherein the main theme returns four or five times, always in the main key. The degree of difficulty was variable, as well. If meant for publication, composers

Figure 5.4 Philippe Mercier, *The Music Party* (1733)
Source: Reproduced by permission from the National Portrait Gallery, London.

needed to recognize that highly virtuoso parts would be difficult for most to execute, and thus they had to tailor their lines to those of moderate ability. For example, in the opening movement of the Violin Sonata Op. 2 No. 1 by Johann Schobert, a popular Parisian composer of such music, one finds that the violin part is relatively simple and not of great difficulty, while the keyboard part is more dominant, though of only moderate difficulty (Example 5.1). This is not unusual for sonatas of this period, for it allows the keyboardist, often the better trained of the pair, to have the most technically difficult portion, while the instrument is often relegated to more of an accompaniment role. As the keyboard was also more versatile in terms of its ability to do both harmony and melody simultaneously throughout, this was not perceived as a detriment or negation of the additional instrument. Indeed, C. P. E. Bach notes in his treatise, "The accompanist will achieve eminence and attract the attention of intelligent listeners by letting them hear an unadorned steadiness and noble simplicity in a flowing accompaniment that does not interfere with the brilliance of the principal part."[17] In other words, regardless of which instrument has the dominant melodic role, each performer is to be considered as a *primus inter pares* or first among equals. This, as Figure 5.4 shows, meant a more intimate and integrated performance practice, with the instrumentalists in synch with each other. The early dominance of one instrument over the other in the thoroughbass duo sonata thus evolved

106 New Developments, Convergences, and Genres

Example 5.1 Johann Schobert, Violin Sonata in B-flat major, Op. 2 No. 1 (Paris, *ca.* 1760), Movement I, mm. 1–15

into a partnership. This also allowed for the rise in ability among the many musicians found in households throughout Europe and elsewhere, not to mention blurring the line between professional court or city musicians and amateurs.

By the end of the century, the sonata had become so commonplace that it was a major portion of the sales of music copyists or publishers, often in sets of four to six works. Composers at the beginning of their careers, such as Beethoven or Johann Nepomuk Hummel, were encouraged both by their publishers and musician friends to turn them out on a regular basis, and many of these appeared to be formulaic in style and structure. Even as early as 1752 Quantz noted that "today no one sees art in composing a sonata," and composer Johann Wilhelm Hässler noted in 1786, "I will not be writing simple keyboard sonatas any more, since I have been urged by everyone towards more important works."[18] This did not mean something similar to what happened to the Baroque sonata, for the market for music that appealed to both professional and amateur remained. Given that the sonata now faced competition from other chamber genres, it had to adapt and modernize, ironically the same position it had been in at the beginning of the Classical Period. Both Beethoven, Hummel, and others realized the need and began the process of evolution as the Romantic Period began.

The Major Instrumental Chamber Genres: Duos, Trios, Quartets, Quintets, and Beyond

While the sonata, whether for solo keyboard or with an additional instrument, remained at the core of chamber genres, composers of the Classical Period were interested in various combinations of colors and timbres. Therefore, they wrote works that exploited the various sounds, even as they adhered to the standard number of movements and formal structures found in the sonata. These works, sometimes published individually, and at others in sets of four to six works, are known by the number of instruments used. Here, too, the trends of the eighteenth century tended to favor certain combinations.

The simplest chamber work in terms of instrumentation was the *duo* or duet. As the name implies, it was for two instruments, and while the duo sonata for a single instrument and keyboard accompaniment noted earlier technically belong to this genre, the numbers written and published exceed other combinations, including works for a pair of keyboards or one keyboard with multiple players. The latter were mostly for two players, one in the upper registers and the second in the lower. One unique work, however, is the satirical *Das Dreyblatt* by Wilhelm Friedrich Ernst Bach, Johann Sebastian's grandson, who composed for pianoforte six hands; two pupils, between whom sat the teacher, playing the lowest and highest notes of the piece (Example 5.2). While this had a humorous effect, almost all the other duos were more serious in nature. Accompanied duos were often included in pedagogical works as examples of timbre and technique, generally for like instruments, with these being relatively simple in form and often quite short. For the larger self-contained duos, they ranged from modest difficulty that allowed for contrasting tone colors, to virtuoso display. Duos were composed for any combination of instruments. These ranged from pairs of the same instrument, such as two violins or two cellos, to various combinations. The most common ones, however, seem to have been for violin and viola or violin and cello. In these, the thin textures could be more like a duo sonata—for example, in the D major violin and viola work by Joseph Haydn in which the violin has the melody and the viola the accompaniment (Example 5.3a)—or more equal, in which both instruments are of equal musical stature, with the violin and viola performing both solo and accompaniment functions, as in the C major duo by Iganz Pleyel (Example 5.3b).

The *trio* was an outgrowth of the Baroque trio sonata, which as noted consisted of a pair of melody instruments and continuo, the upper two of which were often written for performance by several alternative instruments, such as violin, oboe, or flute. The use of the trio sonata in this format continued on into the Classical Period since it, too, had achieved a prominent level of popularity among musicians, both professional and amateur. Quantz notes, "A trio does not require as much labored effort as a quartet, but if it is to be good, it does need almost the same degree of skill on the part of the composer."[19] The reason for this, he states further, is that it has one more obbligato part and thus can be more *galant* (in his sense of the term). Bach's treatise devotes much of his section on accompaniment to how one ought to figure the thoroughbass to allow for both melody instruments to shine, a clear indication that by 1750 even early Classical composers were still thinking of the trio as a work in the Baroque manner.

By 1765, however, the constituent instrumentation began to shift with the advent of the fortepiano, which could provide both an accompaniment and a harmonic foundation against which the other two instruments could be measured. The most common works were now based around the fortepiano (or solo harpsichord), meaning that they could expand their functions both harmonically and melodically. Since these were often intended to be done in more intimate settings of the salon, like the common duo sonata or duet, they had to take into account the variable abilities of amateur musicians. Trios, which also followed generally the three-movement pattern of the sonata in format, had to accommodate a new sense of musical development. Composers not only saw this as a popular opportunity but also knew that it might lead to another opportunity for progressive development. By this time, the keyboard had already taken on a solo role, with a melody instrument, sometimes a woodwind but most commonly the violin, acting as a complement like the duo sonata. The second instrument, however, was often the cello, which sometimes supported the bass line of the keyboard and sometimes emerged as its own voice. For example, a trio by Pater Lambert Kraus from this time has a solo flute, a keyboard (most likely a harpsichord), and a cello, which in the second section of the work emerges from the texture with a nice obbligato (Example 5.4). By 1780, it

108 New Developments, Convergences, and Genres

Example 5.2 Wilhelm Friedrich Ernst Bach, *Das Dreyblatt*, mm. 1–8

had evolved further so that two types of trios could be found: the piano trio, a remnant of the trio sonata with fortepiano, usually a violin, and a cello functioning in a manner exhibited in the Kraus trio, and the instrumental trio consisting of three separate obbligato lines and no keyboard. Here, the first became more standard, while the second offered a cohesive texture. As an example of the latter, one can find the relatively common setting of a string trio for violin, viola, and cello in Karl von Dittersdorf's Divertimento composed probably between 1775 and 1780 (Example 5.5). Here, the violin has the lyrical melody, the viola an inner accompaniment, and the cello the foundation bass line, yet all the textures are calculated to blend. Other instrumental combinations were also to be found as the chamber genre developed.

Example 5.3 (a) Joseph Haydn, Duet for Violin and Viola, Ho. VI:4, Movement I, mm. 1–4; (b) Ignaz Pleyel, Duet for Violin and Viola, Movement III, mm. 1–8

Example 5.4 Pater Lambert Kraus, Trio in C major (*ca.* 1760), Movement I, mm. 44–48

As Quantz noted, the trio was perhaps less difficult to compose than the quartet. For him, a quartet required "a subject appropriate for treatment in four parts, a good, harmonious melody . . . a discerningly devised mixture of the concertante instruments" and "ideas that can be exchanged with one another." He also notes the equal disposition of the parts, and the fact that a good composer should be able to produce

Example 5.5 Carl Ditters von Dittersdorf, Divertimento (Trio) in D major (1775–1780), Movement I, mm. 1–4

a work in which all four voices can and should be used as the melody in turn. While this does not particularly point to the most common of the genres of the Classical Period, the string quartet, it does contain the prerequisites for composers. His model is the six Telemann quartets noted earlier, which, he notes, "may provide excellent and beautiful models for compositions of this sort."[20]

Given the popularity of the Telemann set of works, there can be no doubt that the skill of combining four parts in chamber music could appeal to composers. The rise of the string quartet itself, however, is rather more difficult to determine, given that it seems to have arisen out of several models, from the French *symphonie en quatour* to the Italian *concertino a quattro*, both of which are vague in their characterization as chamber genres. In central Germany and Austria, the four-part divertimento may also have been a model, given that some of the earliest string quartets by composers such as Georg Christoph Wagenseil and Joseph Haydn were published under that title. As musicologist James Webster has noted, many of these early works had the lowest part designated as *basso*, which may or may not contain implications of either an instrument (basso equals violone or contrabasso) or use of a continuo.[21] While it is unlikely that a continuo, including a keyboard, was used in central Europe around 1760, the time when these quartet-divertimenti were published, when these and others from around the continent were published over the next decade and a half, they often included both figured bass and *ad libitum* additional instruments. For example, the six quartets by Pater Romanus Hoffstetter, a Haydn aficionado, published as his Op. 1 in 1772 with Diller in Amsterdam contain both thoroughbass figures and parts for a pair of flutes.[22] While this may have been a publisher's means of expanding the marketability of the set by an obscure monastic composer, the fact that this and works by Haydn and others were sold with the same emendations by major publishers such as Hummel indicates that there was some generic instability at this date as to just what constituted a "string quartet" in the chamber sense.

Joseph Haydn is often considered the "father" of the chamber string quartet. This largely derives from a story by an early biographer, Georg August Griesinger, who states,

> The following purely chance circumstance had led him to try his luck at the composition of quartets. A Baron Fürnberg had a place in Weinzierl, several stages from Vienna, and he invited from time to

time his pastor, his manager, Haydn, and Albrechtsberger (a brother of the celebrated contrapuntist Albrechtsberger) in order to have a little music. Fürnberg requested Haydn to compose something that could be performed by these four amateurs. Haydn, then eighteen years old, took up this proposal, and so originated his first quartet which, immediately it appeared, received such general approval that Haydn took courage to work further in this form.[23]

There can be no doubt that, although his early published quartets were labeled as divertimenti, Haydn became perhaps the leading, and most popular composer of the genre during the last three decades of the eighteenth century. His position as the originator of the string quartet, however, has competition. For example, Franz Xaver Richter published a set of six quartets in 1765 in Mannheim that were actually labeled as such, and given that his works conform to the definition by Quantz of four independent concertante parts, his set may also be seen as important in its development (Example 5.6). In this example, one can see an advancement over the older styles in the independence of all four parts, lending it an integrated texture rather than dividing it between the melody and bass.

Nonetheless, there can be no doubt that Haydn was considered during his lifetime as the main innovator of the string quartet, eventually composing some sixty-eight of them over the course of his lifetime. There can be no doubt that the genre's evolution can be traced specifically in his works, from the early divertimento-derived five-movement format to the final unfinished work (Op. 103). Sets like Op. 9 or Op. 20 were considered models from which other composers throughout the globe took their cues, and Haydn himself was not opposed to offering sets on subscription, such as Op. 33, in which he introduces scherzos into

Example 5.6 Franz Xaver Richter, String Quartet in G major Op. 5 No. 5, Movement I, mm. 1–15

Example 5.7 Joseph Haydn, String Quartet in E-flat major, Hob. III:38, Movement II, mm. 1–10

the format (Example 5.7), as "written in a new and special way." By 1780, the string quartet was a major chamber genre that composers all over Europe were able to compose for a growing group of both amateurs and professionals, who used it for their own edification and entertainment. Perhaps the most famous description of one of these quartets was by Irish tenor and composer Michael Kelly, who while a student in Vienna in the 1780s witnessed a soirée with music performed by a preeminent group of musicians:

> This delayed us a little, and in the interim, Storace gave a quartet party to his friends. The players were tolerable; not one of them excelled on the instrument he played, but there was a little science among them, which I dare say will be acknowledged when I name them: the first violin—Haydn; second violin—Baron Dittersdorf; violoncello—Vanhal; tenor—Mozart. The poet Casti and Paisiello formed part of the audience. I was there, and a greater treat, or a more remarkable one, cannot be imagined. On the particular evening to which I am now referring, after the musical feast was over, we sat down to an excellent supper, and became joyous and lively in the extreme.[24]

The music that was performed on this special occasion is not known, but it does confirm the description of Haydn on the social use of the quartet as an entertainment for both players and audience in the more musically inclined households (Figure 5.5). Mozart himself dedicated a set of six quartets to Haydn, an acknowledgment of that composer's stature as the chief innovator of the genre.

The format of the string quartet was established relatively early; Richter's quartets formed a model for those written in central and northern Germany with two contrasting movements, the first slow and the second either a fast Allegro or contrapuntal. In France and Italy, the quartet followed the three-movement pattern established by the Sinfonia, with a slow movement bookended on either side by faster movements, the last often a rondo or minuet. The quartet model established by Haydn settled into a four-movement format following that set by the symphony; in Vienna this meant dropping one of the two minuets of the divertimento, but elsewhere it seemed to have evolved from the four-movement orchestral quartet or string symphony of the Mannheim composers. By the 1780s, it was not uncommon for the first movement to have a slow introduction appended. Sometimes, this could be strikingly original, such as the highly atonal opening of Mozart's so-called Dissonance Quartet, KV 465 (Example 5.8). While this caused more than a little comment and was uncomfortable for audiences of the time, the main part of the first movement is in a lyrical C major and makes an abrupt and marked contrast to the opening.

The string quartet itself may have been the most popular Classical Period chamber genre apart from the sonata, but it was not the only one, given that the quartet itself could include a wide variety of instruments.

Figure 5.5 Famed Quartet Party as described by Michael Kelly (nineteenth-century painting)
Source: Staatsmuseum Vienna, Public domain.

One of the most popular of these was the piano quartet, which normally consisted of a keyboard instrument (preferably the fortepiano, with its range of dynamics and softer tone) and one each of the violin, viola, and cello. This instrumentation was also followed if woodwinds were added, though these are generally designated by the wind instrument, that is, a flute quartet is for flute and strings, an oboe quartet for oboe and strings, and so on. The same pattern of movements as in the string quartet is followed. These combinations were often done to involve woodwind performers in the salons, especially if they were visiting professionals. Rarely, quartets consisting of four of the same instruments were composed, though these often had more pedagogical uses than entertainment. For example, German-Danish composer Friedrich Kuhlau wrote sets of trios, quartets, and even quintets only for flutes. Finally, for woodwind instruments, the woodwind quartet was also fairly well established. Here, the combination was usually a flute and oboe, or oboe and clarinet, performing the upper two voices, while a bassoon and horn added a bass line and inner harmonies. Since these instruments were often drawn from the outdoors *Harmonie*, this chamber genre represented their entrance into the salon, particularly in courts with outstanding woodwind composers and performers, such as Anton Reicha or Franz Danzi.

The further variation of the string quartet was the quintet, where the number of violas was doubled to provide a thicker texture in the middle registers. The format was the same as in the string quartet, but the added viola allowed for more harmonic exploration, as well as contrasting the melodic function of the first violin and first viola. In the instance of the famed quartet described by Michael Kelly, Austrian composer Maximilian Stadler was sometimes added whenever they needed to perform quintets. In Spain and France, however, a second cello was added instead of a viola. This gave more resonance to the lower registers, which could then be contrasted with the violins. On occasion, famed cellists such as Luigi Boccherini used this combination for special effects, such as the pizzicato opening of the Quintet in C major, G. 324, also called the *Musica Notturna delle strade di Madrid* (*Night Music on the Streets of Madrid*). Here, the instruments are to be strummed in imitation of guitars, a sort of characteristic music evoking the native Spanish music of the time (Example 5.9). Such effects were popular during the Classical Period, and it is due to this that it was included in the film *Master and Commander* as part of the shipboard entertainment performed by the officers on a British warship.

Example 5.8 Wolfgang Amadeus Mozart, String Quartet in C major, KV 465, Movement I, mm. 1–5

Like the quartet, wind instruments or a keyboard could be added to the string quartets to become a quintet. Because of the "symphonic" accompanimental textures of the quartet and the concertante nature of the solo instrument, these were often considered as chamber concertos, though the integration of the inner parts, often with contrasting obbligato lines of their own, made them less displays of the solo and more integrated, as suited the chamber. Two special genres for winds developed during the 1780s: the quintet for fortepiano and woodwind quartet and the woodwind quintet. The latter included one each of the main woodwind instruments of the expanded Classical orchestra: flute, oboe, clarinet, bassoon, and horn. Reicha and others at courts with particularly adept woodwind players often composed for this ensemble, though in terms of structure it did not vary from that of the string quintet.

Larger groups of chamber instruments—sextets, septets, octets, and nonets—were occasionally written, but given that larger numbers produced music that was noisier and therefore less suitable for the intimate chambers in which the works were usually performed, compositions were relatively rare during the Classical Period. Although the sextet was more or less standardized to a pair of horns and a string quartet, the larger chamber genres could be a variety of various instruments, leading to a wide number of settings that were both difficult to obtain in terms of performers and provided little more than timbral contrast without progressive compositional elements.

It can be said that instrumental chamber genres were the core of the social entertainments of the period throughout Europe and abroad. The quartet, especially, was well suited to a variety of innovations, all

Example 5.9 Luigi Boccherini, Quintet in C major Op. 30 No. 6, G. 324, opening sequence

allowable by the standardization of the instruments. Virtually every household of substance during the period had enough family members to perform chamber genres, and the sonata, trio, and quartet were written for both amateur and professional uses. In the sets favored by the publishers, they could be sellable to a wide clientele, and it is no wonder that one finds the chamber genres at the forefront of the expansion of music globally during the Classical Period. One finds instrumental chamber ensembles in the early settlements of the far-flung empires, from Kodiak and Sitka in Russian Alaska to Botany Bay, Australia, from the factors in Nagasaki, Japan, and Bangalore, India to the upper-class households in the Americas. But instrumental music was not entirely alone as the preferred entertainment of the chamber. Most children were also given voice lessons, and during this period vocal music was also frequent during private soirées. Given that it included lyrics, this added a dimension to musical composition, for the poetic nature of the text provided substance and inspiration for both performer and composer.

The Chamber Vocal Genres: The Rise of the Lied

During the Classical Period, young men and women in the aristocratic and upper social strata were well-educated in music, and it was not unusual for this to include voice lessons. Instruction was provided alongside elementary theory and occasionally composition, and while many became adept singers, the purpose was, as in instrumental music, for more intimate entertainment. The pupils were not expected to be at the same level as their professional contemporaries, often their teachers, but were required to be proficient enough to sing a variety of styles and genres.

The most sought-after singing teachers were Italian, largely because they were often either retired or active professionals themselves with knowledge of the most popular language for the voice (see Chapter 6). Rarely were they expected to train their pupils to a standard that would allow them to appear in public, though an exceptional prodigy could emerge who would enter a career in voice. The most popular genre was the song or Lied, which was for a single voice and keyboard accompaniment, but these could either be independent works or published in books containing medleys of popular tunes with titles such as *Liederbuch*, *Recueils*, or *Chansons*.

Songbooks had a long and stable history before the eighteenth century, with predecessors such as the lute song being published over two centuries earlier during the Renaissance. The instrument accompaniment was generally a lute or early keyboard, with the vocal line providing a simple, often strophic melody and the accompanying instrument both bass and inner harmonies. The subject matter was formulaic, often pastoral, though during the Baroque Period didactic and love songs were favored. As a result, the Lied flourished after a fashion, with texts that were poetically solid, though the poetry was often lacking in content or emotion. Simple songs were often linked by short recitatives into secular cantatas, with the idea of presenting a scene or poetic contrast that was both accessible and sentimental, with little of the virtuosity required of its cousin, the opera.

In 1729 Leipzig University professor Johann Gottsched stated in his *Versuch einer kritische Dichtkunst vor die Deutschen* (*Essay to the Germans on a Critical Art of Poetry*): "The Lied is nothing more than an agreeable and clear reading of a verse, which must therefore be equal in the nature and content of the words."[25] Here the song is clearly merely a support of the text, but in 1738 it had become more defined as a genre when recognized composers were enticed into writing "their own melodies," as Johann Friedrich Gräfe put it. The same year Scheibe wrote extensively in his *Critische Musicus* about the song and its role in amateur music-making, noting drily,

> There are a few great spirits who regard even the word "Lied" as derogatory; which, whenever they wish to speak of a musical work that has not been composed pompously or simplistically according to its fashion, is called in their language a song.[26]

This seems more disparaging in the light of the genre's popularity, with the author further stating that "I know that there are certain great and knowledgeable composers who find odes or Lieder far too poor." While these "great composers" are not named, it is clear that in the early part of the Classical Period the song was considered a lesser art for composers. Nonetheless, attempts were made to develop this vocal chamber genre into a viable and both musically and poetically higher-class genre, still without reducing its intended audience of the amateur musician. German and English sources differentiated between the ode and the Lied, the first being defined as music that is set to a verse in praise of someone or something that has interested the poet and is laudatory, while the song is of lesser value, often being a series of stanzas that tell a brief story.

By 1760 Rousseau defined both the content and purpose of the song (here, in French, *chanson*), as being "a type of short lyrical poetry based upon a most agreeable subject and performed as an air to be sung at common occasions, such as at the table, for friends, with one's master and spouse, to pass the time."[27] In other words, it was suitable for multiple occasions, and in educated households the song, whether part of a specially composed collection or a series of arrangements of popular tunes drawn from folk material or the theatre, was a common form of entertainment throughout the European-dominated world. A prime example can be seen in the portrait of the Montegut family by Spanish colonial artist José Francisco Xavier de Salazar y Mendoza from the end of the Classical Period. This family, resident in New Orleans, is gathered for a normal occasion with one daughter seated at a keyboard with one son holding music, another holding a small flageolet, a third with a songbook in her lap (partially hidden by a chair), and the son with a normal transverse flute (Figure 5.6). The social aspects of this scene are typical for the period, a family entertainment in a household far from Europe and yet with the same cultural ties implicit in the setting.

Figure 5.6 José Salazar, *The Family of Dr. Joseph Montegut of New Orleans* (*ca.* 1798–1800, painting)
Source: Louisiana State Museum Collection, loaned by Gustave Pitot.

By 1770 the subject of text and music, the core of the Lied, was a topic of considerable debate, especially in German lands. The term *Liederschule* (Singing School) had become common, though it could range from actual pedagogical institutions focused on the development of professional singers and cantors to groups of composers and poets debating how this chamber genre should develop. One of the earliest of these was the Berlin school, the first generation of which was formed in 1740 by members of Frederick the Great's musical establishment. In 1753 Christian Gottfried Krause published his *Von der musikalischen Poesie* (*On Musical Poetry*), which promoted a simpler, almost folk style with minimal accompaniment. Regarded as the new wave of song composition, it soon fell into disfavor because of its lack of distinctive character or emotional content. As Christian Friedrich Daniel Schubart noted in 1775, "[i]ntemperance, pedantry, alienation from nature, and anxious struggling with art has brought this school down from the pinnacle of its worship."[28] Instead, he proposed a different type of song, one that was more accessible, more akin to the folk song, and meant to evoke various emotions. He notes that the strophic song is better for this, since the tune can be memorized already at the first performance and that if sentimentality is the goal, then the composer has succeeded, for it allows the amateur performer to convey that sentiment to his or her audience.

118 *New Developments, Convergences, and Genres*

Johann Adam Hiller, who founded his own academy of the vocal arts in Leipzig in 1766, also published a series of manuals on the song, one of which is entitled the *Musikalisches Handbuch für die Liebhaber des Gesanges und Claviers* (*Musical Textbook for Amateurs of Singing and Keyboard*). By the end of the century, the Lied had risen to the pinnacle of the vocal chamber genres, being suitable for virtually any social occasion and performable by both families and guests alike.

Perhaps the most prolific composer of the genre was Berlin *Kapellmeister* Johann Friedrich Reichardt, who composed around 1,500 Lieder. As a friend of poet Johann Wolfgang von Goethe, he also sought to create new convergences of poetry and music, as well as publishing volumes of works devoted to specific topics, such as his *Lieder der Liebe und der Einsamkeit* (*Songs of Love and Loneliness*), which appeared in two parts beginning in 1798 (Figure 5.7). The third work, titled "Seufzer" ("Sighs"), consists of three verses and a simple statement of only twelve measures (Example 5.10). The text, by poet Ludwig Hölty, is short and pithy, opening with the sonorous nightingale's call resounding throughout the countryside. In the second verse, young couples stand by a rushing stream to admire the song, but in the third, the singer expresses his or her unease, as they are alone. The sentiment is clear, the music a moody G minor, and the line repetitious and easy. Until the advent of Franz Schubert in the Romantic Period, Reichardt's style represents the sort of song that audiences found both captivating and emotional.

Figure 5.7 Title page of *Lieder der Liebe und Einsamkeit* by Johann Friedrich Reichardt (1798)

Example 5.10 Johann Friedrich Reichardt, Lied "Seufzer." Complete first stanza.

Variety in song forms also existed, as Heinrich Koch noted in his definition of the Lied in his musical lexicon of 1804 (see Document 3). He describes the forms as

> from the oratorio to the sonnet, up to the rondeau, each of the kinds of lyrical poetry has their own differentiated character, even though they also have little more than purpose or form for the most part; the ode and the song are the only ones which differentiate themselves internally.[29]

Indeed, solo songs were not the only sort of vocal chamber music meant for amateurs, especially given that many salons included several singers whose voices might be used for larger or multi-voiced settings. These chamber genres include the *canzonetta*, such as the set published as duets with keyboard by Johann Christian Bach in London in 1780, or short scenes, secular cantatas, that appeared frequently throughout the period. The vocal secular cantata was a remnant from the Baroque Period, but given that it generally included a more complete scene musically, often with short arias and recitatives, it, too, had an appeal for eighteenth-century social groups that could add some sort of impromptu staging or gestures to the performance. In England, composers such as Thomas Arne published series of these cantatas for voice, keyboard continuo (mostly figured), and the occasional accompaniment by an instrument (single violins or flutes, or sometimes pairs or even small ensembles one on a part). One of the more popular chamber pieces of a similar sort was the *notturno*, a work intended for either voices or instruments, the latter either from three to six instruments or as a small chamber orchestra. Both Mozart and Josef Myslivicek wrote works in this style, generally to Italian pastoral texts. Such works were perhaps too large for the normal chamber of the time, but they were too intimate for the concert hall, and thus, they were not common. The usual setting was a pair of voices, generally sopranos, and the accompanying instruments could be woodwinds, as in the case of the former, or a small orchestra, as seen with the Czech composer's works.

With multiple voices of untrained quality, it was not unusual for such singing events to demonstrate the worst qualities of the amateur performers. Fanny Burney laments scornfully their "caterwauling" at salons, while others noted that evening entertainments might deteriorate as other activities such as drinking and gambling proceeded. Though the general performances were rather more sedate and could be quite fine, as Charles Burney noted in his history of music, the more raucous evenings often degenerated into less-than-competent attempts at music-making.

Documents

Document 1. Georg Philipp Telemann, "Autobiography" from Johann Mattheson, *Grundlage einer Ehrenpforte* (Hamburg, 1740), 366–367.

My long-anticipated journey to Paris, where I had been invited several years prior by several noteworthy virtuosos who had found a few of my compositions tasteful, occurred at Michelmas 1737 and lasted for eight months. There I had engraved, according to the royal general privilege I had receive twenty years prior, new quartets on subscription and six sonatas consisting throughout of melodic canons. The wonderful way the quartets were performed by the *Herren* Blavet (transverse flute), Guignon (violin), Forcroy Jr (gambist), and Edouard (cellist) deserves a description here, if words are accessible enough. They made the ears of the court and the city extraordinarily attentive, and in a short time won for me an almost universal honor that was accompanied by a magnificent compliment.[30]

Document 2. Jean-Jacques Rousseau, *Dictionnaire de Musique* (Paris, 1768), II:217.

Sonata: An instrumental work consisting of three or four sequential movements of different characters. The sonata is to instruments as the cantata is to voices. The sonata is usually composed for a single instrument that plays accompanied by a basso continuo; in such a work one emphasizes what is most favorable in showing off the instrument, whether the contour of the line, the choice of notes that best suit this type of instrument, or the forcefulness of the execution. . . . There are many sorts of sonatas. The Italians have reduced them to two main types. One that they call the sonata da camera, which are composed of several familiar airs and dances, about the same as those collections, which in France are called suites. The other type is called sonata da chiesa, in the composition of which one is able to encounter counterpoint, working out of harmony, and melody that is most suitable to the dignity of the place. . . . Today with the instruments being the most important portion of music, sonatas are extremely fashionable, the same as any sort of symphony; vocal music is regarded as only an accessory, and the voice accompanies the accompaniment. We consider this the bad taste of those who want to introduce all of Italian music in a language that is not compatible, and we are therefore forced to seek to do with our instruments, that which is impossible with our own voice. . . . Pure harmonic music is nothing much; in order to please constantly and to be bored, it must rise to the rank of the imitative arts, but its imitation is not always instantaneous, such as poetry and painting. The word is the means by which music most often determines an object though which it conjures an image, and it is through the tangible sounds of the human voice that this image awakens deep in the heart the feeling that it has to arouse. Who does not realize how far from this capability mere instrumental music is when one seeks only to show off the instrument. All of the roulades of the violin of Monsieur Modonville do not affect me the way two notes in the voice of Mademoiselle l'Maure does. The melody animates the song, and adds to its expression but it does not supplant it. To know what all these is acceptable in all of these plethora of sonatas, it would be necessary to do what a painter does, who was obligated to write beneath his figures: this is a tree, this is a man, this is a horse, etc. I will never forget the expostulation of the celebrated Fontenelle, exasperated by these eternal instrumental works, who cried aloud in a fit of impatience: Sonata what do you want from me?

Document 3. From Heinrich Koch, *Musikalisches Lexikon* (Leipzig, 1804), 901–903.

Lied. One designates with this word mainly every lyrical poem of several strophes that is meant for singing and contains a melody that is repeated with each verse, and at the same time has the capability of being performed by any person who is healthy and possesses a not inflexible singing voice, without recourse to artistic training. From this it follows that the melody of a song may not contain either such a great range of notes or that manner of singing or division of the syllables that is meant only for the artistic and trained singing of an aria, but rather that the expression of the sentiments contained within the text can be successfully done through simple, and yet accessible means. The song encompasses various types and genres, whose characteristic differences can be determined partly through content and partly through form . . . there needs be no proof what an important artistic product the song is in terms of poetry and music. If one reflects upon what an influence good and purposeful songs have for the special state and needs of the various classes of citizens of a country, how they are able to reflect the portrayal of the heart . . . thus the song today is the sole product of sound and poetic art in whose content every class of people, and each of the individuals therein can find an immediate interest.

Notes

1. Pater Meinrad Spieß, *Tractatus Musicus Compositorio-Practicus* (Augsburg, 1746), 162.
2. Koch, *Musikalisches Lexikon*, col. 820–821.
3. Johann Heinrich Zedler, *Großes vollständiges Universal-Lexicon* (Leipzig, 1744), Vol. 41: col. 1436.
4. Quantz, *On Playing the Flute*, 315.
5. Little study has been done on the subgenre of chamber symphony. Mary Sue Morrow commented on the chamber symphony, not only noting its existence and contents but also concluding that "[c]omposers should give it more attention because audiences would be giving it more attention." See Mary Sue Morrow, "Eighteenth-Century Viewpoints," in *The Symphonic Repertory: Volume 1 The Eighteenth Century Symphony* (Bloomington, IN: Indiana University Press, 2015), 50. A good manuscript example of a chamber symphony is the Symphony in C-sharp minor by Joseph Martin Kraus, which exists in a set of parts indicating one on a part.
6. Quantz, *On Playing the Flute*, 318. See also Scheibe, *Critische Musikus*, 681.
7. Charles Burney, *A General History of Music* (London, 1789; reprint ed. 1954), II: 924.
8. Daniel Gottlob Türk, *Klavierschule* (Leipzig, 1789), 392.
9. Rousseau, *Dictionnaire de Musique* (Paris, 1768), II: 217.
10. "Sonata, que me veux-tu?" The quote was incorporated by Rousseau in his *Dictionnaire*; see Document 2.
11. Johann A. P. Schulz, "Sonate," in Sulzer's *Allgemeine Theorie der Schönen Künste* (Leipzig, 1783), II: 688–689.
12. Bach, *Versuch über die wahre Art das Klavier zu spielen*, Chapter 3 Performance.
13. Burney, *The Present State of Music in Germany* (London, 1775), II: 270.
14. Schulz, "Sonate," II: 688.
15. Bernard Germain de Lacépède, *La poétique de la musique* (Paris, 1785), 343–344.
16. See Newman, 27–28, for a discussion of the various descriptions of the sonata. Newman notes that though the sonata was noted among the various theorists, it was not discussed in detail
17. Bach, *Versuch über die wahre Art das Klavier zu spielen*, 367.
18. Quoted in Willi Kahl, *Selbstbiographien deutscher Muiker des XVIII Jahrhunderts* (Cologne: Staufen-Verlag, 1948), 74. This was published originally as an appendix to his *Sechs Leichte Sonaten Theil IV* (Erfurt, 1787).
19. Quantz, *On Playing the Flute*, 302.
20. Quantz, *On Playing the Flute*, 317.
21. See James Webster, "The Bass Part in Early Haydn String Quartets," *Musical Quarterly* 63 (1977), 390–424.
22. This set of six quartets has been published in a modern edition; see Romanus Hoffstetter, *Six Quartets Op. 1* (Ann Arbor: Steglein, 2017).
23. Georg August Griesinger, *Biographical Notes Concerning Joseph Haydn*, trans. Vernon Gotwals (Milwaukee: University of Wisconsin Press, 1963), 13. Griesinger's original appeared in 1810. Baron Fürnberg refers to Karl Joseph Weber, Edler von Fürnberg, Haydn's first employer.
24. Michael Kelly, *Reminiscences of Michael Kelly* (London, 1826), 328–329. References are to Joseph Haydn, Carl Ditters von Dittersdorf, Johann Baptist Vanhal, and Wolfgang Amadeus Mozart; Abbé Casti is the poet and Giovanni Paisiello is a popular opera buffa composer.
25. Johann Gottsched, *ersuch einer critischen Dichtkunst* (Leipzig, 1730), 327.
26. See Scheibe, *Critische Musikus*, 539.
27. Rousseau, *Dictionnaire*, I: 78.
28. Christian Daniel Friedrich Schubart, *Deutsche Chronik* (Ulm, 1776), 22.
29. Koch, *Musikalisches Lexikon*, 902.
30. The musicians are Michel Blavet, Jean-Pierre Guignon, Jean-Baptiste Forqueray, and Prince Edouard; the last is not identifiable further.

Part III

Opera! The Development of Popular, Nationalist, and Exotic Entertainment

6 The Structure and Meaning of Italian Opera in the Classical Period

As in the Baroque Period, opera was perhaps the most popular and lucrative entertainment of the age. Over the course of this time, opera was in a state of nearly constant development that changed virtually all aspects of this multimedia genre. From its beginnings as an outgrowth of festive occasions in Italy, it had become a symbol of prestige and power for the courts, as well as a source of economic prosperity for more public houses. Moreover, the expanding popularity of the opera during the Baroque led to increased reputations of singers and composers, many of whom established careers outside their native birthplaces. A prime example is George Frédéric Handel, who began his professional career as a continuo player at the publicly supported opera in Hamburg, went on to establish an international reputation as "the dear Saxon" in Italy and became a fixture in London, where he was associated with several opera houses, some public and others subsidized by the English court, as composer, musical director, and impresario. Another is the castrato Carlo Broschi, known by his stage name Farinelli, who began his career as "*Il ragazzo*" ("The Boy") in 1722 in Rome, where he allegedly competed successfully against a high clarino trumpet in a contest, thus launching a successful career, according to historian Charles Burney. Farinelli performed for the next decade and a half in Vienna, Germany, London, and throughout Italy, gaining both wealth and fame before accepting exclusive employment with the King of Spain in 1737. Here he performed for the Spanish royalty for over two decades before being forcibly retired, living to an advanced age in Bologna, the musical center of the Accademia Filarmonica. While in Rome, he often performed female roles, though his work in London, Spain, and elsewhere featured him as the leading hero (Figure 6.1).

Opera was the main source of entertainment, as well, for it allowed for fantasy, musical display, and social interaction for the audience, as well as being a source of steady employment for musicians. Not everyone was able to rise to the level of fame of a Farinelli or Handel, but so commonplace was opera as a genre that there was room for all, from aspiring talents to the thoroughly professional singer or composer. Moreover, it could be lucrative for all those involved, from both a practical and an artistic standpoint.

Popular Opera as Musical Business and Taste

It was in the world of opera, particularly in Italy, that the new Classical styles of music first emerged, as this multimedia genre was always in need of novelty to attract audiences. Given that many opera houses relied on a stream of new works, the employment of star singers, and the requirement of variable technical demands that served to underscore the required stage effects, opera was an expensive and difficult genre to produce. It needed stages that were substantial enough to host works that included sets of various sorts, in addition to room for audiences who were able to support the enterprise economically. Finally, it had to have room for a substantial orchestra to accompany the singers. Opera was therefore a massive undertaking for the public theatres, and even in the private theatres in courts, palaces, and a few private households, the need for appropriate infrastructure was great, even though the stages may have been substantially smaller than their public rivals. In these places, it became a matter of reputation for performances of operas on a scale that would elicit praise. For example, in Vienna, which had a number of large main stages, Empress Maria Theresia remarked that if she really wanted to see excellent opera, she would visit Esterház, where

Figure 6.1 Caricature of Farinelli in a female role and out of costume by Pier Leone Ghezzi (1724)

Prince Nicholas Esterházy had built a sizable court opera house, with both singers and instrumentalists attached to his *Kapelle* under the direction of Joseph Haydn (Figure 6.2). Berlin's pride and joy was the opera created under the direction of Carl Heinrich Graun for his patron, Frederick the Great, and to ensure its success, he, like so many of his colleagues around Europe, went to Italy to obtain the services of the best musicians he could find. In London, as noted, opera was all the rage, though its fortunes varied over the course of the period, and even in far-flung corners of the Western world, from Malta to Mexico, opera houses catered to supportive audiences and patrons who both reveled in the reputation of their companies and enjoyed the escape that opera provided from real life.

Like in the Baroque Period, Italian opera (or more accurately, opera in Italian) was considered the most popular and widespread of the genre. On the international stage during the Classical Period it was ubiquitous, with virtually every country, city, and court producing it, regardless of whether they had other operas in their local languages. The reasons for this were clear to the eighteenth-century mind; the language was regarded as the most adept for singing, the texts were filled with an extensive variety of terms that conveyed emotional depth, and the natural bent of the Italian style toward lyrical expression was most acute on the stage. This was not just a philosophical point of view, though it provoked polemical debates throughout Europe. The history of the genre provided a solid tradition for both composition and performance going back over a century, while the extensive training of wave after wave of Italian musicians and singers who achieved success across the continent ensured an international acceptance that Italy was a source that seemed inexhaustible in terms of product. In short, Italian opera appears to have dominated the stage in Europe, due to the tastes of its audiences as well as being a thriving business for both popular and court theatres. This, in turn, fueled the constant need for new works, as well as job opportunities, for Italian

The Structure and Meaning of Italian Opera

Figure 6.2 Performance at Esterháza of *L'incontro improvviso* by Joseph Haydn (Anonymous German, *ca.* 1778). Haydn is performing at the keyboard.

musicians both within the peninsula and abroad. Indeed, so important was the dominance that many non-Italians were also sent south to continue or complete their training in the homeland of opera.

Theorists of the period note that the popularity may have been largely due to the beauty of the Italian language, where harsh consonants were lacking and there were a plethora of long vowels that could be used to embellish and ornament. Quantz was succinct when he stated,

> In the vocal composition of modern native Italians, the voice part has the best role. They take the greatest pains with it; they make it comfortable for the singer, and not infrequently introduce charming fancies and expressions . . . you cannot deny that the Italians have the skill in playing, insight into music, and richness in the invention of beautiful ideas, and that they have brought singing to a greater perfection than any other nation.[1]

This is mirrored by the admiration shown by Rousseau for their opera (see Document 1). This sentiment shown by the theorists is, however, not entirely shared when it comes to the staging of the operas themselves. Quantz notes that Italian opera must be properly staged in order to be considered successful. He notes further: "If an Italian opera, or one arranged in the Italian manner, is to please everyone, and is to be held a most agreeable spectacle, it must have the following characteristics."[2] These are defined as a good text treated realistically, good characterization, suitable dialogue divided into recitatives and arias, possibilities for the composer to outline the sentiments through word painting, and an overall refined taste in music that the performers must be able to present with all due expression. Finally, he adds that staging and performance must be of high standard (see Document 2). Given such demands, as well as the need to please both audience and patrons, it is small wonder that the business of opera and opera production was an enormous undertaking, requiring coordination and administration of many parts, not to mention considerable economic support.

Given the logistical needs of mounting an opera, it is not surprising that three different approaches were undertaken: (1) a professional impresario, who organized and sometimes financed opera; (2) a court intendant or theatre director, mainly from the nobility, who was in charge of administration of a permanent company usually supported wholly by the state; or (3) a self-supporting touring company, where the leader fulfilled several roles. These were hired by cities and sometimes courts to assume both artistic and economic risks for the owners of the theatres, who were generally amateurs from noble and upper-class families. The main season for opera in Italy was Carnival, which began in Venice usually on the Feast of St. Stephen, December 26, and lasted until the beginning of Lent. Given that there were secondary festive seasons during Ascension and in the Fall, generally from early October through the end of November, an impresario in that city needed to be aware of the dates so that he would be able to mount productions on time. As he generally held a concession for perhaps as many as two or more theatres, the timetable for obtaining a text, hiring a composer, as well as the singers, musicians, and a technical crew (and dancers, if ballet was needed) had to be adhered to scrupulously. This sometimes meant arranging matters through intermediaries who undertook the matter of negotiations for finances, as well as other contractual issues. In places, such as the smaller theatres in Venice or other Italian cities, he himself would have to judge the success of a production or season several months or more in advance. For the Carnival season, it generally meant, according to historian John Rosselli, that the libretto would have to be ready no later than the first of December, with the composer beginning to work on the music as soon as portions became available. Singers and other theatre personnel would be expected to be in place no later than ten days later so that rehearsals could begin.[3] While many operas were ready for their premiere by the first night, others were not, and if the work did not appeal, the audience often grew unruly, even threatening for the impresario (not to mention the other personnel involved). Therefore, it was not uncommon after 1760 for a work that had been successful, perhaps the year prior, could be substituted, either after a failure or in lieu of a work that had not yet reached its readiness for performance. Given that audience expectations were high, the professional impresario was under extreme pressure to find the best works for the most economical means. This meant juggling budgets and attempting to use local talent for secondary roles. It also meant limiting the amount of time available for all of the artists to prepare for the premiere.

For court productions, the impresario was usually subordinate to the intendant, who, in turn, was often a member of the nobility chosen for the role by the ruler. For example, in 1754 the Genoese diplomat to the Holy Roman court in Vienna, Count Giacomo Durazzo, was appointed by Maria Theresia to oversee the productions at the main opera house (Figure 6.3). Since his family was the owner of the main theatre in Genoa and he himself had considerable experience with the stage, it was only natural that his talents be put to use. In Dresden, however, the court composer Johann Adolph Hasse was given administrative oversight of the Saxon Opera, which was also a natural consequence of his own fame as a composer as well as his marriage to leading soprano Faustina Bordoni. The same could be said for Berlin, where Carl Heinrich Graun served as director of the Prussian State Opera, though here he operated under the watchful eye of Frederick the Great.

The itinerant troupes, on the other hand, had to be entirely self-contained. Many of these were led by entrepreneurial musicians who formed a company and ran it on tours that could last a season or be resident in a city for several. For example, Pietro Mingotti formed a company about 1734 or 1735 that consisted mainly of singers. Initially a resident in Prague, by 1747 he was active throughout central Europe and had hired Christoph Willibald von Gluck as his resident composer and musical director. In 1750 Gluck was replaced by Giuseppe Sarti and eventually Francesco Antonio Baldassare Uttini. Although these companies were sometimes situated for years at a time in a particular city or court, much of their reputation was based on their ability to tour and, in so doing, provided a conduit for Italian opera from St. Petersburg to London and from Scandinavia to Spain. The theatres they performed in ranged from small municipal houses to intimate court theatres, such as the one built in 1747 at Drottningholm in Sweden (Figure 6.4). This venue is still in operation more than 250 years later.

The most difficult part of any company, resident or touring, was its economic viability. Almost all of the companies not directly supported by a wealthy court, such as in Dresden, Berlin, or Vienna, were on

Figure 6.3 Count Giacomo Durazzo (*ca.* 1770, attributed to Martin van Meytens)
Source: Wikipedia Commons from Sotheby's.

a precarious footing when it came to funding. Even in Italy, impresarios were often hard-pressed to turn a profit, given the many hats that they had to wear, not to mention the needs of each opera season. The theatres, too, were expensive to maintain, especially if the audiences clamored for more elaborate sets and costumes, as well as larger orchestras to support larger scoring over the course of the period. Then, too, were the disasters, such as the Venetian theatre called La Fenice (The Phoenix), so called because it burned to the ground in 1774 and was then resurrected from the ashes (Figure 6.5).[4] Economic viability depended on income that was inconsistent, at best. In Italy, most boxes were rented by important families on a more or less permanent basis, and therefore, the income was not necessarily due the impresario. Sometimes, those who rented the boxes would pay for entrance to the theatre but not always, which left the public at large to pay an admission fee (in Italian, *ingresso*), whether or not they actually saw the opera; many came only for social visits or to gamble in the side rooms. To view the work on stage, a second fee was paid to an attendant for seats in the stalls or main floor, where benches were usually set up. At the top of the theatre was the gallery, which had its own entrance and admission fee, though this was generally much less than the main floor or boxes. Box holders were the elite of the audience, and the impresario was often ruled by their demands; they could band together and vote an impresario out of the theatre if the works presented were not up to their standards, for instance.

Figure 6.4 Drottningholm Court Theatre, Stockholm, Sweden
Source: Photo by the author.

Figure 6.5 Eighteenth-Century Engraving of Teatro La Fenice, Venice (*ca.* 1770)

Apart from the various admission fees, the impresarios usually were given the concessions for refreshments or gambling tables. While these could be occasionally lucrative, the theatre owners, too, negotiated them and box holders as to the amount the impresario could obtain from operating them. In the smaller municipal theatres, additional presents and, more rarely, a subsidy was provided by the local rulers (or less often by the municipality itself) if a particular work or season was pleasing, and it was not uncommon for owners to demand a split of the proceeds, even if they provided support for their own theatres. One way of expanding income was to offer dancing or masked ball following a performance, for which an additional entrance fee would bring in money.

Expenses were a constant worry for the impresario or director of a touring group. Production costs could vary considerably, but in order to hire the best composers and musicians, contractual amounts were sometimes negotiated prior to any reckoning of income. A world-class castrato or prima donna, such as Domenico Annibali or Anna de Amicis, could command extraordinary prices, which had to be matched against the income their notoriety or talent would bring in. Important composers such as Giovanni Paisiello or Hasse could also command high fees, so it was not unusual for the impresario to balance such costs by hiring lesser-known people. Finally, in order to maintain a successful season, the income from each night could be split between a number of other constituents, from the impresario to the composer to individual singers, to provide a reward for success or an incentive for future work. For the impresario, this, too, meant a de facto reduction in income.

Finally, there was the matter of popular taste. In the business of opera, the tastes of the audience were of paramount importance in deciding which works to mount. For court productions, the tastes were rather elevated and conventional, which meant that the noble audiences desired works that surrounded highborn characters and showed off the talents of the best musicians. This likely meant Italian serious opera, in which the stories extolled virtue and righteousness, even as the musical focus was on the virtuosity of the singers. For celebratory occasions, such as royal marriages, the *serenata* was preferred, largely because of static plots with allusions to the event and laudatory content. As an example, two operas were commissioned for the marriage of Archduke Ferdinand of the Holy Roman Empire to Princess Maria d'Este in October 1771 in Milan. The first was an opera seria, *Ruggiero*, by one of the most prestigious composers of Italian opera, Hasse, while the second was the serenata (called here a *festa teatrale*, or theatrical celebration) *Ascanio in Alba* by the precocious newcomer Wolfgang Amadeus Mozart. The first work, Hasse's last opera, involved the trials of lovers Ruggiero and Bradamante during the reign of Charlemagne, in which the main theme is faithfulness until death.[5] The second involves Ascanio, the son of Aeneas, marrying Silvia, the descendant of Hercules; here, the only moment of idyllic tension occurs when Silvia has doubts about Ascanio's faithfulness, having only met through visions concocted by Venus. In both cases, the texts were direct allusions to the celebrations and family fealty, and it was easy for the impresario, in this case, Count Karl Joseph Firmian, the governor general of Austrian Lombardy, to choose works that were appropriate for the occasion, knowing that neither would be expected to become a part of the repertory.

Unfortunately, a general season was less certain of a successful outcome. First, the impresario had to ensure that the work would not contain offensive or derogatory allusions to the authorities; even if it passed the censors, the opera had to avoid symbolic or direct comments on the rulers or important patrons. These could and often did demand that the authorities shut down performances, sometimes as they were ongoing, if the insult was grave enough. Second, the performances, if given by under-rehearsed musicians, were subject to the immediate reactions by the paying audiences. Italian audiences were extremely unruly, with bravos being shouted immediately on a successful performance; in many cases, this meant that a particular aria or another number was repeated on the spot, even several times in succession. On the other hand, poor performance elicited mocking laughter or catcalls, and if the audience members took exception to any work or the opera as a whole, they would jeer, shout insults, make noise with whatever was available, or even charge the stage. The authorities, who could shut down a theatre to prevent future disorder, often dealt with such demonstrations of disapproval immediately. In these cases, the impresario was forced to substitute another work in haste, hire new singers, or frantically request a substitute music be composed on the spot, all of which had an impact on his economy. Third, even a success for one night would not guarantee that audiences would continue to attend, which often meant that even the personnel hired were continually worried about getting paid. Finally, if a production was successful and overcame all of the hurdles of popular taste, its success could cause rival theatres envious of the production to hire claques or rowdies to disrupt the performances, forcing them to be canceled. All of this was a catastrophe for the impresario, so it was not surprising that many of their companies, whether resident or traveling, went bankrupt. For example, while not on tour, the Mingotti troupe made its home in Copenhagen in 1747 at the request of Queen Louisa, but he was forced into bankruptcy in 1757, stranding the company in Stockholm; Mingotti himself returned to Copenhagen, where he died penniless two years later, though the musical director, Uttini, was hired by the Swedish court as *Kapellmeister*. As Rosselli notes, "[i]f no one fell ill or sang out of tune, if both the operas contracted for were reasonable successful, if no epidemic threatened and no princely death intervened to close the theatres, the impresario could count himself fortunate."[6]

In all cases, the business of opera in Italy (and elsewhere) was often precarious and uncertain, with great demands made on the directors, even those with permanent positions, to produce a stream of new and successful works. For the courts, entertainment and celebrations provided the opportunity for more serious pieces, the forerunners of which can be found already in the Baroque Period. For the everyday impresario, however, opera had to evolve in a direction that pandered to the popular taste, and for this, historical figures, gods, and heroes could not compete with comedy. This led to a battle of the genres during the eighteenth century, which, in turn, altered both the face and the reputation of Italian opera.

Baroque Opera Versus Classical Opera: The Battle of the Genres

The main type of opera that continued into the Classical Period from the Baroque was the **opera seria**. Designed from the end of the seventeenth century as the epitome of the genre, it featured a standardized format, emphasis on the singers and their virtuoso displays, orchestral accompaniment that was often minimal so as not to interfere with the voice, a large succession of arias and recitatives, minimal purely instrumental movements and ballet, and subject matter generally drawn from Classical history or mythology, "augmented" by the addition of extraneous characters intended to expand the stories by offering intrigue and subplots. The work was generally in three acts, with the first outlining the issues of the story, the second containing the main action, and the third a happy or virtuously moral conclusion. Only the final act had every character on stage all at once in what was called the "coro ultimo" [final chorus, sung by the principal characters]. During the Baroque, opera was called *dramma per musica* or *dramma musicale*—the term *opera seria* did not appear until relatively late in the eighteenth century—and there were often comic scenes that were interpolated into the main story, interrupting the flow.

Librettists were admonished to keep the action limited, often to a period not exceeding an entire day, to present the stories with human conundrums (love vs. hate, forgiveness vs. revenge), and to handle the plot so that the ending would have a moral lesson. Tragic endings were to be avoided; if a death was to occur, then it needed to happen offstage, save if there was a battle scene. Spectacle should be subordinated to nature and more intimate human settings so that the story could take place without interruption or distraction by the locale. Finally, the dialogue was to occur in the recitatives in unrhymed verse (called *versi sciolti*) while the arias concluding each scene were to be in rhymed strophes, generally containing reflections, topical allusions, or poetic commentary. For composers, the main type of aria was the da Capo, with a central section that contrasted in terms of tempo or meter, and the return to the beginning free enough to allow for the singer to ornament the line even further. The recitatives were all *secco* (dry), accompanied only by the continuo, though occasionally there would be an *accompagnato* (accompanied), where the dialogue would be supported by additional instrumentation. The succession of arias ranged from the *continuo aria*, where the voice was accompanied only by the continuo, to the regular aria, where the full orchestra (usually strings with the occasional wind or brass instruments) could be used to fill out a brief opening ritornello.

Given that audiences in the Baroque Period attended the opera mainly to hear the singers, composers such as Alessandro Scarlatti or Giovanni Bononcini would write a huge succession of arias that had little to do with the story or the emotion being displayed in the text but, rather, more to facilitate vocal virtuosity or contrasting styles.

The castrati, whose voices were powerful and flexible, performed the main roles. In cities such as Rome, where women were often banned from the stage, they also acted in female roles, which meant that the tessituras were largely in the alto or soprano ranges for all the characters. Given that the operation caused special growth patterns, it was not uncommon for the castrati to be large and imposing. Female singers, however, were not absent, especially in places such as Venice or Milan, and many such as Bordoni gained fame equal to their male counterparts at the end of the Baroque Period.

By 1700 the need for reform had become significant, with the Arcadian Academy of Rome being at the forefront of creating standards for librettos. Their idea was to bring the texts closer to Classical Greek drama by eliminating extraneous characters and subplots from the opera. This had only a partial success, for in 1720 composer Benedetto Marcello published a brief pamphlet titled *Il teatro alla moda* (*Fashionable Theatre*) in which he savaged the stereotypes of the Baroque opera (Figure 6.6).[7] The librettist, for example, is adjured to "never have read the Greek and Roman classic authors . . . nor should he have the slightest knowledge of Italian meter and verse." Composers are admonished that "noise is what counts in modern music, not harmonious sound . . . every composer should drop the occasional remark that he writes in a popular style and violates the rules frequently only in order to satisfy his audience."[8] There are other suggestions in this satirical pamphlet for singers, impresarios ("He will demand that the singers reimburse him for any wrong notes"), orchestra ("Oboes, flutes, trumpets, bassoons, and other wind instruments should always play out of tune and produce a perpetual crescendo"), and even down to the stagehands and costumers. The result of this is not only a humorous catalogue of the state of Baroque opera; it also points out the need for reform if it is to survive.

The first focus was on the text, mainly through the efforts of Apostolo Zeno and Pietro Metastasio (Pietro Trapassi), both of whom set the standard for the opera seria text as it moved into the Classical Period. Zeno, born of Greek parents, was an early member of the Arcadian Academy, and when he was

Figure 6.6 Title page of Benedetto Marcello, *Il Teatro alla Moda* (1720, Venice)

appointed poet laureate in Vienna in 1718, he dedicated himself to eliminating some of the worst problems of the Baroque opera text. He cut all comic elements, reduced the number of characters and scenes, and made the stories more dignified and sober. Upon his return to Venice in 1729 he had already written thirty-six operas and seventeen oratorios. Emerging Classical composers Carl Heinrich Graun, Hasse, Baldassare Galuppi, and others set his works. The language was still that of the Baroque Period, but he set the stage for his successor, Mestastasio. This poet was educated in Rome, and by 1723 had written his first opera text. Poetry was simplified and made more lyrical. Metastasio continued the evolution begun by Zeno, creating a standard for his librettos that made them models for Italian opera seria for the remainder of the Classical Period. He reduced the number of arias to around twenty, with the principal singers (*prima uomo* and *prima donna*) having the most (usually four or five); the second rank, three or four each; and any of the third rank, whose characters were mentors, advisors, servants, and other extraneous people, only one or two. Ensembles were allowed for the principal characters, and special soliloquies were to be accompanied recitatives. The *Affekt* was to be varied according to the mood or circumstance, with stereotypical arias being lyrical (*aria cantabile*), amorous (*aria d'affetto*), angry (*aria di furore*), noble and virtuous (*aria di bravura*), and somewhere in between (*aria di mezzo carattere*). Although he concentrated on Greek and Roman mythology or history (and biblical stories for his oratorio texts), he was not above making additions if they enhanced the story. His approach was what we would call modular, with each recitative and aria pair self-contained to allow for the composer or singer to substitute works that were to their liking,

Figure 6.7 Title page of Francesco Algarotti, *Saggio l'opera in musica* (1755, Livorno)

that they felt more comfortable with, or that were better suited to their success. This also made it easier for the composers to do last minute substitutions if their original aria was not applauded, as the text had an inherent feeling or emotion that could be expressed in a multitude of ways.

Metastasio was perhaps the most important composer to move opera from the Baroque to the Classical, due mainly to his good poetry, attention to the needs of both the story and singer, and his Enlightenment views on the virtues. He required composers to adapt their music to the drama of the story, rather than just being a conduit for the singers to display their abilities, and he was always careful to conclude the libretto with a rational and moral lesson.[9] It is no wonder that his texts were set multiple times by composers throughout the eighteenth century.[10] Here, Baroque opera was able to transition into the Classical Period due to the reform movements of the librettists, whose work was at the foundation of opera seria from the 1730s on.

One final note on the generic differences concerns the comic opera. In Baroque opera, comic scenes were often interpolated into the opera seria. In addition, in between each of the three acts was a comic play with music called an *intermezzo*. These featured stock characters from the commedia dell'arte tradition, usually with only two or three characters. The stories were largely drawn from improvised comedy, and these were generally performed by a smaller orchestra (mostly strings) and voices that were not on the professional level as the main opera seria. Voice types were more natural, especially in the use of the bass, and the settings were almost always domestic. The intermezzo was used only sporadically in Italian opera until the 1720s, when in Naples and Venice it began to become independent of the main opera seria. Composers such as Domenico Sarro, Hasse, and Giuseppe Sellitto all became known for their short works, but it was Pergolesi's *La serva padrona*, in which a clever maid succeeds in hoodwinking her older employer into marrying her, that achieved international recognition. As Baroque opera began to eliminate the often-raucous comic element from the serious opera, the intermezzo was a halfway house toward developing the comic opera as a genre all its own. As the Classical Period emerged, audiences found the combination of sight gags, familiar domestic situations, improvised comedy, and simple music to their taste, for it provided no illusions of musical development or relied upon the prowess of the singers. As a result, it emerged out of the Baroque opera into its own genre.

Opera in Italy: Old Versus New, Local Versus International

Around 1730 Italian opera had begun to evolve on all fronts. Opera seria still maintained the overall format and structure of the Baroque opera, but it had begun to develop through the reform efforts of poets such as Zeno and Metastasio. By making the texts more standardized and offering composers a variety of good poetry that included opportunities for vocal and emotional display, they extended the life of a genre that had been criticized by many for its stereotypes. Both composers and singers appreciated the new flexibility that allowed for works to be revised quickly and efficiently to take into account popular tastes and the ability of the performers. As this decade progressed, the orchestration also became more attuned to the developing Classical Period orchestra, and as the range of instrumental color supporting the voices increased, so did the need for subgenres such as arias to expand. This often came at the expense of the B section in the da Capo aria, which became less important, and by 1750 was largely seen as anachronistic. Although setting opera seria did not vanish, many of the newer compositions thereafter were less repertory pieces than works done for special occasions at noble courts, such as *Ruggiero* noted earlier. Burney, on the other hand, noted that in 1771 Venice could boast at Carnival time seven opera houses, of which two performed serious opera, and "these were all crowded every night."[11] This indicates that the opera seria in Italy still maintained its stature and popularity, though he does not elaborate on whether the audiences actually liked the works presented or were simply there to be seen socially. Burney later visited Rome and Naples, where in the last city the Teatro San Carlo, the Imperial opera house, was the only place that still produced the opera seria. There he saw Jommelli's *Demofoonte*, the opera of the season, which had as its lead the aging castrato Giuseppe Aprile. He was pleased enough with the performance to state: "Singers such as these were necessary for the music, which is in a difficult style; more full of instrumental effects than vocal."[12] Joseph Martin Kraus, writing over a decade later, was less than complimentary:

> The opera seria this year is called *Adone et Venere* by Pugnani . . . on the whole the music is very mediocre, and the orchestra about which there has been so much noise pitiful; the few women who are debuting in it are nothing but sinners who desire to desecrate coloratura in their autumn days.[13]

It would thus seem that this genre became less popular in Italy as the century progressed, and while the librettos by Metastasio and his followers were set repeatedly, the requirements for composers warred with the need to be current; even providing more ensemble numbers or extended finales did not solve the problem.

Reforms of serious Italian opera were undertaken periodically throughout the century. Neapolitan composer Jommelli and Tommaso Traetta began in the 1760s to insert more movements for the chorus and ballet, taking their cue from the preference of the courts for French grand opera, and both composers made their solo arias less virtuoso and more effective through dynamic contrasts and colorful orchestration of the sort that Burney noted. It was, however, the Venetian nobleman and intellectual Count Francesco Algarotti who in 1755 published his treatise *Saggio sopra L'opera in musica* (*Essay on Opera in Music*). Algarotti, who had observed the opera seria internationally during his sojourns in Berlin, Vienna, and throughout Italy, approached the issues of serious opera from all points of view (Figure 6.7). He had some admonitions for each of the principal parts of the work. He believed firmly that a new cooperation was necessary to reform it for the future. His principal comments are directed toward the librettist and composer, but a general statement reflects his proposals: "Regarding the theatre, a due discipline should regularly be reflected in the different parts that form the opera so that each can have a hand in altering it as needed."[14] He notes that the composer behaves "tyrannically," overwhelming the poetry, so that "people who are dying sing something that has no origins in the text but rather in the harmony, which is laughable." Therefore, Algarotti proposed that "the greater effect of the music comes from the words." He further claimed that a work should "delight the eyes and ears, to arouse and affect the hearts of an audience, without the risk of sinning against reason or common sense."[15] This concept of music being subordinated to the feelings and actions expressed in the libretto gained little traction in Italy, where the conventions of opera seria still remained strong, but in Vienna, two men, Ranieri di Calzabigi and Gluck, met with the intendant of the opera, Giacomo Durazzo; the choreographer Gasparo Angiolini and the set designer Giovanni Maria Quaglio to create a work that would serve as a model for the reforms Algarotti outlined. The first work was a *ballet d'action* (dramatic ballet) titled *Don Juan*, which demonstrated that pantomime could be put to dramatic use instead of conventional stereotypical court dances. When this was premiered in 1761, it caused a sensation, further encouraging Gluck and Calzabigi to complete their test piece, *Orfeo ed Euridice*. When it was premiered at the Viennese Burgtheater the following year, it, too, was successful, and it encouraged both men to create a new work completely in the reform style. *Alceste* appeared in 1767 and when the score was published two years later, it contained a succinct overview of how both conceived of opera reform (see Document 3).

Unlike the well-known tale of Orpheus, *Alceste* was a new work, with the story of the King of Thessaly, Admete, being saved from death by the sacrifice of his wife (Alceste), who offers to perish in his stead. When he learns of her willingness, he is horrified, but the gods will not be denied. At the moment of sacrifice, however, Apollo descends and pardons both as a reward for their faithfulness. While it remains a story rooted in classical Greece, the use of emotional language, a chorus that participates in the action, and a plot that is both logical and conforms to the original story all combined to demonstrate that opera seria could evolve. The reforms limited the recitative and virtuosity of the arias, replacing them with succinct and dramatically inspired works colorfully outlined by Gluck's expanded orchestral palette. Ballets were incorporated within the story at the appropriate places, and the overture was reduced to a single movement that led directly into the first act without pause. It integrated the opera without altering its Classical or historical origins, as well as providing composers with opportunities to write more expressive works. Without these reforms, operas such as Mozart's *Idomeneo* from 1781 would not have been commissioned.

Even the reform works of Gluck and his successors such as Mozart and Antonio Salieri, whose *Axur, Re d'Ormus* from 1787, could not stem the decline in opera seria during the last two decades of the century. Metastasio's texts continued to be composed for both cities and courts (such as Mozart's opera *La clemenza di Tito* composed for the coronation of Leopold II in Prague in 1792). Audiences were less interested in the succession of arias, and with the rise of political events such as the French Revolution, they were more inclined to either escapist operas or works that were more contemporary historically. Also, the role of the castrato declined in proportion to the number of singers, and with the preference for natural voices, the need for conventional opera seria roles made it less viable economically. Finally, neither the continual virtuosity demanded of the da capo aria nor the story lines of the Metastasian opera held any long-term appeal, and by 1800 Italian opera seria, as it was defined at the beginning of the Classical Period, had all but vanished from the stage.

Part of the reason for the decline in popularity of the opera seria was the rise of the **opera buffa**, or comic opera. Although comic operas had been occasionally produced during the Baroque Period, comedy was usually limited to the two-act *Intermezzo* by about 1730. These short, pithy depictions of stock situations drawn from the commedia dell'arte were accessible and, as has already been noted, required little in the way of professional preparation. One work, Pergolesi's *La serva padrona* from 1733, became an instant success following its premiere as an entr'acte to the composer's opera seria *Il prigioniero superbo*. Not only did it become part of the permanent Neapolitan repertory as a work on its own merits, it was also exported internationally throughout the continent and as far away as England and Russia. The music was considered tuneful, the plot easy to follow, the acting filled with pratfalls and simple comic gestures. Two decades after its premiere it even caused a sensation in Paris when the traveling troupe of Eustachio Bambini produced it at a fair theatre, eliciting responses that have become known as the Querelle des Bouffons (War of the Buffoons; see Chapter 7).

It also served as a model for an expanded version, the opera buffa, which retained the two-act format, though it was occasionally in three, with the third act a short conclusion. It began to emerge from the intermezzo around 1730, when Naples needed popular opera for the lesser theatres in the city, such as the Teatro dei Fiorentini. The plots were supposed to show everyday domestic life, with characters that were recognizable to the audiences: the lovers, the wily servants, the pompous merchants or lesser noblemen, the imperious maids, or other extraneous people who would be recognized. The operas used natural voices, though some could have cross-dressing roles, and the music was calculated to be lyrical and filled with stereotypical musical effects. Instead of a succession of arias that demonstrated vocal virtuosity, the opera buffa contained duets, trios, and other ensemble numbers in which the blend of voices enhanced the storyline.

Texts for the opera buffa were written with comic effect at the forefront, and the situations often involved elaborate and sometimes even nonsensical schemes. For example, the text of the popular work *Il mondo della luna* (*The World on the Moon*), written in 1750 in Venice by author Carlo Goldoni for Baldassare Galuppi, satirizes the eighteenth-century mania for scientific discovery. A charlatan astronomer (Ecclitico) wishes to convince the fool Bonafede of his "discovery" of a world on the moon, a ruse that he has concocted with his friend Ernesto to marry Bonafede's two daughters. The two women, Clarice and Flaminia, chafe under their father's stifling restrictions and are let in on the scheme. Ecclitico claims that he has been invited by the emperor of the moon and allows Bonafede to accompany him by drinking a special potion. He awakens in a garden, which is another room in his house disguised to represent the moon. Ecclitico's servant Cecco (in love with Bonafede's maid Lisetta) plays the emperor, and thanks to his clever manipulation, all three of the pairs are married before Bonafede realizes he has been hoodwinked. A clever romp, it contains a bit of exoticism, a social commentary on the mores of the day, the gullibility of the old tyrant, and both disguise and playacting (Figure 6.8). While there is a nod to the commedia dell'arte, the elaborate scheme and its inevitable conclusion were both entertaining and instructive, even as the situation comedy developed.[16]

By 1735, the opera buffa had spread to Rome, where composers Gaetano Latilla and Rinaldo d Capua wrote works that soon established the city as an opera center. Because women were not allowed on stage, younger castrati were recruited to perform the female roles, but within a year, traveling troupes began to export the newly developing genre throughout Italy. Latilla's *La finta cameriera* (*The Pretended Chambermaid*) was one of the first perennially popular works, its plot of transvestite disguises, a fop (Don Calascione, "an idiot who outdoes himself with idiocy"), and a scheming servant made it almost as popular as *La serva padrona*. After its premiere in Venice in 1743, both the Teatri San Moisé and the Teatro San Cassiano became the central performance venues of this genre, now expanded considerably into a full evening. By 1745, Galuppi had entered the lists as a composer of opera buffa, and with the literary genius of comic playwright Carlo Goldoni in residence, Venice soon rivaled Naples as the locus for opera buffa.

Initially, the music of the opera buffa was simple and lyrical enough to appeal to the most common of audiences, and the orchestration was likewise reduced, often to strings in unison. Recitatives were still used, but in moderation and with no other intent than to facilitate the action. Indeed, even the singers would occasionally dance as they sang, providing a more active role than the characters in opera seria. In the early period, the arias were still successive and ensemble numbers rare. Goldoni, however, seems to have used his own comic plays as a model by developing the so-called chain finale or *lieto fine*. Here, all the foibles and

The Structure and Meaning of Italian Opera 139

Figure 6.8 Eighteenth-century engraving of Goldoni's *Il mondo della luna* (*ca.* 1760)

machinations of the work are revealed and resolved in a succession of sections from slow and lyrical to a final chorus in the fastest tempo possible (known as the *più stretto*). He also enlivened the often-tortuous plots with ensemble numbers, which by 1750 had become the norm for the opera buffa. While his own colleague Galuppi and Nicola Logroscino of Naples are credited with the first of these developments—Logroscino (Figure 6.9) was called "*Il Dio del'opera buffa*" (The God of Opera Buffa) for his work titled *L'inganno per inganno* (*Deception Through Deceit*) in 1738—by 1755 it had become a stereotype necessity. This, in turn, led to a succession of works by composers whose fame spread internationally: Pasquale Anfossi, Paisiello, Domenico Cimarosa, Francesco Bianchi, Pietro Guglielmi, Sarti, Niccolò Piccinni, Jommelli, and numerous others. Given that the entertainment value was always high, that positive audience reception was almost guaranteed, and that actor-singers with no pretense to virtuoso skills could perform the music (though many had them), the opera buffa from 1765 to the end of the century became the Italian opera's most visible product. While numerous theorists denounced the absurdity of the plots, the musical stereotypes, and the portrayal of characters in their absurd human condition, the public throughout Europe was drawn to the pure entertainment value of the genre.

The opera buffa resisted change during the last portion of the eighteenth century in its original form, but there were efforts to upgrade its content beyond simple comedy. The first of these seems to have occurred as early as 1749, when Goldoni and Galuppi produced their opera *Il conte Caramella* (*Count Caramel*) in which the characters were redefined as comic (*buffi*), serious (*seri*), and semi-serious (*mezzi*), allowing for a greater musical style to be written than pure comic movements. This was expanded even further in 1760 by Piccinni's *La buona figliuola* (*The Good-Natured Girl*), derived from Samuel Richardson's novel *Pamela*, and in 1789 by Paisiello's *Nina, ossia La pazza per amore* (*Nina, or The Woman Insane with Love*). Both can be seen as introducing sentimentality into Italian opera, something Paisiello termed *opera semiseria*.[17] Another subgenre was the *dramma giocoso* or tragicomedy, in which the plot wavered uncertainly between drama and comedy. The bulk of the text here is a farce, but there are elements of drama and a dramatic conclusion that blur the boundaries between them. It, too, was created by Goldoni as early as 1750, with the best-known examples the two Don Giovanni operas by Giuseppe Gazzaniga and Wolfgang Amadeus Mozart.

By the end of the eighteenth century, opera buffa all but dominated Italian opera both in Italy and throughout the rest of Europe, from Spain to Russia. Audiences, no matter what their nationality, applauded

Figure 6.9 Caricature of Nicola Logroschino conducting from the keyboard by Pier Leone Ghezzi (1753, Venice)

the musical expectations of a colorful orchestration (full-bodied and filled with lush harmonies), stereotyped arias and ensembles (with such things as patter arias, foreign accents, and rapid tempo and dynamic changes), single-movement overtures, and lively recitative dialogue. Opera seria could not compete with the liveliness and was seen as hopelessly old-fashioned, while the intermezzo, no longer needed to fill in between the acts of the seria, had been reduced to parodies or satires on opera practices themselves.[18] While Italian opera dominated the field, it was not without rivals, however. As it spread throughout Europe, operas in other languages soon took up the challenge of competing against it either by imitation or through the creation of their own opera culture.

Documents

Document 1. From Jean-Jacques Rousseau, *Lettre sur la musique française* (Paris, 1753).

Three things seem to me to unite in contributing to the perfection of Italian melody. The first is the softness of the language, which makes all the inflections easy and leaves the taste of the musician free to make a more exquisite choice among them, to give a greater variety to his combinations, and to provide each singer with a particular style of singing, so that each man has the character and tone which are proper to him and distinguish him from other men.

The second is the boldness of the modulations, which, although less servilely prepared than our own, are much more pleasing from being made more perceptible, and without imparting any harshness to the song, add a lively energy to the expression. It is by this means that the musician, passing abruptly from one key or mode to another, and suppressing, when necessary, the intermediate and pedantic transitions, is able to express the reticence, the interruptions, the falterings, which are the language of impetuous passion so often employed by the ardent Metastasio, which a Porpora, a Galuppi, a Cocchi, a Jommelli, a Perez, a Terradellas have so often successfully reproduced, and of which our lyric poets know as little as do our musicians.

The third advantage, the one which gives to melody its greatest effect, is the extreme exactness of time which is felt in the slowest as well as in the liveliest movements, an exactness which makes the singing animated and interesting, the accompaniments lively and rhythmical; which really multiplies the tunes by making as many different melodies out of single combination of sounds as there are ways of scanning them; which conveys every sentiment to the heart and every picture to the mind; which enables the musician to express in his air all the imaginable characters of the words, many of which we have no idea; and which renders all the movements proper to express all of the characters, or at the will of the composer renders a single movement proper to contrast and change the character. These, in my opinion, are the sources from which Italian music derives its charms and its energy.... It is by the aide of these scientific modulations, of this simple and pure harmony, of these lively and brilliant accompaniments that their divine performances harrow or enrapture the soul, carry away the spectator, and force him, in his ecstasy, the cries with which our placid operas were never honored.

Document 2. Johann Joachim Quantz, *On Playing the Flute* (Berlin, 1752), Section 71.

If an Italian opera, or one arranged in the Italian manner, is to please everyone, and is to be held a most agreeable spectacle, it must have the following characteristics. The poet must choose a good subject, and treat it with all possible verisimilitude. He must clearly distinguish the characters of the persons represented from each other, and adjust them as much as possible to the capacities, ages, temperaments, and mien of the singers. He must make each speak in a manner suitable to the character her represents. The recitatives must not be too extended, and the words of the arias must be neither too long nor too bombastic. From time to time some similes should be introduced that may be conveniently expressed in music, and these should be chiefly and necessarily from the language of the passions. The passions must be varied in an adroit manner, both with respect to the augmentation and diminution of their force, and with respect to general diversity. Convenient forms of verse must be chosen for the arias. Reasonable care must be taken to employ words especially suitable for singing, and to avoid as much as possible those that are unsuitable. The composer must have refined taste, and the capacity to express the passions in accordance with the words. He must, without partiality, give each singer the role which accords with his strong points. He must join everything together with the proper coherence, and at the same time observe a suitable brevity. The singers must perform their roles seriously and diligently, in accordance with the characters to be represented, and the intentions of the composer. The accompanists must fulfill the prescriptions of the composer, and discharge their duties properly. Finally, the décor and the ballets must accord well with the content of the opera.

Document 3. Christoph Willibald von Gluck, Preface to *Alceste* (Vienna, 1769).

When I undertook to write the music for *Alceste*, I resolved to divest it entirely of all those abuses, introduced into it either by the mistaken vanity of singers or by the too great complaisance of composers, which have so long disfigured Italian opera and made of the most splendid and most beautiful of spectacles the most ridiculous and wearisome. I have striven to restrict music to its true office of serving poetry, without interrupting the action or stifling it with a useless superfluity of ornaments; and I believed that it should do this in the same way as telling colors affect a correct and well-ordered drawing, but a well-assorted contrast of light and shade, which serves to animate the figures without altering their contours. Thus I did not wish to arrest an actor in the greatest heat of dialogue in order to wait for a tiresome ritornello, nor to hold him up in the middle of a word on a vowel favorable to his voice, nor to make display of the agility of his fine voice in some long-drawn-out passage, nor to wait while the orchestra gives him time to recover his breath for a cadenza. I did not think it my duty to pass quickly over the second section of an aria of which the words are perhaps the most impassioned and important, in order to repeat regularly four time over those of the first part, and to finish the aria where its sense may perhaps not end for the convenience of the singer who wishes to show that he can capriciously vary a passage in a number of guises; in short, I have sought to abolish all the abuses against which good sense and reason have long cried out in vain.

I have felt that the overture ought to apprise the spectators of the nature of the action that is to be represented and to form, so to speak, its argument; that the concerted instruments should be introduced in proportion to the interest and intensity of the words, and not leave that sharp contrast between the aria and recitative in the dialogue, so as not to break a period unreasonably nor wantonly disturb the force and heat of the action.

Furthermore, I believed that my greatest labor should be devoted to seeking a beautiful simplicity, and I have avoided making displays of difficulty at the expense of clarity; nor did I judge it desirable to discover novelties if it was not naturally suggested by the situation and the expression; and there is no rule which I have not thought it right to set aside willingly for the sake of an intended effect. Such are my principles.

Notes

1. Quantz, *On Playing the Flute*, 327–328. He also notes, "Whatever the case may be, good singing style, which extends to a certain extent even to their gondoliers, remains peculiar to the Italians above all other peoples."
2. Quantz, *On Playing the Flute*, 331–332.
3. John Rosselli, *The Opera Industry in Italy from Cimarosa to Verdi* (Cambridge: Cambridge University Press, 1984), 7–8.
4. The real name of the theatre was the Teatro San Benedetto and was operated by the Gimani family after it was built on the site of a former Baroque Period theatre in 1755. Subsequent owners of the theatre included a foundation formed from season box holders and then in 1787 the Venier family, which operated it on into the nineteenth century.
5. See William Mann, *The Operas of Mozart* (New York: Oxford University Press, 1977), 75, 109–110.
6. Rosselli, *The Opera Industry*, 11.
7. Benedetto Marcello, *Il teatro alla moda* (Venice, 1720); English translation by Reinhard Pauly, *Musical Quarterly* 34 (1948) and 35 (1949). The English quotes are from this translation.
8. Benedetto Marcello, *Il Teatro alla moda* (Milan, 1720), 5, 14.
9. The only exception is his text for *Didone abbandonata* from 1724, where the heroine dies on stage at the end instead of being rescued by a deus ex machine or the more common reconciliation. The reason for this was the story itself, where the conclusion was her suicide following her abandonment by Aeneas. Other opera texts on the subject, such as Marmontel's *Didone*, simply add a scene where she is received by Jupiter as a goddess, though this was not entirely satisfactory or would have been permissible in Italian opera. *Didone* was set by composers seventy

times, being eclipsed in popularity by only two of his other texts, *Demofoonte* and *Allesandro nell'Indie*, both of which were composed seventy-five times.
10 Metastasio printed no fewer than sixty-five of his texts for composers to set, which they did up through the beginning of the nineteenth century.
11 Burney, *The Present State of Music in France and Italy*, 151.
12 Burney, *The Present State of Music in France and Italy*, 340. He also notes that for his visit, coinciding with the first rehearsal, there was a substantial audience: "the pit was crowded, and many of the boxes were filled with the families of persons of condition."
13 van Boer, *The Musical Life of Joseph Martin Kraus*, 194. He also heard Aprile, noting that "he pipes a little something to Dear God with his little voice each day."
14 Francesco Algarotti, *Saggio sopra l'opera in musica* (Florence, 1755), 18.
15 Algarotti, *Saggio*, 19.
16 The text was set by several composers, including Joseph Haydn, Giovanni Paisiello, and Gennaro Astarita.
17 In a change that was significant, *Nina* was derived from a French original by Nicolas Dalayrac from 1786, perhaps one of the first times that a French opéra comique made the transition to an Italian opera buffa.
18 These were usually comments on the foibles of producing opera in the Classical Period. For example, Domenico Scarlatti's *La Dirindina* has a conniving young soprano using a castrato to outwit her lecherous music teacher, while Cimarosa's *Il maestro di cappella* has an inept conductor and would-be composer attempting a rehearsal. The most famous is Mozart's *Der Schauspieldirektor* (technically a Singspiel), in which an impresario has to mediate between rival sopranos, while its companion work by Antonio Salieri, *Prima la musica e poi la parole*, introduces a squabble between composer and librettist.

7 Opera in France, Germany, and Elsewhere
Escaping the Past for an Exotic Future

Opera in Italy may have been the dominant type of this genre during the Classical Period, but as in the Baroque, opera in other languages flourished in other guises. It was not just a matter of court preferences, but rather, opera was the main attraction that both courts and cities coveted in establishing their reputations. Moreover, opera was a mirror of life even in the far-flung regions of the globe, where it was one of the first genres to be established in the colonies and, in the case of the United States, newly independent countries.

In all these places, opera took on a role that transcended style to include political statements, lavish spectacle, and progressive musical attributes that were important in progressive musical development. A variety of types coexisted, serving both the courts and countries with the means of international recognition, even as many of the composers were hired across national boundaries to compose works that were meant for local audiences. Singers, too, migrated, often settling in foreign lands, where they achieved recognition for their musical prowess.

In this chapter, we explore the operatic world of the Classical Period beyond the dominant Italian opera, with special attention to venues, styles, and occasionally both composers and performers who ensured that the genre was highly internationalized, regardless of its origins or language.

Opera in France: From Lully to Gluck and Beyond: Crisis, Controversy, and Social Commentary

As the Classical Period began to emerge from the Baroque, opera in France was at a crossroads. The brilliant but autocratic court of Louis XIV, in which the musical dictatorship of Jean Baptiste Lully dominated, resulted in a magnificent spectacle, in which music, drama, and dance were fully integrated. While Lully had passed away in 1687, his successors adhered to the basic style and format—five acts plus prologue, with good texts drawn from classical history and literature, as well as a mixture of tableau, choruses, and ballet—without change. By the 1730s, the court of Louis XV became dominated by the king's mistress, Madame de Pompadour, at whose palace in Fontainebleau a private theatre had been erected. Leading composers of the time, including Jean-Philippe Rameau, were persuaded to premiere their conservative works there before presentation at one of the Parisian performance venues (Figure 7.1). Success meant royal support, but this was not always granted without substantial revisions to any given work to ensure its public success.

As before, the genre of the **opera lyrique** (also known as the **tragédie lyrique**) required a static style of music. Given the assumed limitations of the French language, long lyrical arias were rare, and the bulk of the works consisted of accompanied recitative that merged into arioso that subsequently ended with sung airs, liberally interwoven with choruses and ballet. Originally, the last was done in order that the King could participate, but by the early Classical Period, it was usually left to professional dance troupes. Indeed, one of the hallmarks of this style of opera was the **Divertissement** that concluded the work. It consisted of a series of dances, finishing with a lengthy *passacaille* or *chaconne*. Little action in the plots was necessary, but the music could become quite descriptive. It was not infrequent that exotic settings were displayed, replete with unusual costumes and music.

Figure 7.1 Stage of the Théâtre de Fontainebleau (1740, eighteenth-century engraving)

One of the most performed of Rameau's operas was *Dardanus*, which initially was received with mediocre reviews in 1739. The composer revised it in 1744, but only on its revival in 1760 did it achieve a popular success. The work surrounds King Dardanus, who falls in love with the daughter of his enemy, King Teucer, thanks to the intervention by a magician (Figure 7.2), and ultimately saves her father from a sea monster. It was a grand spectacle, replete with magical effects, exotic characters, and musical depictions with colorful orchestration. The latter inspired Pierre-Louis D'Aquin de Châteaulyon to remark: "Take away the words, and the music no less expresses the accents of suffering and the rigors of a cruel prison. You can change nothing, add nothing, everything is in its place. This is genuine music."[1]

Although works like *Dardanus* held the stage at the Opéra for the next ten years, there was a clear need for this genre to be revitalized. This came in the form of a commission to Holy Roman *Kapellmeister* Christoph Willibald von Gluck in 1770 for a number of works. Marie Antoinette, a Hapsburg princess and now soon to be Queen of France, had arranged this. She had learned of the reforms that Gluck had been part of in Vienna since 1761 and saw in him a composer who would not be beholden to the traditions of the older genres. The first work was *Iphigénie en Aulide* with a text by François-Louis Gand Le Bland Du Roullet, which had its premiere on April 19, 1774. Based on a play by Racine, it both harkened back to the older traditions of Lully and Rameau but contained a more integrated plot that emphasized human emotions, giving life to the Greek story. Particularly effective was the solemn overture, which led directly into the first

Figure 7.2 Costume design for the magician in *Dardanus* by Jean-Philippe Rameau (1744, Paris)

scene of the opera. More controversial, however, was the final monophonic chorus following the traditional celebratory one and divertissement in which the austere orchestration punctuated by a bass drum evokes the savagery of the Trojan War about to begin (Example 7.1). Gluck's subsequent operas included revisions of his *Orfeo* and *Alceste*, as well as a new work *Armide* in 1777. At this time, the Académie de Musique, possibly at the request of Marie Antoinette, brought Italian composer Niccolò Piccinni to Paris, pairing him with Jean-François Marmontel, to write operas in an artificial rivalry with Gluck. His first work, *Roland*, which premiered at the Academy on January 27, 1778, had the effect of dividing audiences between the two composers, artificially creating what has become known as the Gluck–Piccinni controversy. American envoy Benjamin Franklin noted that Parisian audiences became almost viciously partisan, often eliciting the greeting in the streets of "Sir, are you a Gluckist or Piccinnist?" In 1779 both composers were commissioned to set Nicholas-François Guillard's sequel to *Iphigénie en Aulide* (titled *Iphigénie en Tauride*), and the performances of both works, Gluck's in May 1779 and Piccinni's in January 1781, presented a comparison that audiences agreed favored the German.

Despite the partisanship of their adherents, both Gluck and Piccinni remained on relatively cordial terms, and after Gluck left Paris in 1780, Piccinni remained a solid supporter. This stopped the rivalry, but several

Example 7.1 Christoph Willibald von Gluck, *Iphigénie en Aulide*, Act III, Final Chorus, mm. 1–6

attempts were made to reinvigorate it. Marie Antoinette invited Piccinni's compatriot Antonio Sacchini to work in Paris under her protection. Sacchini had been a visitor to the city during the height of the Gluck–Piccinni controversy, and each side thought that his music would support his cause. The first work, *Renaud*, was performed in February 1783, and the resultant criticism demonstrated that neither faction was supportive. The Piccinnist considered it a Gluck clone, while the Gluckists found it too Italian. In the meantime, Gluck was allegedly working on an opera, *Les Danaïdes*, but both the failure of his flaccid *Echo et Narcisse* in 1780 and the aftereffects of a stroke left him with little desire or will to fulfill the commission, and thus, he received permission for Antonio Salieri to help him. The work was completed and performed on April 24, 1784, with great success; it was to become one of the main forerunners of the grand operas of the nineteenth century at the Opéra. Sacchini's final work, *Oedipe à Colonne*, was a failure at first, though following the death of the composer it was revived successfully.

The French grand opera, however, had to compete in popularity with comic opera, even though the French aristocracy heavily supported it. This genre was called the **opéra comique**, and initially it had been created in an attempt to define a French form of the Italian intermezzo. The War of the Buffoons had been started because of the contrasts that had been created in 1752 when Pergolesi's *La serva padrona* was performed by an Italian troupe at the Académie royale. Shortly thereafter Rousseau premiered his work *Le Devin du village* (*The Village Magician*) at Fontainebleau and within a short span of time, the polemics began between the adherents of French and those of Italian music. Rousseau himself noted,

> I believe to have been made to see that there is neither measure nor tunefulness in French music, because the language is not sensible; that French singing is only continual barking, insupportable for all unprejudiced ears; that the harmony is brutal, without expression and feeling uniquely like the cobbling of a schoolboy; that French airs are not airs; that French recitatives are not recitatives. Thus, I must conclude that the French have and can have no music; or that if ever they acquire one, it would be so much the worse for them.[2]

Rousseau's work was meant to "Italianize" and simplify the French comic or pastoral opera but was not intended by its composer to be a model. He noted to visiting German author Christian Felix Weisse in 1759, "It is a bagatelle, which I only did to see what beasts the French are, and to allow them to taste a wretched dish."[3]

148 Opera! Popular, Nationalist, Exotic Entertainment

Figure 7.3 Copper engraving of a performance at the Foire St. Laurent (*ca.* 1770)

Regardless of the debate, comic operas in French continued to be written and performed in such venues as the fair theatres at St. Germain and St. Laurent (Figure 7.3). These were originally intended as theatrical entertainment for agricultural fairs held during the early spring and late summer. The theatre at St. Germain was in a covered building, while the St. Laurent, which took on the air of a flea market, was held outdoors. Both performed comic operas under the auspices of the Opéra-Comique, and by 1743 Charles Simon Favart (Figure 7.4) had been hired by the impresario, Jean Monnet, to write pieces for both stages. His first important work following the Querelle des Bouffons was *Les troqueurs* (*The Tradesmen*), which premiered in July 1753 to music by Antoine Dauvergne. It had been advertised as a "translation" from the Italian but was actually one of the first of a series of popular works that became popular successes. This was followed by *Le Diable à quatre* in 1756, which was a French adaptation of the English ballad opera *The Devil to Pay*. Favart's arrangement, for which Pierre Baurans assembled music in pasticcio fashion, was an instant success, and several composers, including Gluck, wrote original scores as the text was spread abroad. Perhaps the most important of the early works was Favart's *Soliman II, ou Les trois sultanes* (*Soliman II or The Three Sultanas*) in 1761. The story revolves around the vying of three harem women (a Circassian, a Spaniard, and a Frenchwoman) for the hand of Sultan Soliman II. The former woos him with her song,

Figure 7.4 Engraving of a portrait of Charles Simon Favart (*ca.* 1760)

the second with her dance, but the winner of the contest is Roxelane, the Frenchwoman, who cajoles him through her stubbornness and force of character. Paul Gibert composed the music, but what drew audiences was the sets and costumes imported from Constantinople and the vivacious choreography of a new ballet master, Jean-Georges Noverre. Other works that attained international popularity were *Ninette à la cour*, *Annette et Lubin*, and *La Rosière de Salency*, with music by a stable of composers including Egidio Duni, François-André Danican Philidor, and Pierre-Alexandre Monsigny.

The fair theatres were limited venues in terms of their productions, and the music was intended to be sung by actors and actresses who were not professionals. The tunes were simple and memorable, with the bulk of the music being short strophic *ariettes*, accompanied mostly by strings (with the occasional woodwinds and horns, depending on the mood). All the dialogue was spoken, and the choruses were usually made up of the cast alone. Duets and ensemble numbers began to appear more frequently, as these indicated the continuation of the dialogues, and at the conclusion a popular finale called the *vaudeville* appeared. In this each character sings a strophe followed by a choral refrain.

In 1762, when the theatre at St. Germain fell victim to fire, the Opéra-Comique merged with the Comédie-Italienne and moved to a new building called the Hôtel de Bourgogne, which had a larger stage and orchestra pit, as well as room that increased audience access by providing three rows of boxes and seating on the main floor. Although the St. Germain theatre was rebuilt the following year, the new facility became the central venue that allowed for substantially larger performances to be mounted (Figure 7.5). Although called the "Italian" comedy (and known as the Théâtre Italien), the repertoire became much more internationalized, with an emphasis on new works by French composers being produced alongside older favorites.

The pieces began to evolve from simple pastoral plots to more adventurous and contemporary stories. The first success of Belgian composer André-Ernest-Modest Grétry, *Le Huron* from 1768, for example, features the cross-cultural relationship between a girl from Brittany and a man raised in New France by

Figure 7.5 Engraving of the stage interior of the Théâtre Italien (1765)

the Huron indians. His most popular opera, *Lucille*, was produced the following year. This was called a **comédie mêlée d'ariettes** (comedy strewn with little arias), meaning that the dialogue was spoken, but it was interspersed with songs, for which Grétry wrote a substantially expanded score that features colorful orchestral effects, has no lengthy repetitions of themes, and avoids virtuoso display for the singers. These were now trained both as actors and singers, removing the last vestige of amateurism from the comic opera. Grétry also rescored some of the earlier works, producing his own version of *La Rosière*, but his most important contribution to the field came in the form of exotic operas such as *Zémire et Azor* from 1771. This work was called a **comédie-ballet mêlée de chants et de danses** (comedy-ballet strewn with songs and dances) and was based on a tale we now know as *Beauty and the Beast*. This work, with its tale of magical transformation, its exotic costumes (Figure 7.6), and its powerful score, became an international success,

Figure 7.6 Engraving from André-Ernest-Modest Grétry, *Zémire et Azor* (1771, Paris)

being performed as far away as Russia and Sweden over the next several years. It also became one of the forerunners of a subgenre of the comic opera known as the **rescue opera**. This type of work features a hero or heroine forced into an untenable situation but who is rescued through adventure and luck. Grétry's *Richard Cœur de lion* (*Richard the Lionheart*) from 1784 relates the story of King Richard, who is held for ransom by an evil governor, Florestan. His faithful troubadour, Blondel, recognizes his song and, with the help of Countess Marguerite, frees the king and turns the tables on the governor. Musical innovations in this work include adding a section of chorus to the overture and imitating a medieval song.

In 1782 the Comédie-Italienne was renamed the Opéra-Comique again, and it moved into a new building called the Salon Favart. Here it would remain until late in the nineteenth century. In 1786 a new composer, François Dalayrac, premiered his opera *Nina, ou La folle par amour* (*Nina, or The Woman Insane with Love*), representing a new generation of French comic opera composers. An instant success that soon achieved popularity outside France, the work demonstrates both a lyrical style of vocal writing and a colorful orchestration.

By the time of the French Revolution in 1789, a third competing theatre had emerged in Paris. This was the Théâtre de Monsieur, founded in January of that year by the Duke of Provence (later Louis XVIII, the brother of Louis XVI). Initially it was meant to produce plays at the Tuileries Palace, but within a few months it had moved due to civic unrest to the St. Germain Fair and subsequently to a new building in 1791, when it was renamed the Théâtre Feydeau (Figure 7.7). Its first musical director was Luigi Cherubini, an Italian who had already begun to make a name for himself as a composer of dramatic operas. The initial repertory of the theatre was a mixture of Italian opera buffa, French comic opera, plays, pasticcios, and nontheatrical events such as public concerts of instrumental music. In 1791 the new directorate abolished all royal theatrical privileges, and Paris was soon awash in new venues, many of which were meant to support the revolution (as well as provide income during times of economic difficulties). The Théâtre Feydeau, therefore, had to focus its productions on works that would be both appealing and yet avoid political controversy. The rescue opera was a perfect choice for this, and in 1791 Cherubini produced his *Lodoïska*, set in Poland. The success of this work was due to the excellence of the orchestra and singers, the realistic sets, and the subject matter, which appealed symbolically to the citizens of Paris. Although Cherubini continued to produce Italian opera buffa, he also encouraged a new generation of French composers, Jean-François Le Sueur, François Devienne, and Pierre Gaveaux, to compose works that would establish the Théâtre Feydeau as the main opera house in the city. In 1801 Napoleon revoked the right to establish theatres willy-nilly, but the Théâtre Feydeau was confirmed as one of the four official Parisian operatic establishments.

Both Cherubini and LeSeur were later to become well known for their pedagogical work at the Conservatoire, but they also mentored a new generation of opera composers into the Romantic Period, whose works and popularity continued to place French opera at the international forefront. These include the dramatic composer Etienne Méhul and François-Adrien Boieldieu, whose 1800 opera *Le calife de Bagdad* became both a connection between the old Turkish opera and a new exotic style with tales drawn from *A Thousand and One Nights*.

Figure 7.7 Engraving of the Théâtre Feydeau (1790, Paris)

152 *Opera! Popular, Nationalist, Exotic Entertainment*

Given the history of French opera in the eighteenth century, there is usually a tendency to place it as a rival to the Italian opera genres. Although at the outset the merits of both were debated in the Querelle des Bouffons and the Gluck–Piccinni controversy, French opera evolved along its own path. By the middle of the century it had achieved a solid foundation on two levels: first, it reaffirmed the power of the *tragédie lyrique* on the main stage Opéra, and second, it demonstrated that the popular form of comic opera could be formulated in a typically French fashion with tuneful yet simple songs, pastoral plots, and accessible music. As the century headed toward the inevitable chaos of the French Revolution, French opera developed an international dimension, with popular works being exported elsewhere in Europe. It evolved into pieces that incorporated the exotic and magical, as well as deeply gripping dramas, such as the rescue opera. The colorful orchestration, the increasing lyrical and technical demands of the singers, and the story lines all pointed the way to the Romantic period.

Opera in Germany: Defining Nationalism Without a Nation

It may seem that German opera ought to have been, like the German style of music, in general, a blend of the French and Italian, but in the case of opera, there was an element of national pride that directed an original course. Germany existed as a language and culture throughout the period, but politically it failed to unify the various states and principalities into a single entity. Prussia dominated the northern part of today's Germany, but the states of Saxony, the Palatinate, Bavaria, and Hessia (among other smaller ones) exercised equal political and cultural power, for which opera was ideally suited. In the remainder of the Holy Roman Empire, German opera was often less evident; although Vienna had a long and illustrious tradition of works in the language, other provinces often lacked even the basic performance venues for opera, meaning that if anything theatrical was produced, it was the provenance either of traveling troupes performing on impromptu stages, university productions generally surrounding academic events, or of what may be determined to be folk operas, sometimes in local dialect and produced by religious orders such as the Jesuits for religious or moral purposes.

The most performed operas in Germany of this period were, as noted, Italian. In Dresden, as noted, the power couple of composer Johann Adolph Hasse and his wife, soprano Faustina Bordoni (Figure 7.8), made the city a magnet for opera, and since both were well regarded in Italy, as already noted in the last chapter, the

Figure 7.8 Faustina Bordoni and Johann Adolph Hasse (1740, engravings)

interchange of works between Saxony and the opera centers of Italy was constant. In Berlin, Carl Heinrich Graun's main duty as *Kapellmeister* was to perform Italian opera, for this was a hallmark of Frederick the Great's cultural establishment. Although the king attempted to "reform" the conventional style with the opera *Montezuma* in 1755, it was still in Italian and retained the conventional forms, such as the da capo aria, even though Frederick paid particular attention to the text and Graun offered a more colorful score. The same can be said for other venues, such as Munich or Stuttgart, where Italian composers such as Nicolò Jommelli were employed. But opera in German had a long, if checkered, history that was largely moribund by 1740. The famed Hamburg Opera on the Gänsemarktplatz had ceased to exist in 1739—its place was taken over until the theatre burned down in 1750 by an Italian troupe headed by Pietro Mingotti—and earlier city opera companies in Leipzig, Frankfurt, and elsewhere had suffered the same fate. As a renewed interest in German literature began to appear about that time with the *Empfindsamkeit* authors, such as Gotthold Ephraim Lessing, it was only a matter of time before opera in German was resurrected.

In 1749 Scheibe had decried the demise of native opera,[4] proposing a text that would revive it, but it had to wait for several years before a new style that was uniquely German emerged. This came in the form of a translation of Charles Coffey's *The Devil to Pay*, a ballad opera that had premiered in London in 1731 and subsequently become one of the most popular works of the eighteenth century. The plot of this work was immediately successful, as it had no pretense to either sophistication or morality. It involves an abusive cobbler (Jobson) married to a meek, pretty wife (Nell), while close by Lord Loverule, a generous and enlightened nobleman, is plagued by his shrewish wife. Both the cobbler and Lady Loverule turn out a magician, and in revenge, he switches their places. Both learn a lesson in behavior before the magician switches them back again. From a musical standpoint, the work is unremarkable, but the plot, with its moral but entertaining plot, resonated with European audiences, as we have already seen with its French equivalent, *Le Diable à quatre*.

In 1743 a theatrical troupe performed a version in Berlin intending it to be the inaugural work in a new Prussian National Theatre established by Frederick the Great. This was not a success, but in 1752 a troupe led by Heinrich Koch in Leipzig performed a revised version by Christian Felix Weisse, with new music by Johann Georg Standfuß. This inaugurated a brief controversy known as the Comic War, in which the **Singspiel**, as it was known, was popular enough to attract the ire of university professor and playwright, Johann Christoph Gottsched. Gottsched, whose hope was to establish German literature and opera based on high moral principles, railed against the lowbrow new genre in a series of pamphlets, one of which stated bluntly: "Opera is the most absurd work that human understanding has ever conceived" (Document 3).[5] Koch met these with public replies that sometimes bordered on the slanderous, in the end, a public lawsuit forced a compromise whereby Koch could continue to produce opera without invective against Gottsched and the professor would cease his diatribes against opera.

While the Comic War can be considered a miniature version of the War of the Buffoons in Paris, it did demonstrate that a popular form of opera, in which simple tunes often resembling folk music were accessible to audiences and rather easy to produce, and in 1766 the genre was given a more professional standing through the work of Johann Adam Hiller. Hiller's idea was to expand the spoken dialogue, compose arias that were mostly either strophic or contained simple tunes, and clothe it in light and tuneful orchestration. The subject matter was to be focused on the life and locations of common people, with plots that were reduced to bucolic love stories. His subsequent operas *Lottchen am Hofe* (*Little Lotta at Court*, 1767), *Die Jagd* (*The Hunt*, 1770), and *Der Dorfbarbier* (*The Village Barber*, 1771) were enormous successes.

The characters of this Singspiel were ordinary people, with plots that incorporated stock comic situations, often in a country setting. The melodies of the musical portions were simplified and memorable so that they took on the aspect of folk tunes. The orchestration was often simple, and the vocal lines were meant to be performed by actors, much like musicals today.

In order to train the actors to a higher standard, Hiller instituted a school of Singing in 1771, from which some of the most important German singers of the period, such as Elisabeth Mara, and composers, such as Johann Christian Friedrich Haeffner, graduated. He also came under the influence of a troupe of actors under Abel Seyler, who not only specialized in the Singspiel, but also promoted its development throughout northern Germany. His work soon came to the attention of prominent literary figures, such as Goethe, who in 1773 wrote a text for his first Singspiel, *Erwin und Elmire*. It was premiered at the Liebhabertheater in Weimar to music by Duchess Anna Amalia in 1776. The text, later set by no fewer than five other composers, including Johann Friedrich Reichardt, *Kapellmeister* at the Berlin court of Friedrich Wilhelm. Goethe's next libretto, published in 1774, was *Claudine von Villa Bella*, but Reichardt did not first set that until 1789. During the last two decades of the eighteenth century, the German Singspiel took on many of the aspects of the French opéra comique, including larger orchestration, stories that included magic or fantasy, and increasing difficulty for the vocalists. Unlike the French models, however, dramatic intensity drawn from the literature of the period formed a focal point. Reichardt's *Die Geisterinsel* (*The Isle of Ghosts*), for example, is filled with scenes of wild nature and supernatural manifestations. By 1780 the Singspiel was being performed by both wandering and stable theatrical troupes, from Reval (now Tallin, Estonia) in the north to Bayreuth in the south.

German Singspiel was not the only form of this opera to have been developed in German-speaking lands. From the late Baroque Period a popular form had developed in Vienna, where it was produced at the Kärntnertor Theatre. Here, the main characters were borrowed from the Italian commedia dell'arte, the plots usually versions of Harlequinades, and the performers comic actors whose musical abilities were nominal. The language was almost always in dialect, and the principal character was named Hanswurst, whose appearance and antics dominated the works (Figure 7.8). While a low class of entertainment, it offered composers learning their craft an opportunity to write works that would appeal to audiences. For example, Joseph Haydn's first stage work titled *Der krumme Teufel* (*The Lame Devil*) from 1751 was of this genre.

By 1770, the Viennese Singspiel had evolved into a more sophisticated genre, with design improvements at the Kärntnertor Theatre allowing for larger productions. Despite the preference for Italian opera, and the competition in the realm of comedy offered by the opera buffa, the Viennese Singspiel nonetheless provided an alternative for the ordinary citizens of the city. In 1778 Emperor Joseph II decided to elevate the theatre into the German National Singspiel with the appointment of Ignaz Umlauf, a violist in the Hofkapelle, as its director. His inaugural work, *Die Bergknappen* (*The Mountain Boys*), was an instant success, and it was followed by several more in the following years by local composers, including Antonio Salieri. The most famous work, however, was Wolfgang Mozart's *Die Entführung aus dem Serail* (*The Abduction from the Harem*), which had its premiere in July 1782. Its librettist, Gottlob Stephanie Jr., was the inspector at the National Singspiel, and he adapted his work from a German author, Christoph Friedrich Bretzner, who had written it originally for Johann André a year earlier. As it was Mozart's first opera commission in Vienna, he lavished a considerable amount of time on its composition, and the details thereof, as well as the personnel required to sing in it, are described in detail in the composer's letters.

Although *Die Entführung* soon became a permanent part of the repertory in Germany, in Vienna the emperor's zeal for German opera soon waned in favor of Italian opera. In 1783 Umlauf's company was disbanded, and the director became Salieri's assistant rehearsing the normal Italian works at the Hofoper. The reasons for this included a poor economy, a lack of court patronage, and the increasing dependence on German translations of French opéra comique. In 1785 there was a revival of sorts, this time along the models of the successful Singspiel in central and northern Germany, with works incorporating pastoral plots (mainly villages and forests), fantasy, and the supernatural. These were performed in the Leopoldstadt theatre that had taken over the local Singspiel and plays (known as "*Wiener Posse*") in 1781. The first *Kapellmeister* was Wenzel Müller, who persuaded Viennese composers to create new works for this stage. These include Dittersdorf's fairy tale *Das rote Käppchen* (*Little Red Riding Hood*) from 1788, and perhaps his most internationally known Singspiel, *Doktor und Apoteker* (*Doctor and Apothecary*), which became an international success. This work, with a plot in which the children of two rivals in the medical practice outwit their elders to come together, incorporates such comic interludes as a snoring aria ("Nun mag der Herr kommen"; Example 7.2). A fantasy work, Paul Wrantizky's *Oberon* from 1789 achieve a popularity that lasted on into the nineteenth century. A final company formed by Emanuel Schickaneder took over a new theatrical enterprise in the Viennese district of Wieden in July 1789, being persuaded of its economic viability by size (large enough for between 500–800 spectators) and location near the center of the city. A

Example 7.2 Carl Ditters von Dittersdorf, Aria (from Finale Act I) "Nun mag der Herr kommen," mm. 800–820

few months earlier Mozart's *Entführung* had been revived with some success, and Schickaneder, who had known Mozart from the latter's Salzburg days, was eager to capitalize on its popularity. Noting the trend at the Leopoldstadt Theatre for fantasy operas, Schickaneder began to compete with works of his own. He did not have, at first, his own director or *Kapellmeister*, so his earliest efforts, such as the pasticcio *Der Stein der Weisen* (*The Philosopher's Stone*), were collaborative works that included Mozart and several other singer-composers in the troupe. Several other works followed, but the most popular was Mozart's *Die Zauberflöte* (*The Magic Flute*), which premiered in the fall of 1791. Other fairy tale works by Franz Süßmayer and Peter von Winter followed, but the theatre proved to be too costly to maintain or update; Schickaneder moved to a new location (Theater an der Wien) that was larger and better built in 1801, whereupon his old stage was torn down.

During the last decades of the century, the realization that a more viable and progressive type of German opera was needed apart from the popular Singspiel. A work with a plot drawn from a Classical Greek story, *Alzeste*, premiered in Weimar in May 1773. This opera, commissioned by the Seyler troupe as a model for their concept of German serious opera, was more conventional in musical style, and both the text by Christoph Martin Wieland and music by Gottfried Schweitzer received less critical acclaim. *Sturm und Drang* author Johann Wolfgang von Goethe noted particularly in his satire "Gods, Heroes, and Wieland" that the work failed to achieve its purpose.[6] Another lengthy review by Joseph Martin Kraus in *Etwas von und über Musik* from 1778 was likewise ungenerous in its criticism, but the work encouraged other composers to attempt more serious works in German. Given the trends in the literature of the time, a Jesuit priest in Mannheim, Pater Anton Klein, then proposed a work based on a twelfth-century historical incident in German history. Titled *Günther von Schwarzburg*, it paralleled the need for national identification in the plays of the period and was intended to be composed for the famed Mannheim orchestra. *Kapellmeister* Ignaz Holzbauer was entrusted with the music, but concerns over the symbolism of a national German hero being betrayed by both his prince and others led to a delay in its premiere. When it finally appeared on stage on January 5, 1777, it became an instant success, prompting critics to advocate for new works in the same vein. The scoring for this opera was generous, given that the orchestra was the famed Mannheim *Kapelle*, but the recitatives are integrated, the arias more fully developed, and the action portions in the work depicted through instrumental interludes and dramatic choruses. While it may have seemed to use the operatic spectacle of Gluck as its model, Gluck himself was impressed enough to begin work on a similar nationalist work, *Hunnenschlacht* (*Battle of the Huns*), which remained fragmentary due to the composer's ill health. It also encouraged composers of the Romantic Period to explore more nationalist subjects beyond the generic structure of the Singspiel, which nonetheless remained the main genre of German opera.

The Singspiel, however, was not the only original German opera genre to be created during the Classical Period. In 1774, Georg Anton Benda, a member of the talented Bohemian family and already a well-known composer of the Singspiel, created a new and distinctly German brand of theatre piece called the **melodrama** (or **duodrama**). Given the interest in Germany for spoken theatre, which often included incidental music such as entr'actes, an overture, and the occasional insertion song, aria, or chorus, it is perhaps not surprising that the concept of merging theatre and opera was considered. For both composers and actors, this was a particularly effective, if difficult subgenre, for it consisted of a spoken play with orchestral punctuations throughout the dialogue. Benda's first effort, *Ariadne auf Naxos*, was premiered at the court theatre in Gotha on January 27, 1775, and became an instant success for its novelty. This work was followed by his *Medea* a few months later, and within a few years both were heralded as a unique German form of theatre music. Few realized that the creation of the subgenre was the result of practical considerations; the tiny court theatre in Gotha was simply too small to have both singers acting out a plot and an orchestra together (Figure 7.9). Regardless of the necessity of adapting to the venue, the commission by the Seyler troupe meant that it was the perfect theatrical piece to take on tour, and within two years both works had been performed throughout Germany.

The genre itself had a limited life span, however, though the notion of music emphasizing spoken theatre has continued on into the present day. Benda's works did influence a number of similar pieces, such as Christian Cannabich's *Electra* being expanded to include sung choruses. Even Mozart was so taken with it, that he reported enthusiastically to his father that he found Benda's music "excellent" and that "most operatic recitatives should be treated in this way—and only sung occasionally, when the words can be perfectly expressed by the music."[7] He even contemplated his own work, *Semiramis*; while his music to this work has not survived, he later used melodrama in his incidental music to Thomas von Gebler's play *Thamos, König von Ägypten*, KV 345, and the Singspiel *Zaide*, KV 344, and remnants of it appear in the stage works of Carl Maria von Weber, Ludwig Spohr, and Ludwig van Beethoven in the early Romantic Period.

In opera, the German style may have borrowed from both the Italian and French, but unlike the general definition, these models allowed it to evolve in its own direction. The Singspiel and the melodrama were both original developments, and the historical focus on national history in the more serious operas in Germany gave rise to a subconscious need for cultural identity. This, in turn, was not precisely idiomatic with opera in this region of Europe but, rather, was symptomatic of the trends elsewhere in the world.

Figure 7.9 Eckhof Court Theatre in Gotha, Schloss Friedenstein
Source: Photo courtesy of Schloss Friedenstein.

Opera Goes Global: The Importance of National Cultural Definition

Italian, French, and even German, no matter how popular internationally, hardly fit all the needs of countries on the outside. As noted, Italian opera and performers were commonly found throughout Europe, and courts imitating the culture of the *ancien régime* of France meant that French musicians, dancers, and singers performed regularly there, as well as the latest operas from Paris (even in translation). It can be said, however, that local needs influenced the development of styles of operas, which could be more accessible to audiences, whether at court or public. Each country, province, or colony had its own particular culture, for which opera could serve as an important identifier. Opera in the local language was a good tool to inspire a sense of national identity, encourage the literary efforts of local authors, and give resident composers an opportunity to write music using material derived from their unique environments. As a result, national opera became a trademark of a country, with considerable advantages for both economic and political movements. These included a fad for exotica, often associated with an eighteenth-century orientalism, and works that were based on local literature often using folk or folk-like material.

"Turkish" Opera

Perhaps the most international of the exotica were the so-called Turkish operas, in which the clash between European and oriental cultures was presented. The dressing in costumes from all around the world and the use of "foreign" music to depict the setting or plot were part of the Baroque Period. We have already seen an example from Rameau's *Les Indies galantes* in Chapter 2 in which the "savages" from North America are depicted musically in a lively galant manner, as well as Classical Period works such as Favart's *Soliman* and Mozart's *Entführung*. This sort of playacting may have been seen as quaint by audiences of the day, and even in Italian opera settings in non-Western cultures were not unknown; *Montezuma* is set in Mexico, even though the principal singers are castrati and the music filled with opera seria display arias.

The plots of these works were generally simple, with the infidel ruler (usually a sultan or caliph) portrayed as a magnanimous and prescient monarch. There was usually a foil in the person of an overseer, and one of the common comic scenes was to get him drunk, as it was known that alcohol was prohibited in Moslem countries. Finally, there was usually a European who either was involved in rescuing a maiden taken into the harem or a strong-willed woman who humbles the chauvinist foreigner. For librettists, it was either an opportunity for complete comedy unfettered by social rules or a way to "instruct" those above him or her socially on behavior. For composers, it offered the possibility of using a variety of percussion instruments such as the bell tree (*Schellenbaum*), tambourine, or various drums along with high piccolos and trumpets to give the work an exotic tone color. Moreover, the use of modal harmonies allowed for more unusual modulations and melodies, though many of the works are conventional in terms of form and structure.

Operas such as Grétry's *La Caravane du Caire* (*The Caravan of Cairo*), Haydn's *Incontro improviso*, or Mozart's *Entführung* were each popular when premiered, but such works quickly became a stock in trade, with many composers seeking to exploit the setting and coloristic possibilities of the works, without any real nod to realism. It was not unusual for excerpts from such operas to be arranged for wind band or appear in characteristic symphonies, though these were devoid of specific allusions to the stage works themselves.

Turkish operas were considered a mainstream style as the period progressed, a depiction of the interest in orientalism that paralleled contacts, both official and peripheral, with non-European powers. As the bulk of the Turkish operas were comic or Westernized to some extent, any other type of opera needed to focus on native subjects, which often included historical or mythical events, folk material, and specialized musical forms. To discuss this world is a difficult task, for much of the research into this area is only available in local languages, but a few examples can give an idea of the global reach of indigenous opera.

Opera in England

Perhaps one of the most influential opera types of the period was the English ballad opera. As noted earlier, one work, Coffey's *The Devil to Pay*, was not only popular throughout English-speaking regions, it was translated into a number of languages and performed successfully all over Europe. As *Le diable a quatre* or *Der Teufel ist los*, it had a tremendous influence on the development of comic opera genres in both France and Germany, and in these various guises was possibly the most performed work internationally. The genre began, however, as a parody of the fad for Italian opera in England early in the century. On January 28, 1729, the first work, titled *The Beggar's Opera*, premiered in London at the theatre of Lincoln's Fields. With a text written by John Gay and music arranged by violinist Johann Pepusch, it is a satire on the opera seria. Instead of characters drawn from classical history, it featured the lowest classes in London; whores, thieves, and reprobates. The plot was rather amoral, surrounding the seduction of Polly Peachum by a highwayman, Macheath, and the result ending up not in an Arcadian grove or Roman palace but in the insane asylum of Bedlam. The music was drawn from outside sources, apart from the overture, and included parodies of Handelian opera arias, folk tunes, and popular ditties. The orchestration was limited to minimal forces, allowing performances to be done by a variety of ensembles, originally, only strings and continuo; lines could be performed with the occasional woodwind, if available. It was so successful that it had a negative impact upon serious opera, as well as spawning imitations such as Coffey's work.

By the 1750s this English genre had expanded to include more extended and cohesive plots based on longer stories and novels, and within two decades ballad operas were not only the most popular form of musical theatre in England; they were also exported to the English colonies. The new style of opera can be seen in *Thomas and Sally* by Thomas Arne, which premiered in 1760. This work was entirely without the spoken dialogue of the ballad opera, yet its plot was reminiscent of the popular genre. The libretto by Isaac Bickerstaff was intended as an afterpiece, a musical work that often followed a spoken play. The two brief acts are similar to the Italian intermezzo, but the story is particularly English. Thomas is leaving on a sea voyage, and in his absence, a country squire decides to woo Sally. Aided by her friend Dorcas, he persists

Example 7.3 Thomas Arne, *Thomas and Sally*, Hunting Aria, mm. 141–48

in his quest, but just as he is about to succeed, Thomas returns. He and Sally are then to be married, and the squire admits defeat. The libretto is quite rustic, but Arne's score is rather more complex than the usual ballad opera in that it employs woodwinds such as clarinets. The music is simple and often strophic, and there are hints of native English melodies in the hunting song and sea chanties (Example 7.3). Two years later Arne composed his *Artaxerxes*, which was premiered with considerable success at Covent Garden. Unfortunately, this success led the management to eliminate a special half-price discount for tickets, and the revival the following year was marred by one of the most destructive riots in English theatre history (Figure 7.10). The *Gentlemen's Magazine* in 1763 noted,

> The mischief done was the greatest ever known on any occasion of the like kind: all the benches of the boxes and pit being entirely tore up, the glasses and chandeliers broken, and the linings of the boxes cut to pieces. The rashness of the rioters was so great, that they cut away the wooden pillars between the boxes, so if the inside of them had not been iron, they would have brought down the galleries upon their heads.[8]

Artaxerxes was Arne's imitation of a Metastasio libretto, its purpose both to imitate the opera seria genre in Europe and to revive the popularity of the recently deceased Handel. It was successful, being performed throughout the British Empire over the next several decades, but imitations were not numerous.

Figure 7.10 Engraving of the 1763 riot attending Thomas Arne's *Artaxerxes* (1763)

Instead, the ballad opera evolved into a more cohesive form, with music newly composed instead of popular tunes. Arne himself began the transition with his 1762 *Love in a Village*, which, like *Thomas and Sally*, has a libretto by Bickerstaff. Although he only composed a few of the pieces, they became the more popular, and within a few years, works with specially written music were commonplace. The most important composer in the 1770s was Thomas Linley Sr., who wrote the music to *The Duenna* in 1775 along with his son, the prodigy Thomas Linley, Jr. This work, now in three acts imitating the opera buffa, incorporates some Scottish tunes, even though it is set in Spain. The plot, in which a lovestruck son of a local nobleman plots to extract his paramour, Donna Clara, from the clutches of her overbearing father, is Italian in all but language, but the work was an immediate success, remaining in the repertory in London until the end of the century and beyond. It was also exported to the English colonies, being performed as far away as Jamaica in 1779. Toward the end of the century, a trio of composers—Stephen Storace, Michael Kelly, and Thomas Attwood, all of whom were trained in Vienna (Attwood was one of Mozart's star pupils)—began their careers writing English opera at the King's Theatre on Drury Lane. Storace further expanded the operatic style to include works of a more serious nature, such as *The Iron Chest* (1796) and *The Pirates* (1792), all of which reflected his training in Italy. In a foreshadowing of modern composers for film and television, Kelly wrote out the tunes for sixty-two works for the stage but relied on professional orchestrators, such as Attwood, to complete the scores. These composers set the stage for Henry Bishop and others by composing in a popular style that reflected a gift for memorable, and often popular, tunes in their operas

Opera in Scandinavia

Scandinavia is often overlooked when discussing opera of the Classical Period. Consisting of two realms, Sweden (which included Finland) and Denmark (with Norway and Iceland), it was a region that was both connected to the European core and yet on the periphery. Both countries nurtured an indigenous opera in the local language that, due to their relative isolation, was both imitative of mainstream styles and differed in interesting and unexpected ways.

Denmark's development of opera (*syngespil*) began with the popularity of Danish playwright Ludvig Holberg, who during the late Baroque was famed for his comedies. One of these included an opera parody, *Kilderejsen*, where the only "music" was a few interpolated popular songs and a character, Leonora, cannot speak but answers in virtuoso coloratura. Other plays included local songs in Danish, but it was not until 1747, when the Pietist monarch was replaced by his sybaritic son, Fredrik V, that a rebuilding of the opera house at Charlottenburg Palace in Copenhagen was undertaken. At this time, the Mingotti troupe began seasonal performances of opera there. At the same time, Italian composer and singer Scalabrini arrived in Denmark and soon formed a singing school to train Danish voices. In 1755 Fredrik appointed the musical director of the Mingotti troupe, Giuseppe Sarti, as Royal *Kapelmæstare*, with the sole intent that he devoted his time to creating a viable resident opera at a new theatre on Kongens Nytorv. Although he mainly produced Italian opera over the next decade, in 1757 he collaborated on the first opera in Danish, *Gram og Signe*, to a text by Niels Bredal. Sarti was unfamiliar with the language, so another, probably Carl August Thielo, composed the recitatives. Sarti was to write several more Danish operas during his time in Copenhagen, but these were simple works with spoken dialogue.

In 1766, Christian VII was crowned king, but his mental state was precarious, and soon Denmark was embroiled in a scandalous affair that saw a German physician, Johann Friedrich von Streuensee, rise to political power.[9] In the aftermath of this affair, the new Prime Minister, Ove Guldberg, needed a means of uniting the Danish people and directing their attention away from the precarious political situation. He appointed an up-and-coming composer, Thomas Christian Walter, as head of the opera with instructions to elevate the national stage as a nationalist symbol. His 1774 *syngespil Den prøvede Troskab* (*Faithfulness Tried*) to a text by Dorothea Biehl was an instant success, not only for its lyrical melodies but also for its symbolic content. Walter was married to Denmark's leading soprano, Carolina Halle, and together they

Example 7.4 Johann Ernst Hartmann, *Balders død*, No. 8 Terzett, mm. 1–10, vocal score

formed a sort of power couple for the next several years, with the composer writing several works for her. In 1775, however, Walter's public abuse of his wife cause them to separate, and the composer was sent abroad, first to Italy to hire musicians, then to France as legate, and finally to the Danish colony of Tharangabadi in India. At the time, Guldberg was keen on creating a uniquely Danish national work, and Walter's successor, Johann Ernst Hartmann, was chosen to set the mythological *Balders død* (*The Death of Balder*). The text by Johannes Ewald created a hodgepodge of myth (including the god Thor) and Danish Viking prehistory, but the work was successful, not least due to Hartmann's expansive score and powerful Germanic harmony. As an example, Brunnhilde sings a paean to the Norse gods in an F-minor aria that has an uncanny foreshadowing of an opera the following century (Example 7.4).

Hartmann's success led to a second work, *Fiskerne* (*The Fishers*) in 1780, in which the rural setting of Danish citizenry is juxtaposed against a royalist message. The music is simpler, with a plethora of folk-like tunes and ballads, but the nationalist view is stressed by the inclusion of "Kong Christian stod ved højen mast (King Christian stood at the high mast)" later to become a national anthem. His third Danish opera, *Gorm den gamle* (*Gorm the Old*), from 1785, was likewise based on Nordic mythology. While the next several years were devoted to adaptations of French and German operas, by 1789 a new wave of Danish operas appeared with the next generation of composers. German Friedrich Kunzen's *Holger Danske* (*Holger the Dane*)[10] was premiered that year but withdrawn after only six performances due to a controversy over the influence of Germans in Danish opera, a remnant of the Struensee affair. Although it had been hailed as a masterpiece of national opera, it was Johann Abraham Peter Schulz, who in 1790 produced *Høstgildet* (*The Harvest Festival*) and three years later *Pers bryllup* (*Peter's Wedding*) and finally succeeded in reviving the popularity of Danish opera without the stylistic controversy, leading to an active and continuous series of works in the nineteenth century by Friedrich Kuhlau, among others.

In Stockholm, a native comic troupe led by Petter Stenborg in 1747 produced the earliest Swedish opera. Titled *Syrinx, eller then uti Wass förvandlade Wattennymphen* (*Syrinx, or The Water Nymph Transformed from Reeds*), it was a pasticcio that began a popular theatre in Swedish, though it had little effect on stimulating native opera. The same year a theatre at a former tennis court was completed to cater to the tastes of the Crown Princess Louisa Ulrika, sister of Frederick the Great, later augmented in 1766 by a new stage at Drottningholm built to replace an earlier one that burned (See Figure 6.4). She invited the Mingotti troupe to Sweden for several years, and when it went bankrupt, she kept its director, Francesco Uttini, as her court *Kapellmästare*. Over the next years he composed both opera seria and opéra comique for the court, the former mostly to texts by Metastasio.

When Gustav III ascended the throne in 1771, one of his first acts was to focus the Royal Spectacles on the creation of a fully fledged opera (Document 4). He established both a literary and musical academy, the latter of which expanded to include a self-sustaining curriculum for the new Royal Opera. The first stage work was *Thetis och Pelée* by Uttini, which demonstrated the viability of Swedish as an operatic language. Two other works in 1773–1774, a nationalist play with music *Birger Jarl* and an adaptation of Gluck's *Orpheus*, all of which were successful, followed this. With these works Gustav launched the publicly supported Royal Spectacles, and over the years that followed, this developed into three trends (all in Swedish): new works with Classical subjects to appeal to the Francophile nobility, new works in Swedish with plots based on national history or mythology, and arrangements of the latest works from Paris by Gluck, Piccinni, and others. The leading tenor, Carl Stenborg, was allowed to compete at his own Swedish Comedy by creating works that were either nationalist or translated arrangements of opéra comique, many to localized texts by Carl Envalsson. All were presented from August through May in a revolving repertory to allow for members of the *Hovkapell* and singers to perform a variety of works in all of the venues.

In 1782 a new opera house opened, designed by Carl Fredrik Adelcrantz as the most modern and largest in Europe (Figure 7.11). Its main stage was wider and deeper than the Opéra in Paris, and it had room in the orchestra pit for an expanded ensemble of up to seventy-five. The inaugural work was to have been the monumental six-act *Æneas i Cartago* (*Æneas in Carthage*) by the newly arrived Joseph Martin Kraus, but the lead singer, Carolina Müller, fled to escape debts, and *Cora och Alonzo* by Dresden *Kapellmeister* Johann Gottlieb Naumann was substituted. In 1787 a sister institution, the Royal Dramatic Theatre, was founded to produce stage plays that often contained operatic musical portions. By 1790, Stockholm's citizens could enjoy several operas each week of the long season, creating a reputation throughout Europe for a vibrant and progressive Swedish national stage.

The four types of operas found in the Gustavian opera (as it was called), included works that were meant to foster support for the king, who was known for both his literary acumen and his political adventurism. In 1777 Stenborg produced *Gustaf Adolphs Jagd* (*Gustav Adolf's Hunt*), a *sångspel* based loosely on a French model but incorporating Swedish folk songs. In 1786, Gustav produced a strongly nationalist work, *Gustaf Wasa*, with music by Naumann that stirred patriotic feelings against Denmark (and later Russia), while the following year Abbé Vogler produced *Gustaf Adolf och Ebba Brahe*, a work that reached back into Swedish history. Both works extolled the national sentiments of the realm; the first harkening back to Sweden's fight for independence and the second to the magnanimity of the powerful ruler during the Thirty Years' War. That same year Stenborg produced his *Gustaf Eriksson i Dalarna* (*Gustav Ericsson in Dalarna*), which incorporated Swedish folk songs, and Olof Åhlström the opera *Frigga*, which adapted Norse mythology to a Classical realm.

When Gustav III was assassinated in 1792 at a masked ball, the Royal Opera turned toward models based on French operas or the plays of August von Kotzebue; the brief concept of the national stage lay dormant for two decades. Unlike Denmark, Sweden did not have the political crisis that helped develop their national opera, but given the proclivity of Gustav toward the stage, it nonetheless created works that highlighted national aspirations to become a European power.

Opera in Russia

The Westernization begun under Peter the Great led to the development of a culture that looked abroad for its musical identification. His successor, Empress Anna, imported Francesco Araja to write opera for the St. Petersburg court. His first work, *La forza dell'amore e dell'odio* (*The Power of Love and Hatred*), was translated into Russian by Vasily Trediakovsky in 1736. Thereafter followed a series of opera seria, all in Russian translation, until 1755, when librettist Alexander Sumarokov provided Araja with a new work entirely in Russian but based upon a Classical subject, *Tsefal i Prokris* (Procris and Cephal). Araja continued to compose Russian translations of his works until he left in 1762, but the importation of major figures of Italian opera continued through the reign of Empress Catherine the Great. These included Baldassare Galuppi, Tommaso Traetta, Giovanni Paisiello, Giuseppe Sarti, Domenico Cimarosa, and Vincente Martín y Soler, all of whom had established international careers in Europe for their works, mainly opera buffa, as we have seen in the previous chapter.

Figure 7.11 Watercolor by Gustav Nyblæus of the interior of Gustav III's opera house from *ca*. 1810, Stockholm, Sweden

Source: National Museum, Stockholm.

Catherine, a German princess from Saxon-Anhalt-Zerbst, was a significant patron of opera, and she made it possible for the major composers of the genre to spend time in Italy to compose works by offering them handsome salaries, the freedom to compose without the usual restrictions, and an audience of the nobility that was both critically aware of and focused on the latest trends and styles in the European core. The last also followed the preference for the opéra comique, adapting French models for court productions. The first of these was *Anyuta*, which was a Russian opera to a text by Mikhail Popov. The composer of the work is unknown. The story surrounds a young woman taken in by a peasant family but finds out she is of noble birth and therefore able to marry her noble love, Viktor. Since the music has not survived, it is difficult to say whether this work, one of the first truly Russian operas, incorporated the folk idiom.

Initially, the performances of opera in Russia were held in the Imperial theatres, mainly attached to the court in St. Petersburg. In addition, there were private theatres that could be found in the palaces of the nobility, which were allowed to produce the operas once they had premiered at court. In 1742 the court had instituted a government office to oversee Imperial productions to be financed by the state, but it was not until 1783 that Catherine established the Imperial Theatre on the foundations of the Winter Palace. This was meant for official use only, with no public access, but the performances by the court opera company drew praise from visitors and the intelligentsia alike. The house open to the public was the Kamenny Theatre (also known as the Bolshoi), which had opened in a small house in 1775, but in 1783 it was redesigned in Classical fashion as a public venue. In Moscow, Prince Peter Ouroussoff had organized a theatre company in 1776 and, in 1780, built a large structure on Petrovka Square that was to house a public theatre, the Petrovsky. The royal privilege lasted for a decade before this stage was absorbed into the Imperial Theatres. A final St. Petersburg theatre was that founded in 1772 by Karl Knipper, who turned a riding stable into a stage, performing works for the public using mainly students from his music academy. The music initially was a Russian translation of Hiller's *Singspiels*, and in 1783 it was acquired by the Imperial court theatres to be the main venue for the second stream of Catherine's operatic establishment.

Catherine, herself a librettist like her cousin Gustav III of Sweden, also fostered the development of Russian opera. She and her nobility wished to be seen as important patrons of European culture, but as the ruler of a polyglot country that included serfs and peasants who had their own indigenous stories, she was aware that a native form of opera based on the folk tales needed to be created. In order to facilitate this, she sent promising young composers to complete their education in Italy, with the promise of official positions upon their return. One of the earliest of these was Ukrainian Maksim Berezovsky, who was the first Russian elected to the famed Accademia Filarmonica in Bologna. Upon his return to St. Petersburg in 1772 he was appointed to the staff of the Imperial theatres, but it is not known what Russian operas he wrote, if any. His successors, Vasily Pashkevich, Mikhail Sokolovsky, Ivan Kerzelli, and Yevstigney Fomin,[11] were all active composing Russian folk-style operas, beginning in 1779 with Pashkevich's *Neschast'e ot karety* (*Misfortune from Owning a Coach*). This was followed by one of the most popular folk pieces, *Sankt Peterburgskiy Gostinyi Dvor* (*St. Petersburg Bazaar*), in 1782. Fomin, who like Berezovksy was trained in Italy, was the most prolific composer of Russian opera of his day, with more than thirty works. His most famous was *Yamshchiki na podstave* (*The Coachmen at the Relay Station*) from 1787, with its characteristic folk tone (Example 7.5).

It is a curious twist of fate that Catherine rarely allowed Russian works drawn from history or her Italian imported composers to write works in Russian. The first work, to a text by the empress, was Fomin's *Novgorodskiy bogatyr' Boyeslayevich* (*The Novgorod Hero Boyeslayevich*) of 1786, but with a grander opera, *Nachalnoye upravleniye Olega* (*The Early Reign of Oleg*) she first approached Cimarosa and then, when he was unable to fulfill the commission, Sarti, who collaborated with Pashkevich to complete it in 1789. Thereafter, interaction between the Russians and Italians was allowed more frequently.

Opera in Russia was a curious mixture of continental and domestic national types, and while these often lacked the political overtones of Catherine's Scandinavian rivals, they nonetheless demonstrate the dual nature of Russian society, boyars and serfs.

Example 7.5 Yevstigny Fomin, *Yamshchiki na podstave*, Duet, mm. 4–16

Opera in Iberia

Opera in the Iberian Peninsula followed much of the periphery in that it imported the leading Italian styles. Given the close association with Italy, it is not surprising that composers were invited to the courts in Madrid and Lisbon to write for the Spanish and Portuguese courts, in turn influencing local composers to develop their own works.

Opera in Spain had been prominent during the Baroque Period, when it had ruled Naples, home to the leading conservatories of the day. Although castrato Farinelli spent over a decade in Madrid his appearances there on the stage were limited, and the Teatro Real was mainly concerned with the performance of Italian opera by Italian composers. Philip V had an interest in opera and in 1737 had a stage inaugurated as the Teatro de los Caños del Peral, where it was home to Italian troupes (Figure 7.12). Only two years later, these ceased performing at the venue, and during the intervening years only the occasional Spanish company performed there; they also did Italian opera. The main theatre was the Teatro Buen Retiro, which was next door to the royal palace. It was intended to be the main opera house in Madrid, especially since it bordered onto the expansive gardens where productions could be taken outdoors. Farinelli did administer a troupe, but in 1759 Carlos III terminated his employment, and the theatre was rarely used. In 1786 the king allowed the reopening of the Caños theatre, not for entertainment purposes but, rather, for it to serve

Figure 7.12 Copper drawing of the front of the Teatro de los Caños del Peral (1788)

as a source of income for charity cases. Both it and the Buen Retiro were enlisted, but the performances were not successful. An English traveler, Joseph Townsend, noted in 1792 that "the play-houses of Madrid are not much frequented; the genius of the people does not assimilate this sort of amusement."[12] In 1799, Carlos IV prohibited foreign opera, and the dominant international type was no longer performed.

Spain did have, however, two native types of opera, the *zarzuela* and the **tonadilla**. The former was similar to the opera buffa in that it was generally in two acts and featured comic plots. The latter was a much smaller genre specifically focused on satire; it could be staged or not. The zarzuela first appeared during the Baroque Period, but by the time of Philip V had expanded to become similar to its Italian counterpart by including arias, recitatives, and ensemble numbers, all in Spanish. Performances were held at the Teatro del Principe and the Teatro del la Cruz. Both were popular and featured partisans, known locally as the *chorizos* (sausages) and the *polacos* (Poles), each of which argued for the primacy of their venues. Composers such as Antonio Rodriguez de Hita, Antonio Litares, and José de Nebra, composed both heroic and burlesque zarzuelas, incorporating ensemble numbers, dances, and orchestrations that often featured Spanish instruments. Spanish rhythms also appear, such as Nebra's *Viento es la dicha de Amor* (*Wind Is the Poetry of Love*) from 1743. Luis de Misón is credited with the first tonadilla, and eventually composed over 100 works in this style. Many pieces excerpted from both subsequently became well known as folk music. This indigenous pair of Spanish stage works were local, with the exception that a few were subsequently produced in Portugal.

In Portugal, the first opera house in Lisbon dates from 1735 and, like Spain, was devoted to the production of Italian opera. João V was an enlightened ruler who favored the composition of what he called "divine operas," that is, works based on liturgical stories, but he allowed for the opening of a larger house, the Teatro da Rua dos Condes in 1738 for the public. These were presented in the original languages, but at a rival marionette theatre, an international company produced works by Portuguese composers such as Antonio Teixeira and António José da Silva in Portuguese. Although the plots, such as Silva's *Vida do grande Don Quixote*, are still Spanish in origin, the local language provided enough incentive for them to become popular. In 1750, three new theatres were opened following a dearth of entertainment for the last several years of João V's reign, during which the monarch was indisposed due to mental illness. His successor, José I, was a keen supporter of opera and had Giovanni Bibiena design the Teatro do Salvaterra, Teatro do Ajuda, and the Teatro do Tejo to accommodate a new emphasis on the genre. The last was intended to be the main Lisbon house, but within a few months of its opening with David Perez's *Allesandro nell'Indie*, the great Lisbon Earthquake destroyed much of the city.

The theatres at the Rua dos Condes and Bairo alto reopened in 1761, but their repertory consisted mainly of a mixture of Portuguese plays and Italian operas, along with the occasional Spanish zarzuela. It was not until 1782, with the inauguration of the Teatro do Salitre, that Portuguese language works were promoted under the direction of a composer with a most fortuitous name, Marcos Antonio Portugal. However, these were generally only translations of Italian texts, and no native form of opera emerged despite an active and vibrant opera culture.

Opera in the Americas

The continents of North and South America had thriving musical centers during the Classical Period. Opera, however, seemed to appear only sporadically. Theatres were neither as ornate nor as expansive as in Europe, and musical developments were mainly in other genres. Nonetheless, one can discern the beginnings in lands that were mostly provinces or colonies of European lands.

In Canada, the changeover from French to British rule in the aftermath of the French and Indian War had little influence on the settlement of the colony along the St. Lawrence River. While towns such as Quebec and Halifax had few or no theatres, Montreal became home to Joseph Quesnel, who emigrated from France in 1779. Trained as a musician, he composed the first Canadian operas, *Colas et Colinette* and *Lucas et Cécile*, based on opéra comique models. The tunes are simple and direct, with allusions to the frontier, though these could also reflect rural France. Neither complete librettos nor full scores have survived.

In the United States, prior to independence, the English ballad opera was considered the main theatre work in the colonies. Popular operas were frequently staged here within a few years of their premieres in England itself, indicating that in many of the colonies, namely, from the Carolinas up through New York, society and its entertainment needs mirrored the home country. With the conclusion of the War for Independence in 1783, the Continental Congress banned theatrical entertainments, though some continued to be performed as "private lectures" in unstaged versions. The first American opera was *The Disappointment*, composed probably around 1760. The "composer," Andrew Barton, is a pseudonym for "a son of Philadelphia College," possibly Thomas Forrest or John Hopkinson. The main interest in the work is the appearance for the first time of the tune "Yankee Doodle." In 1789 the ban on theatrical productions was lifted, and immediately, new companies formed, including the New American Company of Philadelphia and the John Street theatre in New York. British immigrants Alexander Reinagle, James Hewitt, Raynor Taylor, and Benjamin Carr all contributed works imitating the ballad opera, though some, like the 1797 *Columbus, or The Discovery of America*, were focused on their new adopted homeland. The theatres in both Philadelphia and New York (and eventually Boston) were able to field orchestras of modest size, and given the simplicity of the arias, mostly strophic songs, no professional talent was needed.

Opera was also produced in New Orleans in the 1790s, though the city had no permanent venue; the works were entirely French opéra comique, and information on singers or orchestras is lacking. Elsewhere in French America, on the island of Hispaniola, both Port au Prince (Sainte-Domingue) and Cap Hatiën (Cap François) boasted opera houses during the Classical Period. Although virtually all the repertory was imported from France, there were two local composers, Dufresne (first name unknown), who produced his *Laurette* in October 1775, and Bissèry (likewise first name not known), who composed his *Le sourd dupé* (*The Deaf Fool*) that was performed in June 1777. Bissèry's last work, *Bouquet disputé* (*The Disputed Bouquet*), was premiered in a new 750-seat opera house constructed by François Mesplès in 1782. The orchestra was of similar size to the Parisian comic stages, and the main roles were taken both mulattos and émigrés from Paris. Unfortunately, opera activity ceased in the aftermath of the French Revolution in 1791.

Opera in the Spanish provinces of New Spain and Portuguese Brazil was likewise spotty. Mexico City had the Teatro Coliseo Nuevo. There the *maestro di capilla*, Ignacio de Jerusalem, wrote music for productions, including several operas, but the main repertory continued to be drawn from the zarzuelas imported from Spain. Opera also existed in Lima, the other provincial capital, since the Baroque Period, but during the Classical Period, little is known about the productions. Jesuit operas based on the lives of saints, however, have surfaced in various locations in the Bolivian and Paraguayan mission fields, with the possibility that some of the works were either the product of the priests themselves or native composers. Brazilian opera, however, does not appear until the nineteenth century, though there were several Portuguese operas performed in Rio de Janeiro and elsewhere earlier.

This chapter is intentionally more expansive than some of the previous and following, but the domination of opera throughout the globe warrants a more intensive exploration. As the most important form of entertainment during the Classical Period, it was a source of pride, not only for public venues in cities such as Paris, Stockholm, or London, but it also generated much of the economic prosperity and artistic reputations of the places where they were performed. Courts were noted for their musical theatre, as were the large houses, and both singers and composers made much of their reputations from the composition of opera, whatever the language. Opera was not, however, the only ubiquitous genre to hold sway over the people of the period. Even though the Enlightenment was more humanist, religion was still important, and the music that was written to glorify God was a major source of inspiration for composers.

Documents

Document 1. Jacques Cazotte, Excerpt from *La guerre de l'opera* (Paris, 1753). P. 3–4.

Madame, fire has erupted in all corners of the Opéra. Italian music is fighting it out with French music. Imagine the entire mess of a war that is at the same time alienating and civil. Intrigues, cabals, factions, the high, the low, the surprising twists; fortune declares itself for the stranger without giving itself time to choose, then wavers between the two sides, soon to yield without knowing why. The extreme joys, the intoxication, the triumphal passages, the unexpected descents, the foiled plots, the extravagant hopes. Behold the faint thread of what passes before us beneath our eyes at the Théâtre Lyrique. It is interesting that your taste should make you accept all of these motions, which you will no doubt read with pleasure in the newspapers. At the end of the summer, there were two Italian comic actors that were part of a troupe of this sort, engaged in Strasbourg. This is probably not to tempt the taste of the public on this new kind of pleasure. These comedians presented first at the Opéra one of these small pieces in two acts, which are called *intermèdes*. The work is by a very esteemed musician. . . . The new performance was more advantageous for it; little by little, the ears were accustomed to the music, and the connoisseurs declared themselves for it. Anyone who was anyone followed them to this spectacle, along with the curious, the indolent, and the rest of the nation.

Document 2. Jean-François Marmontel, *Essai sur les révolutions de la musique en France* (Paris, 1777).

Why should we not do in music what was done in poetry? With cries, howls, sounds ripped and terrifying, one expresses the emotions, but these accents will abide, if they are not embellished in imitation, as they would be in nature, of expressions of pain. If we only wished to be moved, we would want to hear, among the public, a mother who loses her son, and the children who lose their mother; without doubt, this is the expression of sorrow without artifice, but it is also quite powerful. But what pleasure would we derive from trusting this wrenching of emotion? It is necessary to put balm on the wound when the feeling of pain is reached in the spectacle. This balm is the pleasure of the spirit, and of the senses; the origin of this pleasure in poetry is the sublimity of thoughts, sentiments, and images, the noble elegance of expression, the charm of beautiful verses. In music, the same pleasure must be blended with sorrowful impressions; the reason for this lies in the art of the musician, like that of the poet; in this art of giving to the musical expression a voice that does not resound in nature; the cries, the laments, the funereal accents or the painful deliriums. Thus, is it such a strange idea that we want to ban from lyric theatre the harmonious singing that we want to forbid the beautiful in favor of tragedy? But an even stranger notion is to blend the fragments into a mutilated song. Why not complete the song we began? Or, why start a song that you do not wish to finish? What is an intermittent declamation, which begins swiftly, then suddenly ceases, and finishes heavily? There is a plethora of excuses for the imitator to move away from nature in order for us to perceive the pleasures of art. In two words: the melody without expression is wanting, but the expression without melody is something that does not move. Expression and melody, the tune and all else must be elevated together: this is the difficulty with art. It remains to be seen who will give us a solution to this problem.

Document 3. Johann Christoph Gottsched, from the *Critische Dichtkunst* (Leipzig, 1742).

Opera is the most absurd work that human understanding has ever conceived. . . . A poem or fable must be an imitation of a human situation through which a specific moral lesson is fashioned. A situation which is not natural is not appropriate. . . . The characters in an opera think, speak, and act completely differently than would in normal life, and we would be taken for fools if we acted even slightly in the manner Singspiels present to us. . . . Thus the Singspiel is a work for the senses; the mind and heart gain nothing from it.

Document 4. Gustaf Johan Ehrensvärd, From his *Dagboksanteckningar* (Stockholm, 1878).

An opera that contains a pleasant and attractive music, a well-conceived ballet, decorative costumes, pretty and well-painted decorations, is so captivating that the eye, ear, and other senses are pleased all at once. Through this one eventually becomes used to the language, whose harshness is softened by a captivating music; one eventually finds words and expressions more gentle, one should find them more serviceable, and eventually one comes to like his own language. An opera can be given many times in a row; one always seems to find something new to see and hear.

Notes

1 Pierre-Louis D'Aquin de Châteaulyon, *Siècle littéraraire de Louis XV* (Paris, 1753), 219.
2 Jean-Jacques Rousseau, *Lettre sur la musique de la françoise* (Paris, 1752), 494.
3 Quoted in Christian Felix Weisse, *Selbstbiographie* (Leipzig, 1806), 73.
4 Scheibe's text was titled *Thusnelde*, which clearly was not amenable to composers as a possibility, not even Scheibe himself.
5 The entire episode is explained in Bertil van Boer, "Coffey's *The Devil to Pay*, the Comic War, and the Emergence of the German Singspiel," *Journal of Musicological Research* 8 (1988), 119–139.
6 Goethe's entire parody, created while drinking a "bottle of good burgundy," was intended to diffuse the anger he felt at Wieland's promotion of the work as a model for good German opera.
7 Robert Spaethling, *Mozart's Letters, Mozart's Life* (New York: Norton, 2000), 193–194.
8 Although unusual, riots of this sort persisted until the abolition of discounts was revoked, but these generally occurred at the houses presenting spoken plays.
9 Without going into the involved politics, it should be noted that Streuensee had an affair with Queen Caroline Matilde, making Denmark and its king the objects of ridicule.
10 Also referred to as *Ogier the Dane*, based upon the original French sources.
11 The name missing here is Dmitry Bortniansky, who composed four operas between 1786 and 1788, but these are all in French. Ivan Khandoschkin, another prominent composer, did not write opera.
12 Joseph Townsend, *A Journey Through Spain in the Years 1786 and 1787* (London, 1792), II: 158.

8   Sacred Music in the Era of Secularism

Throughout the Classical Period there was a decline in interest in sacred music, largely as Enlightenment thought turned more toward secular humanism and away from the rigid dogma of the established religions. That is not to say the music in the churches was abandoned or ignored, but there was a trend beginning during the 1740s to treat sacred works in a much more secularized symphonic style, generally in opposition to the controls that each of the four main European religions sought to impose. The result was often a freeing up of these controls, and not infrequently, the excesses led to various reform movements that sought to return music in the church to a simpler and more participatory form for congregations.

Theorists noted that sacred music often reflected the public taste, meaning that it imitated opera and other concert pieces. This, in turn, meant that composers who were obligated to write for worship services often had to conform to the expectations of both the ecclesiastical requirements and audience expectations. The requirements were different not only between the two dominant churches, the Roman Catholic and Lutheran, but also within these the notion of church music varied widely. The only relatively static sacred music was that of the Anglican Church in England, where a more conservative style was observed. Apart from this example, the debate over what constituted "appropriate" music for worship continued up through the Napoleonic era, with local traditions were often diametrically opposed to efforts for reform.

One should first note that not all sacred music was the sole provenance of the various churches. Devotion in the eighteenth century was not limited to a particular venue or time, though religious calendars played an important role. Sacred songs were composed and published for personal use, and larger works such as oratorios were most often performed in other places outside the church. Hymns of praise or salvation were meant for larger settings, such as courts or public out of doors, while funeral music, such as Requiems or cantatas, could be done in a variety of places. These were occasional works, for which there was no set season or liturgical reason. For instance, a Te Deum could be either Catholic or Protestant, performed in a church or public venue, and reflect an immediate need (a military victory, a royal birth, a marriage, etc.) or recall a historical event of national significance. It could be simple and direct or monumental and celebratory. In short, it could reflect both piety and glorification, depending on the circumstances.

Church Music for Secular Glory or Devout Worship

Since medieval times, music's place in the church has been a subject of debate. By the Baroque Period, however, it had become commonplace, and it was expected even in the most Pietist of centers that sacred works would be performed as a means of enhancing devotion. The dominant divisions of Christianity, Roman Catholic and Protestant (here defined mainly as various forms of Lutheranism), all incorporated substantial amounts of sacred music, both in regular worship services and on special occasions such as Christmas, Easter, Lent, or feast days. These were required throughout the year according to a sacred calendar, with the most active times of musical composition being the period between December and whenever Easter fell during the year. Lent, especially, was a fertile time for new musical works, as in Catholic countries the opera houses were closed. In the Classical Period, the public concerts, such as the Concerts Spirituels in Paris, were initially devoted to the performance of sacred works in a concert setting, while elsewhere oratorios kept musicians active during the closures. In Protestant countries, the Baroque composers such as Christoph Graupner, Georg Philipp Telemann, Johann Sebastian Bach, and others were required in their positions to compose cantatas in cycles for every Sunday of the year and Passions during Holy Week. Telemann, in particular, was aware of the constant need for such works even in the smallest of Lutheran churches, thus forming the rationale for his compendium *Harmonischer Gottesdienst* (*Harmonic Worship Service*) published in 1725–1726 as a cycle of seventy-two cantatas in simpler settings.

By the emergence of the Classical Period, sacred music had a long and popular tradition, yet two issues began to arise: a revival of popular secularized music in the church and the role of religion in Enlightenment thought. These, in turn, brought up issues of music and liturgy, as well as how music could be "reformed" to accommodate the various styles and trends without remaining staid and overly conservative. Catholics and Protestants (and others) were cognizant of this development and sought to evolve their sacred music accordingly.

Sacred music in the Roman Catholic Church was still loosely governed by the suggestions of the Council of Trent held over a century earlier. The council, however, did not specifically issue directives but, rather, sought to minimize the secularization of sacred music.[1] Given that the precise fulfillment of the recommendations was left up to individual diocesan preferences, the restriction of "abuses" in favor of a return to pure polyphony and plainchant was meant to relate principally to the Vatican. This *stile antico* (or ancient style) was generally acknowledged as the model that ought to be imitated. Cities such as Naples and Venice had their own traditions, and both the Imperial capital of Vienna and major archbishoprics such as Salzburg maintained a larger and more extensive use of music in the worship services.

This, in turn, led to a division in music for the church, where control was lax. Where churches had the wherewithal to field larger ensembles, such as Dresden or Salzburg, sacred music flourished and evolved to include works of substantial length and expanded settings, many of which were calculated to complement the highly ornamented churches (Figure 8.1). This was also evident in the larger monasteries, especially those that served as centers of pilgrimage, such as Mariazell near Vienna or Einsiedeln in Switzerland. Here, the musicians could often include both the clergy and local performers. Chant was still practiced, but it was frequently of lesser importance than the concerted music, leading to concerns over whether music had deviated from its principal purpose of supporting piety, not to mention the issue of *a cappella* music or the inclusion of instruments. In short, the direction of sacred music seemed on a trajectory toward what some critics decried as complete secularization.

By 1749, the often-brilliant music in the majority of Catholic churches necessitated Pope Benedict XIV to issue the encyclical *Annus qui hunc* to address the current traditions and to offer some guidelines for the composition, performance, and use of sacred music.[2] This document is particularly interesting in that Benedict, an intellectual humanist, brings to bear a substantial amount of historical commentary in support of his recommendations. As always, the foundation is Gregorian chant, which is to be performed unaccompanied. However, in the fifth section, citing Pietro Anello Persico, he notes, "The universal use of the organ and other instruments in the Divine Office is praiseworthy in its favor, and useful in raising the souls of the imperfect toward the contemplation of God." He admits further that "the use of polyphonic chant and musical instruments in Masses and during Vespers, and in other ecclesiastical functions, has proceeded a long way thus far." This is a tacit admission that instruments are to be allowed in church on a wholesale basis, something he clarifies in Sections 10 and 12:

> We shall produce no admonition save that these should only be used to strengthen in a certain manner some force of the words to the chant, that their sense be more instilled into the minds of the listeners, and the minds of the faithful be moved towards contemplation of spiritual things, and be stirred towards God and the love of divine things.

Benedict does restrict the use of what he calls "theatrical" music as inappropriate, but rather urges all music be "solemn and contemplative." With this encyclical, sacred music in the Catholic Church was freed to be as extensive and brilliant, or as compact and simple, depending upon the traditions and needs of whatever

Figure 8.1 Baroque interior of the Engelberg Monastery, Switzerland
Source: Photo by the author.

was required or needed on a local basis. Only in Rome were the recommendations of the Council of Trent retained, though larger sacred works were performed outside the churches themselves, often in private chapels of the ruling families or in the oratories that were maintained outside the sanctuaries.

With the freedoms noted in *Annus qui hunc*, Catholic sacred music was able to incorporate both the expanded instrumentation and genres of the worship service. While this opened the doors both to new and augmented music, it also did not quell the occasional call for a return to traditional simple music such as hymns or chant, either unaccompanied or supported only by an organ. The most effective of these reform movements was that proposed by Salzburg prince-archbishop Hieronymus Colloredo in 1782 in a pastoral letter. Colleredo, the nominal confessor of the Holy Roman Emperor Joseph II, proposed that the trappings of opulence that had become the rule were to be replaced by a studied simplicity, particularly due to the poor quality of music available to the individual parishes. For the emperor, this meant a return to music that was both accessible to the people and removed the excessive secular elements in favor of simple hymns and short, focused pieces for everyday use.[3] In his *Gottesdienstordnung* (*Rules of the Worship Service*) of 1783, he limited masses with instruments, the so-called concerted masses, to High Mass on Sunday and feast days, further prohibiting musical vespers, litanies, and other ancillary portions of the liturgy (Figure 8.2). Chant was to be the mainstay for the Catholic service for most days, while he reiterated the desire of his mother, Empress Maria Theresia, for widespread use of German hymnals to replace the Latin texts so that the citizens of the empire could have a greater participation in the devotional services. While this was to be limited to Vienna initially, it was the emperor's intent that it be adopted throughout the Holy Roman

Figure 8.2 Title page of the *Gottesdienstordnung* (1783, Vienna)

Empire as the norm. Two years later further restrictions in other regions, such as Upper and Lower Austria took effect, thus limiting the amount of concerted sacred music to the principal parish churches. The result was a precipitous decline in Catholic music during this time, even though the restrictions were often ignored or deliberately flouted, and what was written was intended for special feast days or restricted to works with only an organ as accompaniment.

By 1790, their unpopularity was such that Joseph II's successor, Leopold I, rescinded the restrictions on the use of instruments in the worship service, and although there was a revival of interest in concerted masses and other liturgical genres, the level of compositional activity never achieved was never the same as the time before the reforms were instituted. Indeed, the concept of musical simplicity formed a direction for Catholic sacred music in the nineteenth century, leading to a decline in the larger musical forms.

Elsewhere, the vibrant secularized sacred music flourished alongside other less expansive genres, so that the Classical Period can be seen as a kaleidoscope of various ways of using music to expand and support religious services.

Catholic Church Genres: Liturgical and Nonliturgical Music

Whether one views Catholic sacred music of the Classical Period as mainly secularized or adhering to a more conventional set of forms and genres, it can be said that it was a time when some of the most significant works were composed for the church. The main genre was the Mass, the core of the worship service. By the eighteenth century it had stabilized into three types: the *missa longa*, often called the cantata mass, in which each of the six parts of the Ordinary (Kyrie, Gloria, Credo, Sanctus, Benedictus, Agnus Dei) were subdivided into separate solo and choral movements; the *missa brevis*, or short mass, in which the parts were performed each as a single movement; and what might be called the *missa ordinarius*, or regular mass, in which each of the six movements was longer and subdivided into sections of varying tempos. The text of the Ordinary was unchangeable, and there were certain formulaic traditions that were common. For instance, the final portion of the Gloria was often contrapuntal, as was that of the Credo. This was an opportunity for composers to demonstrate their ability even if briefly, as seen in the final portion of the Gloria in the Mass in G major by Pater Roman Hoffstetter (Example 8.1).

More reflective moments were usually found in the *Et incarnates est* and *Crucifixus* of the Credo, in which the life of Christ was paraphrased; here, even in the shorter missa brevis this was cause for composers to slow the tempo to reflect the solemnity of the text (Example 8.2). On the other hand, the final portion of the Agnus Dei, the Dona nobis pacem (Grant us Peace), was sometimes set in a meter that seems to imitate a dance, such as the minuet from the Hoffstetter Mass (Example 8.3).

The missa longa was generally used for more celebratory occasions, and often it would include a thicker orchestration, as well as requiring singers who would be able to perform the frequent virtuoso arias. The missa brevis was the more common style of Mass, especially in central Europe during the period, with its longer cousin becoming the norm toward the end of the century, particularly in the late Masses of Joseph Haydn. In Italy it was not unusual for several composers to set separate movements, but the general practice was that a single person would compose the entire ordinary.

Instrumentation for the Mass Ordinary was quite variable, though most of the solemn masses (labeled generically *missa solemnis* but structurally either long or short types) included brass instruments to supplement the normal four-voice chorus and strings (always with an organ continuo). For the keys of C and D major, these were usually trumpets and timpani, although horns could also be included; for other keys, horns were usually employed. Woodwinds (flutes or oboes) also appeared more frequently after about 1750, and by 1780 it was not unusual for a full woodwind and brass complement to be used, if the ensemble was able to provide it. For example, the D major Mass by Johann Stamitz featured the full forces of the famed Mannheim *Kapelle*, including clarinets (Example 8.4). In central Europe, a trio of trombones could reinforce the vocal lines (with the occasional solo), and in some instances, two pairs of trumpets were used, the upper pair (*clarino*) providing brilliant melodic lines while the lower pair (*tromba*), often written in a C clef (alto or tenor), were mainly used for harmonic support. From central Europe, too, came the convention

Example 8.1 Pater Roman Hoffstetter, Mass in G major, Gloria: Cum sancto spiritu, mm. 94–105

of a homophonic chorus with the main theme against nonthematic running violin parts, called occasionally "violins à la Reutter," after a stereotypical pattern established by the *Kapellmeister* at St. Stephen's Cathedral in Vienna, Johann Georg von Reutter. Finally, in many Masses (and other Catholic sacred works), composers omitted an independent viola part, though it is a matter of conjecture whether this instrument was eliminated entirely or simply doubled the bass line at the octave, as Quantz seems to imply.[4]

Of course, the Mass itself had other musical portions called the Proper, the text of which changed from day to day. The most popular were the gradual and the offertory, both of which provided an opportunity for composers to fill time in the Mass with both simple and sometimes more expanded works, labeled generically as motets. There were generally set individually and most often were shorter homophonic choruses, though they retained the instrumentation of the main Mass Ordinary. Michael Haydn, for example, composed 130 graduals and sixty-five offertories, many scored only for four-part chorus and organ

176   Opera! Popular, Nationalist, Exotic Entertainment

Example 8.2 Baldassare Galuppi, Mass in C major, Credo: Et incarnates est (complete)

Example 8.3 Pater Roman Hoffstetter, Mass in G major, Agnus Dei: Dona nobis pacem, mm. 1–8

(Example 8.5). In accordance with the directives from Colloredo, Haydn's employer in Salzburg, many of these are simple, homophonic works that can be performed with limited musical forces, though other works by Haydn's predecessor, Johann Ernst Eberlin, and colleague Leopold Mozart are larger and more florid. Given the focus on accessibility, Haydn also wrote music for the Mass, both the Ordinary and various Propers, in German; the main Mass was titled *Detusches Hochamt* (*German High Service*) while the other individual works ranged from simple sacred songs to a cappella choral works. Finally, it was not uncommon in

Example 8.4 Johann Stamitz, Mass in D major, Agnus Dei, mm. 1–7

the central regions of the Holy Roman Empire to have instrumental interludes, such as the Epistle sonata. This genre, often orchestrated for a solo organ with string accompaniment, could also be performed by the organ alone or, in the case of several churches, including the main cathedral in Salzburg, by multiple organs (Figure 8.3). This instrumental work could be augmented in the more secularized churches by the **sinfonia da chiesa**, a single-movement orchestral work generally performed either between readings or to fill time to allow the celebrant to proceed from the pulpit to the altar. While it could be a special genre all by itself (see Chapter 4), it could just as easily be drawn from the many secular symphonies composed during the Classical Period.

A fourth type of Mass was the **Requiem**, reserved for funerals and memorial services. Requiems were quite popular during the Classical Period, largely because the musical portion substituted the Gloria and Credo with a twelfth-century sequence, the Dies Irae. This was often set as several movements and consisted of graphic text depicting a range of emotions from the Day of Judgment to prayers for supplication. In addition, in included an Introit (*Requiem aeternam*), an offertory (*Domine Jesu Christe*), and a benediction variant of the traditional Agnus Dei. For composers, the pictorial elements of the Sequence especially provided inspiration for musical compositions. The most famous of these is the unfinished Mozart Requiem, KV 626, about which much scholarship has been written. But the genre was widespread, with more than a thousand works from all countries. In many instances, most were written in minor keys, with a succession of movements in slower tempos. The exceptions were often the Kyrie, which was mainly contrapuntal, and the Dies Irae, which was often an Allegro or Presto.

178 *Opera! Popular, Nationalist, Exotic Entertainment*

Example 8.5 Michael Haydn, Gradual *Tribulationes cordis mei*, mm. 1–6

Figure 8.3 Salzburg Cathedral interior during the millennial celebration of 1680, engraving by Melchior Küsel (*ca.* 1680); instrumental and vocal ensembles are on the four pillars.

Special sacred music was required for feast days of the saints, as well as other services outside of the Mass. Perhaps the most common was the text associated with the liturgy of the Virgin Mary. These could be simple individual motets or were traditional texts from the standard liturgy. Motets include *Ave Regina coelorum*, *Salve Regina*, *Ave Maria*, and *Regina coeli*. These could be either set as single movements or broken into sections like a short cantata. The standard liturgical works include the *Magnificat* and *Stabat mater*. The first was generally sung at the Feast of the Annunciation and like the motets could be a single, expansive movement, or broken into individual movements with solo and choral portions. The second was more appropriate to Easter and was cast in a more solemn and reflective mood, given the subject matter of Mary weeping at the crucifixion. One of the most popular works was the powerful and emotional Stabat mater of Giovanni Pergolesi, a work in twelve movements that is one of the most poignant and emotional pieces written. It dates from 1736 and was composed only a short time before Pergolesi's death at the age of twenty-six. The close harmonies, the insistent rhythms, the emotional textures, and the lyrical lines, as well as the brief and often-stark counterpoint, were all trademarks of the emerging Classical style, and even Johann Sebastian Bach was so taken as to compose a paraphrase when the score came into his hands. As an example, the opening movement's vocal entrance with the suspensions and mysterious anachronistic walking bass are a memorable vision of the sorrow of Mary weeping at the cross, while the stark fugue of the "Fac ut ardeat" is harsh and implacable (Example 8.6).

Example 8.6 Giovanni Pergolesi, *Stabat mater*, (a) No. 1 *Stabat mater dolorosa*, mm. 12–16; (b) No. 10 *Fac ut ardeat*, mm. 1–7

Example 8.6 (Continued)

It is not surprising that Pergolesi's work was performed and even revised posthumously throughout the period as the quintessential work Catholic work for Easter. The Magnificat, on the other hand, contains a variety of emotions, from humility to exultation, and it is not surprising that compositions of this text were common in both Catholic and Protestant regions. One particularly interesting motet was the *Stella coeli*, which was meant as a prayer of thanksgiving against the plague from the twelfth century.

Genres meant for the other services include the **litany, vespers,** and **responsories,** the last of particular importance during religious seasons such as Lent or Easter. Each of the first two consists of various Psalm texts, often set to music with four-part chorus and orchestra. For example, the Loreto Litany (in Latin, *Litaniae laurentanae*), a work dedicated to the Virgin Mary, dates from the sixteenth century and was popular in both Italy and the Holy Roman Empire. Consisting of four movements (Kyrie, Sancta Maria, Regina Angelorum, and Agnus Dei), it was set by numerous composers during the period, including Mozart, Michael Haydn, Cajetan Adlgasser, and a number of Benedictine monastic composers. The style is mostly homophonic, with a final "Amen" fugue finale, but the orchestration is festive and often uses trombones to support the voice lines. Vespers, on the other hand, were a popular part of the canonical hours to be sung in the evening. It consists of several movements, including the minor doxology (*Gloria patri et filio*) after each movement, concluding with the *Magnificat*. Psalms form the bulk of the remaining movements. For example, Wolfgang Mozart's *Vesperæ Solemnis de Confessore*, KV 339, written in 1780 for the Salzburg cathedral has six movements; the Psalms 110 through 113, 117, and the Magnificat.[5] The settings, scored for woodwinds, horns, and strings, are a mixture of homophonic and contrapuntal choruses, save for the *Laudate Dominum*, with its soaring and languid solo at the beginning (Example 8.7). Responsories were especially popular during Holy Week, where a sequence of three sets of Psalms were performed on Maundy Thursday, Good Friday, and Holy Saturday. Each of these consisted of nine movements, thus emphasizing the Trinitarian symbolism of the season; the subdivisions into three movements performed during each of the three nocturns of the celebration reinforces the symbolism. Responsories could also be performed on special feast days, such as that for John the Baptist. From a musical standpoint, the responsories are generally less extensively orchestrated and often composed for choir or double choir singing alternatively with only a continuo (organ and bass instruments). A fourth genre that was as popular during Holy Week was the Lamentations of the Prophet Jeremiah (also known as the *Leçons de Ténèbres*), usually performed during Matins on Thursday, Friday, and Saturday. These settings begin with the intonation of the announcement *Incipit Lamentatio Ieremiae Prophetae* ("Here begins the Lamentation of Jeremiah the Prophet") or a simple statement of the book itself. Thereafter, each section is denoted by the sung Hebrew letters *aleph* through *he*, following which the verses form the text. It concludes with the brief colophon *Ierusalem, convertere ad Dominum Deum tuum* ("Jerusalem, return unto the Lord thy God"). The composition of this

Example 8.7 Wolfgang Amadeus Mozart, *Vesprae Solennes de Confessore*, KV 339 (1779), *Laudate Dominum*, mm. 11–19

Example 8.8 Franz Xaver Richter, *Lamentations of the Prophet Jeremiah*, No. 1 Introduction, mm. 1–20

set of verses was especially popular in eighteenth-century Iberia, set mainly for four-voice chorus and continuo, but in other regions, namely, Bohemia, Italy, and Germany, the settings could contain a more solemn and emotional affect, requiring expanded instrumentation. One such example is those composed by Franz Xaver Richter for Strasbourg, the opening movement of which is scored for the darker timbres of violas, cello, and bass (Example 8.8).

Two of the remaining Catholic genres that were popular during the Classical Period were the Psalm *Miserere mei deus* (Psalm 51) and the twelfth-century hymn *Te Deum Laudamus*. The former was used during solemn occasions and known as a Penitential Psalm, while the latter was more spontaneously composed for special celebrations, including military victories, battles, coronations, births, and other events that required laudatory music. The *Miserere* was usually performed at Lauds, though it was also done more frequently during Holy Week to supplement the responsories and Lamentations. The most famous work was a seventeenth-century setting by Gregorio Allegri, which contains sections of chant, full choir, and a high-range solo voice. It was allegedly the sole purview of the Vatican, but according to one story, the young Wolfgang Mozart was able to copy it out by memory after only two hearings.[6] The usual arrangement of the Psalm text is to divide it into five or more movements of varying tempos, including the short doxology.[7] Composers of the Classical Period found the text compelling, and many set it in cantata style, replete with large instrumentation, even though the penitential prayers have a grave and solemn text. For the Te Deum, however, the main expression is jubilation, meaning that the majority of works are written in the keys of C or D major to take advantage of the brilliance of high brass and timpani. These can be composed either as a single movement, usually with several tempo changes, or a large-scale cantata-like structure with multiple movements. In some instances, there is sometimes even an introductory brass fanfare to mark

Example 8.9 Joseph Haydn, *Te Deum*, Hob. XXIIIc:2 (1798), mm. 9–12

the celebratory nature of the piece. A prime example of this practice can be seen in the opening of Joseph Haydn's late 1798 Te Deum, in which he paraphrases the original twelfth-century chant with a powerful brass accompaniment (Example 8.9).

There was also a movement to provide nonliturgical sacred music of a simpler nature, particularly in central Europe. This took the form of a text in the vernacular (Italian, German, or other languages), sometimes in a local dialect, and music that was simple and uncomplicated. Arias or simple choral works were the main genres used, with the voice declaiming the text above a lighter accompaniment of strings, with horns or woodwinds sometimes added in a style called *stylus rusticanus*.[8] In Bohemia and Moravia, as well as Austria, these short pieces were titled **pastorellas**, and the usual season for their performance was Christmas. Similarly, in Iberia and New Spain the **villancico** was used for special nonliturgical works. First appearing during the Baroque Period, these works in the eighteenth century were composed by local composers according to local performance practices; often written for voices, they incorporated a lighter accompaniment of strings and continuo, though some texts might call for a more elaborate instrumentation. For example, the vibrant *Pastorales alegres* by Guatemalan composer Rafael Castellanos reflects the simple vocal and instrumental accompaniment from about 1750, showing that even in the remoter areas of New Spain, such local secularized music was performed (Example 8.10).

Example 8.10 Rafael Castellanos, *Pastores alegres*, "Villancico de Navidad" (1778), mm. 20–26

Finally, during the Classical Period composers in Catholic countries developed the **oratorio** or **azione sacra** along the lines of the opera seria. Given that opera was usually proscribed during Lent, to keep the singers and musicians who were employed by the theatres active, composers turned toward the oratorio. As Quantz notes, oratorios were distinguished mainly by subject matter, namely, that the stories and plots were drawn from the Bible (see Document 1). During Easter, a special type of oratorio called a **sepolcro** (or *sepolchro*) was developed as a sort of Passion play or reflection (see Document 3). As an example of the plots developed by librettists such as Metastasio, *La Passione di Gesù Cristo* presents a series of questions presented to the Apostle Peter by his colleague John, Joseph of Arimathea, and Mary Magdalene. It is particularly nonactive, and yet it was deemed suitable when first composed in 1730 by Antonio Caldara for Vienna in an operatic style, in which a succession of recitatives and arias outline the questions and the allegorical commentary on the replies. Within three years it was given its second setting by Roman composer Carlo Sodi, and by the time the last by Francesco Morlacchi was done in 1812, no fewer than sixty-one composers had done their own oratorios on the same text. These include important Classical Period figures as Johann Gottlieb Naumann, Niccolò Jommelli, Antonio Salieri, and Johann Friedrich Reichardt. Other generic works by Metastasio were *La Betulia liberata* (*Betulia Liberated*, set by Wolfgang Amadeus Mozart, among others), *Gioas re di Giuda* (*Gioas, King of Judah*), and *Isacco figura del Redentore* (*Isaac, Redeemer Figure*). His works also served as models for other librettists of the period.

Music in the Monasteries and Elsewhere: Serving God and the Flock

Mainstream churches in the larger cities were not the only places where composers devoted their efforts at writing useful and accessible sacred music. Many smaller towns, particularly in Central Europe, were dominated by the various Catholic monastic orders: Franciscans, Cistercians, Premonstratensians, and, most important, Benedictines. To these can be added a nonmonastic order, the Jesuits, whose work in the various educational and mission fields spread Catholic sacred music to all parts of the globe.

While many of the monasteries performed music that was for their inhabitants alone, thus being a self-sufficient musical establishment, others located either in cities or towns functioned as religious centers, often with the monks serving as priests to the local parishes in the surrounding region. As a result, the music for their services had to be functional, accessible, and adaptable to local performance practices. Moreover, there were many towns where music was needed but where no local composers lived to provide it. This

Figure 8.4 Organ at the Benedictine Abbey at Ottobeuren
Source: Photo courtesy of the Benediktinerabtei Ottobeuren.

circumstance led to monastic composers creating works in sets or collections that could be generically used by a wide variety of people but without excessive demands on brilliance or virtuosity.

Music in the monasteries was usually led by a *regens chori*, who sometimes also functioned as the organist. Many of the larger institutions, such as the Benedictine monastery in Ottobeuren in Bavaria (Figure 8.4), were capable of fielding large ensembles during the period, while some of the smaller ones relied upon a mixture of monks and townspeople. Most of the monastic churches in the Classical Period were characterized by highly ornate and brilliantly decorated chapels, a style termed **rococo** for its intricacies. Part of this decoration often included the organ, and it is not surprising that monasteries were able to acquire some of the largest and most powerful instruments of the time. While Gregorian chant was considered the main type of music suitable for all types of services, more festive occasions required a more elaborate setting, especially during the seasons of Easter and Christmas. Historian Wilhelm Kosch noted that in the Benedictine monastery in Ottobeuren, "the choir was well-attended day and night, and kept in order by educated men's voices." Moreover, he found that forty of the brethren comprised the voices, with two organs providing a foundation and a larger instrumental ensemble available for the feast days. In 1765, the abbot Rupert Neuss also favored musical theatre on sacred subjects for the end of the school year and High Holy days, and "on special festive occasions."[9] Finally, in the evenings after supper it was not uncommon to have the brethren perform symphonies or other chamber works for their own amusement.

This sort of vibrant musical life in the monasteries was also noticeable outside in the small towns that surrounded them, and it was not unusual for monks to perform in secular venues. Where these were located in larger towns or cities, it was also common for members of the local court (*Hofkapelle*) to supplement the ensembles. As a result, the secularization of sacred music became commonplace, and in turn, this created a demand for new works that were composed both by professional musicians outside the monasteries and by capable monks within. Musical libraries in many places were extensive, with a steady stream of works exchanged between them. For example, Pater Andreas Schröfl of Aiblingen made it his duty to collect as many works as possible for the Benedictine monastery there: "Along with such copies Schröfl collected contemporary prints or manuscript copies from the region (Augsburg, Regensburg) or directly from the workshops of known composers (Salzburg)."[10] Given that Salzburg was the site of a large Benedictine school where many monks from throughout the Empire studied, as well as having a well-regarded composer, Michael Haydn, in residence, it is not surprising that a sort of trail of his music and that of his students can be linked to the many monastic collections from this century.

Given that monasteries had a broad range of duties to the various communities in which they were located, it is not surprising that many monastic composers (and a few lay people involved in music in the abbeys) conceived the idea of publishing sets of generic music for all liturgical occasions. The chief publisher of such works was Lotter in Augsburg, and beginning already in 1740 numerous collections of simple Masses, Litanies, Te Deums, and other sacred works, usually scored for four-voice choir and accompaniments that ranged from simple organ continuo to larger ensembles including trumpets, horns, and timpani (see Figure 8.5). These sets were so popular that they not only provided a substantial income for the monasteries, they also appeared regularly, beginning with the Ten Masses Op. 1 by Pater Marianus Königsperger in 1740.[11] By 1799, a regular issuing of the sets had so dominated central Europe, that one of the composers, Pater Eugen Pausch, noted drily,

> Even more short Masses? For what reason has the musical world been inundated for more than a decade by reams of such bagatelles? That is what I hear the critics cry, but myself I find the plethora of short Masses of some worth less large that one might believe. Because I myself direct music in a monastery, then I can base my argument mainly on the needs of my own and other monasteries and abbeys, where one needs a whole raft of short Masses throughout the year, and each has a love of variety.[12]

In this way, the monasteries were not only centers of sacred music internally, but they also served as the origin of broader popular works that served the larger communities of which they were a part.

The Protestant Church Genres: The Fall of the Cantata and Rise of the Secular

During the Classical Period music in the Protestant churches was subject to convention, which meant that over the course of the eighteenth century it experienced a steep decline. During the Baroque Period, the core of the Lutheran musical liturgy was the **chorale**, containing a text that was often set homophonically, as well as appearing in improvisatory **chorale preludes** or with other texts embedded within **church cantatas**, **Passions**, or other larger works such as **oratorios**. Congregational hymn singing was the norm in the period, with hymnals (in German, *Choralbuch*) being published regularly in Protestant regions. Indeed, in places dominated by the conservative Pietists, hymns were almost the only music that was allowed in church, and in such places, sacred music declined or was deliberately unchanged from earlier times.

Music for organ was central to the worship service in most Protestant churches, especially those whose liturgy did not allow or minimalized any other form of extensive musical portions. Because most of these were intended to support the hymns of the day, they often included elaborations on the tunes, and not infrequently they required some sort of counterpoint. Although improvisation was a common practice, development of this skill required extensive instruction. Some of the leading figures of the day composed manuals for this. For example, Johann Ludwig Krebs, a pupil of Johann Sebastian Bach, published a three-volume set titled *Clavier-Übung bestehend in verschiedenen Vorpielen und Veränderungen einiger Kirchengesänge* (*Keyboard Exercises Consisting of Various Preludes and Arrangements of Some Sacred Chorales*). When the first volume was published in 1744, it consisted of thirty-nine well-known chorales that formed a core for the remainder of the set, which, in turn, became a seminal work for prospective organists in Lutheran German churches (Figure 8.6). This was only superseded by the three-volume set *Der angehende praktische*

Sacred Music in the Era of Secularism 187

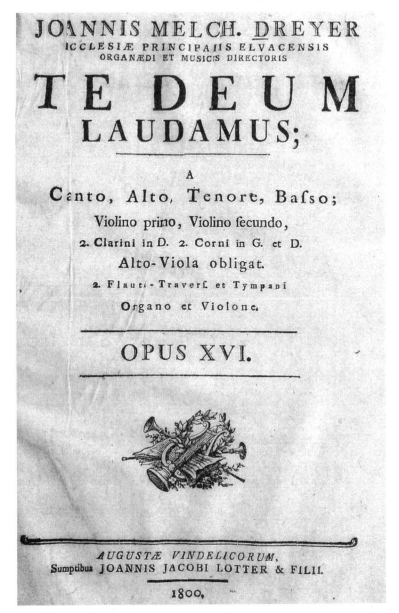

Figure 8.5 Johann Melchior Dreyer, Title page of the Lotter print of a generic *Te Deum* (Augsburg, 1800)

Organist (*The Involved Practical Organist*) by Johann Christian Kittel, the last important student of Bach in Leipzig, first published in 1801. The style was basically unchanged from the Baroque Period, meaning that the style and ways of elaborating the music changed little during the Classical Period.

The central musical portion of the Lutheran liturgy was the cantata, again a holdover from the Baroque. Consisting of a chorus and succession of recitatives and arias, concluding with a chorale in its most basic form, cantatas continued to be performed throughout the Classical Period. Bach's pupils or adherents, such as Gottfried August Homilius, Johann Kirnberger, Wilhelm Friedemann Bach, and many others, endeavored to expand the cantata through more homophonic textures, enlarged orchestration, and the use of the

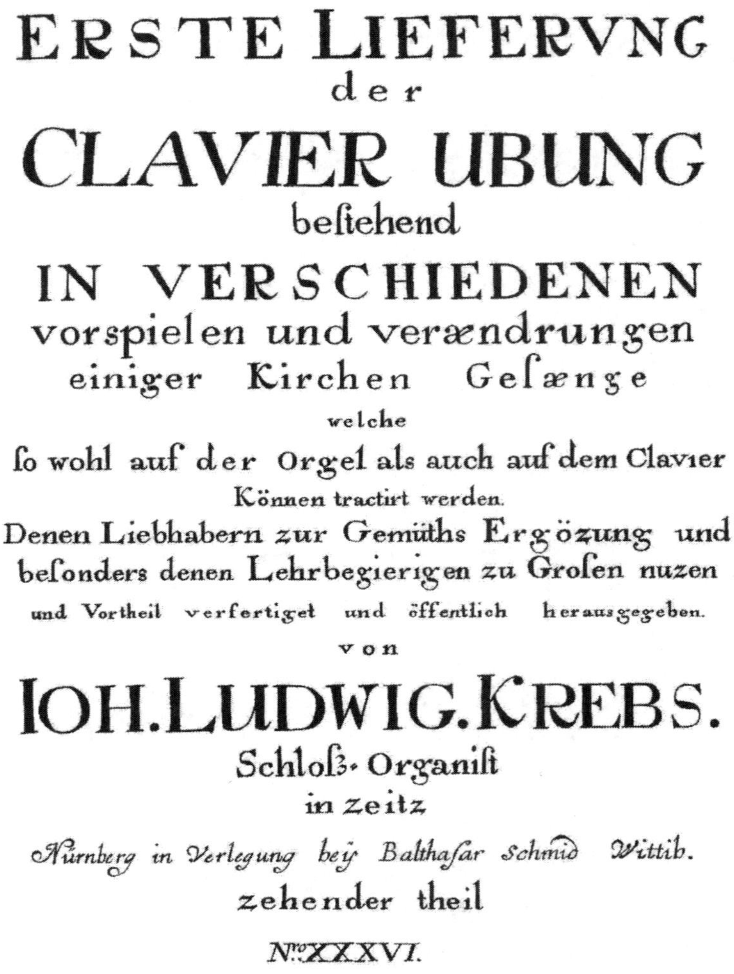

ERSTE LIEFERVNG
der
CLAVIER UBUNG
bestehend
IN VERSCHIEDENEN
vorspielen und verændrungen
einiger Kirchen Gesænge
welche
so wohl auf der Orgel als auch auf dem Clavier
Können tractirt werden.
Denen Liebhabern zur Gemüths Ergözung und
besonders denen Lehrbegierigen zu Grosen nuzen
und Vortheil verfertiget und öffentlich herausgegeben.
von
IOH. LUDWIG. KREBS.
Schloß-Organist
in zeitz
Nürnberg in Verlegung bey Balthasar Schmid Wittib.
zehender theil
N.º XXXVI.

Figure 8.6 Title page of Johann Ludwig Krebs, *Clavier-Übung bestehend in verschiedenen Vorspielen und Veränderungen* (Nuremberg, 1744)

styles of the *galant* or *Empfindsamkeit* with considerable success. Yet the form and structure remained linked to the Baroque, and as the century drew to a close, the Lutheran cantata had become less adaptable to the changing liturgy, even as it imitated the secular forms derived from the theatre.

Like the cantata, the Passion too became old-fashioned during the Classical Period, even though in Lutheran practice it still was required during Holy Week. C. P. E. Bach was required in his position in Hamburg to continue to write one each year, but after only a short while he resorted to cobbling together the work from various sources. Only in the case of the oratorio did Lutheran church music advance. Here, there was more flexibility in terms of content and structure. In 1755 a collaboration between poet Carl Ramler and Carl Heinrich Graun produced *Der Tod Jesu* (*The Death of Jesus*), consisting of a series of reflections on the crucifixion for Easter. Here, the Enlightenment sentiment prevailed to such an extent that only a few years later Johann Adam Hiller was to remark in his 1791 *Beyträge zu wahrer Kirchenmusik* (*Essays on True Sacred Music*) said simply that the work, now performed throughout Northern Europe, was a "masterpiece" and admonished any worthy church or library to have it in their collection. Ramler went on to produce two other texts to make this series a trilogy (*Die Hirten bei der Krippe zu Bethlehem* [*The

Example 8.11 Carl Philipp Emanuel Bach, *Auferstehung und Himmelfahrt Jesu*, Wq 240 (1778), Introduzione

Shepherds at the Manger in Bethlehem] and *Die Auferstehung und Himmelfahrt Jesu* [*The Resurrection and Ascension of Jesus*]), both of which were set by multiple composers; the last was especially gripping in the setting by C. P. E. Bach, with its spare and ghostly monophonic introduction (Example 8.11). Its success encouraged other composers to collaborate with authors to produce works that were both emotionally intense and musically progressive; examples include *Die Kindheit Jesu* (*The Childhood of Jesus*) by Johann Christoph Friedrich Bach and Johann Gottfried Herder and two powerful large-scale works, *Der Tod Abels* (*The Death of Abel*) and *Abraham in Moria*. By Johann Heinrich Rolle.[13]

Finally, Lutheran musical practice continued to use Catholic genres, such as the Te Deum, motet, and even an abbreviated Mass Ordinary (Kyrie and Gloria), all of which were set in either in Latin or in the vernacular and accompanied by orchestral ensembles.

Church Music of Other Realms: Between the Orthodox and Paradox

Sacred music was not just written for Catholic or Protestant churches. While these two were the dominant forms of Christianity during the Classical Period, other regions were of different faiths or were considered offshoots of the mainstream religions. In Russia, for example, the Russian Orthodox Church was dominant, and it inspired local composers to write specialized works for the liturgy. These usually had texts in Old Church Slavonic, an early language that was the equivalent to Latin in the Catholic Church. The United Kingdom was dominated by the Anglican Church, the result of the break with Catholicism that took place under Henry VIII during the sixteenth century, and its musical traditions were still adhered to during the Classical Period without much alteration. There were also various Protestant sects, many suppressed or banned outright in Europe that managed to flourish both in the mission fields and in the New World, where freedom of religion and tolerance were part of Enlightenment thought in places like the new United States of America during the latter part of the century. Finally, there were the non-Christian faiths that had their music absorbed into the missions, were sometimes viewed with curiosity and even satirized in Europe as contact with these mostly non-Western cultures increased, and were developed in some of the oriental cultures, such as the Ottoman Empire as part of the Eastern Orthodox rite.

In the regions dominated by the Russian Orthodox Church, services both in public and in the monasteries were, like the Catholic Church, dependent on hymns and chants that had developed as part of the Orthodox rite. These included special chants for all of the feast days, as well as religious holidays, and their performance practice was codified long before the Classical Period. There was, however, a newer form that developed in the eighteenth century called the *choral concerto* or hymn. These were *a cappella* works based usually upon the Psalms for single or double four-part chorus. One composer who specialized in this was

190 *Opera! Popular, Nationalist, Exotic Entertainment*

Example 8.12 Dmitri Bortniansky, Choral Concerto No. 6, mm. 1–6

Dmitri Bortniansky. His choral concertos were usually in three movements, dividing the texts according to both affect and formal structure. Although traces of Orthodox chant can be traced in a few of the works, most were diatonic, homophonic, and without displays of complex counterpoint or virtuosity. For example, the sacred concerto "Slava v vyshnih bogu" (No. 6, "Glory to God above") shows the attention to clear four-part textures and smooth flowing vocal lines, with some brilliant touches, such as the soprano beginning on a high sustained G (Example 8.12).

Special occasions, of course, required more expansive music, especially during the reign of Catherine the Great. The most brilliant composer of these works, oratorios or heavily orchestrated hymns, was Giuseppe Sarti, who was brought to St. Petersburg to write opera buffa. His work sometimes reached monumental proportions, such as a Te Deum composed in honor of the Russian victory at Ochakov in 1788. This piece included double chorus, a huge orchestra, an entire Russian horn choir, carillons, fireworks, and even military salutes by the artillery. Another work is his massive Easter oratorio, the final movement of which outlines the text from Psalm 150 with a double chorus and orchestra that includes an expanded brass section, percussion, a solo organ, and even an ostinato that imitates a bagpipe.

The core of the Anglican musical tradition was the Service, generally for chorus and organ drawn from the Book of Common Prayer. Here, the liturgy was set in simple homophonic fashion, often with some limited imitation or canon. Similarly, other worship services, such as Evensong or Matins, were set in a similar fashion. The music includes versicles, responsories, and anthems, with the conclusion of the Service having an organ voluntary. The writing was often quite conservative, following models from earlier periods. Charles Wesley Senior, an Anglican minister, himself composed more than eight thousand hymns, while his son, Charles Wesley Junior, called an "obstinate Handelian" by his brother Samuel, also a noted composer and organist, focused on anthems. Perhaps the best known of these works was a collection titled *Cathedral Music* published by William Boyce in 1755, completing a work done by his teacher Maurice Greene. In his preface, Boyce notes the historical importance of his work:

> One advantage resulting from this publication, will be the conveying to our future composers for the church, these excellent specimens of what has hitherto been considered as the true style and standard of such compositions; and as this style in Writing is at present but little studied, it is become necessary to publish some reputable models of it, lest it should be totally neglected and lost.

Example 8.13 William Boyce, Te Deum from the *Short Service*, m. 1–13

An example from this collection is a Te Deum written for four voices and organ (Example 8.13). While the day-to-day services were not intended to be developed beyond tradition, the larger works for special occasions, the odes and anthems, could take on larger forms and structures, particularly if they were meant for celebratory performances.

Finally, the English oratorio too followed the traditions established by Handel during his focus on the genre during the first half of the century. Religious in content and message, they were nonetheless intended to be performed outside the church if necessary. Operatic in format, they did not avoid the use of virtuoso vocal music in the arias, but the inclusion of the chorus helped to create a dramatic context that was more intense than on stage. The orchestration was often brilliant, with extensive use of woodwinds and brass, though the formal structures and sound could seem old-fashioned as the century progressed. As this dominated the public face of English religious music, it is not surprising to find examples of the oratorio written in the far-flung colonies of Great Britain by local resident composers, such as Samuel Felsted in Jamaica, who composed his short work, *Jonah*, in Kingston around 1774. The main examples of colonial music,

192 *Opera! Popular, Nationalist, Exotic Entertainment*

Example 8.14 William Billings, "Morning Hymn" from *The Continental Harmony*, mm. 1–8

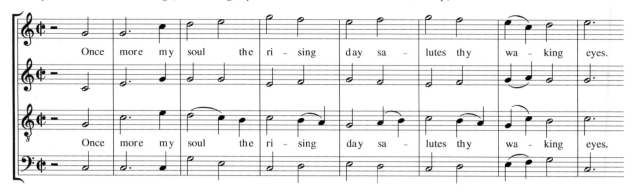

however, continued to be relatives of the simple four-part-plus-organ hymns or services, many of which were composed locally.

Another particular aspect of religious music was the publication in the American colonies (and later the United States) of music based on religious themes but meant to be performed communally by local townspeople and choral societies. These were titled anthems, or *fuging tunes*, and were set for multiple voices (usually four part), sometimes with a bass line that could be performed with whatever instruments were available. These works were characterized by a succession of tempos and a texture that ranged from simply hymn-like homophony to imitative counterpoint. These were published in various collections and composed mainly by amateurs, with the bulk of composers coming from New England or New York. The earliest of these was *Urania. A Choice Collection of Psalm-Tunes, Anthems and Hymns* compiled in 1761 by James Lyon, who included a few of his own melodies. The first real collection by an American composer was by William Billings in 1770. His most famous published series was from 1794, by which time a number of other singing masters had imitated his work (Example 8.14).

Religious tolerance was not especially widespread in a Europe dominated by the two major branches of Christianity, even though in the eighteenth century a more tolerant attitude had developed. The concept of reform had been continuous since the separation of Protestantism from the Catholic Church during the time of Martin Luther and before, but even in the eighteenth century, such movements were heavily restricted in Europe, resulting in sacred musical traditions being established wherever and whenever circumstances allowed. Perhaps the most interesting of these were the Moravians, a reform movement called the *Unitas Fratrum (United Brethren)*. They found a sympathetic patron in Count Nicholas von Zinzendorf, a counselor at the court of August the Strong of Saxony (Figure 8.7). Raised as a Pietist, he became intrigued with the theological message of the Moravians, and in 1722 he arranged for them and some of his more forward-thinking Pietist fellows to establish a town called Herrenhut on his estate in Saxony. In keeping with Enlightenment principles, he encouraged a broader, more tolerant form of Christianity whose intent was to bring a message of harmony and global unity. Although he was often autocratic, he nonetheless encouraged self-sufficiency and education, as well as often traveling abroad to help establish both colonies and missions in Europe and the Americas.

Music was a focal point from the earliest congregations, with education in music being considered paramount in the expression of their faith. The school established at Herrenhut taught music as an integral part of the theological preparation for the mission field, educating adherents in both choral and instrumental music. By 1738 the Moravians began a worldwide mission with the establishment of a site in Genadendal, South Africa, and eventually this numbered thirty settlements in as far-flung regions as Labrador, the West Indies, North America, and South America. One main emphasis was the creation of sacred works that reflected their sense of piety and devotion. In these missions, musical works were created in the local

Sacred Music in the Era of Secularism 193

Figure 8.7 Portrait of Count Nicholas von Zinzendorf by Balthasar Denner (*ca.* 1735)

languages, with the missionaries teaching the local populations hymns and four-part singing as well as instrumentalists with the limited number of instruments that could be found. For example, in 1740 they established a mission to the Mohicans, an Algonquin nation, composing hymns in that language; they were expelled from the New York colony only four years later when antipathy toward the Mohicans led to a rumor that the Moravians were "secret Jesuits." But in 1741 Zinzendorf himself helped establish a colony in Bethlehem, Pennsylvania, where the colony was more tolerant of various sects, which, over the course of the next two decades, emerged as a main center for Moravian music. A second center in Winston-Salem, North Carolina, was developed in 1766, becoming the second-largest missionary community for the Moravians. In both of these centers, as with the other dozen smaller missionary outposts in the American colonies, music was used judiciously as a means of enhancing the Moravian message of peace, equality, and devotion.

The main music performed in Moravian centers was the hymn, often a simple four-voice work in strophic format. Since the immigrants from Europe often brought with them both instruments and the knowledge of the music of the period, it was common for a higher level of competency than simple congregational singing to be done. As part of the daily liturgy, the *Singstunde* (or Singing Time) was an important opportunity to sing and expand on well-known hymns, but larger groups and ensembles were often formed to provide music for both liturgical and social functions. In Bethlehem, for example, the collegium musicum incorporated not only a trombone choir but also both wind and string ensembles that could be broken down into smaller chamber groups as needed or expanded into a mass whenever several nearby churches congregated for special occasions. One such communal event was the *Liebesmahl* (Love Feast), where music and social interaction, generally involving food and drink, were mixed. Works performed would include chamber music, such as trios, quartets, or quintets, choral singing, and even larger orchestral works drawn from the more popular genres and composers of the time. Music in the main centers was a combination of such works with pieces composed by local Moravian composers. In the more remote missions, however, it was not uncommon for anonymous native composers to create both arrangements of known works or even write their own compositions for local performances.

Conclusion

Sacred music in the Classical Period can be seen as both omnipresent and an important part of the social structure, even as it varied considerably in terms of its liturgical use. The one common denominator as the eighteenth century progressed was that it had become so secularized that some sort of reform was continually proposed. The documents reflect this view, noting that the differences in many cases between opera and church music were small, and while theorists and theologians decried what they saw as its decline, the more elaborate and festive pieces were symbols of the glory and brilliance of the various genres. Moreover, thanks to an effort to make it appeal to the population as a whole on the part of monasteries, religious sects, or even the reformers, it formed an important facet of music of this period.

Documents

Document 1. From Johann Joachim Quantz, *On Playing the Flute* (Berlin, 1752).

Church music is of two kinds, namely Roman Catholic, and Protestant. In the Roman church, the Mass, the Vesper Psalms, the Te Deum laudamus, the Penitential Psalms, the Requiem or Mass for the Dead, some hymns, the motet, the oratorio, concerto, sinfonia, pastorale, etc. are found. Each of these pieces in turn has its own particular parts, and each piece must accord with its purpose and with its text, so that a Requiem, or Miserere does not resemble a Te Deum or a composition for Easter, the Kyrie resemble the Gloria in the Mass, or a motet a happy opera aria. An oratorio or dramatically treated sacred history is ordinarily distinguished from a theatrical composition only by its content and, to a certain extent, by its recitative. In general, the introduction of more liveliness is permitted in the church of the Catholics than in that of the Protestants. The extravagances sometimes encountered in this regard, however, should probably be entirely ascribed to the composers. . . . In general, a serious and devout style of composition and performance is required in church music of any type. The style must be very different from that of an opera. To attain the desired objective, it is to be hoped that this point is always properly considered, especially by composers. In judging a church composition, which ought to stir us to praise of the Almighty, excite devotion, or engender gravity, one must consider whether its designated purpose is observed from beginning to end, whether the character of each type is maintained, and whether anything contrary to this character is introduced.

Document 2. From Johann Adolph Scheibe, *Der Critische Musikus* (Leipzig, 1745).

It is rather the main goal of sacred music principally to enlighten the listener, to encourage him to devoutness, and thus to awaken a quiet and holy awe of the heavenly Being. This goal was already sought by the Jews of the Old Testament from the admonition of eternal Providence; furthermore, it was also to be seen at the time of the first church, and it would be propitious for the virtue and worth of music if one made the effort to take it into consideration in a more precise manner in our sacred music than heretofore. We would recognize the best means of attaining this sacred intention through the main divisions of the sorts of church music. One can discern three divisions mainly according to the nature of its uses, of which two are common to all nations, but only one more usual among the Protestants. We thus note first the regular sacred pieces or the sacred cantatas that are found only in Protestant congregations. Second, the Masses, motets, odes, and whatever else belongs to it; third, the oratorios or such pieces that have been created in a dramatic manner, and thus introduce a sacred plot. These last are also found outside of the church. . . . Certainly, our sacred music is in such need of betterment, and one has become used to so many errors and excesses that one cannot be grateful enough to the various persons who loathe these and withdraw from listening to them. The arrogance and a massive noise that we have learned from the Italians has not crept into our houses of worship alone, and a particular dance-like and darting manner that normally is used for other occasions has snuck into the sanctuary as well. No wonder! If a few monomaniacal clerics have considered music as an unnecessary and distracting piece of the worship service, and desire to ban it from the altar to where it undoubtedly belongs, musicians have promulgated and strengthened this madness.

Document 3. From Joseph Martin Kraus, *Etwas von und über Musik füs Jahre 1777* (Frankfurt, 1778).

The sacred music of our times is varied according to the religions. Concerning the chant, the old usage remains among the Catholics in its most faithful form, and they are correct to seek to retain this treasured remnant of ancient times as a matter of great worth. I would only wish that they took better care of this important piece of their worship service with more diligence and not superficially as so often happens when transmitted through the taste of inexperienced practitioners of music. By itself, figural music is nonsense for the church—pure nonsense.

If music is meant to awaken spirituality and consummate devotion and contribute to it, then it is not possible to accomplish it through the Masses of today's masters. I have heard one such performed in a not average place and wonder even today, and cannot wonder about it to my satisfaction. Before the first Kyrie began a noisy overture with trumpets and timpani was heard; thereupon the chorus jubilantly fell into it with full force, and with this in order that nothing be spared in order to glorify the thing, the organist let loose all of his registers, and with every chord he brought to bear all ten fingers. Schmidt, Holzbauer, Brixi, Schmidt in Mainz have all delivered Masses: set other words underneath, and you could make short operas of them. One accepts the more solid (or however you call it!) worked-out material of Wassmut, Pögel, Richter, the great Fux, Gassmann. Why on earth does one need to repeat a simple Amen several hundred times? Should not music in the church be primarily for the heart? Are fugues appropriate for this? . . . Among the Protestants, the chorales are mostly embellished, and they will become even more so if they are considered something great, or are able to be performed in variation or four-voiced, etc. They have much more and better stuff for their church music, but unfortunately the *Cantores ad beneplacitum* themselves are able to choose. They have great masters who have given them magnificent pieces according to our taste. Graun, Agricola, Bach, Rolle, Schweitzer, Benda, Grünert, Homilius are all proper people in their craft, but; must I repeat myself? If the music in Church ought to be for the heart, are busy choruses appropriate? Are canons and contrapuntally worked-out themes according to the rules? Or even fugues?

Notes

1. For further information, see Karl Gustav Fellerer, "Church Music and the Council of Trent," *Musical Quarterly* 39 (1953), 576–594. Although the article is dated, it still gives a good overview of what the council did or did not do with respect to music. It also provides a discussion of the various following decrees that specify the rather vague precepts in the council recommendations.
2. Pope Benedict XIV.
3. The reforms, immensely unpopular in Vienna, even caused the Vatican to question their validity, and in March 1782 Pope Pius VI visited Joseph II in order to get him to rescind the dissolution of the monasteries and the institution of the reforms. The emperor refused. The reform of music was embedded within a general overhaul of the worship services.
4. See Quantz, *On Playing the Flute*, 237. He states specifically: "If he must play the bass part . . . he must adjust his performance of the high bass to each sentiment, and accommodate it to the upper part." Quantz, however, does not mention sacred music here.
5. These are *Dixit Dominus* (Ps. 110), *Confitebor tibi* (Ps. 111), *Beatus vir* (Ps. 112), *Laudate pueri* (Ps. 113), *Laudate Dominum* (Ps. 117).
6. After the first visit, he wrote it out, using the second to correct errors.
7. These are *Miserere mei Deus, Amplius lava me, Tibi soli peccavi, Ecce enim, Asperges me, Auditui meo dabis, Averte faciem, Cor mundum crea, Ne projicias, Docebo iniquos, Domine labia mea, Sacrificium, Tunc acceptabis,* and the *Gloria patri*. Other divisions of the text can occur.
8. See Geoffrey Chew, "The Austrian Pastorella and the *Stylus Rusticanus*," *Music in Eighteenth Century Austria*, ed. by David Wynn Jones (Cambridge: Cambridge University Press, 1996), 133–193. In Alpine regions, sometimes local instruments, such as alphorns (*tuba rustica*), could be used. In Bohemia and Moravia, the language was Czech, elsewhere German. Some pastorellas were intended only as instrumental works, giving rise to some generic confusion.
9. See Gertrud Haberkamp, *Die Musikhanschriften der Benediktiner Abtei Ottobeuren* (Munich: Henle, 1966), 11–13.
10. See Siegfried Gmeinwieser, *Der Musikhanschriften in der Theatinerkirche St. Kajetan in München* (Munich: Henle, 1979), xii.
11. Other monastic composers include Pater Isfrid Kayser, Pater Lambert Kraus, Pater Meinrad Spieß, but lay composers such as Johann Melchior Dreyer, Johann Anton Kobrich, and Johann Lederer, all of whom were associated with

abbeys, also contributed sets. The forerunner of this publication series was Valentin Rathgeber, who published no fewer than twenty sets of various sacred works with Lotter beginning already in 1726.
12 Preface to Eugen Pausch, *VI Missæ Breves solemni Tamen Quarum ultima de Requiem* Op. IV (Augsburg: Lotter and Sons, 1799), ii. Pausch was the *regens chori* at the Walderbach Benedictine monastery.
13 Rolle devoted much of his compositional career to the Lutheran oratorio, eventually composing fifteen of them, including a *Der Tod Jesu*.

Part IV
Capitals and Centers of Music-Making in the Classical Period

9 Urban Musical Centers and Their Musical Establishments

The Proud Hubs: Vienna, Paris, Berlin, London

The main musical centers were, as one might expect, the capitals of the most powerful states of the eighteenth century: Vienna (Holy Roman Empire of the German Nation), Paris (France from Louis XV to Napoleon), Berlin (Prussia under Frederick the Great), and London (United Kingdom under the Hanoverians). In each of these cities, musical establishments abounded, offering both employment and opportunity for musicians, even those not connected to the courts themselves. Moreover, the ruling classes supported music in a variety of ways, ranging from being performing musicians and composers to expanded royal patronage. In addition to the court cultures, all four cities offered concerts, multiple theatres, and a vibrant musical culture for the public. Given their political importance, all four capitals indulged in government-supported spectacles that focused on the state's position and power.

Vienna

As the capital of the largest European empire, Vienna held a primary status as the center of musical culture on the continent. Not only was it the principal city of the Holy Roman Empire, a status it achieved back in 1452 under Frederick III, it was a unique feudal system whereby each emperor had to be "elected" by prince-electors, who, in turn, governed their own states in Germany and elsewhere. Vienna was also the capital of Austria (*Österreich*, or Eastern Empire), and as such controlled additional domains in Hungary, the Balkans, and Italy. The geographical sprawl during the eighteenth century ranged from Belgium (the Duchy of Lorraine) in the west to Transylvania in the east, from Poland in the north to Sicily in the south. This confederation of petty states and principalities, all with an eye toward Vienna, meant that there was a confluence of musical culture there that was so vibrant that the term *Viennese Classical* (*Wiener Klassik*) has become almost synonymous with the entire period as a whole.

Sidebar 9–1 Rulers of the Holy Roman Empire During the Classical Period

Charles VII	1742–1745
Franz I	1745–1765
Joseph II	1765–1790
Leopold I	1790–1792
Franz II	1792–1806

Although Maria Theresia was supposed to inherit the crown per the Pragmatic Sanction of 1713 by her father, Charles VI, the War of the Austrian Succession (1740–1748) and the Seven Years' War (1758–1763) required her to be co-ruler with her husband, Franz I, and son Joseph II. She nonetheless reigned as absolute sovereign for forty years (1740–1780) in reality, if not in title. Her cousin Charles, Duke of Bavaria, ruled briefly during the first war.

202 *Capitals and Centers of Music-Making*

The most important patron of music was Empress Maria Theresia, who inherited a monarchy that was divided and weak politically. Although her father had attempted to ensure her succession as early as 1713, when he died much of central Europe was embroiled in an eight-year war during which territories belonging to the realm, such as Silesia, were poached by rivals such as Frederick the Great of Prussia. Maria Theresia, however, prevailed, being co-ruler in the eyes of the electors with her husband and son Joseph. Nonetheless, she wielded considerable power, with titles as Queen of both Bohemia and Hungary, as well as Archduchess in no fewer than six Habsburg lands: Austria, Tyrol, Milan, Carinthia, Styria, and Slovenia (then known as Carniola). Moreover, she created powerful alliances with France by marrying her daughter Marie Antoinette to the future Louis XVI; another to the Bourbon King of Naples, Ferdinand IV; a third to the Duke of Parma (also a Bourbon); and a son to a daughter of the Italian Este family. This extended her political and cultural reach into most of Europe.

Her father had established a court musical establishment modeled, like so many others, on Louis XIV, with opera at its center. The Kärntnertor Theatre (Figure 9.1), located alongside the main palace wall in Vienna, had been founded in 1709 and catered to the public at large, whereas a private court theatre was the domain of Italian opera seria. Major Baroque artists were encouraged to relocate to Vienna; these included Antonio Caldara, one of the chief rivals of Alessandro Scarlatti and Antonio Vivaldi, as well as the prolific librettist Pietro Antonio Trapassi, who wrote opera texts under his pseudonym, Pietro Metastasio. Along with Styrian composer Johann Joseph Fux and Johann Georg Reutter, they formed the core of a vibrant stable of composers who focused on creating Vienna as a Baroque musical center to rival France.

When Maria Theresia and her husband, Franz I, became rulers in 1745, they turned their musical tastes toward the more modern styles, a direction that could be seen as in keeping with her wish that Vienna

Figure 9.1 Theater am Kärntnertor, Vienna from the *Deutsche Schau-Bühne zu Wienn* (copper engraving, 1756)

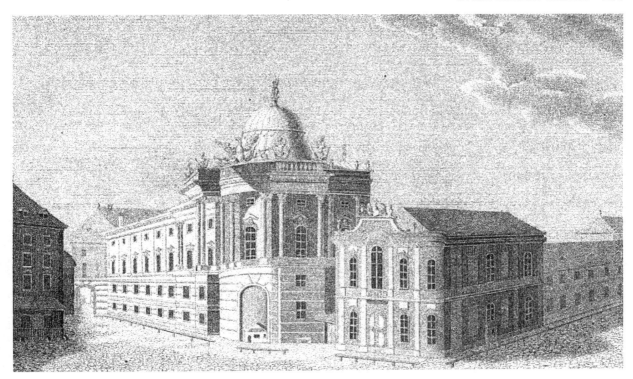

Figure 9.2 The Burgtheater in Vienna about 1765 (copper engraving)

become even more of a cultural focal point for the realm. Her first major act was to replace the court theatre by a new building, called the Burgtheater (Figure 9.2), designed by French architect Jean Nicholas Jadot de Ville-Issey, which, while administered by the court, was open to the public, thus creating a rival to the Kärntnertor. In order to maximize its use, she brought the leading composers of the day to write works for the new venue. Although opera seria continued to compose the bulk of the repertory, French stage works began to be performed by 1752, when a troupe of actors was imported from Paris. Like opera houses elsewhere, it also functioned as a concert hall on occasion.

Although the nobility preferred Italian and French opera, the court also encouraged a native form of Singspiel, with stock characters drawn from commedia dell'arte in German guise, (see Chapter 7). Although Maria Theresia banned improvisation in 1753 after she found the remarks vulgar and insulting, performances of German theatre and opera continued, with a gradual improvement in both quality and substance until by the 1770s it had metamorphosed into a sort of national theatre. Here, as early as 1748 an Imperial decree recognized the popularity of German works among the nobility by dictating how seating should be done according to social rank, with the Imperial box located just in front of the proscenium. As Charles Burney noted, the theatre was an impressive structure that served the city well (see Document 1).

Instrumental music was often performed in the palaces of the nobility, such as the Esterházy or Saxe-Hildeburghausen. Here new talents, such as Carl Ditters von Dittersdorf or Georg Matthias Monn were able to display their virtuosity, accompanied by the ensembles that each court supported. Moreover, musical soirées were commonplace among the minor nobility, and both professionals and amateurs indulged in nightly concerts, leading to the development of popular chamber genres, such as the divertimento or string quartet. There were also regimental bands, many supported by the nobility, which were called the *Harmonie* and consisted of mixed ensembles ranging from pairs of woodwinds, horns, and bassoons to much larger groups. Finally, Vienna was home to street musicians (*Gassenmusikanten*), who formed impromptu groups to offer daily entertainment at gatherings and other venues, both indoors and out. Their music featured either dances or the divertimento, and the Viennese tradition was widely imitated throughout the realm. Charles Burney notes that the quality of this was variable:

> There was music every day during dinner and in the evening at the inn where I lodged . . . but it was usually bad, particularly that of a band of wind instruments . . . all so miserably out of tune that I wished them a hundred miles off.[1]

On the other hand, without these musicians, composers such as Haydn would not have achieved success, as they were the initial stages of many a career.

Vienna was also partial to private performances open to the public. For example, Russian ambassador Dmitri Galitzin held concerts at his palace, while Baron Gottfried van Swieten, a diplomat and administrator, encouraged both exploration of earlier Baroque composers and their music, as well as served as a patron for large-scale works such as Haydn's *Creation* and *Seasons*. He held regular concerts at the Imperial Library and was one of the main supporters of the *Tonkünstlersozietät* (Society of Composers), which had been founded in 1771 by Florian Gaßmann as a means of providing funds for the widows and children of Vienna's musicians. Mozart was one of many freelance composers who contributed to this organization, in addition to promoting his own works at private academies.

In terms of the musicians available to composers in the cities, many of the courts had their own private *Kapelles*, whose personnel was sometimes available for outside performances whenever they were in town. The *Hofkapelle* itself was thirty-two players strong in 1772 (increasing by five more twenty years later), with additional members of the resident regimental band available to supplement as needed. The orchestras available for the Tonkünstlersozietät performances could double or triple the size of the *Hofkapelle*, though these were special benefit concerts.

Given the richness of the musical culture in Vienna, it is no wonder that it was considered the center of music throughout Europe. Burney noted in his diary:

> Vienna is so rich in composers and encloses within its walls such a number of musicians of superior merit, that it is but just to allow it to be, among German cities, the imperial seat of music as well as of power.[2]

Paris

If Vienna was regarded as the European musical center during the Classical Period, then its closest rival was Paris. Unlike Vienna, Paris had long maintained a position as the model for civilization and culture ever since the rule of Louis XIV in the Baroque era. The continuity that the music had achieved, especially in the world of opera (see Chapter 7), as well as the intellectual discussions of the Enlightenment ideals of savants such as Voltaire, Diderot, and Rousseau, meant that it was seen as the determinant of a polite (or *galant*) society that other courts sought to imitate.

Sidebar 9–2   Rulers in Paris During the Classical Period

Louis XV	1715–1774
Louis XIV	1774–1792
French Republic	1792–1804
Napoleon I	1804–1814

Although dominated throughout the period by the developments in opera, Paris retained its position by virtue of being the main center of music publishing. It was here that Rameau developed modern theory, that virtuosos from all over Europe came to be heard and make their reputation, and the latest symphonies, sonatas, and other genres were to be discussed and critiqued.

The control of the musical establishments in Paris by the court declined over the course of the eighteenth century. When Louis XIV passed away in 1715, the dominance of Versailles over the culture of France was weakened, and with the reign of Louis XV, society began to be centered on Paris. It was here that encyclopedists such as Diderot and Rousseau began to create philosophical and aesthetical discussions on music and its relationship to the other arts. Rousseau, in particular, outlined what he considered to be the weaknesses of the French style in is works *Lettre sur la musique françoise* (1753), and *Dictionnaire de la musique* (1768), the second being acknowledged as the foundation of music lexicography and widely imitated.

Music in Paris was divided between opera and instrumental music. Venues for French-language opera have already been discussed, but instrumental works were important in that they were the mainstay of the music publishing business. It was in Paris that engraving practices on thin copper or pewter had developed, with the engravers often being noblewomen who sought extra income. After about 1750 numerous publishers were active in the city, each of whom both advertised their editions and sought composers directly for works to publish and disseminate. While some works were done on subscription to the wealthiest patrons, many were available in bookshops throughout the city, and music was often shipped abroad to customers around the world. Haydn's own pupil Ignaz Pleyel became one of almost a hundred music publishers in the city by 1790, lending support to Paris as the center for international music publishing throughout the century.[3]

Musical activity outside of the various theatres was vibrant through the reign of the monarchy up to the French Revolution in 1789. In particular, public concerts proved especially popular, enough so that the *Mércure de France*, the main newspaper of the city, noted a rapid increase in the number of concerts, public and private, further stating "musical taste has never been so universal."[4] In 1725 Anne-Danican Philidor obtained a royal privilege to conduct public concerts during Lent. These became known as the *Concerts Spirituels*, and although the earliest repertory was devoted to sacred music, only a few years later secular music was introduced. Although it retained its name, by 1730 much of the music was secular, and it became the main venue for new works both from French composers and foreigners. The concerts were held in the Tuileries Palace and by about 1775 the number of performers, both orchestra and choir, increased to over a hundred (Figure 9.3). The main component of the repertory by this time was the symphony, though oratorios in French were also popular. In 1748 composer and courtier Antoine Dauvergne managed to obtain the privilege, but his incompetence allowed it to be passed on to several other enterprising men, such as François Gossec and Joseph Le Gros. It is here at the Concerts Spirituels that composers such as Mozart hoped to make their reputation, and successes, such as the symphonies of Johann Stamitz in 1755, earned them international acclaim.

As crucial an organization as the Concerts Spirituels was, its success spawned rivals. In 1770 a competing series called the Concerts des Amateurs was formed with an orchestra of forty-eight musicians performing the latest in the symphonic repertoire. Held at a room in the Hôtel de Soubise, the series remained popular until 1781, when the Société de la Loge Olympique, concerts organized by the Masonic lodge of that name, replaced it. An even closer competitor to the Concerts Spirtuels, its concerts were held in the same Tuileries

Figure 9.3 Poster for a Concert Spirituels at the Tuileries Palace in Paris (1754)

Figure 9.4 Etching of the Chevalier de Saint-Georges by Gabriel Banat after a painting by Mather Brown and William Ward (1787)

Palace under the direction of famed violinist Giovanni Battista Viotti. It was this group that scored a coup by a special commission to Haydn for six symphonies, now known as the Paris Symphonies, in 1784.

Like Vienna, private concerts were often held in the homes of the nobility, where a regular gathering of prominent musicians patronized by the upper classes performed frequently. The social structure was such that invitations were tendered to the most important visitors, as well as local high-class people such as the famous West Indian violinist and swordsman, Joseph Boulogne, the Chevalier de Saint George (Figure 9.4). Few, if any, however, indulged in more than chamber music, but the exceptions were the Prince of Condé, Louis Joseph de Bourbon, and the Duc d'Orleans, Louis-Philippe-Joseph. Both of these noblemen supported their own small chamber orchestras, and in many cases provided juries for eventual performances at the Concerts Spirituels.

Music education also played an important role toward the end of the Classical Period. In 1784 the École Royale du Chant (Royal Singing School) was established under Gossec, with the intent that singers would be trained in the latest operatic styles of Piccinni and others. The 1789 revolution and the establishment of the first French Republic a few years afterward dealt a critical blow to music in Paris, which was now forced to become a servant of the state, consisting of works that extolled the virtues of the bourgeois citizenry. Composers such as Gossec, Cherubini, and Grétry all wrote cantatas, oratorios, operas, and orchestral works that had political ramifications, but in perilous times, the vitality of Parisian musical life that had existed prior to 1789 waned. It was not until the reestablishment of order following the chaos of the Reign of Terror that a systematic revival of music in Paris was undertaken. In 1792, Bernard Sarette established the Institut National de Musique (National Institute of Music, originally the more politically correct École gratuité de la garde nationale, or Free School of the National Guard), which was meant to develop music in the service of the state. Realizing that both institutions had the same goal, these were merged into the Conservatoire de Paris in 1795, with Sarette as the director. The goal of the Conservetoire was to provide for a solid curriculum for future musicians under the tutelage of the foremost composers and performers of the time, including Cherubini, Méhul, violinists Pierre Rode and Rudolphe Kreutzer, and others. In 1803 the Prix de Rome, established in the Baroque Period by Louis XIV, was extended to music, becoming the major prize for aspiring musicians and composers to the present day.

Paris, as a musical center, rivaled Vienna as a place where music was omnipresent and performed continuously for the public, as well as being the source of much of the printed music of the Classical Period.

Berlin

As a musical capital Berlin was also a major center, although the culture was less well-developed than in either Vienna or Paris. For much of the period it was dominated by Frederick the Great, whose own peculiarities, as a rule, dictated a different sort of musical establishment, particularly since the king was often at the forefront of many wars that involved Prussia during the eighteenth century. As the heir to the throne, his father, Friedrich Wilhelm I, who had suppressed Frederick's interest in the arts in favor of military training, had dominated him. When Frederick was able to obtain his own residence at Rheinsberg, he began to surround himself with musicians, in particular Johann Joachim Quantz, who became his flute teacher. Upon the succession to the Prussian throne in 1740, Frederick provided permanent employment for a covey of musicians, whose job was to provide for the king's own pleasure and gratification. These were all of the first rank and included the violinists Johann Gottlieb Graun and Franz Benda, both already considered virtuoso players and adept composers. In addition, he hired Carl Philipp Emanuel Bach as his personal accompanist, as well as Christoph Schaffroth as accompanist to his sister, Anna Amalia, herself a composer and collector of music. His own personal *Kapellmeister*, Carl Heinrich Graun, accompanied him from Rheinsberg and was put in charge of the Berlin musical establishment.

Sidebar 9–3 Rulers of Prussia During the Classical Period

Friedrich (Frederick) II the Great	1740–1786
Friedrich Wilhelm II	1786–1797
Friedrich Wilhelm III	1797–1840

Frederick was himself a notable composer, whose major works were written in the *galant* or *Empfindsamkeit* style, both of which he learned from Quantz. He also encouraged the musicians in his employ to devote themselves to the progress of musical composition, though not at the expense of his own tastes or needs. For example, he held nightly soirées in which he was the featured soloist, often in works he himself had written (Figure 9.5). The audiences were generally limited to his immediate family or special guests, and his passion for music was noted by visitors. In 1772 Charles Burney noted, "His performance surpassed, in many particulars, anything I had ever heard among the *Dilettanten* or even professors: His Majesty played three long and difficult concertos successively, and all with equal perfection."[5]

208 *Capitals and Centers of Music-Making*

Figure 9.5 Copper engraving of Frederick the Great performing at a concert by Johann Peter Haas (*ca.* 1786)
Source: Used by permission of the Bildarchiv Preussischer Kulturbesitz.

Frederick's control over music in Berlin was regimented and strict, but he was often on military or diplomatic missions, so his private musicians were often left to their own devices. This led to a three-tiered musical establishment. His personal concerts were held regularly at his favored palace San Souci in Potsdam, but he supported both opera and concerts in Berlin itself. Because he disliked German theatre, he ensured that his *Kapellmeister*, Graun, made Berlin a center of Italian opera by hiring the best singers and musicians from Italy for a new opera house inaugurated in 1741 with Graun's opera *Cesare et Cleopatra* (Figure 9.6). Thereafter, it was to produce two new works each season, culminating in 1755 with Graun's *Montezuma* to a text by the king himself. Only toward the end of his life did the king allow for German Singspiel to be performed but only by visiting troupes such as Koch's and only if intermingled with plays. The third tier was the establishment of Berlin as a musical intellectual center, where the future of music itself would be debated and developed. Quantz, C. P. E. Bach, and Johann Philipp Kirnberger all published seminal treatises on music in the city, with Quantz's work on the flute and Bach's on the keyboard serving as models for both performers and composers throughout the rest of Europe. Composer and contrabassist Johann Gottlieb Janitsch created the *Freitagsakademien* (Friday Academies) at his home in which chamber music for both professionals and amateurs was performed and discussed, and Christoph Nichelmann, Bach, and author-composer Christian Gottfried Krause formed the first Berlin *Liederschule* (School of Song) to develop the solo song as a popular genre.

During the last years of Frederick's life, his own musical tastes became moribund, and with the succession of his nephew Friedrich Wilhelm to the throne in 1780 the control and ossification of Berlin's musical

Figure 9.6 Copper engraving of the Opera House in Berlin (*ca.* 1745)

establishment was relaxed. The king was an avid cellist and loved an easygoing lifestyle. His teacher, Jean-Pierre Duport and violinist Ivan Jarnovic were hired to lead the orchestra, and he had the services of a new *Kapellmeister*, Johann Friedrich Reichardt, though this composer was often away on his travels. Also in residence was Carl Christian Fasch, conductor of the opera, who succeeded Janitsch in hosting singers, composers, musicians, and intellectuals regularly at his home. In 1789, he made his gatherings legitimate by assembling them into the *Berliner Sing-Akademie* (Berlin Singing Academy), one of the most important organizations and libraries of the Classical Period. Fasch's successor, Carl Friedrich Zelter, was one of the first music professors at the Royal Academy of the Arts, a position from which he supervised the establishment of music conservatories throughout Prussia.

Although tightly controlled, the musical establishment in Berlin was intellectually progressive, and throughout the Classical Period served as a northern center, drawing composers to create new works, particularly in vocal and chamber genres. It was led for much of the time by a peculiar, autocratic, but musically-gifted monarch, whose discipline was legendary.

London

From a political standpoint, the capital of the United Kingdom, London, served as one of the major cities in Europe. For much of the century it had been subject to turmoil, beginning with the establishment of the Hanoverian dynasty of George I in 1717. Throughout the century, England had gone to war innumerable times, first with other European powers during the War of the Austrian Succession, then internally with the Jacobite rebellion in 1745, and then both the Seven Years' War and American Revolution, all of which created political crises within the kingdom. When added to the occasional disengagement of George III due to a hereditary illness, and the continual infighting in Parliament, one might not have been surprised if music in London was of little consequence. This, however, is not the case, for in the city and its surrounding regions, musical life was an important and present part of the English culture.

Sidebar 9–4	**Rulers in London During the Classical Period**
George II	1727–1760
George III	1760–1820

As the Classical Period emerged from the Baroque about 1730, Handel was regarded as the main musical figure in the city. In 1728 his Royal Academy of Music had become bankrupt due to the popularity of new works such as *The Beggar's Opera* and the high expenditures necessary to mount the Italian opera seria. As noted earlier, successive opera companies, such as Handel's own revived Academy, the Opera of the Nobility, and other smaller theatres, continued the tradition of opera in London thereafter, but the repertory of these gradually turned to works in English as they were cheaper and more accessible to audiences than were Italian works. Handel's music, however, left an indelible mark on composers, and many of his contemporaries, such as Thomas Arne, Maurice Greene, and William Boyce all only cautiously expanded their style in new directions.

Following Handel's death in 1759, English musical life was altered only slightly in terms of the theatre. During the last decade or so of his life he had begun to drift from Italian opera seria toward an Anglicized version that was more akin to the popular English oratorio he had fostered. His English opera *Semele* had demonstrated that this more nationalist work could be popular, even if it conformed to a well-known foreign model. Both the King's Theatre in Pall Mall under a privilege awarded to Edward Vanbrugh and the Royal Theatre in Covent Garden took to producing more English opera, with each building designed to accommodate suitable audiences. This superseded the Baroque custom of taverns offering performance

Figure 9.7 Illustration (etching) of Vauxhall Gardens, by Thomas Rowlandson (*ca.* 1785)

venues alongside their drinking establishments, in essence giving Londoners a good choice for regular entertainments. To ensure that these proved economically viable, a mix of Italian and English opera was performed, with Arne's works being particularly popular. The venues were substantial and often served for both stage works and the occasional instrumental concert. As noted in Chapter 7, the public was allowed in at heavily subsidized rates, and a number of attempts on the part of the private management to raise them resulted in riots and mayhem.

During the summers and early fall when the weather was good, music took place outdoors in one of several gardens in London, the most important of which were Ranleigh and Vauxhall. These were outfitted with large pavilions hosting a variety of entertainments, though the main concerts were held in the largest and most ornate ones (Figure 9.7). Audiences had the opportunity to stand or sit and listen to the concerts, or to wander about with the music in the background. These pleasure gardens were host to impromptu orchestras and singers, with an eclectic variety of music available to audiences, and by the middle of the century had become an important center of music in the English capital. In 1762 German composers Karl Friedrich Abel and Johann Christian Bach, the latter who arrived from Italy to compose Italian opera seria for the London stage, became residents in the city. Three years later, they teamed up with Venetian-born soprano and entrepreneur Teresa Cornelys to offer a public concert series at her opulent series of rooms at Carlisle House in Soho Square.[6] Cornelys, one of the most colorful figures of her time, had extensively renovated the building to include a variety of rooms for socializing, drinking, and gaming. In addition to concerts in the main ballroom, she hosted a variety of dances, masquerades, and other communal activities. As Francis Burney noted in 1770, "[t]he magnificence of the rooms, splendor of the illuminations and embellishments, and the brilliant appearance of the company exceeded anything I ever before saw." Her luck changed in 1772 when she began to present operatic performances in violation of the royal privilege, which in turn led to her bankruptcy a year later.

In 1774 the Bach-Abel concerts were held in the Hanover Square Rooms in the same neighborhood until Bach's death in 1782 (Figure 9.8). This concert hall had been purchased by both composers as a venue for their series, and in 1783 a new series was started by violinist Johann Wilhelm Cramer called the Professional Concerts. These began to feature a talented violinist by the name of Johann Peter Salomon,

Figure 9.8 The Hanover Square Rooms, London (nineteenth-century engraving)

who gradually took the reins of the public concerts from Cramer, who devoted his time toward charitable concerts for the Music Fund, an organization similar to Vienna's *Tonkünstlersozietät*. It was Salomon who persuaded Joseph Haydn to make two trips to London in the 1790s. In the meantime, the former patron of the Professional Concerts, Willoughby Bertie, known as Lord Abington, threw his support to the rival concert series held in the Pantheon, a large and imposing building modeled on the Pantheon in Rome (Figure 9.9). Here in 1789 opera was presented after the King's Theatre burned, but despite the rival patronage that brought Haydn's pupil Ignaz Pleyel to London to compete with Salomon's concerts, the popularity of this venue was short-lived.

The most famous international event of the Classical Period in London, however, was the Handel Centenary held in the Pantheon, Westminster Abbey, and other venues around the city to celebrate the centennial of Handel's birth. After its first success in 1784, it continued to be held for several years thereafter. Burney noted in 1787 that the festival, now known as the Grand Musical Festival, numbered more than eight hundred performers, further stating, "Such is the state of practical music in this country, that the increase of performers, instead of producing confusion, has constantly been attended with superior excellence of execution."[7]

In London during the period, private music-making was also an important social event that occurred in most households on a regular basis. Thanks to Burney, the Earl of Sandwich, and others, the Concerts of Ancient Music, begun in 1776, also provided a historical occasion to revive the music of the past, and social clubs, such as the Catch Club from 1761, also provided an opportunity for members to engage in musical interactions. As Burney states,

> [t]he spirit and liberality with which this establishment has been since supported has not only much improved the manner of performing the catches, canons, and glees of old masters, but been productive of innumerable new compositions of that kind, which are still of a more ingenious and elegant texture.[8]

In short, London was an active environment for music, with its share of publishers, brilliant public concerts, opera, and private music salons, and given that it was a favorite destination for foreign musicians and composers, beginning with Handel and lasting up through Haydn, there is no doubt that it deserved its reputation as a main musical capital.

Figure 9.9 Masquerade held in the Pantheon Theatre, London, with the concert stage in the background (*ca.* 1798, copper engraving)

The Italian Rivals: Naples, Venice, Rome

Given the dominance of Italian music during the Classical Period, it is not surprising that the major cities of the Italian peninsula all competed against each other, particularly in the realm of opera. Although these were politically diverse, they all subscribed to a similar cultural identity, and even though there were local differences, each maintained a tradition of music that was often imitated elsewhere in Europe.

Naples

During the Classical Period Naples was arguably the center of music in Italy. Through its four conservatories, it provided a steady stream of musicians—composers and performers—who achieved international recognition. In 1735 Charles VII, the son of the King of Spain, inaugurated Bourbon rule over Naples and the Two Sicilies (Sicily and Sardinia). He inherited a vibrant musical culture that had been in full flower since the Baroque Period.

At the core of the musical establishment in the city were the four conservatories (as noted in Chapter 1), which not only offered employment to the many musician-teachers but also trained musicians in every instrument and voice. Many of these students, who were required to demonstrate both proficiency and progress during their education, came from outlying regions around the Mediterranean from as far away as western Greece, Malta, and the Iberian Peninsula. Their teachers not only achieved fame for their pedagogical ability but also supplied a steady stream of music for not only the main opera house, the Teatro San Carlo but also venues from the many churches in the city to improvisatory street theatre. As the largest city in Italy, it was both a cultural and economic powerhouse.

Composer-teachers such as Francesco Durante and Leonardo Leo established Naples as one of the main centers of the new Classical Period style. However, despite the activity at the main opera houses supported by the nobility and the churches, there appears to have been little in the way of actual organized musical activities. The led the many visitors on a grand tour to regard Naples in a less than favorable light. For example, Burney notes in 1772,

> The national music here is so singular as to be totally different, both in melody and modulation, from all that I heard elsewhere. This evening in the streets there were two people singing alternately; one of these Neapolitan *canzoni* was accompanied by a violin and a *calascione*. The singing is noisy and vulgar, but the accompaniments are admirable and well performed.[9]

There were no public concerts or concert venues during the period. Nonetheless, many performances occurred at private entertainments in the villas of the wealthy. Visiting musicians were often asked to play there, but the main entertainments were held at the various summer outdoors fairs, such as that held at Mergellina on the shores of the bay. An Italian visitor described it:

> Each summer for about two months the night is illuminated by an infinity of torches, and in the middle is placed an orchestra composed of students of the three music conservatories in our city to play the most beautiful sinfonias and notturnos until after midnight.[10]

In the seaside resort of Posillipo, boat and shoreline concerts were also heard, with special concerts arranged at the Casino di Delizia from around 1770 onward. Composers and singers engaged at the opera houses regularly performed at these venues, and after 1777 at the Accademia de'Cavalieri, an organization devoted to pleasure (gambling, drinking, dancing, music) that organized concerts for their members and guests. Naples was also famed for its religious holidays, when processions were led through the streets, culminating with sacred music in one of the churches written especially for the occasion.

After the revolution of 1798, the short-lived republic replaced the Italian music culture with one derived from Revolutionary France, but in the aftermath of its demise after only half a year, the restoration of the monarchy brought a return to an enlightened culture, with the exception of those composers who had served the Republic. Domenico Cimarosa found himself imprisoned and Giovanni Paisiello escaped to France.

As perhaps the most important musical city in Italy, Naples did have a variable reputation. It turned out scores of composers and musicians from its conservatories, some of whom had international careers, and no opera composer of note could expect a reputation for success unless their work was produced at least once in the city. Charles's successor, Ferdinand IV, was a strong supporter of the arts, especially opera, himself being a player of the lira organizzata or hurdy-gurdy (for which he commissioned Joseph Haydn to compose pieces). It was a necessary stop for all traveling musicians on the grand tour, who favored the various native and ex-patriot aristocrats with their talents. It was, however, contradictory to note that, as musical as the populace was, the lower classes had a reputation for low-brow comedy that bordered on the vulgar.

Perhaps the only real competition Naples had as a musical center was from the second-largest city, Venice.

Venice

The Venetian Republic was a declining power during the Classical Period. As an independent entity, it held little more than a fraction of its economic sway from previous centuries, and politically it had no power at all since the Treaty of Utrecht in 1718. It was still a major cultural center, however, and during the Classical Period it maintained a reputation for musical entertainment. Given that opera was the dominant genre, performed in a variety of houses that were operated under license from the various leading families. The usual season was during Carnival, a brief period around Ascension, and a sort of preseason during the late fall. There were six theatres in the city, though not all of them performed opera; the most resplendent was the Teatro San Benedetto, which opened in 1755. The Venetian houses were relatively small until the establishment of La Fenice (The Phoenix) in 1792 but were used for a variety of purposes, such as masquerade balls during the Carnival season. New works were commissioned for every season, though, as noted in Chapter 6, not all succeeded. Nonetheless, it was an important city for composers to premiere their latest works, especially if these were to be exported to cities such as Dresden or Vienna.

Given that the opera season was so short, musical activity needed other venues to function year around. While Venice lacked the street music or the opulent seaside escapes of the wealthy found in Naples where music could be heard, there was a certain popular element that did exist, particularly among the boatmen (gondoliers) and street musicians. Burney notes, "The songs of the *Gondoleri*, or Watermen . . . are so celebrated that every musical collector of taste in Europe is well furnished with them."[11] Burney's first encounter with Venetian popular music was

> performed by an itinerant band of two fiddles, a violoncello, and a voice . . . performed so well that in any other country in Europe, they would not only have excited attention, but have acquired applause, which they justly merited.[12]

While this sort of impromptu music was found everywhere, the main centers of music-making apart from the theatres were the famed Ospedales (called by Burney and others "conservatories") and the many churches. While no doubt musicians found employment outside the theatres in private functions for the wealthy families or special occasions, these were subordinated to the impressive musical concerts given at these institutions. The four Ospedales (della Pietà, dei Mendicante, degli Incurabili [Figure 9.10], and the Ospedaletto a San Giovanni e Paolo) were originally hospitals run by monastic orders, but by the Classical Period had become both orphanages and schools for the well-to-do young women, who were trained in music and the other fine arts. It was in music, however, that they achieved an international reputation for excellence, already beginning in the Baroque Period under teachers such as Antonio Vivaldi. The *maestri di cappelli* of each institution regarded their positions as vital to the cultural atmosphere and reputation of Venice, and each not only trained the young women to a degree of excellence; they also composed music both for their charges and for the city at large. Ferdinando Bertoni and Baldassare Galuppi were the main figures, but internationally famed composers such as Traetta, Sacchini, Jommelli, Sarti, Pasquale Anfossi, and Cimarosa were all appointed to posts at these institutions. As the music as exclusively performed for sacred occasions, such as the regular Saturday and Sunday Vespers concerts, it is not surprising that the Ospedale system was regarded as an important one for the city, even though the musicians themselves generally did not perform outside of the buildings. In early years, they performed behind screens from the audiences, who paid to attend the concerts, thus providing support for the Ospedales. By 1750, however, newer facilities were furnished where the audiences were admitted to a ground-floor salon, with the performers

Figure 9.10 Engraving of the Ospedale degli Incurabili, Venice (*ca.* 1750)

Figure 9.11 Concert at the Ospedale della Pietà, Venice (*ca.* 1765, Venice, Fondazione Querini Stampaglia)

separated above, either in boxes or on a special raised stage (Figure 9.11). Although many of the pupils went on to fulfill the usual roles in Venetian society, a number of the protégés remained behind, taking the veil and becoming well-regarded musicians and teachers in their own right. These took the name of the Ospedale, and composers such as Agata della Pietà and Samaritana della Pietà became popular for their extensive abilities on the organ and violin, as well as their pedagogical work.

Visitors to the Ospedale concerts marveled at the talent, though there may have been a tinge of the exotic about choruses and orchestras made up solely of young women. Charles de Brosses wrote of one such concert,

> The transcendent music here is that of the conservatories. . . . [They] are raised at the expense of the state and are uniquely trained to excel in music. They both sing like angels and play the violin, flute, organ, oboe, cello, bassoon; in short there is no instrument big enough to daunt them. They are cloistered like nuns. They perform entirely by themselves, and each concert is composed of about 40 girls. . . . Their voices are exquisite in agility and context with each other.[13]

The main church was St. Mark's Basilica, though Burney and others witnessed a constant parade of sacred music in all of the many churches. The English visitor reported that, although much of what he heard was set for nothing more than voices and organ, the music was still "so well executed and accompanied, that I do not remember ever to have received more pleasure from this kind of music."[14] In St. Mark's however, the Mass he heard included instruments placed in the various balconies about the church, just like during the Renaissance.

If Naples and Venice were the Italian music capitals, the center was still Rome, where different notions of how music was to be performed prevailed.

Rome

During the Classical Period, Rome was a contradiction in terms of music. The city was dominated by the Vatican, and, as noted in Chapter 8, Pope Benedict XIV issued his encyclical *Annus qui hunc* in 1749 legitimizing the use of a more secular style in Catholic sacred music. At the same time, the Vatican itself (and those churches closely associated with it) were adjured to maintain the strict Council of Trent *stile antico*. As Pope Pius VI told visitor Joseph Martin Kraus, he feared that Italian music had not progressed to any extent, with Kraus who commented further on a performance at the Sistine Chapel: "The cappella consists of sixteen to twenty singers, among whom hardly four castrati have bearable voices. . . . I have not found a single good Italian organist."[15]

Sacred music elsewhere in Rome was less constrained. In other churches a larger setting was allowed, and in 1716 Pope Clement XI had ordered all musicians practicing in Rome to become members of the Confraternity of Santa Cecilia, originally founded back in 1585. This gave the Holy See a limited control over music in the city, and in the special venues, such as the Oratory of St. Fillipo Neri, regular musical concerts were held during church feast days and Lent. Indeed, the term *oratorio* itself derives from these venues during the Baroque Period, and by the Classical Period they regularly featured concerts that were regarded more secular than sacred.

Venues in Rome would include private theatres such as the Cancelleria Apostolica or the various palaces of the cardinals or nobles who maintained residences in Rome. These were mostly smaller theatres, but there were also times when the churches themselves served as to host works such as oratorios or other liturgical works. One such was the Capella Palatina, which was attached to the Spanish legation, which produced works during Lent.

One of the leading proponents of musical and poetic development was the Arcadian Academy. During the Classical Period, it debated the connection of poetry and music, with one of the members, Metastasio, taking a leading role. They met and heard cantatas and oratorios performed in the Cancelleria, though their efforts were spread about the city in the different palaces of the Cardinals.

Rome also became a leading center of opera, with large venues (Teatro Argentina [Figure 9.12], Teatro Valle, Teatro Capranica) located throughout the city. Here mainly opera seria was produced. The pope, however, forbade women to appear on stage, so female roles were taken on by males in transvestite roles.

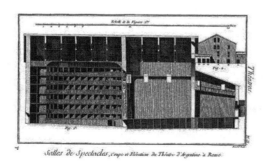

Figure 9.12 Engraving of the architectural cross-section of the Teatro Argentina, Rome (*ca.* 1760)

Furthermore, he allowed opera to be produced only during Carnival, and while this may have limited the normal season, it did have the effect of leading singers being able to accept other commissions and engagements elsewhere in Italy during the other times of the year.

Audiences in Rome were known for their often-raucous criticism of stage performances, so much that a number of famous singers, such as the castrato Manzuoli, hesitated to appear for fear of their comments. Moreover, audiences often confused the musical performances with the various aspects of their appearance, particularly since this created sexual ambiguity and what the philosopher Montesquieu described as a "bad effect on morals." Nonetheless, Burney noted that Roman audiences were the most "fastidious" in Europe, and despite the limited opera season and capriciousness of the audiences, most composers would gravitate there, if nothing else, for the variety of music that could be commissioned in the various churches, oratories, and private palaces.

The Musical Centers of the Holy Roman Empire: Dresden, Prague, Mannheim/Munich

Dresden

If Berlin was considered a progressive musical city in the Classical Period, its main rival was Dresden, the capital of Saxony. Here under the rule of August the Strong, music thrived as a part of the city and court culture. At the end of the Baroque Period, the main focus had been on music for the church. Dresden was in a unique position in eighteenth-century Europe, in that Saxony was split almost evenly between Catholics and Protestants; moreover, enlightened rulers such as Count Zinzendorf supported smaller offshoots such as the Moravians. All of these groups were active musically, and it is not surprising that a degree of overlap in opportunities awaited composers, whatever their personal religion. Dresden also had direct connections with other Imperial musical centers, such as Prague and Vienna, from which they drew musicians to the city. Its *Hofkapelle* was considered one of the most proficient, led by violinist Johann Pisendel and organist Johann David Heinichen, and it is not surprising that many of the later stars in places such as Berlin, like the Graun and Benda brothers, began their careers in Dresden.

Sidebar 9–5   Rulers in Dresden During the Classical Period

Friedrich August I the Strong	1694–1733
Friedrich August II	1733–1763
Friedrich Christian/Maria Antonia	1763–1768
Friedrich August III the Just	1768–1806

Friedrich Christian passed away after only a few months, leaving his wife, Maria Antonia of Bavaria, as regent for his underage son.

By 1745, sacred music had largely been supplanted by opera, as Johann Adolph Hasse and his wife, soprano Faustina Bordoni, arrived from Italy as musical superstars. The Dresden Hofoper became one of the most celebrated venues for performance under their guidance, with large numbers of Italian singers and musicians imported to perform. Hasse also formed strong musical ties with Vienna and Italy, places he continued to return to fulfill commissions. In 1764, realizing his own age had passed, Hasse recommended Johann Gottlieb Naumann as his successor. Naumann, initially occupied the post of church composer. After a successful tour of Italy, he succeeded Hasse as *Kapellmeister* in 1776, winning international fame for his Italian operas. Under his direction, the Hofoper gained prominence as one of the main opera houses in Germany, with a large orchestra and extensive company of singers recruited both locally and from Italy.

The two other venues that offered employment and regular music were the two main churches in town, the Catholic Hofkirche and the Protestant Frauenkirche. Both were redesigned in the 1740s as part of a renewal of the city center, and both were prime objects for musicians wishing jobs. The Frauenkirche had a 1736 Silbermann organ of forty-three stops, and Bach's son Wilhelm Friedemann was one of the secondary organists who obtained his first position there. At the Hofkirche, the reconstruction of 1751 included a Silbermann organ of forty-seven stops, a direct competition with the Frauenkirche. Both these venues could count on the services of the *Hofkapelle*, which was one of the strongest and most proficient in German. Burney noted that resonance of the Frauenkirche, stating, "The singing here, with so fine an instrument, has a very striking effect."

Virtually all major composers were associated with Dresden at one time or another: Johann Pisendel, the Graun brothers, the Bendas, Gottfried August Homilius, Quantz, Hiller, and many others. Thought they proceeded beyond Dresden, their main education and employment there enhanced their further careers. As a draw, Burney noted, "For such is the insinuating power of music, that to acquire friends and admirers it needs only to be heard." He proclaimed the Dresden musical spirit to be universal, and that it served as a beacon, despite the occasional depredations of the Prussians, who seemed to attack the city regularly.

Prague

As the capital of Bohemia, Prague can be considered one of the major musical centers of the Holy Roman Empire, though many Czech composers made their careers elsewhere. Burney noted the musicality of the Bohemians, called the region "Europe's conservatory." He considered the entire population as one of the most educated and creative in Europe, and during his travels encountered schools of children who were not only literate but also well trained on instruments of all sorts. Many of these rural students went on to study, as Johann Stamitz did, at the University of Prague, where they were exposed to numerous opportunities to practice their craft. As many of the Bohemian nobility, the Lobkowitz, Clam Gallas, and other families, had palaces in Prague as well as Vienna, there was a constant exchange between these two Imperial capitals, with native composers such as Vanhal, Kozeluch, Mysliviček, and Wrantizky eventually establishing their musical lives in the latter. Nonetheless, when in town, the nobility used the musical talents of their servants to perform in public all manner of concerts.

For those remaining in Prague, the main churches of St. Vitus and St. Nicholas, as well as the Strahov monastery. Here composers such as František Brixi and František Ignác Antonín Tůma wrote significant amounts of sacred music. Musicians such as Jan Ladislas Dussek and František Dušek (similar names but not related), the latter who was married to famed soprano Josepha Dušek (born Hambacher), held musical salons, where chamber music was performed on an almost daily basis. Even composers from rural Bohemia, such as Jan Ryba, had their works performed in some of the smaller venues in the city.

The city has been known mainly for its relationship to Wolfgang Mozart, who was commissioned to provide two operas there, beginning in 1787 with *Don* Giovanni (see Chapter 11). Prague hosted two main theatres, the City Theatre and the Estates Theatre, both of which had been placed under the direction of Italian impresarios. The former was organized by Count Anton Sporck during the Baroque Period, and by the early 1730s had already begun to produce works (in Italian) lauding Czech themes. In 1738 the Kotce Theatre was created in the old town with Locatelli as its impresario. Although there were performances by the occasional Bohemian composer, the bulk of the repertory consisted of opera seria, and after 1781 German Singspiels. In 1781, however, Count Franz Anton Nostitz-Rieneck provided the land for a new theatre called the Estates Theatre, which was completed two years later (Figure 9.13). Under the direction of Italians Pasquale Bondini and then Domenico Guardasoni, it became the dominant venue in Prague (and the only one after 1798). A brief fourth theatre, the Patriotic Theatre, flourished briefly in the 1790s, producing Czech language Singspiels by Ondřej Holý and Jan Tuček.

As a result, the citizens of Prague had ample opportunity to view the latest operas, especially since many were imported directly from Italy or from Vienna. Though it maintained an active and vibrant musical culture, it became more famed for the export of Bohemian composers and musicians, some like Stamitz who were instrumental in the founding of significant court ensembles, such as Mannheim.

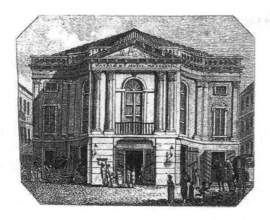

Figure 9.13 Engraving of the Nostitz Estates Theatre, Prague (*ca.* 1787)

Mannheim/Munich

In 1745 Carl Theodor became the Prince-Elector of the Palatinate, with his main seat in Mannheim at the junction of the Rhine and Neckar Rivers. These were natural trade routes in all directions with the city at its crossroads. This meant that the electorate was in a position to profit handsomely from the trade, and given that close by was the independent city of Frankfurt am Main, the university town of Heidelberg, and other courts such as Darmstadt and Zweibrücken, it was surrounded by places where music thrived during the Baroque Period. Composers such as Christoph Graupner and Telemann were well regarded during their years at these places, and given Mannheim's importance as a commercial center, Carl Theodor soon realized that it had to have a musical establishment worthy of its new stature. Fortunately, he was able to hire a Bohemian violinist, Johann Stamitz, who set about creating a legendary orchestra. He hired the most progressive musicians of the age, creating a discipline as concertmaster that was the model for orchestras for several generations. As noted in Chapter 3, this rapidly evolved into an ensemble that was not only well endowed from the standpoint of virtuoso performers—an "army of generals," as Burney put it—but also self-sufficient in terms of their ability to write music that was new and innovative, with orchestral devices such as the famed layered crescendo (also known as the Mannheim Steamroller), as well as increasing the colors of the orchestra through the permanent additions of instruments such as clarinets and an additional pair of horns. The number of musicians in the orchestra was around fifty-five, but these were augmented from time to time by talented students from the Jesuit Gymnasium and Music Seminar nearby.

There were three generations of Mannheim composers who were also members of the orchestra, with Stamitz and Anton Filz being the most important members of the first generation. Upon Stamitz's death in 1757, the second generation raised the level of musicality to its peak through the new concertmaster Christian Cannabich, Carl Toeschi, Johann Stamitz's two sons Anton and Carl, and Ignaz Fränzl. In addition, Franz Richter was hired as a bass singer and chamber musician, and though he did not interact directly with the orchestra, he nonetheless provided it with a reputable composer who had already been recognized as one of the early pioneers of the symphony. Finally, a German polymath, Abbé Georg Joseph Vogler from the city of Würzburg, was sent by the Elector to hone his skill in Italy, returning in 1776 as an organist and theorist, who wrote the treatises on theory and pedagogy called *Betrachtungen einer Mannheimer Tonschule* (*Observations of a Mannheim School of Music*), which set rules for music theory and analysis that are still to be found today in the concept of chords by Roman numerals and the movable and fixed *do*.

Figure 9.14 Mannheim Electoral Palace (eighteenth-century engraving)

The main venue for the performances of the orchestra was in a wing of the expansive electoral palace itself (Figure 9.14). In addition, the orchestra also performed for sacred services at the Jesuit church and the main cathedral, as well as the Jesuit Gymnasium and Music Seminar.

Stamitz's position as **Konzertmeister** (concertmaster) was as leader of the orchestra, but during his early years Carl Grua was *Kapellmeister*. In 1753, however, Carl Theodor imported as his successor Viennese-born composer Ignaz Holzbauer from nearby Stuttgart, where he had been serving the Elector of Baden-Württemberg. Holzbauer was a seasoned composer of opera, and when playwright Gotthold Lessing and stage designer Lorenzo Quaglio were imported to Mannheim, it also became a center of opera, where, as noted, the first significant Classical Period German opera *Gunther von Schwarzburg* was premiered. In 1778, however, Carl Theodor moved to Munich as the new Elector of Bavaria following the War of the Bavarian Succession. At that time, the majority of the Mannheim orchestra moved with him and were amalgamated with the court orchestra in Munich. While Cannabich transferred his position, Holzbauer remained behind in Mannheim, and other members of the musical establishment, such as the two Stamitz brothers and Vogler embarked on solo careers as virtuosos. In Munich, a third generation of composers, including Franz Danzi, Peter von Winter, and Franz Beck, emerged to carry on the tradition.

Munich's reputation as a musical center was high prior to the arrival of Carl Theodor. During the Baroque Period, Agostino Steffani had led the *Hofkapelle*, performing Italian opera and festive music for the Bavarian court. Performances were relatively rare for the public, however, and by the early Classical Period such performances at the court opera were restricted to the nobility. In 1755 Italian composer Andrea Bernasconi was appointed as *Kapellmeister*, having served as chorusmaster at the Ospedale della Pietà in Venice. His tenure did little to develop the court musical establishment, though he did compose and perform opera seria in a small theatre attached to the palace, called the Cuvilliés Theatre, which the Elector had built to replace a temporary stage set up in a large interior room. This was designed by François de Cuvilliés and proved to be an adequate, if not expansive stage in the French style (Figure 9.15). There court operas were performed as required by the court, but the theatre was not open to the public. In 1772 Bernasconi withdrew from active service, though he continued to compose sacred works, mainly for the several important monasteries in the city. His predecessor, Neapolitan composer Giovanni Porta, revitalized the orchestra, eventually raising the numbers to forty musicians, as well as importing singers from Italy. He also instituted the commissioning of new operas during the carnival season; for 1775 the work was Mozart's *La finta giardiniera*, an opera buffa to a text by Giuseppe Petronsellini. This was performed for the public in the Salvator Theatre. Upon the arrival of Carl Theodor, however, further consolidation occurred. Thirty-three members of the former Mannheim orchestra accompanied the elector to Munich, where they were combined with thirty-two musicians of the *Hofkapelle* there, and their duties under Cannabich were to perform for both the smaller Salvator and the palace theatres, in essence splitting their activities. In 1784, Bernasconi passed away and the musical establishment was passed on to Paul Grua, with Abbé Vogler as the honorary *Kapellmeister*. The same division between court and public, with the latter being able to enjoy opera only during the Carnival season, continued until 1795, when the elector merged the two operations and opened the palace theatre to the public. Grua's successor was Peter von Winter.

Figure 9.15 Cuvilliés Theatre in Munich, view from the stage (eighteenth-century engraving)
Source: Universal Images Group/Art Resource, NY

As a final word about the Munich musical culture, orchestral concerts were rare during the eighteenth century and generally only for the court. However, the public could find on any given day new sacred works that were performed by monastic ensembles in both the accessible monasteries and the churches, such as the Mariankirche, in the city. Munich was home to Augustinians, Benedictines, Premostraterians, and Cistercians, all of whom used the city as a central educational location from which monks were sent to numerous locations throughout central Europe. Unlike nearby Augsburg, where the Benedictines provided both monastic and civil music, in Munich they were distinct from the court ensembles and yet were able to produce music that served the sacred needs of the city and region.

The importance of the Mannheim School composers cannot be underestimated, even though their famed orchestral devices were derived from Italian operatic practice and the structural elements of the music developed simultaneously in several other European centers, such as Paris or Berlin or Vienna. As Burney noted, they were renowned for their discipline, progressive musical creativity, and effect. What is more, they were able to spread their style throughout Europe by way of successes in Paris, where music from Mannheim was famed as "*La melodia Germania*," or German style. Publication of their instrumental works spread abroad so that composers like Stamitz were performed in places such as Philadelphia or Stockholm, and imitators such as Scottish composer Thomas Erskine, Earl of Kelly, absorbed and expanded on the stylistic devices they developed. Their introduction of instruments such as the clarinet expanded the color and size of the orchestra, and even in terms of opera, the Mannheim theatre continued this progressive trend by being a center for the development of German opera, both national and the unique form called melodrama. While Munich prior to Carl Theodor was relatively normal in terms of its musical establishment, after 1778 it took over the creative impulse of Mannheim, making that city a center for musical excellence in the period.

All the cities in this Chapter were major population or national centers during the Classical Period, and all of them had important roles to play in the development of musical style, each with its own focus and reputation. These were, however, not the only places where musical development was undertaken, and in many courts and cities, music progressed at an equivalent pace, even cross-fertilizing musical culture in the centers.

Documents

Document 1. From Charles Burney, *The Present State of Music in Germany, the Netherlands, and United Provinces* (London 1775).

The theatre is lofty, having five or six rows of boxes, twenty-four in each row. The height makes it seem short, yet, at the first glance, it is very striking: it does not appear to have been very lately painted, and looks dark; but the scenes and decorations are splendid. . . . The orchestra has a numerous band, and the pieces which were played for the overture and act-tunes, were very well performed, and had an admirable effect. . . . The first time I went to the cathedral of St. Stephen, I heard an excellent Mass in the true church style, very well performed; there were violins and violoncellos though it was not a festival. . . . That which I heard in the choir this morning was much out of tune; it was played, however, in a very masterly, though not thoroughly modern style. . . Indeed, Vienna is so rich in composers and encloses within its walls such a number of musicians of superior merit that it is but just to allow it to be the Imperial seat of music.

Document 2. William Beckford, *Italy with Sketches of Spain and Portugal* (London, 1834). Collected letters and diaries from 1790.

People are scarcely awake until dinner time. But, a few hours thereafter, the important business of the toilette puts them gently into motion; and at length, the opera calls them completely into existence. But it must be understood that the drama, or the music, do not form a principal object of theatrical amusement . . . if there be some actor, or actress, whose merit or good fortune happens to demand the universal homage of fashion, there are pauses of silence, and the favorite airs may be heard. But without this cause, or the presence of the sovereign, all is noise, hubbub, and confusion, in an Italian audience.

Notes

1. Charles Burney, *The Present State of Music in Germany, the Netherlands and United Provinces* (London: T. Becket, 1775), I: 335.
2. Burney, *The Present State of Music in Germany*, I: 368.
3. Given the number, there was an increased need for new music from all over Europe, but the Parisian publishers, aware that not every composer would be a household name, frequently substituted the names of known figures, thus forging attributions that composers outside France often needed to contravene. The most famous example of this is the Op. 3 string quartets attributed by the publisher Bailleux in 1777 to Joseph Haydn after eradicating the name of Pater Romanus Hoffstetter, a Benedictine monk from Germany.
4. *Mércure de France* 1727, quoted in Jean Mongrédien, "Paris: The End of the Ancien Régime," in *The Classical Era* (Englewood Cliffs, NJ: Prentice-Hall, 1989), 66.
5. Burney, *The Present State of Music in Germany*, II: 152–153.
6. The first concert was actually held in 1764 in the Spring Garden Rooms, whereupon Madame Cornelys persuaded the composers to begin offering their concerts at the Carlisle House on a regular basis.
7. Burney, *A General History of Music*, II: 1023.
8. Burney, *A General History of Music*, II: 1022.
9. Burney, *The Present State of Music in France and Italy*, 307–308. The Calascione is a fretted instrument similar to a lute.
10. Giuseppe Sigismondo, *Descrizioni della città di Napoli e suoi borghi* (Naples, 1788), II: 136; quoted in Dennis Libby, "Italy: Two Opera Centres," *The Classical Era*, see Note 4. Corrected from the original.
11. Burney, *The Present State of Music in France and Italy*, 144.
12. Ibid.

13 Charles de Brosses, *L'Italie il y a cent ans, ou Lettres écrites d'Italie à quelques amis en 1739 et 1740* (Paris, 1836).
14 Burney, *The Present State of Music in France and Italy*, 151–152.
15 See Boer, *The Musical Life of Joseph Martin Kraus*, 182. He writes this in a letter to his parents, noting that he should have diplomatically responded—"I am extraordinarily enchanted with the divine nature of Italian music"—but instead evaded the questions by telling Pope Pius that his answer proved he was a connoisseur.

10 Cities and Courts on the Periphery

As vibrant as the main urban hubs were as centers of music during the Classical Period, other places were equally as important. These were the cities and courts that maintained musical establishments on what may be determined as the periphery of the main centers, and indeed, in a number of instances had reputations that were comparable and even occasionally influenced music in the main cities. These were places that rose to achieve a stature far beyond their peripheral locations, creating music that was sometimes acknowledged for its particular cultural contributions.

General histories usually pay scant attention to these peripheral places, largely because their reputations as musical centers were either regional, national, or did not proceed into the Romantic Period that followed, at least from a conventional historical point of view. As Neal Zaslaw notes in his study of the cultural history, music in these places has been little studied in the general context of the Classical Period as a whole, but this does not make them any less a part of the cultural and social environment, given that deep connections can be made with main centers. Moreover, few were isolated in the literal sense of that term; most retained close interaction with colleagues and musical developments throughout the period, on one hand. On the other, their positions often led to innovations that were quite progressive. To paraphrase Joseph Haydn, who spent a greater portion of his years at Esterház, a rural palace carved out of the Hungarian marshes, isolated as he was, he was forced to become original.

In order to view the music in these places, a definition of the periphery needs to be made. There are two "peripheries," one that defines it literally as on the edges of the eighteenth-century world and a second that regards any city or court outside the main centers as peripheral to the musical world of the period. Neither really can be seen as isolated, for both musicians and composers traveled about. For example, we speak of Haydn visiting England toward the end of his life, but one rarely hears of his stops along the way. In another, virtually anyone who achieved a reputation in Italy as a composer of opera wound up in Russia, which although a major political power, is geographically on the edge of the Western world of the time. Giuseppe Sarti, for example, not only spent time in Vienna, London, and Paris; he was also active for many years in Denmark and Russia, a truly international figure. Italian composers Domenico Scarlatti, Luigi Boccherini, and Gaetano Brunetti spent the bulk of their careers in Spain, even though their music was well known elsewhere in Europe. A theorist such as Johann Baptist Cramer could list Antonio Rosetti as one of the six major composers of the age, and yet his career was spent almost entirely at a small court in southern Germany, and then there is the case of Haydn (who admittedly did spend a portion of the year in Vienna), whose journey to England only took place later in his life, long after he had become famous throughout Europe. In other words, to look at the period as a whole, one has to view the periphery not as lonely outposts of sometimes primitive music but, rather, as an integral part of the musical culture of the period. Moreover, some of the places were neither small nor unimportant from an eighteenth-century geopolitical standpoint; some, as has already been noted, in the previous chapters on opera and sacred music. These include the countries or realms in the north, which were major participants in both the cultural and economic development of Europe. Indeed, these could be considered as rivals to the main centers to some degree.

The Northern Rivals: The Netherlands, Scandinavia, Russia

There were essentially four places that comprised the northern periphery: the Netherlands, Denmark, Sweden, and Russia. The first was hardly the economic powerhouse it had been during the Baroque era, though it was still an important center of trade and commerce. Denmark saw its stature diminish steadily mainly as the result of a weak monarchy, though a prime minister, Ove Guldberg, refocused the artistic culture on defining Denmark as a nation. In Sweden, King Gustav III created a cultural establishment that emphasized both the arts and the country's position as a European power. In Russia, Empress Elizabeth and her successor, Catherine the Great, imported Italian musicians for the court, but also developed native Russian opera. As noted earlier in Chapter 7, the main focus in Scandinavia and Russia was on opera, a genre that incorporated a multimedia approach to national identity. The main venues here were the opera houses, as has already been discussed, but the musical establishments in all four cases helped to achieve a degree of musical culture that was often original, focused on national priorities, and merged the latest musical trends of the continent with indigenous developments.

Sidebar 10–1 List of Rulers in the Netherlands, Scandinavia, and Russia During the Classical Period

Stadtholders of the Netherlands

Willem (William) IV	1711–1751
Willem V	1752–1806

Kings of Denmark

Christian VI	1730–1746
Frederick V	1746–1766
Christian VII	1746–1808

Kings of Sweden

Frederick I	1720–1751
Adolph Frederick	1751–1771
Gustav III	1771–1792
Gustav IV Adolph	1792–1809

Emperors/Empresses of Russia

Anna	1730–1740
Ivan IV	1740–1741
Elizabeth	1741–1762
Peter III	1762
Catherine the Great	1762–1796
Paul I	1796–1801
Alexander I	1801–1825

Amsterdam/The Hague

Amsterdam's position as the economic and political center of the Netherlands was undisputed. Charles Burney noted that the city was prosperous and clean, as befitted "a brisk commerce and an affluent people."[1] He did not, however, find much in the way of a normal concert life but, rather, restricted his observations

Figure 10.1 Engraving of the Schouwburg Theatre, Amsterdam (*ca.* 1738)

to organs in the various churches, the carillons in the towers, and even a concert in a synagogue.[2] Burney's commentary might have given the impression that Amsterdam was devoid of musical life, but it was a center of music publishing, and such firms as Hummel, Witvogel, De Céne, and Roger had an international following with branches in other European centers. For instance, virtually all the most important composers of the period had their music published by Hummel, including Haydn, Mozart, Kraus, Johann Christian Bach, and many others. As this sort of mercantile effort was in keeping with the main commercial focus of the city, it brought international acclaim.

Burney's claim that Amsterdam was without musical entertainment was not entirely correct. In 1729 Pietro Locatelli took up residence in the city, often finding both public and private venues to dazzle audiences with his virtuosity on the violin. The Schouwburg Theatre was a lively hall for both stage and instrumental musical performances (Figure 10.1). Few Dutch composers made their home in Amsterdam, however, finding that it was difficult to make more than a hard living as a teacher. Most, like violinist Willem de Fesch or Pieter Hellendaal, established their careers elsewhere. The musical taste of the city was decidedly old-fashioned, and the transient nature of musicians mitigated against a progressive musical culture. It did have close associations with the residence of the *Stadtholder* in The Hague, where a more conventional court could be found. The *Kapellmeister* there, Christian Ernst Graaf, presided over four performance venues for opera in addition to private salons. As Burney noted, it was more of a waypoint than a home for many composers, although Graaf was himself a prolific composer. One of the more interesting musicians in his orchestra was Francesco Zappa, a Milanese cellist who held the title of *Maître de musique à la Haye*. He made his home in The Hague, though he toured extensively in northern Europe. Other musicians employed by the court often performed in Amsterdam, and the musical traffic between the two cities was continuous.

Copenhagen

The musical life of early Pietist Copenhagen was relegated mainly to chorales, if done at all, and even royal celebrations did not require more than a minimal musical support. Nonetheless, Queen Sophie Magdalene persuaded her husband to appoint composer Johann Adolph Scheibe as *Kapelmæstare* in the city in 1739. Scheibe threw himself into developing a musical life in the city and in 1744 he founded *Det Musikalske*

Societet or *Selskab* (The Society of Music), which began to perform public concerts in imitation of the Concerts Spirituels in Paris. Since these featured mostly sacred works, they were tolerated, although the orchestra and vocalists were generally local amateurs.

In 1746, the new monarch Fredrik V made clear his intention to reopen the *Det Danske Skueplats* (Danish Theatre) to produce both plays and comic operas for the public. Scheibe was not comfortable with this direction, preferring more serious instrumental and church music, and in 1748 Fredrik brought Italian singer Paolo Scalabrini to Denmark as Scheibe's replacement. Scalabrini opened a school for singing the following year, with the intent that artists would be trained for the new opera theatre, which was inaugurated at Kongens Nytorv (Figure 10.2) in 1749. In 1755, Fredrik appointed the *maestro di cappella* of the Mingotti troupe, Giuseppe Sarti, as *Hovkapelmæstare*, at which point Scalabrini stepped aside to devote himself to his school. Both Scalabrini and Sarti collaborated on reviving the public concerts and theatre, in effect dominating musical life in Copenhagen. Their local competition came from a group called the collegium musicum, which was organized in 1749 by Johan Erasmus Iversen, precentor at the main church in the city.

In 1762 Scheibe returned to Copenhagen where he mainly concentrated upon the composition of sonatas, concertos (composing more than two hundred of them), and symphonies. At the death of Fredrik V in 1766, Sarti was on a journey to Italy to recruit singers for the Danish opera, and decided not to return as he was having some success in Rome; he was finally dismissed in 1769 after an absence of three years. Scalabrini was reinstated as *Hovkapelmæstare* and began creating opportunities for native Danish

Figure 10.2 Woodcut of the Danish Theatre, Copenhagen (*ca.* 1765)

musicians. Scheibe's pupil Thomas Christian Walther was elected to the *Nye Musikalske Selskab*, an organization that had been formed to promote a Danish musical style. In 1773 he was promoted to director of the Royal Opera, a post that had become more important after the infamous Streuensee incident, as noted in Chapter 7.[3]

A new concert series called *Det harmoniske Selskab* led by violinist Johann Ernst Hartmann was also instituted, performing public instrumental and vocal music for the public at the Royal Theatre. Although Hartmann focused his attention on opera in Danish with nationalist themes, he and a colleague, Simon dell'Croubelis, wrote instrumental works for the series, including symphonies that reflected a blend of continental and exotic styles. The orchestra was increased under Hartmann to around forty-five players, allowing for larger works, both vocal and instrumental, to be performed.

Hartmann's colleague at the public concerts, flautist Hans Zielche, became known for his quartets and sonatas shortly after his arrival in Copenhagen in 1761, and by the end of the century had become known as one of the chief composers of woodwind music. In 1787, a new *Kapelmæstare*, Johann Abraham Peter Schulz, he arrived in Copenhagen from Prussia. A proponent of the French opéra comique, he pandered to the tastes of the Danish citizens and court, while at the same time developing charity concerts to benefit the musicians and their families, as well as expanding the music education of the capital. He found Danish folk song interesting, promoting a new style of folk opera that resulted in the two nationalist works, *Høstgildet* and *Pers Bryllup*, noted earlier. The simple, direct tunes of these works became perennial favorites among the Danish public as concert pieces and in private salons. Under his leadership, Copenhagen's musical life began to achieve a reputation equal that of Stockholm. His colleague Friedrich Ludwig Æmelius Kunzen arrived in Copenhagen in 1784 to reorganize the public concerts in conjunction with Hartmann and Zielche. When his 1789 Danish nationalist work, *Holger Danske*, failed due to a scandal about musical style, the composer left Denmark, only to return in 1795. His subsequent work for *Det harmoniske Selskab* and the Royal Opera was successful, and he achieved an international reputation for Denmark through two oratorios, *Opstandelsen* (*The Resurrection*) and *Das Hallelujah der Schöpfung*, the last which anticipates Haydn's monumental *Creation*. Christian Felix Weyse followed his mentor Schulz's footsteps in exploring folk idioms, eventually inserting them into his six symphonies, Lieder, and cantatas. By the end of the century, Copenhagen had a well-established and vibrant musical life, with a regular nationalist repertory at the Royal Opera, several public concert series, and a focus on work that reflected a Danish musical identity. It achieved its final high point in the early nineteenth century with the arrival of a controversial figure, singer and violinist Eduoard Dupuy, as well as progressive ballet master Antoine Bournonville from Stockholm.

Copenhagen's musical life was extensive throughout the Classical Period, though it depended a great deal on the influences of foreigners, mainly Germans. The orchestra was of decent proficiency, and groups such as the various societies kept music-making alive through some awkward political times, with the result that music was more urban than centered upon the Danish court. Most important, the political situation moved stage music strongly in the direction of nationalism, extolling the culture and rulers of Denmark through mythological and folk musical worlds.

Stockholm

Stockholm was Copenhagen's rival in terms of Scandinavian cultural cities during the Classical Period. Unlike its Danish counterpart, it had a progressive sense musical culture and taste. With the death of Carl XII, the orchestra employed at court could count only a paltry ensemble of four singers, eight violins, two basses, and a few woodwinds.[4] Indeed, such was the debased state of music there that in 1720, Johan Helmich Roman noted in a memorandum that it was due to "the excesses of sloth, indulgence, and drunkenness; a hate for all things native and an enthusiasm for the foreign, poor education, native language being seen as distasteful, and the rest of such barbarisms."[5] With the election of Duke Fredrik of Hesse-Kassel to the Swedish throne, however, a revival was undertaken.

Roman introduced the music of Handel at a new series of public concerts held at the Riddarhus beginning in 1731 (Figure 10.3), performing "all manner of solo and instrumental as well as vocal music."[6] A few

230 *Capitals and Centers of Music-Making*

Figure 10.3 Riddarhus in Stockholm, site of the Cavalierskonserter (*ca.* 1800, engraving)

years later he undertook a journey to Italy, where he purchased music and observed the change in musical style, which changed his own from Baroque to *galant*. The *Hovkapell* consisted of a string core (up to twelve players plus continuo), as well as trumpeters and woodwinds. With the arrival of Hinrich Philipp Johnsen, *Kapellmästare* to crown prince Adolf Fredrik, an additional orchestra was resident in the city, causing some considerable competition, both musically and stylistically, since Johnsen was a proponent of the newer style of *Empfindsamkeit*.

In 1747 Adolf Fredrik built for his wife, a Prussian princess, a court theatre at the country estate of Drottningholm (Figure 10.4), a venue that even today offers performances of eighteenth-century music in a preserved theatre. In order to cater to her desire for Italian opera, mainly buffa, Adolf Fredrik hired Francesco Uttini as his personal court musical director in 1757. The old core of Roman's ensemble continued to function as a court orchestra, while Johnsen was able to expand his as a public orchestra by giving concerts at the Riddarhus. At this time, a concerted effort was undertaken by Roman, Johnsen,

Figure 10.4 Stage of the Drottningholm Court Theatre
Source: Drottningholm Theatre Museum.

and a Swedish military commander and amateur composer, Arvid Niklas von Höpken to explore the adaptation of the Swedish language to music: the first concentrated on sacred music, the second on a collection of songs to texts by "our best native poets," and the last on a Christmas oratorio he titled a *försök* (experiment). All these efforts resulted in the audiences acknowledging the adaptability of the language for music, but it was not until Gustav III, who inherited the throne in 1771, that an emphasis on purely Swedish music took root.

The musical situation at the beginning of Gustav's reign was a varied one. Apart from the divided *Hovkapell*, a private musical society Utile dulci was able to produce regular concerts with members of both royal orchestras beginning in 1766. It had been founded in honor of Olof Dalin, one of the strongest proponents of a native Swedish literature, and could count as members the most important singers and musicians in Stockholm, with performers often numbering thirty to forty. With this society, Gustav intended to create a musical establishment that was focused on the stage, though he also encouraged both the private and public concert series held at the Riddarhus. The Royal Academy of Music, instituted by the king in 1772 with a mission to supply talent for Stockholm's musical venues, employed a comprehensive training program using the members of the *Hovkapell* and Royal Opera as instructors, thus providing Stockholm with a continuous supply of professional musicians. To stimulate musical development Gustav imported both foreign singers and musicians, like Naumann, Abbé Vogler, and Kraus, as well as instituting polemical debates on music and literature in the local newspapers. By 1786 he had made Stockholm into a major musical center, with an orchestra of some sixty-five players producing stage works two or three times each week in a revolving repertory, as well as year-around public concerts, these generally led by members of the *Hovkapell*, such as violinist Johan David Zander and woodwind player Johann Friedrich Grenser, the son of Europe's most famous wind instrument maker.

Gustav also encouraged private salons among the intelligentsia, such as that which formed around architect Erik Palmstedt and his wife Gustava about 1784. To cater to this growing trend, a new musical magazine, *Musikaliskt tidsfördrif* (*Musical Pastimes*) appeared in 1789, remaining in publication for almost fifty years and featuring a compendium of songs, chamber works, and popular opera excerpts from Stockholm and abroad. Contributing to this were local musicians such as popular troubadour Carl Michael Bellman, who created a following with his Order of Bacchus and who also was a welcomed guest at the Palmstedt circle, where he collaborated in substantial works, such as the *Fiskarstugan* trilogy praising an Arcadian life (Figure 10.5).

After the assassination of Gustav in 1792 the vibrant musical life continued, though at a reduced pace. In 1799 Anders Fredrik Skjöldebrand founded a society called *Nytta och Nöje* (Utility and Pleasure) to encourage amateur performance of mainly stage works; this was followed by several others, including in

Figure 10.5 Aquarelle engraving of Carl Michael Bellman welcoming the Palmstedt Circle to his Fisher's Cottage (*Fiskarstuga*), 1789 (Stockholm, Kungliga Bibliotek)

1805 *Nytta och Enighet* (Utility and Unity), which created musical entertainments for the increasingly affluent middle-class society. In these groups, the singers and instrumentalists were amateurs, but their quality was good enough to give popular concerts. Regimental bands also were common, often performing in special public events, as well as lending their musicians, such as clarinetist Bernhard Crusell, to the public concerts.

During the Classical Period, Sweden must be considered the main northern center of musical culture, with an all-encompassing society that ranged from almost daily performances at the theatres, including nationalist works in Swedish, to amateur circles and weekly year-round public concerts. If there was a rival to this, it was in the Russia of Gustav's cousin, Catherine the Great.

St. Petersburg

Peter the Great had little interest in music, though his push to westernize Russian brought musicians to his new capital of St. Petersburg on the Baltic Sea.[7] His successor, Empress Anna, began the importation of Italian composers, the first of which were traveling troupes, but by 1735 she had invited Italian composer Francesco Araja to compose operas; Araja was followed by a parade of Italians, each of whom was mainly tasked with composing Italian works for the court theatres, in the winter at the Hermitage and during the summer at Tsaritsa Meadow (Figure 10.6). With the exception of Giuseppe Sarti, who displayed a special love for Russian musical idioms, these composers focused on music of the prevailing Italian operatic styles.

In 1762, Catherine expanded the court orchestra, and as in Stockholm, musicians performed in the city theatres both opera and instrumental music, though a true public concert series was lacking.[8] Special Imperial events, however, required performances on a monumental scale. For example, to celebrate the victory at Ochakov in 1788, Sarti composed a Russian Te Deum for Moscow that required a massive ensemble consisting of double chorus, two complete orchestras with full winds and percussion, a carillon (provided at the time by St. Basil's Cathedral), and even cannon and fireworks. Also included in this gigantic musical event was a unique musical ensemble, the Russian horn band. It was a group of as many sixty musicians, each playing a single-pitch instrument. The music, derived from the hunt, was kaleidoscopic in nature (Figure 10.7), though foreign visitors often thought it quaint that the ensemble could work with each player coordinating their music for the whole (see Document 3). The horn band was occasionally also used both in folk operas at the Little Theatre and in other private concert venues, in addition to such events.

Many of the early musicians in Russia were foreign-born, hired for a contractual period. Beginning during the reign of Empress Elisabeth, efforts were made both in St. Petersburg and Moscow to train Russian musicians, many of whom came from the serf class. The earliest of these seems to have been Josef Kerzelli, who, along with his sons Frants and Ivan and grandsons, developed the Moscow music academy to train

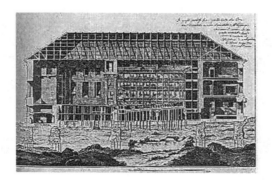

Figure 10.6 Cutaway drawing of the opera house in St. Petersburg (*ca.* 1760)

Figure 10.7 Illustrated engraving of a Russian Horn Band (*ca.* 1800)

string players. Josef also edited a journal, *Muzykalye useveniya* (*Musical Amusements*), that brought the music of Russian composers to the public eye alongside Western chamber works. The concertmaster of the Knipper theatre orchestra, Ivan Khandoshkin, was known as the best violinist and teacher at Prince Potemkin's musical academy at Yekaterioslav, which also supplied musicians to the court orchestras in St. Petersburg. In 1793, Sarti founded the Russian Conservatory, with branches both in St. Petersburg and Moscow, and with this a stable supply of capable musicians for the Russian ensembles was assured, making the foreign imports redundant.

Private households, too, encouraged musical entertainments, and to provide music, publications of collections of pieces suitable for the boyar class families were undertaken. Although much of these consisted of occasional pieces, generally for keyboard and one or two melody instruments, Russia's foreign ambassadors, such as Counts Lichnowsky and Galitzen, both supported foreign composers such as Haydn and Beethoven; they also commissioned works that would become popular chamber music back home. Even resident composers, such as Arnošt Wanzura, were encouraged to standardize chamber literature for private music-making; Wanzura, a Pole, published national pieces such as symphonies based on Russian, Polish, and Ukrainian folk tunes arranged both for keyboard and orchestra.

All four of these cities demonstrate that music in the Classical Period in the north was every bit as vibrant and progressive as elsewhere on the continent. Although each approached the development of music in a different manner, the variety brought acclaim to each that was recognized even in the major centers. The north, however, did not represent the only periphery; music was also an important part of the culture of the Mediterranean region, even though here Italy and Italian music dominated the musical landscape.

Some Exemplary Courts: Esterház, Regensburg, Oettingen-Wallerstein, Salzburg

No discussion of music in the Classical Period would be complete without acknowledging the importance of the musical establishments at the courts that were outside the main urban centers. These were often in smaller towns or even rural areas, yet they not only maintained extensive and highly professional orchestral and theatrical venues; they also achieved reputations that spread beyond their geographical or political boundaries. The eighteenth century was still a time when the nobility of the era still exercised considerable sway over their domains and, as a result, were expected both to demonstrate the appropriate standards of living and autocratic rule that were theirs by rights. Well-to-do courts with extensive lands could maintain music for their private entertainments, to which the public was rarely invited, while those of lesser dominion often had difficulty supporting extensive cultural establishments on a continual basis. Nonetheless, music was always a prerequisite for the nobility, whether performed by a professional ensemble or by immediate family members.

> **Sidebar 10–2 Hereditary Princely Rulers of the German and Holy Roman Courts**
>
> Esterházy
>
> | | |
> |---|---|
> | Prince Paul Anton | (1711–1762) |
> | Prince Nicholas I "the Magnificent" | (1762–1790) |
> | Prince Anton | (1790–1794) |
> | Prince Nicholas II | (1794–1833) |
>
> Thurn und Taxis
>
> | | |
> |---|---|
> | Anselm Franz | (1714–1739) |
> | Alexander Ferdinand | (1739–1773) |
> | Karl Anselm | (1773–1805) |
>
> Salzburg Prince-Archbishops
>
> | | |
> |---|---|
> | Leopold Anton Eleuthnerius, Baron Firmian | (1727–1744) |
> | Jakob Ernst, Count Liechtenstein | (1745–1747) |
> | Sigismund Christoph, Count Schrattenbach | (1753–1771) |
> | Hieronymus Josef Franz de Paula, Count Colloredo | (1772–1803) |

Esterház

Perhaps the most famed court of the Classical Period was that of the Esterházy family. They were the hereditary treasurers of the Holy Roman Empire with vast holdings in today's Austria and Hungary. While they maintained a residence in Vienna, their main palace was in the town of Eisenstadt, though there was a smaller one in Sopron. At the beginning of the Classical Period, Prince Paul Anton maintained a core of musicians led by Gregor Joseph Werner, whose main task was mainly to provide sacred music for the Eisenstadt church. His successor, Prince Nicholas I, was a culturally enlightened ruler, who was determined to make his musical establishment the best in the Empire. To that end, he hired a young, energetic composer, Joseph Haydn, along with a number of musicians in order to achieve this goal. The aging Werner considered Haydn an upstart, but the prince, himself a performer on the baryton, largely deflected his complaints, and in 1766 Haydn was promoted to *Kapellmeister*. At this time, he was able to bring the number of musicians to twenty-eight, and their abilities earned them the name "Band of Professors."

In 1772, Prince Nicholas renovated an isolated hunting lodge called Esterház into a summer palace, moving there each year for several months (Figure 10.8). This included an opera house that was of such renown that even Empress Maria Theresia noted that if she wanted to see a first-rate performance, she had to come to Esterház. The musicians performed under strict protocols, with Haydn functioning both as leader and administrator. One of the clauses in Haydn's contract states that he is to be considered a "house officer," an overseer of the musicians, music, and musical instruments. He also was to inquire daily about music for the Prince and the court: "The party of the second part [i.e., Haydn] agrees to perform any music of one kind or another in all the places, and at all the times, to which and when His Highness is pleased to command."[9] On a social level, this meant that at Esterháza, the musical establishment served at the whim of the prince, but since he was both knowledgeable and enthusiastic about music, the private performances were to be done on an almost daily basis, even when the musicians were sequestered out at the summer palace. In one particular instance, this isolation was cause for Haydn to compose one of his most famous works, the Farewell Symphony, Hob. I:45, through which he informed his Prince of the anxiety of the musicians to return home to their families.

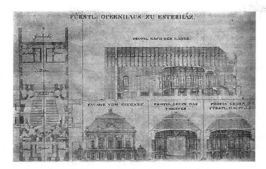

Figure 10.8 Architectural rendering of the opera house as Esterház (18th century drawing)

After Prince Nicholas's death in 1790, his successor, Prince Anton, dissolved the musical establishment, only to have it revived on a smaller scale in 1794 through his heir, Prince Nicholas II.

Regensburg

Although not as powerful politically as the Esterházy family, the Thurn und Taxis rulers were of equally important a stature, being largely in charge of the postal services throughout the Holy Roman Empire, as well as being an Imperial representative in the region. Their main court was in the city of Regensburg in Bavaria, though one branch of the family had estates in Bohemia. This meant that there was a direct conduit for Czech musicians to be hired for the large twenty-eight-member orchestra in Germany. The court theatre was a lively one, with its heyday being reached during the rule of Prince Karl Anselm. It varied between German and Italian productions, and finally in 1786 he dissolved it altogether. From a musical standpoint, however, the Regensburg court orchestra continued almost daily performances, mainly of small vocal and larger instrumental works.

The musical administrator was Baron Theodor von Schacht, who himself was both an avid collector of music and a composer of note. He was in charge of creating a unique entertainment for the Imperial ceremonies and administrative functions, which included opera performances on Mondays and Fridays, the days when the meetings were in session. Since Regensburg was a "free" city, the relationship with the city in which the court resided was a symbiotic but separate one, with the performances usually taking place in a rented town theatre. Spectacles on important days, such as the prince's birthday, were held regularly with musical pageantry, as one description from 1797 noted: "On such days an open table, concerts, etc. are held at the Prince's [estate]."[10] A continual round of private concerts, which achieved a reputation similar to Esterház for the exceptional performances, complemented the outdoors festivities.

The musicians were of high quality, with the orchestra being led by violinist Joseph Touchmoulin, while violinist Joseph Riepel became known for his theoretical work on form and structure in the Classical Period. Perhaps the most interesting musician from the court was violinist Franz Pokorny, who began and concluded his career at the court as the principal second violinist (Figure 10.9). Trained in Mannheim by Stamitz, he spent the last two decades in Regensburg, where his compositions were especially esteemed. This success, however, caused a degree of envy from Baron Schacht, who made a deliberate effort to eradicate his name from compositions in the princely library.

Oettingen-Wallerstein

The court of the Counts (and later princes) of Oettingen-Wallerstein is an example of an expansive and highly regarded musical establishment under the control of a less prominent noble family. The main centers of this *Hofkapelle* were the smaller castles in the towns of Harburg, Oettingen in Swabia, and Wallerstein

236 *Capitals and Centers of Music-Making*

Figure 10.9 Engraving of a portrait of Franz Pokorny (*ca.* 1780)

Figure 10.10 (a) Silhouette of the Harmoniemusik (Wind Band) at Oettingen-Wallerstein; (b) engraving of a portrait of Antonio Rosetti (*ca.* 1780)

in Bavaria. These were rural domains, whose main ruler, Kraft Ernst, was raised from a count to a prince in 1776. Like Esterház, the court life was restrictive and private, with the musicians being hired to serve their ruler and his family, as well as the frequent visitors. It was through them that their reputation for excellence was achieved, and it was not unusual for travelers to witness special performances, such as the wind band (Figure 10.10a). The most illustrious composer of his *Kapelle* was Antonio Rosetti, who arrived in 1773 (Figure 10.10b). Like the composers attached to Mannheim, he made a success in Paris in 1781, earning international acclaim for his works. His predecessor, Joseph Reicha, was also famed for his music, but in 1785 he had left for another position in Cologne and Bonn as the *Kapellmeister* to Elector Maximilian Franz. Both were illuminated by the composer Neefe as among the top composers of Germany in the eighteenth century.

Salzburg

The city of Salzburg, today inevitably associated with Wolfgang Amadeus Mozart, was a major musical center in Austria during this time. The Prince-Archbishops were chosen from among the ruling families of the Holy Roman Empire, and their main position was as the confessor to the Emperor. The Salzburg court

Figure 10.11 Main organ at Salzburg Cathedral

had a large and vibrant musical establishment during the Baroque Period, even though it was concentrated mostly on sacred music, performed regularly at the main cathedral or in one of the several churches around the city. As an important center at the crossroads of the empire, it also boasted several monasteries, the most important of which, St. Peters, was established by the Benedictine order. Finally, the city hosted a university, whose purpose it was mainly to train students in theology and philosophy. Despite the fact that it was quite conservative, the fact that it combined both secular and sacred rule meant that the music was required to serve both church and state.

The *Kapelle* in Salzburg had been continuously modernized throughout the eighteenth century, beginning with the long-serving *Kapellmeister* Johann Ernst Eberlin. This composer had by 1757 achieved a reputation as "a thorough and accomplished master of composition," and his productivity was compared to both Telemann and Alessandro Scarlatti. The main venue was the cathedral, which had no fewer than five organs; four smaller ones attached to the pillars of the main dome of the Romanesque church and a large one in the loft (Figure 10.11; see also Figure 8.3). The musical ensemble, at times numbering forty musicians, consisted of four groups; the first choir consisted of the director, vocal soloists, and three or four trombones, while the second included a string ensemble, the third the trumpet and timpani corps, and the fourth the regular chorus (made up usually of choirboys and men from the Benedictine monastery) and organ continuo. To these would be added various woodwind as needed. The same group without the choir would also perform in the archbishop's palace for secular occasions.

By 1760 Archbishop Schrattenbach had begun to shift the musical interest away from sacred works toward instrumental music, and in Salzburg the Italian style became more popular. His *Hoffkapellmeister* Giuseppe Lolli focused on music for the church, but composers such as Leopold Mozart and Cajetan Adlgasser enjoyed careers that were geared toward instrumental music such as symphonies and serenades (though they too wrote for the church). By the end of Schrattenbach's life, the *Kapelle* had hired a new organist, Michael Haydn, as well as the prodigy Wolfgang Mozart, to enhance the stable of composers.

Archbishop Colloredo, however, was more reform-minded, and he curtailed the musical establishment both in quantity of music and genres in his zeal to reform the liturgy, as noted in Chapter 8. Haydn subsequently felt more at home with the Benedictines, who not only had a large number of monks who were being trained for musical activities in monasteries throughout central Europe but also were in charge of school dramas at the university. While there was no functioning theatre in Salzburg, itinerant troupes did perform at the various salons, and festive occasions such as graduation and feast days allowed for some pageantry to be undertaken. Music-making was also done frequently at the houses of the various wealthy citizens, and not infrequently did people come together to form their own private orchestras for private invitational concerts. Leopold Mozart, writing to his son, notes in 1778 that one of these put on by Count Czernin had a string section of no fewer than twenty-five strings, in addition to pairs of oboes and horns, as well as his daughter Nannerl on the harpsichord. Here both the nobility and commoners mingled to produce a concert where symphonies, concertos, arias, and at least one chamber work were performed.

Salzburg therefore had both the world of the professional court and an intense amount of private music-making at the same time, in turn providing the opportunity for composers to write new works. Daniel Schubart may have dismissed the musical establishment as having little style of its own, but Burney noted that "the archbishop and sovereign . . . is very magnificent in his support of music."[11]

These four courts are only samples of the types of musical establishments that could be found during the Classical Period. They represent both urbanized and rural courts, with a range of venues and performance cultures. As all four were relatively wealthy, they exhibited their wealth by showing off their musical ensembles. It should be noted, however, that they were not the only courts in Europe to do so.

Music on the Periphery: The Mediterranean Sphere

During the Classical Period it is impossible to define music in the Mediterranean region—defined as the lands surrounding the Mediterranean, Aegean, Adriatic, and Tyrrhenian Seas—without acknowledging that the major influence stemmed from the Italian Peninsula. Italian composers dominated music in this arena, with even non-Italian composers often being trained in the conservatories of Naples or Venice, as well. The main European center outside of the peninsula was Iberia, but there were other outposts of European domination that pushed up against the non-Western Ottoman Empire in the east and the Arabic caliphates to the south. Venetian control over the Dalmatian coast and the relationship of Malta with the Vatican were examples of the close ties to Italian culture, and from a political standpoint, these interrelationships demonstrate the close contacts that allowed a free flow of music around the region. In Iberia, the War of the Spanish Succession that ended in 1713 had established a Bourbon on the throne of Spain, but Portugal remained an independent kingdom. Both of these countries, moreover, had their own vast colonies in the Americas. Malta, a pair of heavily inhabited islands south of Sicily, was under the rule of the Knights of St. John, with close religious ties to the Vatican, while Venice maintained commercial and cultural interests in the Adriatic all the way down to the island of Corfu. Ties with the Islamic lands were particularly strong economically, and it is not surprising that cultural interactions were frequent.

Iberia

The Iberian Peninsula was divided into two separate kingdoms; Spain and Portugal, both of which maintained vibrant musical cultures, including an indigenous opera (see Chapter 7). While the Italian style dominated court music, it was by no means monolithic. Italian composers and musicians were frequently called to Spain; Queen Elisabetta had hired the castrato Farinelli in 1737, believing his voice could cure Philip V of morbid depression, while Domenico Scarlatti accompanied his pupil Portuguese princess Maria Barbara from Lisbon to Madrid in 1733. It was not until the reign of music-loving King Carlos III that Spain was to receive important composers Gaetano Brunetti and Luig Boccherini, both of whom were particularly fond of Spanish musical genres. Indeed, dances such as the fandango became a fad throughout Europe, showing up in compositions by Gluck and Mozart. Other musicians arrived in Spain's southern cities of Seville and Cadíz, the latter a disembarkation point for further travel to New Spain. Composers such as Ignacio de Jerusalem and José de Campderrós spend the early parts of their careers as violinists in the city.

Local composers, however, were not neglected. Padre Antonio Soler, a Hieronymite priest, functioned as musical director in Madrid at El Escorial, a royal palace known for its several salons and courtyards surrounding an old monastery in which music for the court was regularly performed. Soler himself functioned as *maestro di capilla* at the church at Lleida in Catalonia, composing a huge number of single-movement keyboard sonatas that rivaled those of Scarlatti in complexity and structure. Catalonia served as a center for educating composers in sacred music throughout Spain, with schools in Barcelona and Monserrat. The *escolania* at the monastery featured composers Benet Esteve and Benet Julià, both of whom were important teachers promoting the enlargement of church orchestras to include wind instruments. At the end of the century, Carles Baguer and Anselm Viola both became significant composers of instrumental works, especially when they moved to Madrid to take up employment for the royal court. Elsewhere in Spain, much of the city music-making was either at the local theatres or in wealthy houses, for which chamber works, including some featuring the guitar, and dances were preferred.

Sidebar 10–3   Rulers of Spain and Portugal During the Classical Period

Spain
House of Bourbon

Philip V	(1724–1746)
Ferdinand VI	(1746–1759)
Carlos III	(1759–1788)
Carlos IV	(1788–1808)

Portugal
House of Braganza

João (John) V	(1706–1750)
José I	(1750–1777)
Maria I	(1777–1816)
Pedro III	(1777–1786)

Maria, also known as the Mad Queen, married her uncle Pedro but in 1777 became the de facto sole ruler, despite their joint throne.

In Portugal, Scarlatti was brought to Lisbon by João V to reorganize the Capela Real and establishing a music school at the Basilica Patriarchal. The promising students from this school were sent to Rome to finish their studies, returning to become either members of the Capela or teachers at the school. Most music up to the great Lisbon earthquake of 1755 that destroyed much of the city was performed in households or churches, however. The king's illness in 1742 had closed almost all the theatrical productions, and after the disaster, foreign composers such as David Perez helped to revive the musical culture through the rebuilding of the theatres in Bairro Alto and the national theatre of São Carlo, as well as reestablishing a school at Vila Viçosa. After Perez, native Portuguese composers—João de Sousa Carvalho and Marcos Antonio Portugal—took up the reigns of local musical production.

While much of Portuguese music retains an Italian style, the development of a love duet, the *modhina*, served to stimulate an interest in popular styles that were absorbed into more classical genres. While Portugal may have been on the periphery of Europe, it, like Spain, was a destination for musical culture, and with the direct connections to Brazil, its colony in the New World, musical styles were widespread between the continents.

Malta

The island of Malta was musically tied to Naples, to which it sent promising musicians for training in the conservatories. Musical opportunities in these islands were extensive, though they were mainly concentrated

Figure 10.12 The Manoel Theatre, Valetta, Malta
Source: Photo courtesy of *The Times of Malta*.

on the large number of churches and monasteries that dotted the countryside. The main city, Valetta, could boast an opera house in the Classical Period, the Teatro Manoel (Figure 10.12), but the works performed there were exclusively by visiting troupes; there appears not to have been much in the way of public concerts done, although the opera season was relatively active. In 1724 the cathedral of St. John in Valetta hired Italian Giuseppe Sammartini as their *maestro di cappella*, but it was not until 1789 that a native Maltese, Francesco Azzopardi, was appointed to the position.[12] His work includes extensive sacred music composed for churches in Rabat, Valetta, and Mdina, for which the composer recruited a substantial orchestra from the Neapolitan conservatories. While his musical style reflects the close connection to Italy, he excelled at all genres for the church. A colleague, Benigno Zarafa, also composed for numerous churches, especially in his hometown of Żebbug and Mdina; both participated in establishing the occasional instrumental concerts performed in the churches, for which they both composed symphonies. Of particular interest is Azzopardi's laudatory cantata *Malta felice* (*Happy Malta*) from 1775.

Music on the Periphery: Music Outside Europe

The music of the Classical Period was not just restricted to Europe. Music-making was a vital part of culture in the far-flung regions of the globe. Although exploration in its strictest sense had largely given way to colonization, there was still considerable interest in the musics of these places as a result of contact or local customs. For example, Louis Antoine de Bouganville visited Tahiti in 1767, returning to France with a native who introduced the French Academy of Sciences to his musical world; one of his songs was transcribed (Example 10.1), though the unfortunate man fell victim to disease before he could return home. It has already been noted how in the less settled and more rustic colonies, such as Russian Alaska or English Botany Bay in Australia, chamber music was performed, but by the eighteenth century, colonies in the Americas had already been in existence for several centuries. Even though the European powers still ruled the majority—the exceptions were the United States of America, which gained its independence in 1783, and Haiti, in 1798—and even though vast regions populated solely by indigenous peoples still existed in both the north and the south, relatively large and culturally active places could be found throughout these continents and the islands between. During this period, European proxy wars were still fought on American

Example 10.1 Transcription of the "Aria dell Isola della Società" (Tahiti) from the original manuscript (British Library).

soil, colonial oversight changed hands, and the raw materials of the continents still provided goods to the European homelands, yet from a musical standpoint, some rather interesting developments took place here in Spanish lands (the *Virreinato* or Viceroyalties), the French settlements (Québec and Louisiana), Portuguese suzerainty (Brazil), and the English colonies (North America and the Caribbean). Of these, the largest was the territory comprising New Spain, ranging from the missions of California to the Tierra del Fuego.[13]

Music from the New World was not unknown in Europe prior to the Classical Period, for Marin Mersenne had published several "Canadian" tunes in his *Harmonie Universelle* the previous century. Native American musics appeared regularly in places such as Diderot's *Encyclopéde*, and visitors were brought to cities like Paris to demonstrate their music and dances. Given that slaves from Africa were used in the colonies of all the European powers in the New World, African music was also known. But the Europeans themselves found a need to establish their own musical ensembles, not only to maintain a connection with Europe but also to provide what they determined was a civilized society.

New Spain

New Spain was already well settled along Spanish models during the eighteenth century. As noted earlier, Mexico City and Lima could boast opera houses that performed both works from Europe, mainly Italian, and the occasional piece by local composers, such as Ignacio de Jerusalem. Festive events resulted in cantatas, many performed outdoor, and as the Jesuit missions became established, local musicians performed remote locations such as Santa Cruz, Bolivia, both didactic opera and sacred music. This resulted in a rich but relatively little-studied repertory that is only now beginning to be explored.

For example, in the establishment of a series of missions along the Camino Real in Alta California (from today's San Diego up through San Francisco), the mainly Franciscan monks brought with them music to be taught to their native neighbors. Hymns like the *Alabado* were sung polyphonically, and hymns of praise (*Gozo*) and villancicos were part of every celebration. A report from 1815 concerning mission music states, "The neophytes have a lot of musical talent, and they play violins, cello, flutes, horn, drum and other instruments that the Mission has given them . . . the Indian converts sing Spanish lyrics perfectly."[14] Orchestras at the missions by 1792 could reach the same proportions as the smaller European ones, with music both locally written and imported from both Spain and Mexico.

Almost all of the main churches in the cities had ensembles that ranged from Mexico City and Puebla, where the sizes and number of instruments were equivalent to European orchestras, to some smaller churches, where they were limited to pairs of violins and a bass (*bajo*). Some of the larger churches, such as in Durango, as musicologist Drew Davies had noted, could boast active and vibrant musical groups, with local composers such as Santiago Billoni writing music that reflected the community needs. The villancico was the most popular form of music to be written, and given that many musicians were trained in Italy,

Figure 10.13 Engraving of Ignacio de Jerusalem y Stella (*ca.* 1760)

the Italian style was prevalent. Ignacio de Jerusalem y Stella (Figure 10.13) and natives such as Oaxacan composer José Abella wrote in the galant style, but Manuel Arenzana developed late Classical genres such as the *verso* into large-scale symphonic works.

To the south lay the Viceroyalty of Peru, where the main cathedral in Lima provided a core for music-making in the European style, while the cathedral in Bogotá, Colombia, boasted both native and Spanish composers writing special music for it. In Bogotá in 1784 a large orchestra called *La banda de la corona* was formed that both provided weekly church music and served festive occasions. In Venezuela, however, a priest, Padre Pedro Palacios y Sojo, traveled to Europe in about 1768 to obtain music for a new group of composers now known as the Chacao School. Music had been a subject taught at the university in Caracas beginning in 1725, but Palacios y Sojo was the first to establish a society of both composers and musicians who, according to his own admonition, were to "play the game of balls and give concerts." His contemporaries, Juan Manuel Olivares and José Caro de Boesi, served as teachers in a new school that has survived to the present day, while the second generation, led by José Angel Lamas, contributed music toward the independence movements of the nineteenth century. This school was noted for symphonies and sacred works, all presented in public in Caracas. In Lima, music was largely relegated to the cathedral and monasteries, but with a strong influence by the native Inca, much included performances with both European and native instruments. Choral singing by the native populations had been observed since the conquest, but in the Classical Period, it was harnessed to the needs of the state. Roque Ceruti, originally from Italy, became *maestro di capilla* in 1717, and by his retirement in 1758 had changed his style to conform to the *galant*. His colleague, José de Orejón y Aparicio was a native Peruvian who composed one of the most popular villancicos of the period, *Mariposa de sus rayos*. Even farther south was the cathedral in Santiago de Chile, where José de Campderrós was in charge of the musical establishment. He not only wrote sacred music for the church; he also organized public concerts there, sending for the latest symphonic works from Paris for public performance during the last quarter of the century.

The Viceroyalty of Havana included a significant post at the cathedral in Havana, Cuba, but the most important school was in the city of Santiago. Here, organist Esteban Salas y Castro formed a school at the Seminary of San Basilia a Magro, where he trained musicians, mainly vocalists and violinists, for service in churches and towns throughout Cuba and the Caribbean. His music, known for its simplicity and lyricism, was especially popular. Although constrained by economic circumstances, he was able to teach several generations of organists, such as Juan París and Francisco Hierrezuelo, both of whom contributed significantly to the musical life of the islands.

The musical life in New Spain was neither primitive nor scattered, with the upper classes having access to the same musical culture that could be found in Europe, often importing musical instruments for chamber works, as a painting from the 1790s in Spanish New Orleans demonstrates (See Figure 5.6). The Jesuits and other were able to bring music to their missions, training both musicians and composers in some of the more far-flung regions of the territory, such as today's Paraguay and Bolivia, while in the main centers and northern missions, native music was sometimes blended to create new sounds while adhering to the genres of the Classical Period.

Brazil

The portion of South America colonized by Portugal was likewise home to musical development on a large scale. Brazil supplied an enormous amount of gold and other commodities to Europe, but it was by far no exotic frontier, though much of the area known as Amazonas remained unexplored (and unexploited). By the Classical Period, cities such as Belo Horizonte and Ouro Preto in the province of Minas Gerais could boast important musical cultures, helped in part by the establishment of a system of guilds known as the *irmandades* (or brotherhoods). Given that most of the population were mulattos, mixtures of European and African parents, these educational institutions served to provide both composers and musicians for a wide variety of public festivities without the oversight of European immigrant composers. Much of the music was liturgical, though marches and dances also formed part of their works, and many of the towns had orchestras that mirrored the same size and functions of those in Europe. Composers such as Manoel Dias de Oliveira and José Lobo de Mesquita achieved local reputations for tuneful and accessible music, as well as being known for their teaching abilities; Oliveira, for example, taught at the Irmandade de São Miguel e Almas in the town of Tiradentes. During the Classical Period, more than a thousand musicians were active in Minas Gerais.

The main cities, Rio de Janeiro and São Paulo, had more extensive musical establishments since these were the provincial capitals. Here, the ensembles were larger, there was a theatre that performed operas (mainly drawn from Italian works), and the need for civil music for a wide variety of occasions was great. Many of the composers were also mulattos, but they were also mostly clerics. Fra João de Santa Clara Pinto, for example, spend much of his life teaching at the Franciscan monastery while providing music for the cathedral in Rio de Janeiro. The most important composer was José Maurício Nunes Garcia, one of the first to establish an Irmandade in Rio in 1784. By 1798 he not only composed operas for the theatre; he was also named as *mestre di capella* at the main cathedral. When the court of Dom João fled to Brazil to escape the Napoleonic wars, he was appointed as court composer, as well, though European colleagues undermined his position within a few short years. His musical style was highly original, with a good sense of orchestration and a novel approach to form and harmony. In São Paulo, an up-and-coming city dependent on trade, the new cathedral imported composer André da Silva Gomes, who arrived as an ordinary musician but by 1774 had been appointed as *mestre di capella*. Not only did he teach several generations of Brazilian composers; he also functioned as a leader of the Societas Ordem Terceira do Carmo, a Carmelite group that was dedicated to simplifying sacred music (Figure 10.14). His liturgical works are either a cappella or accompanied only by an organ, similar to those in Russia by Bortniansky (see Chapter 9).

Figure 10.14 Nineteenth-century view of the church of the Societas Ordem Terceira do Carmo in São Paulo, Brazil, postcard (*ca.* 1890)

New France and English North America (the United States)

The Iberian colonies were not the only ones settled by the European powers. In North America, France and Britain established a presence and, in the last portion of the century, became a focal point as the United States of America gained its independence through a war that ended in 1783. After the defeat of the French in 1756, Britain had controlled much of the settled continent, though French influence in Quebec remained strong. We have already seen a native Canadian composer, Louis-Joseph Quesnel, who was one of the first to compose comic operas in Montréal, but the main towns of the time were Québec City and Halifax. Little has been done to outline the musical life in these places, though the merchant classes all considered music as an important part of their culture. Military bands were the main source of public concerts in both cities after 1760; unlike modern bands, these included both singers and string sections so that larger ensembles could be created to perform the latest works from Europe. In 1790, for example, a series of public concerts was announced in Halifax that included some popular symphonies, and in Québec Joseph Glackemeyer, who had immigrated in 1779, announced in the local paper his availability as a music teacher and purveyor of music. He also wrote works for orchestra, though information is particularly scarce.

In the American colonies, music was divided into the urban and rural spheres. Many of the latter were either community performances of *a cappella* music by composers such as William Billings or the Moravians or meant to be social occasions, as noted in Chapter 8. The urban areas, however, had both public concerts and theatres that provided entertainment to the newly emerging middle classes and immigrants. In 1769 a public concert was held in Philadelphia, followed the next year by Boston. In Charleston, the St. Cecilia Society was formed in 1762 both to present music to the public of this port city and to provide both social and educational support. The main venues were either common rooms or outdoors locations, mirroring the open-air concerts in London. In Williamsburg, the Governor's Palace was home to smaller musical events, and virtually every estate had its own instrumentarium, including keyboards. For example, Thomas Jefferson was himself a proficient violinist, and he not only collected music during his time in Europe for performance at Monticello; he also occasionally indulged in attempts at amateur musical composition.

When independence seemed assured, music was revived throughout the new country. In 1778, however, the Continental Congress issued a proclamation that closed all the theatres in the new country. To circumvent this, subscription concerts were held in places such as City Tavern and the "closed" Chestnut Street Theatre (Figure 10.15), along with "lectures" at private rooms and homes, where vocal music could be performed, including the latest works from ballad operas. By 1789, however, the prohibition was rescinded and theatres could present works once again. This led to a thriving musical environment, which in turn enticed immigrant musicians James Hewitt, Alexander Reinagle, Benjamin Carr, Joseph Gehot, and others to come. Reinagle and Carr settled in Philadelphia, where they also sold music instruments and published

Figure 10.15 Plate print of the Chestnut Street Theatre, Philadelphia (*ca.* 1800)

works for popular consumption. Hewitt moved to New York, where his theatre had an orchestra of 16 on the payroll. Native composers like Francis Hopkinson and Philip Phile wrote patriotic and chamber music for Congress and President George Washington, while the von Hagen family revived the musical entertainments in Boston. This also allowed for traditions, such as the Moravian congregations, to continue their solemn musical festivities.

The practice of music in the new United States was not often considered even by its audiences to have been at a high level. Jefferson is known to have stated that music "is the favorite passion of my soul, and fortune has cast my lot in a country where it is in a state of deplorable barbarism." George Washington regarded music as essential, stating, "nothing is more agreeable, and ornamental, than good music." Given the deplorable state of music in the military, he threatened to withhold pay if it did not improve. Even with the creation of professional ensembles in the 1790s, the audiences could be uncontrolled. Conductor James Hewitt had the misfortune in New York of having a knife thrown at him, as well as being physically assaulted when he refused to accede to audiences demands for political music (see Document 4). Regardless of the unruly listeners, music was an important and vital part of American society in the new country, and as the nineteenth century dawned, politics and patriotic music began to become all the more popular.

The cities in this Chapter were major population or national centers during the Classical Period, and all of them had important roles to play in the development of musical style, each with its own focus and reputation. These were, however, not the only places where musical development was undertaken, and in many of the lesser courts and cities, music progressed at an equivalent pace.

Documents

Document 1. From Charles Burney, *The Present State of Music in Germany, the Netherlands, and United Provinces* (London, 1775).

Upon the whole Amsterdam does not seem to be a very amusing residence for idle people; there is so little for them to see in the way of pleasure, and so much for the mercantile part of the inhabitants to do in the way of business, that they seem very unfit company for each other. . . . Though Amsterdam is the capital of the United Provinces, yet this [The Hague] being the residence of the Stadtholder, and the place where his court is constantly kept, it should, of course, be likewise the seat of the polite arts. The musical establishment of His Serene Highness consists chiefly of German musicians. . . . The Hague seems more calculated for musical birds of passage than natives. . . . It is common for German and Italian musicians in their way to or from England to visit . . . but they seldom remain here longer than a ship, which enters a port merely to wood and water.

Document 2. From an article in the *Almänna Tidningar* by Carl Christoffer Gjörwell (Stockholm, 1770). Translation by the author.

For Swedish genius can thus be found to not only equal, but often surpass foreigner with respect to both vocal and instrumental music, and recently one has seen in those published literary works to what degree the Swedish language has achieved both strength and taste in poetic art and perfection, and [therefore] the establishment of a Swedish theatre and opera, which would be useful, pleasant, and do honor to the nation as a whole, should also be possible.

Document 3. From William Coxe, *Travels into Poland, Russia, Sweden, and Denmark* (London, 1792). Comment on his travels in Russia.

The postilions sing from the beginning of a stage to the end; the soldiers sing continually during their march; the countrymen sing during the most laborious occupations; the public houses re-echo with their carols; and on a still evening I have frequently heard the air vibrate with the notes from the surrounding countryside.

Document 4. From the *New York Evening Register* for March 6, 1794

The *junto* were kept aloof, and to make up for their absence (and determined to have *some* fun) the prelude was commenced upon an *individual*, poor Hewitt, the leader of the band and a very respectable, inoffensive character. They quarreled with him, because as a foreigner, he did not know the music called for, nor would they wait until he could recollect himself, and make up the tune from the rest of the band, which was afterwards done. Perplexed as the leader of the band always is by the variety of calls from every busy creature who is fond of the sweet sound of his own voice at a theatre, how *pleasant* a situation would he be if every call not instantly complied with was thus resented. But it did not matter, something was necessary for a beginning, "a word and a blow" did the business and afforded excellent sport.

Notes

1 Burney, *Present State of Music in Germany*, I: 284. Burney's discussion of his visit can be found on pp. 284–303.

2   Burney, *Present State of Music in Germany*, 301.
3   Johann von Streuensee was the personal physician to King Christian IV and involved in a scandalous affair with Queen Charlotte Matilda. He sought to establish an absolute control over Denmark but was deposed and executed.
4   Reported by Joseph Martin Kraus in a letter to his employer dated May 14, 1792. See the present author's *The Musical Life of Joseph Martin Kraus*, 291.
5   Manuscript memorandum in Stockholm, Roman-samling; quoted in *Musiken i Sverige II: Frihetstiden och Gustaviansk Tid* (Stockholm: Fischer, 1993), 16. Translation by the author.
6   A list of concerts is provided in Patrik Vretblad, *Konsertlifvet i Stockholm under 1700-talet* (Stockholm: P. A. Norstedt, 1918).
7   Indeed, in 1729 the *St. Petersburg Gazette* published a definition of opera that was felt necessary to educate the local inhabitants of a major entertainment in Europe in anticipation of importing it to Russia.
8   That is not to say that all public spectacle was lacking. The 1789 commemoration by Sarti has already been mentioned, and he and his colleagues also wrote massive oratorios for public church performances.
9   See Landon, *Haydn Chronicle and Works*, II: 42.
10 Albrecht Kayser, *Versuch einer kurzen Beschreibung der kaiserlichen freyen Reichsstadt Regensburg* (Regensburg, 1797), 51.
11 Burney, *The Present State of Music in Germany*, II: 324.
12 Two earlier talented native Maltese musicians, Giuseppe Arena and Girolamo Abos, were both sent to Naples with the intent that they return to Malta, but both remained in Italy; Abos became an instructor at the San Loreto, while Arena achieved success as a composer of Italian opera.
13 Technically speaking, New Spain was the northern viceroyalty, with Mexico City as its capital, while the southern portion was the Viceroyalty of Peru and the Caribbean, the Viceroyalty of Havana.
14 Taken from an 1814 questionnaire, translated in Craig Russell, *From Serra to Sancho* (New York: Oxford University Press, 2009), 256.

11 From Universal Composer to Icon
Joseph Haydn and Wolfgang Amadeus Mozart

There can be no doubt in the mind of today's public that two composers are viewed as synonymous with the Classical Period; Joseph Haydn and Wolfgang Amadeus Mozart. Indeed, according to the German tradition of "great masters" formulated even as early as the beginning of the nineteenth century, these two composers were considered as the epitome of music of the period against which all others (reckoned as *Kleinmeister*, or "Masters of Lesser Light" as musicologist H. C. Robbins Landon once noted) were to be measured, and this, in turn, led to the prevailing view that Vienna was the predominant musical center and the entire mature style was called the Viennese Classical style. This triumvirate was promoted as early as 1809 by Ernst Theodor Amadeus Hoffmann, who that year began a widely read and international career as a music critic writing for the journal *Allgemeine musikalische Zeitung*. In his inaugural outing, a review of Ludwig van Beethoven's Fifth Symphony, Hoffmann offers what can be considered one of the first, and perhaps the most seminal, views on the importance of all three composers, including Beethoven. He notes,

> Haydn grasps the natural in the life of mankind, more easily accessible for the majority; Mozart rather takes into account the supernatural, the miraculous that lives within the inner spirit; Beethoven's music moves the rising of fear, of terror, of turmoil, of pain, and awakens each and every eternal longing that is the soul of the Romantic.[1]

It should be noted that all three composers are considered by Hoffmann to be "Romantics," yet the trio are noted to have risen above all others by the author at the time as harbingers of the future of music. As Hoffmann was widely read internationally, the elevation of all three gained in prominence over the course of the next several decades until their iconic status as the standard-bearers of the Classical (and Romantic) Periods was universally recognized.

Without deconstructing their importance or the origins of their iconic status, it should be noted that, while Beethoven was considered even during his lifetime as a major developer of a new direction of music we might term "Romantic" (in the current definition of this historical term), the status of both Haydn and Mozart were viewed differently during their lifetimes. For Haydn, the current popular image of "Papa Haydn," a fatherly figure of music, derives from the esteem in which he was held toward the end of the century. Indeed, Haydn was regarded as the principal composer of that time. In 1785, one of Beethoven's teachers, Christian Gottlob Neefe wrote in the collection *Dilettanterien* the following: "Haydn is the master, and Mozart, Kozeluch, Kraus, Pleyel, Reicha, and Rosetti all stand alongside him or follow in his worthy footsteps."[2] Here, Mozart is given stature as one of the major German composers of the day in Neefe's view, though he is listed among five others. Haydn's importance at the time can also be seen in the following quote from the *European Magazine and London Review for October, 1784*:

> The universality of Haydn's genius cannot be more strongly proved than by the vast demand for his works all over Europe: there is not only a fashion but also a rage for his musick; and he has continual commissions from France, England, Russia, Holland, etc. for his compositions, expressly written for individuals, or for the music-sellers resident in these kingdoms.[3]

This gives Haydn the distinction of being one of the most important international composers in the eyes of his contemporaries. Despite this high reputation, Haydn regarded Mozart as "the incarnation of music," considering him to have been the more original and gifted composer. Mozart reciprocated his admiration of Haydn, dedicating six string quartets to the elder composer as a mark of high respect. Mozart, however, only achieved his international reputation at the same level posthumously.

> **The Music of Haydn and Mozart: The Catalogues**
>
> The exact number of compositions composed by both Joseph Haydn and Wolfgang Amadeus Mozart is still a work in progress, given that there exist references to a number of lost works as well as misattributed or spurious compositions.
>
> For Haydn, the three-volume catalogue *Joseph Haydn, Thematisch-bibliographisches Werkverzeichnis (Joseph Haydn: Thematic-bibliographic Catalog of Works)* by Anthony van Hoboken, published between 1957 and 1978, lists the compositions in systematic order by genre. These are designated as Hob. numbers.
>
> For Mozart, the first catalogue of his musical works was done in 1866 by Ludwig Ritter von Köchel and is titled *Chronologisch-thematisches Verzeichnis sämtlicher Tonwerke Wolfgang Amadé Mozarts* (*Chronological-thematic Catalogue of the Complete Musical Works of Wolfgang Amadeus Mozart*). These are designated by K or KV (used here) numbers, standing for Köchel or Köchel Verzeichnis. The sixth edition from 1964 (reprinted as the seventh and eighth in subsequent decades) is current, although a ninth edition, edited by musicologist Neal Zaslaw, is forthcoming.

Over the course of the next two centuries, Mozart's reputation rose to iconic status, a position still maintained somewhat today, while Haydn's has been variable, mainly resting upon his symphonies and string quartets. It is noteworthy that both were, however, universal composers who wrote professionally and extensively in most genres and styles of the period, developing their own musical voices as their careers progressed. Their lives intertwined for a few years prior to Mozart's early death, yet their professional lives were perhaps as different as one might imagine

Haydn

Joseph Haydn was from a family of musical amateurs, and two of his brothers, Michael and Johann, also sought careers in music. He was born in the small town of Rohrau, Austria, on the Hungarian border on March 31, 1732. The son of a wheelwright, he was instructed by a local schoolmaster by the name of Johann Matthias Frankh in music as he displayed an unusual talent. After a few years he was recruited by Johann Georg von Reutter as a member of the choir at St. Stephen's Cathedral in Vienna (Figure 11.1), where he spent a decade performing both in church and at court. His musical training included lessons in voice and instruments such as the violin and keyboard, and he soon was one of the main soloists. By 1745 he was replaced by his brother Michael, who apparently was equally or perhaps more talented a musician than he, and for the next several years he attempted to adjust his own abilities to accommodate the changing circumstances. In 1749, he apparently made his first attempts at composition, a Mass in F major, Hob. XXII:3. This first work demonstrates the influence of his years singing at St. Stephen's under Reutter, featuring a mostly homophonic chorus against which a pair of violins weave a nonthematic arabesque (Example 11.1). While not entirely groundbreaking, it does demonstrate both a solid knowledge of Reutter's Viennese church style and, as Haydn himself stated later in life, contained "much youthful fire."

It is clear that Haydn and Reutter did not see eye to eye, and the same year the *Kapellmeister* used a pretext to dismiss the young musician. Albert Dies, one of Haydn's first biographers, noted that this dismissal came about when the young composer cut off the queue of another choirboy and then refused punishment, while another, Georg August Griesinger, says nothing at all about any incident, though noting that he left the choir abruptly "on a cold November day in 1749." His first lodging was a garret room with a close

Figure 11.1 St. Stephens Cathedral, Vienna

friend, Johann Michael Spangler, and for the next three years he spent time as a freelance musician in Vienna. He joined the ranks of street musicians, and because these often-impromptu groups were invited in to perform music for various houses, both merchant and aristocratic, he made important contacts with potential employers. He also did odd jobs such as singing briefly in a choir in Mariazell, teaching music lessons, and performing as an organist and violinist, both at various venues in Vienna, including the rare occasion at St. Stephen's, and private homes. One of these in 1752 led to his first opera, the Singspiel entitled *Der krumme Teufel* (as already noted), the success of which brought a measure of success. He also self-taught himself from Fux's *Gradus ad Parnassum*, treatises by Johann Mattheson and David Kellner on instrumentation and thoroughbass, as well as absorbed the *Empfindsamkeit* style of C. P. E. Bach through the famed composer's keyboard sonatas. Haydn himself noted later that "whoever knows me well must have discovered that I owe much to Emanuel Bach, for I have understood and diligently studied him."[4]

In 1752 one of the most important breaks in his heretofore transient lifestyle came when he was hired by Metastasio as the teacher of his musically talented ward, Marianna Martines. This employment came with room and board, and within a short time opera composer Niccolò Porpora moved into the same house.

Example 11.1 Joseph Haydn, Mass in F major, Hob. XX:1, Gloria, mm. 1–6

Martines was extremely gifted as a composer and performer, and Porpora became her main voice teacher, with Haydn as accompanist. In exchange for various "menial" services as a valet, Haydn soon became Porpora's student as well and, through him, came into contact with the most important composers resident in Vienna at the time; Christoph Georg Wagenseil, Giuseppe Bono, and, most important, Christoph Willibald von Gluck. Haydn later stated that he learned "the genuine fundamentals of [musical] composition" from Porpora during the three years he spent under his tutelage. During this time, Haydn began to write and perform pieces ranging from sonatas to sacred music, in effect "something can come out of nothing,"[5] as he later noted.

About 1755 or 1756 Haydn began to become associated with prominent Austrian families, thanks to his introductions to society through Porpora and others, freelance work as a supernumerary at the various court functions, as well as the dissemination of his music. These included the Count Haugewitz, for whom he served briefly as an organist at the Bohemian chancellery, Countess Thun, who hired Haydn as her music teacher following her obtaining one of his keyboard works, and Count Carl Joseph von Fürnberg, who invited Haydn as part of a string quartet to his summer estate to perform chamber music. As his reputation grew, Haydn became an active and popular figure in the musical world of Vienna.

Haydn's style at this early stage demonstrates his study of Bach and Fux, even though it tends toward accessibility and formal simplicity. For example, in the Sonata in F major (Hob. XVI:9) composed around 1757–1758, the opening movement is a rounded binary form with a simple 2+2 bar theme that has little development (Example 11.2). The modulatory patterns do not stray beyond the dominant, and the use of small motives shows the influence of Bach.

Example 11.2 Haydn, Sonata of Keyboard in F major, Hob XVI:9, Movement 1, mm. 1–15

In 1758 Fürnberg, himself unable to afford a permanent musical employee, recommended Haydn to Count Karl Joseph Morzin, who took him to Lukavice in Bohemia as his *Kammercompositeur* (Chamber Composer) during the summers; winters were spent in Vienna. He led an orchestra of sixteen players and wrote chamber works, mainly sonatas and wind band music (*Harmoniemusik*), for the Morzin family. His first symphonies date from this period and demonstrate already a mastery of the genre. Haydn varies these works between three and four movements, the common practice modeled after those he had no doubt heard in Vienna by his predecessors, Wagenseil and others. The formal structures of these works show an increasing interest in monothematic development, in which Haydn uses a single principal theme, varying it as a secondary theme in a new key. The central sections are developed from this main theme, which is often expanded through sections of sequences and the occasional insertion of minor-key episodes. The structure is an expansion of the rounded binary form, with the beginning of careful attention to modulatory sequences. He also experimented with changes in format, sometimes beginning with a slow movement and placing the minuet in either second or third position when used. One can also discern his interest in providing obbligato solo moments, as the Symphony in A major, Hob. I:5, demonstrates (Example 11.3).

Haydn's employment at Lukavece was also to be short-lived when the count found it necessary to disband his orchestra due to financial difficulties. Apparently, one of the major members of the nobility, Prince Paul Anton Esterházy, attended a concert in 1760 in which Haydn's first-known symphony was performed. While information is sketchy, it is apparent that he learned of Morzin's troubles and arranged for Haydn to come to Eisenstadt for a trial run. A contract dated May 1, 1761, was made with the composer, employing him as Vice-Kapellmeister with the stipulation that he continue the expansion of the Esterházy court orchestra that had begun under the *Kapellmeister* Gregor Joseph Werner (Figure 11.2). Well known as a composer of church music, Werner was unable to function due to age and health, so Haydn was to take over most of his duties. The contract notes that the composer is to be regarded as a "house officer" of the court, to have "sole direction" of the court musical ensembles, including a new theatre, and to allow the prince to be the only authority regarding Haydn's music written for the court. It also adjures Haydn to "conduct himself in an exemplary manner" and to "take charge of all music and musical instruments." Prince Paul Anton died less than a year later, and his brother Nicholas inherited the position, thus providing Haydn with a musically knowledgeable and magnanimous patron.

The years that Haydn spent at the Esterházy Court, 1766 to 1790, saw his stature rise from musical servant to celebrated composer, all without leaving the region. In winter, Haydn often accompanied his Prince to Vienna, but in the summer he stayed at the palace of Esterház, located in the Hungarian marshlands

Example 11.3 Symphony in A major, Hob I:5, Movement 1, mm. 59–63

Figure 11.2 Joseph Haydn as Vice-Kapellmeister (*ca.* 1765, copper engraving)

254 *Capitals and Centers of Music-Making*

near the city of Fertőd (after 1766). The remainder of the year was spent at Eisenstadt, where compositions from the period when he was Vice-Kapellmeister focused mainly on instrumental works. Here he first began to insert programmatic elements into his symphonies. First and foremost among them are a trio of works based on the times of the day: Hob. I:6 "Le Matin," Hob. I:7 "Le Midi," and Hob. I:8 "Le Soir." These works include the rising of the sun in a slow introduction to the first (Example 11.4) and a tempest that

Example 11.4 Haydn, Symphony No. 6, *Morning*, Hob I:6, Movement 1, mm. 1–10

From Universal Composer to Icon 255

concludes the last. He includes sections for obbligato instruments, demonstrated by the use of solo violins, flute, bassoon, and cello.

Werner died in 1766 but not before issuing a rather nasty letter of complaint against Haydn, whom he regarded as frivolous and lazy, calling him a "scribbler of songs." The prince admonished his young Vice-Kapellmeister, telling him to exercise discipline among his musicians and to "apply himself to composition more diligently than heretofore."[6] Since Prince Nicholas was fond of playing the baryton, a large stringed instrument (see Chapter 3), Haydn took special pains to write music especially for it, including more than a hundred trios. Upon Werner's death, he was elevated to the post of *Kapellmeister* and given the wherewithal to expand the Esterházy orchestra and singers in anticipation of the completion of a new opera house at Esterház, the prince's summer estate then under construction. With its completion in 1768, much of Haydn's efforts were dedicated toward the writing and production of operas there (Figure 11.3).

Haydn's two-and-a-half decades at the court were marked by considerable musical changes, not to mention the development of an international reputation as his music was disseminated throughout Europe. Haydn himself was often at the core of this, for in several instances he was personally involved in direct

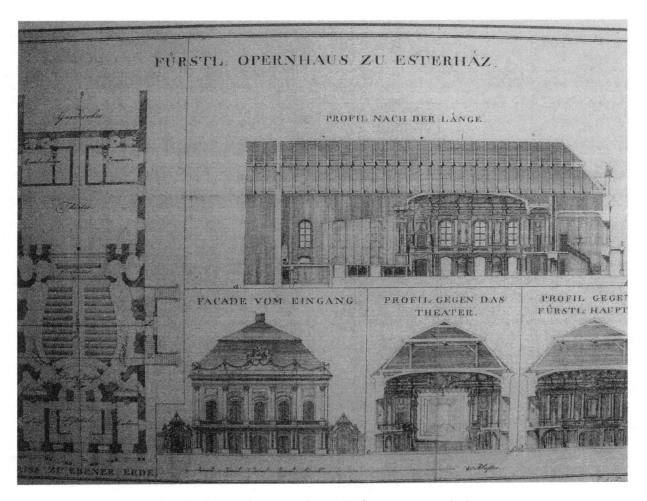

Figure 11.3 Architectural plans for the Esterház opera theatre (18th century engraving)

marketing. As an example, in 1781 he wrote to Swiss physician Johann Caspar Lavater offering him a personal subscription to his Op. 33 string quartets:

> As one reads, hears and is told, I am not without ability myself, since my name (as it is) is known and appreciated highly in every country. Therefore, I take the liberty of asking you to do me a small favor. Since I know there are in Zürich and Winterthur many gentlemen amateurs and great connoisseurs and patrons of music, I shall not hide from you that I am issuing, by subscription for the price of 6 ducats, a set consisting of 6 Quartets for two violins, viola, and violoncello solo, correctly copied out and written in a new and special manner (for I haven't composed any for 10 years). . . . Subscribers who live abroad will receive them before I publish the works here.[7]

This letter parallels others sent to Prince Krafft Ernst of Oettingen-Wallerstein, whose *Kapellmeister*, Antonio Rosetti, was in correspondence with Haydn, as well as his publisher, Artaria, in Vienna.

One can divide the first years as *Kapellmeister* into two musical phases. The first occurs from about 1766 to 1778, when Haydn embarked on a series of bold experiments in terms of his own compositional development. These took the form mostly of instrumental works, mainly symphonies and string quartets, in which he probed the breadth of styles, creating his own brand as he spent months in the remote, isolated Esterház palace. Although he also spent a portion of the year in both Eisenstadt and Vienna, his work for Prince Nicholas was meant to appeal to the court rather than the public at large. In 1776 the new opera house at the estate began the series of annual seasons over the next decade and a half that saw almost a thousand performances. The works produced were mainly Italian opera buffa by the leading composers of the day, but Haydn himself contributed a goodly number of works for the small, intimate stage (see Figure 6.2). Empress Maria Theresia is alleged to have remarked that she would visit Esterház if she wanted to hear good opera. Haydn's musical style evolved during this period, with expanded use of the bifocal cadence at the end of expositions, the sometimes-unusual keys of F-sharp minor and B major, (Hob. I:45 and I:46), respectively, for which special adaptations had to be made for the horns, and the inclusion of periodical structures, such as in the last symphony mentioned the return of melodic fragments from other movements in the finale. He also experimented with minor keys, where modulatory sequences were more fluid, such as the Symphonies in G minor, Hob. I:39; E minor, Hob. I:44; and C minor, Hob. I:52. Obbligato instruments are used frequently with spectacular effects, such as in the second trio of the Symphony in B-flat major, Hob. I:51, where the horns rise to the top and descend to the bottom of their registers (Example 11.5).

The second phase lasted until his retirement in 1790. In 1779, the opera house at Esterház burned down, and for a couple of years performances were held at the smaller marionette theatre. It was replaced in 1781 with a larger and more magnificent stage, and the composer wrote his last three operas (*Armida, Orlando Paladino, La fedeltà premiata*) for special occasions. His time spent in Vienna during the winter months was both socially and compositionally productive. His music was being regularly performed throughout Europe, from Stockholm in the north to the Iberian Peninsula and from Russia to the new United States. In 1784 the Olympic Loge in Paris, which supported subscription concerts under the direction of the Duke of Orleans, commissioned him to write a set of six symphonies (Hob. I:82–87), while the director of the Concerts Spirituels, Joseph Le Gros, reported that Haydn's *Stabat mater* had achieved considerable success at that famous venue. Offers to publish his music came from Paris and London, while in Spain the Duke of Alba, along with other members of the aristocracy, entered into a multiyear agreement to purchase music directly from Haydn. Indeed, in 1786 the archbishopric in Cádiz commissioned him to write seven sonatas based on the seven last words of Christ on the cross (Hob. XX:1, see Chapter 8). The composer himself noted, "It was no easy task to compose seven adagios lasting ten minutes each, and to succeed one another without fatiguing the listeners."[8] In 1787 he was approached to travel to England, and the newspapers were filled with rumors of his impending arrival. Haydn was not able to undertake the journey due to his official duties, but he sent a steady stream of works abroad by way of visitors, by his own subscription, and directly to publishers. Indeed, his music was so popular that the publishers in London, Paris, and elsewhere

Example 11.5 Haydn, Symphony in B-flat major, Hob. I:51, Movement 2, mm. 1–8

often put Haydn's name as composer on works by other composers.[9] In short, Haydn was perhaps the best-known and most popular composer of his time (Figure 11.4).

In September 1790, Haydn's patron, Prince Nicholas, passed away, and his successor, Prince Anton, found it necessary to dissolve the famed musical ensemble. Haydn, his concertmaster Luigi Tomasini, and a couple of others were retained, but they had few official duties at court. Haydn's service, however, was nominal, for both Esterházy princes endowed him with a substantial pension that allowed him to move to Vienna and retire. At the age of 58, he was approached by a number of courts, such as King Ferdinand IV of Naples, to enter their service, but the composer accepted a proposal by Johann Peter Salomon to visit London instead. Salomon was the director of a concert series held in the Hanover Square Rooms, and an important violin virtuoso in his own right. Haydn arrived in Dover on New Year's Day in 1791 and immediately became a celebrity. Given that London was a magnet for musicians from throughout Europe, Haydn's circle of acquaintances grew considerably, and he soon found himself immersed in activity. The newspaper *Morning Chronicle* in December 1790 noted: "A concert [series] is planned under the auspices of Haydn, whose name is a tower of strength, and to whom the amateurs of instrumental music look [upon] as the god of the science." In July, it was arranged by Charles Burney that Haydn would receive an honorary doctorate at Oxford University. The papers described this as a "murderous harmonious war," but both remained friendly with each other, and soon the rivalry fizzled.

258 Capitals and Centers of Music-Making

Figure 11.4 Portrait of Joseph Haydn as *Kapellmeister* (*ca.* 1780)
Source: Haydn Museum: Erich Lessing/Art Resource, NY

Haydn's style during this first visit to London expanded considerably, especially in the realm of the symphony. The orchestra was the largest he had ever had and included clarinets. He remarked that "never in my life have I written so much in one year," attending to both the needs of his host Salomon and the various works written for others and for publication. He expressed his outside interests by visiting Sir William Herschel, himself a talented composer, and viewing his telescope, as well as the naval yards at Plymouth, where he sketched in his diary a fire ship (Figure 11.5). A year later, he was back in Vienna with a handful of commissions and a promise to return to London. On his way back, he stopped in Bonn, where the elector induced him to take on a young talent, Ludwig van Beethoven, as a future pupil.[10]

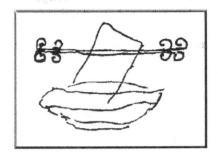

Figure 11.5 Haydn's drawing of a British fire ship from his *London Notebooks* (1792)

In January 1794, Haydn returned for a second visit to London. As before, he was greeted with applause, met with fellow musicians new to the London music scene, and created a sensation with his last symphonies. Although celebrated, Haydn refused a longer stay, for the new Prince Esterházy, Nicholas II, had written him about reinstituting the orchestra and required him to return at his earliest convenience. However, the new prince did little to revive the musical life at Esterház, instead preferring Vienna and Eisenstadt has his residences, and while he was fond of music, he was more interested in art. His support of Haydn was often grudging, and the composer was left with little to do than sacred music. In 1796 he nonetheless began a series of Masses, the first of which, *Missa in angustiis* (also known as the Lord Nelson Mass) was produced for the princess, though the necessary woodwind players had not yet been employed (Example 11.6). This left Haydn with considerable freedom to do his own work in Vienna. He had received an oratorio text based on the Bible and Milton's *Paradise Lost* titled *The Creation*, with the notion that it would be premiered in London. Haydn, however, probably felt his English was not up to the task, and so he asked his friend, court librarian Baron Gottfried van Swieten, to translate it into German. The work that he described as his being "never so devout as when composing [it]"[11] was given its premiere in April 1798 at the palace of Prince Schwarzburg in Vienna (Figure 11.6). A critic in the *Neuer teutscher Merkur* noted, "Three days have gone since that mesmerizing evening, and still the music resounds in my ears and heart; the mere memory of the flood of emotions experienced then still grips my chest."[12] *The Creation* (in German *Die Schöpfung*) was such a success that it was immediate engraved in score and performed throughout Europe. Baron van Swieten, who sought to take as much credit from its text as possible, then persuaded Haydn to write a second work based on the seasons of the year. The text, described as "stiff as the Baron himself," was a monumental task that cost the composer much of his remaining strength. Only a few compositions date from after 1802, though he helped secure his legacy through participating in biographies by Dies and Griesinger, as well as compiling his own catalogue of works with the help of his copyist Joseph Elssler. In May 1809 Haydn passed away as French forces occupied Vienna.

Haydn was a universal composer of the Classical Period, important because his music not only was considered the model for numerous composers of his time but also because it had an international audience. His symphonies, many written in isolation at Esterház exclusively for his patron, evolved into being the epitome of the genre, while his string quartets (all seventy-two of them) demonstrate a consistent evolution over the course of his lifetime. As a composer of Masses, the final works written late in life are viewed as landmarks in the style of what might be called the missa ordinarius, retaining the basic six movements of the missa brevis but expanding them through tempo and metrical changes, colorful and expressive orchestration, and operatic vocal parts. The two late oratorios are equally magnificent in their monumental scope, their expressiveness, and their precise attention to each musical detail. Haydn was one of the first to write for the keyed trumpet and did not hesitate to compose music for instruments that were obscure, such as the baryton or lira organizzata. His aforementioned explanation—"I was cut off from the world. There was no one to confuse or torment me, and I was forced to become original"[13]—has an important resonance for his contributions to the development of music during this time.

Example 11.6 Haydn, *Missa in angustiis*, Hob. XII:11, Kyrie, mm. 16–27

Figure 11.6 First performance of Haydn's *Creation* in Vienna, 1798
Source: bpk Bidagentur/Museum der Stadt Wien/Art Resource, NY

Mozart

The life and musical-stylistic development of Wolfgang Amadeus Mozart took a rather different route than that of Haydn. While both were born into musical families, Mozart's father Leopold was a highly esteemed professional at the court of the Prince-Archbishop of Salzburg. The year of Mozart's birth, 1756, Leopold Mozart published the first edition of his *Versuch einer gründlichen Violinschule* (*A Treatise on the Fundamental Principles of Violin Playing*), a work that Charles Burney called "well-digested and useful,"[14] particularly with regards to his promotion of *Affekt*; by 1770 it had been reissued in two further editions and translated into French, Italian, and Dutch. The result of this is that the young Wolfgang Amadeus grew up in a professional musical household, and even though his father never achieved a position beyond Vice-Kapellmeister, he was a composer who was both prolific and thoroughly versed in all of the musical styles of the time.

The fact that Wolfgang Mozart was gifted has become almost synonymous with his identification as a child prodigy. He and his sister Maria Anna (nicknamed Nannerl) demonstrated unusually precocious musical talent; in one of the numerous anecdotes about the child Mozart, he even began "composing" a concerto at the age of five. Leopold Mozart decided to take his children on tour, displaying their talent at the various courts where such prodigies were welcomed with some awe. At the age of seven, therefore, the Mozart family embarked on a three-year journey (Figure 11.7). Their initial concerts were at important German courts in Munich, Stuttgart, and Mannheim, where they met both the nobility and notable court composers. By January 1764 they performed before Louis XV at Versailles and made the acquaintance of musical figures in Paris as well as having Wolfgang's first works published as a means of establishing his reputation in the center of music publishing. Thereafter, they moved on to England for fifteen months, where concerts were given at the court of George III as well as public concert venues such as Ranleigh Gardens. Here he was taken under the wing of Johann Christian Bach and composed his first symphonies. The return to Salzburg in 1766 was by way of the Dutch court at The Hague, Paris, Switzerland, and Bavaria. At each stop, the young child was lauded, in some cases for the "progress" made since the earlier visit.

In terms of the performance culture, it has been a source of debate whether their father exploited Mozart and his sister at too young an age. While this period of his life meant no formal schooling, he was immersed in the musical culture of some of the principal centers in Europe, and his own efforts at musical composition reflect this environment. For example, to learn how to compose concertos (and possible for his own public display) he orchestrated three sonatas by J. C. Bach (KV 107), and then produced four more based on movements cobbled together from sonatas by popular composers of the period, including Hermann Raupach, Johann Schobert, and Johann Eckard (KV 37, 39–41). In London he came under the mentorship of Bach, as well as demonstrating his precocious ability with a short motet in English, *God is our Refuge and our Strength*, KV 20, for the Royal Academy of Music (Example 11.7). When he returned home to Salzburg following an absence of three-and-a-half years, he not only had achieved a reputation as a prodigy but also had a portfolio of his compositions. Archbishop Sigismund von Schrattenbach was skeptical that an eleven-year-old child could have written the symphonies, concertos, and other works, so he made Mozart compose a work, probably the *Grabmusik*, KV 42, in isolation. Thereafter, he embarked upon an ambitious succession of works, including two for the stage, *Apollo et Hyacinthus*, KV 38, for Salzburg University and the first part of an oratorio, *Die Schuldigkeit des ersten Gebotes*, KV 35. The works composed during this early period were impressive, though in some cases there is evidence that they were "tidied up" by Leopold to eliminate awkward passages.

In September, Leopold Mozart embarked upon a journey to Vienna to introduce the child to the Holy Roman court. The entire move was ambitious, for not only was the child introduced to the Imperial family; he was also able to compose two operas, *La finta semplice*, KV 51, and *Bastien und Bastienne*, KV 50, one an opera buffa in Italian and the second a German Singspiel that was a gloss on Rousseau's *Le Devin du Village*. The second was performed at a private theatre at the residence of Anton Mesmer, who gained fame for his work on magnetism and hypnosis, but the latter's intended production at the Hoftheater was canceled; it was produced in Salzburg a few months later. His continued productivity in all genres led to

Figure 11.7 Painting of Mozart as a boy by Pietro Antonio Lorenzoni, 1762–1763
Source: © Internationale Stiftung Mozarteum/ISM.

Example 11.7 Wolfgang Amadeus Mozart, *God is our Refuge and our Strength*, KV 20, mm. 1–9

the appointment as honorary concertmaster in October 1769. Both the operas and other works such as symphonies and the Mass in C minor, KV 139, demonstrate that the young Mozart was making progress, learning both the simple style of the Singspiel and the more fluid style of the opera buffa, as well as the necessary contrasting material in his instrumental works that reflected the evolution of the symphony in central Europe of the time.

The second phase of Wolfgang Mozart's musical education came at the end of that year, when both father and son began a year and a half journey to Italy. This was less about displaying the talents of Mozart as a prodigy and more about giving him the opportunity to be influenced by Italian music in the various cities on this Grand Tour. Mozart did concertize regularly, often in towns or by invitation of the nobility. Word of his talent led him to be examined by the musical societies (Accademia Filarmonica) in the major northern Italian towns such as Verona, Mantua, and Bologna. He was also introduced to some of the leading composers of the day, such as Sammartini in Milan (who helped arrange for him to compose the opera *Mithridate* for the 1770 Carnival season), Piccinni, Farinelli, and Padre Martini. In Rome, he was introduced to the Pope, demonstrating his skill by copying out the proprietary Miserere by Gregorio Allegri by memory and being introduced to the Roman nobility. In June 1770, the Pope, in an honor that only rarely bestowed on composers from outside Italy, made him a knight of the Order of the Golden Spur (Figure 11.8). The Mozarts also spent time in Naples, where a painting allegedly shows both performing with violinist Tommaso Giordani in a private concert (Figure 11.9). In July he was admitted to the prestigious Accademia Filarmonica in Bologna after the acceptance of a test antiphon, *Querite primum*, KV 86, and spent the fall in Milan

Figure 11.8 Mozart as a Knight of the Golden Spur, painting by Antonio Nardi after an oil by della Croce (?) in 1777
Source: © Internationale Stiftung Mozarteum/ISM.

Figure 11.9 Painting by Pietro Fabris of a concert at the home of Kenneth Mackenzie, Earl of Seaforth, in Naples, 1771, allegedly showing Leopold and Wolfgang Mozart at the keyboard and Tommaso Giordani playing violin

Source: Reproduced with permission from the Scottish National Gallery.

composing the commissioned opera. This was performed with some success on December 26, 1770, earning him a second commission to be performed the following year at the Regio Ducale theatre; the forthcoming marriage of the governor, Archduke Ferdinand, in 1772 also elicited a second commission, this one for a serenata titled *Ascanio in Alba*, KV 111. Charles Burney met the Mozarts in Bologna, noting,

> I must acquaint my musical reader that at the performance just mentioned, I met with M. Mozart and his son, the little German, whose premature and almost supernatural talents so much astonished us in London a few years ago, when he had scarce quitted his infant state. Since his arrival in Italy he has been much admired at Rome and Naples, has been honored with the order of the *Speron d'Oro*, or Golden Spur, by his Holiness and was engaged to compose an opera at Milan for the next Carnival.[15]

A few months in Salzburg resulted in a special commission for the elevation of Archbishop Hieronymus Colloredo as Prince-Archbishop of Salzburg in March 1772 following the death of Archbishop von Schrattenbach, as well as his being appointed as a salaried concertmaster in July. The third journey to Italy began in October, only this time he did not tour, but rather went directly to Milan to produce his third opera, *Lucio Silla*, KV 135. Noting that there were warning signs that Colloredo would be less tolerant than his predecessor, the Mozart family hoped that Archduke Ferdinand would see Mozart's success in Milan as a reason to extend employment. However, when the archduke petitioned his mother, Empress Maria Theresia, the answer was not positive.[16]

Between 1772 and 1777, Wolfgang Mozart was a colleague of his father at the Salzburg court. No longer precocious, he earned a salary, was on good terms with the local nobility, and exercised his craft with considerable skill and ability in most genres. Having a natural gift for melody and orchestration, he was adept at both vocal and instrumental works, as the iconic "Allleluja" from his motet *Exultate, Jubilate*, KV 165, shows (Example 11.8). While Salzburg did not have an opera house, visiting troupes did occasionally appear, and the Mozarts were allowed in 1773 to visit Vienna, where Wolfgang Mozart was able to do some limited concertizing, renew friendships from prior to his Italian journeys, and probably meet other professional colleagues. Here the influences of Joseph Haydn were being felt, particularly in the genres of chamber music, and a set of quartets (KV 168–173) were probably composed under the influence of Haydn's latest works, the Op. 20. Here he also began to perform as a soloist, composing his first keyboard concerto (KV 175) for his own use. There has been speculation that this Viennese visit was intended as a means of finding another position for the teen-aged composer, but if so, it too was unsuccessful. The influences of composers such as Vanhal, Dittersdorf, and Haydn in genres such as the symphony were felt on his return to Salzburg, where Mozart wrote several works in quick succession that demonstrated a good knowledge of the Viennese works by these composers. In particular, one might note the powerful and dramatic Symphony in G minor, KV 183 (one of only two symphonies he wrote in a minor key) or the lively and humorous Symphony in A major, KV 201, with its surprising thematic twists and expanded sonata form sections. The only other outside commission, however, was for an opera, *La finta giardiniera*, KV 196, for Carnival in Munich in 1774. As an opera buffa, it was so much a success that a German translation was done for the Böhm theatrical troupe, who toured it throughout central Europe for a number of years.

During this Salzburg period, Mozart also received the occasional commission for concertos for violin, violoncello, keyboard, oboe, and bassoon, as well as a "grand concerto" for two violins, the Concertone, KV 190. He also experimented within this genre with a work for the Lodron family featuring three solo keyboards (KV 242). The stimulation of various visiting artists also provided Mozart with the incentive to continue to develop his own musical style. The only difficulty was the decree by Colloredo that limited church music. Salzburg had a long tradition of festive music for the three churches, but in the main cathedral, the archbishop seemingly had little tolerance for either extensive Masses or services, decreeing that even the most solemn occasions should last no more than forty-five minutes. He still required complete music, which had to be tailored to the timeframe. This resulted in Mozart condensing his missa brevis into short, cohesive movements, which were complemented by equally brief and succinct Epistle sonatas

Example 11.8 Mozart, *Exultate, Jubilate*, KV 165, Movement 3, mm. 9–16

for organ. The young composer chaffed at the impositions, made all the more intolerable by Colloredo's insistence on strict social protocol. As Mozart noted, musicians were to be placed higher than the cooks but lower than the valets.

The third period of Mozart's musical education came as the result of a petition in August 1777 to the archbishop offering his resignation.[17] His purpose, prompted by his own developing musical craftsmanship and self-awareness of his abilities, was to seek his fortune outside Salzburg, preferably at one of the musical centers of the time. Vienna was not considered, mainly because the archbishop was the official confessor of the Holy Roman Emperor, and thus, any official tender of a position would have entailed considerable diplomatic maneuvering. In the company of his mother, Wolfgang Mozart turned his attention westward, going first to Munich and then to Mannheim, the prestigious court of Elector Karl Theodor. It is not entirely clear whether Mozart himself considered this journey to be a search for a position or the touring of an independent artist and composer, since he both sought employment and concertized throughout.

His first stop as at the court of Prince Krafft Ernst of Oettingen-Wallerstein in Hohenaltheim, but here he apparently only performed a brief concert. At Mannheim, Mozart spent almost five months in the city. While he did interact with members of the famed *Kapelle* and did the occasional teaching and commission, his petitions for a position went unrewarded. He did make good connections with some of the leading members, such as Christian Cannabich and Ignaz Holzbauer, but given that the *Kapelle* was self-sustaining, he probably never had much hope of obtaining a post. What we know of his visit comes mainly from Mozart's own copious correspondence with his father, but petitions to Elector Karl Theodor by way of his court musical director, Count Louis Aurel von Savioli, were met with ambivalence. Savioli did dangle the offer of chamber composer to Mozart, but no official appointment was forthcoming. Mozart at the time fell in love with Aloysia Weber, daughter of a court copyist. While this is generally viewed from the standpoint of Mozart's letters, which contain various schemes involving their future together on tour and Leopold Mozart's admonitions against the affair, there can be no doubt that it complicated his prospects. His father finally succeeded in stirring his son into action, for on February 12, 1778, he wrote: "Off with you to Paris! And that soon! Find your place among great people. *Aut Caesar aut nihil.*"[18]

Mozart was resident in Paris from March to September 1778. On his way to the city, he visited Franz Xaver Richter in Strasbourg, noting that this elderly composer's works contained much "fire." Upon his arrival in Paris, he approached Baron Friedrich Melchior von Grimm, who was one of the respondents in the War of the Buffoons. Grimm introduced him to Joseph Le Gros, the administrator of the Concerts Spirituels, who, in turn, immediately commissioned Mozart to compose a symphony (KV 297), additions to a Miserere by Holzbauer, and several other works. Among them was a sinfonia concertante for woodwind quartet and orchestra (KV 297B), the soloists for which were friends he had met in Mannheim. He was also introduced to the famed choreographer Jean-Georges Noverre and through him with Anne-Pierre-Jacques de Vismes du Valgay, the director of the Opéra. He also began to give lessons to the daughter of the Duc de Guines, insinuating that this connection in the highly complex Parisian social structure would lead to further possibilities.

It has been said by Mozart scholars that his visit to Paris was unsuccessful, though this notion, which appeared as early as 1798 in the biography of Franz Niemetschek, has been called into question by musicologist Simon Keefe. Although Mozart did have some personal success with various commissions and contacts, it was not his intolerance for the complex social mores of Paris, as Niemetschek and later biographers have intimated, that led to his inability to obtain a formal position here. Rather, his arrival coincided with a number of events over which he had no control. Opera in Paris was in the midst of a turbulent period under Vismes's stewardship. The Gluck–Piccinni controversy was at its height, leaving little room for other works by unknown composers; furthermore, the enterprise was running a terrible deficit, which meant that new pieces were a gamble that would be economically difficult.[19] The other theatres in the city had their own stable of composers, such as Grétry or Monsigny, and therefore, the venues were not options. Le Gros, as director of the public concerts, was deeply concerned about the need for novelty among his paying audiences, but this did not include permanent employment of composers; indeed, Mozart himself was asked to provide a new slow movement to his symphony, because the original "did not have the good fortune to

Example 11.9 Mozart, Symphony in D major, *Paris*, KV 297, Movement 1, mm. 1–12

win his approval."²⁰ He did, however, include popular clichés such as the *coup d'archet* at the beginning of the same work, which did cause a sensation with its unison rushing up the scale (Example 11.9). In other words, as important as the performance of works at this venue was for one's reputation, it was not intended as a means of continual support unless one carved out a special niche with a particular genre.²¹ It was possible to make a living as a teacher in Paris, but Mozart apparently had little inclination to focus on this route. Although he wrote to his father of an offer of the post of organist at Versailles due to the efforts of composer Jean-Josephe Rodolphe, even detailing the conditions and salary, it is still not known whether this was legitimate. There were also personal considerations in Paris that undermined his focus; his mother passed away in July, and there seems to have been a coolness with his love for Aloysia. Although musically active and moderately successful in terms of audience appreciation, the possibilities for permanence did not seem to appear, and therefore, Leopold Mozart interceded with Archbishop Colloredo for his son to return to Salzburg to a regular court post. In September, he began the return journey, stopping in Mannheim for several months, where he gave concerts and reconnected with old friends. He was approached by the head of the new German Theatre, Baron Herbert von Dalberg, to compose music for a pair of melodramas, but since the court of Karl Theodor had in the intervening months moved to Munich, there was little left in the way of employment there.

While one can debate the professional success of Mozart during his travels, there can be no doubt that he came into contact with a wide variety of styles and genres to which he had heretofore not been exposed. In Paris he was able to witness both Gluck and Piccinni's reform operas, while both in Mannheim and at the Concerts Spirituels he found that a new sound world was opened up to him by the use of clarinets. The effects he found faddish, but he was able to study the popular symphonies of the time, as well as learning how to compose a sinfonia concertante in the Parisian manner. In Mannheim he also learned about the melodrama, and while the works that he hinted would be commissioned have not survived, the technique of spoken dialogue with orchestral background did make its appearance in movements of his later theatre works from the next stage of his life.

His position upon his return to Salzburg was a court organist, which meant performing and writing for religious services and teaching. He lamented that there was no permanent opera house in the city, but when a visiting troupe led by Johann Heinrich Böhm arrived in the summer of 1779, he was able to exercise his musical-dramatic skills in incidental music for Thomas Gebler's play *Thamos, König von Ägypten*, KV 345. He also composed the bulk of a Singspiel *Zaide*, KV 344, based on a text titled *Das Serail* adapted by court trumpeter Andreas Schachtner, perhaps in anticipation that another troupe would appear the following year.[22] Other efforts in the genres of sinfonia concertante, missa brevis, serenade, and symphony reflect a much-expanded sense of form and design, as well as orchestration. In particular, the entr'actes for *Thamos* feature a dramatic element that hints of Gluck.

The connections with the Mannheim–Munich orchestra finally paid off in 1780, when Mozart was commissioned to compose a large-scale dramatic opera titled *Idomeneo*. Based on a work by French Baroque composer André Campra from 1712, the text was revised by Abbé Gianbattista Varesco, who may well have been engaged as part of the negotiations between the elector and the archbishop for Mozart's absence for several months in Munich to compose the work. The work was successful, largely in part because it merged both the French and Italian styles into a hybrid form that includes bravura arias, dramatic choruses, and a complex, yet powerfully human plot. The influence of Gluck, Piccinni, and Holzbauer can be seen throughout, as noted by musicologist Julian Rushton.[23] In March 1781, however, Mozart was summoned to Vienna as part of the official retinue of the archbishop, and while he was there found that in his spare time he was allowed to explore the musical environment of the city to his own success. An inevitable parting of the ways between an insubordinate Mozart and the implacable archbishop came in May ended with the composer being tossed onto the street. From this point onward, he was a freelance composer.

He had been warned that the Viennese were changeable in their tastes and that his fortunes would be subject to this fickleness. Mozart, on the other hand, had already prepared himself to profit from his abrupt departure from the Archbishop's service. He taught both composition and keyboard, with a large clientele drawn from the most prominent families in the city. He also offered subscription concerts called academies at the *Mehlgrube*, a converted flour depot, or in the Augarten, a public space, the first of which occurred in May 1782. He made contact with the publisher Artaria and the music distributor Johann Traeg, both of whose international connections allowed a large distribution of his works. A further friendship with composer Franz Anton Hoffmeister, who also published music, enhanced his musical reach so that within the space of a couple of years Mozart's reputation had been revived as one of the main composers of the period.

Joseph II had harbored the idea of establishing a German National Opera to compete with other courts in the Holy Roman Empire. As noted previously, the Viennese Singspiel was a rather lowbrow and localized genre of opera, and the emperor wished to raise the standards. He inaugurated it with *Die Bergknappen* by Ignaz Umlauf in 1778, and in July 1781 the director of the Kärntnertor Theatre, Gottlob Stephanie Jr., approached Mozart to write *Die Entführung aus dem Serail*, KV 384. Although the premiere did not take place until a year later, it was an immense success, and within a few years, performances were held in many cities throughout the realm, from Amsterdam to Warsaw, and from Hamburg to the southern provinces of Austria. It also catapulted Mozart into the highest rank of Viennese composers, and though the Emperor's interest in German opera waned shortly thereafter, he was aware of Mozart's talent in opera. Much of Mozart's instrumental music of the Viennese years, from 1781 to 1787, was written for his own concerts or for publication, though his own preference was for the more lucrative opera. Following *Entführung*, he sought a more comfortable commission in Italian opera, and though he did not have a firm commission from the Burgtheater for a work, several were begun and abandoned, such as *L'oca del Cairo*, KV 422. He continued to be successful as an arranger of his own concerts and as a teacher. Coupled with this was his marriage to Constanze Weber, the sister of Aloysia. Much has been written about the match, but it appears to have been an important stage in stabilizing his career in Vienna. In 1783, he and his new wife even paid a visit to Salzburg, an important step in reconciling familial issues.

One of the most important events of 1784 was Mozart's entrance into the Masonic lodge *Zur Wohltätigkeit*, led by Baron von Gemmingen, who had written the text to a melodrama for the composer several years earlier. He also frequented the most important lodge in Vienna, *Zur wahren Eintracht*, whose master was the prominent freemason Ignaz von Born. Much has been written about his involvement with this society, but it can be said that Mozart was an ardent supporter who believed in the ideals they promulgated. Indeed, he freely wrote special music for his fellow masons, but his membership also allowed him to interact with the leading nobility and citizens of Vienna. These connections began to pay off, for Mozart probably began to be considered for a court post in early 1786.

The search for a suitable opera text came in 1785. Poet Lorenzo da Ponte had arrived in Vienna in 1781 and established himself as a librettist for Antonio Salieri, but within a few years, he was asked to write texts for other composers, including Mozart. Knowing that Mozart was in need of a work that would gain him attention in the world of Viennese Italian opera, he opted to rewrite a libretto based on a banned work, Beaumarchais's *Le marriage de Figaro*, part of a controversial trilogy of plays. The anti-nobility theme was revised, and censorship issues overcome. On May 1, 1786, it was produced with some success at the Burgtheater, whereupon it was disseminated to other venues in the Holy Roman. Although he was well known in Vienna, he was adored in Prague, where *Figaro*'s success was especially large. They had invited Mozart to witness the production, and another opportunity to compose an opera was presented to him by the director of the Estates Theatre, Pasquale Bondini. Da Ponte was again chosen as the librettist and on October 29, 1787, *Don Giovanni* premiered to equal success. As a composer, however, for Mozart, the year 1787 seems to have been unusually slow, no doubt due to the need to work on the opera and his father's death. In November, however, he was appointed as one of the two Imperial music posts, Court Chamber Musician (*Kammermusikus*), succeeding Gluck, who had just passed away. Mozart how had a stature equal to that of Antonio Salieri in terms of the Viennese musical establishment, though his actual duties were minimal. During 1788, however, Mozart was actively engaged in revising oratorios for Gottfried van Swieten's *Gesellschaft der Associierten* (Society of Gentlemen), conducting works by C. P. E. Bach and Handel. He also contemplated a series of private concerts, for which he most likely composed his last three symphonies (E-flat major, KV 539; G minor, KV 550; C major, KV 551). The last of these contains an ingenious fugue with triple counterpoint in the final movement (Example 11.10). While these attempts came to naught, he embarked on a journey with Prince Karl Lichnowsky to Berlin. He visited Dresden, where he was hosted by Johann Gottlieb Naumann, viewed Johann Sebastian Bach's works in Leipzig, and met with King Friedrich Wilhelm II in Berlin, before returning in June 1789. His final opera for the Burgtheater, *Così fan tutte*, was again to a text by da Ponte. It is difficult to say whether this work would have equaled the other two operas in success, for successive performances were interrupted by the death of Joseph II in February 1790.

270   Capitals and Centers of Music-Making

Example 11.10   Mozart, Symphony in C major, *Jupiter*, KV 551, Movement 4, mm. 384–387, showing all four contrapuntal themes simultaneously

It is about this time that Mozart began his association with the Theater auf der Wieden, whose leader, Schickaneder, Mozart had known back in Salzburg. Initially he was part of a stable of composers providing pieces of the pasticcios the director produced, such as *Der Stein der Weisen*. A brief journey to Frankfurt in the fall for the coronation of Leopold II was a moderate concert success, and during this same season, Mozart often performed or participated in various academies in Vienna. In April, he had submitted a petition to be named *Kapellmeister* at St. Stephen's Cathedral, succeeding Leopold Hoffmann, who was aging and infirm. In the meantime, Schickaneder had commissioned a fairy tale opera, *Die Zauberflöte*, which was produced with immense success in 1791. In July of that year, Domenico Guardasoni arranged for Mozart to compose a coronation opera, *La Clemenza di Tito*, for Prague. This was an official commission, and only Mozart and Salieri, as Imperial composers, were eligible to write it; Salieri turned the work down, but Mozart was required to accept it. The work was composed in only eighteen days, with the recitatives mainly done by his pupil, Franz Xaver Süßmayr, and using at least one pre-extant movement. This work had a moderate success.

In November, Mozart took ill and passed away on December 5. He left a Requiem unfinished, and in later biographies, the work took on the aura of a mystery. A short while later, Constanze Mozart received word that his petition to replace Hoffmann at St. Stephen's had been granted. As musicologist Christoph Wolff has noted, Mozart's financial position at the end of his life was less precarious than biographers have made it out to be, and his musical reputation during his lifetime was considerable. This was due not just to his early life as a prodigy, but rather his music continued to be performed throughout the Holy Roman Empire and beyond during the last two decades of the eighteenth century. While the iconic status he enjoys today may have developed posthumously, there can be no doubt that the music he wrote during the last decade of his life was significant, in terms of both breadth and stylistic development. It must be remembered, however, that neither Mozart nor Haydn wrote outside of their environments, the former in the fertile musical world of Vienna and the latter for a discerning and generous patron who allowed him considerable leeway to develop in a stable position.

A chapter devoted to the biographies of two composers might seem out of place in the overview of this book, but it is necessary because both composers, Haydn and Mozart, have achieved iconic status as the main representatives of the period in the eyes of the public. While it is a matter of controversy on whether this status is entirely justified from the point of view of contemporary history, there has always been a

From Universal Composer to Icon 271

Figure 11.10 Unfinished portrait of Mozart by Joseph Lange, 1789
Source: © Internationale Stiftung Mozarteum/ISM.

view that music should be seen in comparison with their works. From an eighteenth-century standpoint, however, they must be seen as consummate professionals, musicians whose own creativity was stimulated by and achieved through knowledge and craftsmanship of their contemporaries. They existed in an age of musical plenty, and though history has elevated them beyond their original musical and stylistic contributions, both composers have come to represent formal purity, structural symmetry, and a forward-looking approach to the development of music of this era.

Documents

Document 1. From Johann Wilhelm Cramer, *Magazin der Musik* for April 1783.

Mr. Joseph Haydn, who in his exquisite sonatas has given to many a keyboardist an antidote to grief and ill-fortune, certainly would not take it amiss that the large number of yearning violinists dare most humbly to ask him to keep them in mind and to honor them with a few violin sonatas. As to the labor expended by the great artist, would it not be payment enough if any violinist could offer the good man his sincerest gratitude? According to newspaper reports, Haydn has undertaken a trip to England. Crowned with laurels and, if his merits are rewarded sufficiently, paid in good cash, he will return to his affectionate and admiring fatherland. Should this note then come into his hands, he might fulfill the wishes of German violinists, who hold him in great esteem.

Document 2. From Michael Kelly, *Reminiscences* (London, 1826).[24]

He [Mozart] was a remarkably small man, very thin and pale, with a profusion of fine fair hair, of which he was rather vain. He gave me a cordial invitation to his house, of which I availed myself, and passed a great part of my time there. He always received me with kindness and hospitality. He was remarkably fond of punch, of which beverage I have seen him take copious draughts. He was also fond of billiards, and had an excellent billiard table in his house. . . . He gave Sunday concerts, at which I never was missing. He was kind-hearted, and always ready to oblige; but so very particular, when he played, that if the slightest noise were made, he instantly left off. . . . Mozart was very liberal in giving praise to those who deserved it; but felt a thorough contempt for insolent mediocrity.

Notes

1 Ernst Theodor Amadeus Hoffmann, *Schriften zu Musik* (Berlin, 1878), VII: 46–47.
2 Christian Gottlob Neefe, *Dilettantarien* (1785), 131. Besides Mozart, the references are to Leopold Kozeluch from Vienna and both a rival and colleague of Haydn and Mozart, Joseph Martin Kraus, *Kapellmeister* to Gustav III in Sweden, Ignaz Pleyel, a Haydn student and later friendly competitor in London in the 1790s, Josef Reicha (1752–1795), one of Neefe's colleagues in Bonn and another teacher of Beethoven, and Antonio Rosetti from the court of Oettingen-Wallerstein.
3 *European Magazine and London Review for October,* 1784, Col. 4.
4 Georg August Griesinger, *Biographische Notizen über Joseph Haydn* (Leipzig, 1810), 13.
5 Albert Dies, *Biographische Nachrichten von Joseph Haydn* (Vienna, 1810), 14.
6 Quoted in Karl Geiringer, *Haydn: A Creative Life in Music* (Berkeley: University of California Press, 1982), 53.
7 Letter of December 3, 1781, copied out by Haydn's secretary. See H. C. Robbins-Landon, *Collected Correspondence and London Notebooks* (London: Thames and Hudson, 1959), 32–33. This retranslation offers some slight differences from Landon's original.
8 Noted in H. C. Robbins Landon, *Haydn: Chronicle and Works* (Bloomington, IN: Indiana University Press, 1978), II: 617.
9 The result is that there are more than 157 symphonies attributed to Haydn that are by other composers. Haydn himself can be blamed for a few of these; he sent music by his student Ignaz Pleyel, as well as one symphony by Joseph Martin Kraus, to Parisian publishers with his recommendation; these then unscrupulously put his name on the printed works. Moreover, when a set of quartets arrived from a Benedictine monk, Pater Romanus Hoffstetter, his name was erased and, as already noted, the set printed as Haydn's Op. 3. Haydn unwittingly later "recognized" them as his own compositions.
10 A letter from Count Waldstein to Beethoven dated October 29, 1792, notes: "Labor assiduously and receive Mozart's spirit from the hands of Haydn." Beethoven had met Mozart during a brief visit in 1787 but was unable to study with him due to family issues back in Bonn.
11 Griesinger, *Biographische Notizen*, 101.
12 *Neue teutsche Merkur* for 1799, ed. Martin Wieland, et al., 32.

13 Griesinger, *Biographische Notizen*, 24–25.
14 Burney, *A General History of Music*, II: 950.
15 Burney, *The Present State of Music in France and Italy*, 236–237.
16 In a letter dated December 12, 1771 the empress wrote a scathing letter to her son, specifically saying that "what I say is intended only to urge you not to burden yourself with useless people . . . it gives one's service a bad name when such people run about like beggars." Another petition to Ferdinand's brother Leopold, the Duke of Tuscany, yielded no result as well.
17 Colloredo regarded this as highly insolent and insubordinate and, in reply, dismissed both Leopold and Wolfgang from service. Leopold was forced to grovel to retain his position and was reinstated.
18 "Either Caesar or nothing." Leopold Mozart also states in the same letter: "From Paris the name and fame of a man of great talent resounds throughout the whole world."
19 See Mark Darlow, *Staging the French Revolution: Cultural Politics and the Paris Opera 1789–1794* (New York: Oxford University Press, 2012), 41–42.
20 See Spaethling, *Letters of Mozart*, 167; the comment is quoted in a letter to Mozart's father Leopold dated Paris, July 9, 1778.
21 One of these semipermanent composers was Giuseppe Cambini, who wrote more than ninety sinfonia concertantes in an easily accessible style. Mozart blamed Cambini for the suppression of his own woodwind quartet work and probably with some good reason. Mozart himself, however, was contemptuous about the Parisian tastes, noting about the *coup d'archet* that "they begin all together here just like everywhere else."
22 Another troupe led by actor Emanuel Schickaneder, later librettist for Mozart's *Zauberflöte*, did appear, but there is no indication that *Zaide* was to be performed.
23 Julian Rushton, *Mozart* (New York: Oxford University Press, 2006), 80–81.
24 Richard Sheridan noted about composer and tenor Michael Kelly that his visitor's card should read: "Michael Kelly. Composer of Wines and Importer of Compositions."

Part V

Music for the People

Music as a Social Phenomenon in the Classical Period

12 The Folk and Their Music

Music was not just an art form that was meant for formal or informal concertizing. It was useful as a social tool for the common person, and the "folk" were involved in the development of music during the Classical Period in many ways. Actual folk music was, of course, practiced everywhere throughout the world, being one of the common denominators of ordinary life that involved everyone, from village festivals to traditional pieces sung or played in the home. These were often the main means of creating a cultural identity, especially if the people were in the minority or were striving for a way of keeping their culture alive during political changes. For composers, folk music was a good source of inspiration and material that could be adapted for their own more upscale works, enlivening them with interesting and well-known melodies and sometimes unusual harmonies and rhythms. Finally, during the Classical Period there began a systematic effort to collect and study popular music, sometimes with a more global perspective in mind.

As the control of absolute rulers diminished, to pay attention to the music of the people as a social phenomenon was a means of retaining one's position as the head of the local government, especially if that ruler obtained their position through heredity or election. Examples of this abound in the eighteenth century. The Hanoverian kings of England were German, as were Empress Catherine of Russia and King Gustav III of Sweden. The first and last were "elected" by the parliaments of their respective realms from the eligible nobility that were peripherally related. The Duke of Tuscany was Austrian, while the Dukes of Savoy in Northern Italy were French, as was the Bourbon King of Spain. Each of these and other rulers who were not native to the places they governed used music as a way both to identify themselves with their citizens and to increase the sense of patriotism in the broadest sense of that term. Moreover, as new nations arose in North America and France through revolution, music was put to popular use to increase political support.

Popular music, whether it was from the folk or composed for political or nationalist reasons, had an appeal to the ordinary citizen and therefore a good source for the music business that developed during the Classical Period. Composers were commissioned to arrange popular tunes in a variety of ways to create a repertory that both demonstrated local music and make it accessible to both the public and connoisseurs alike.

Folk Music as a Source and Repository of Popular Cultures

The first interest in folk music appeared with the early encyclopedists during the Baroque Period. In 1636, Marin Mersenne had published several "Canadian" tunes in his *Harmonie Universelle*, equating them with the music of savages, and a bit later German savant Athanasius Kircher noted that various "nations" had their own "*complexio*," or specific styles of music that suited their cultural environment.[1] As the eighteenth century dawned, Jean Chardin published a number of pieces in his 1711 travelogue *Voyages en Perse, et Autres Lieux de L'Orient*, also noting the tuning, scales, and use of various instruments in dance music. In 1735, Jean Baptiste du Halde published the *Description Géographique, Historique, Chronologique, Politique, et Physique De L'Empire de la Chine et de la Tartarie Chinoise* that presented for the first time a Chinese tune that was to be reprinted a number of times in diverse places throughout the century. Du Halde himself probably based his knowledge on the popular Jesuit travelogues of the time, many of which

278 *Music for the People*

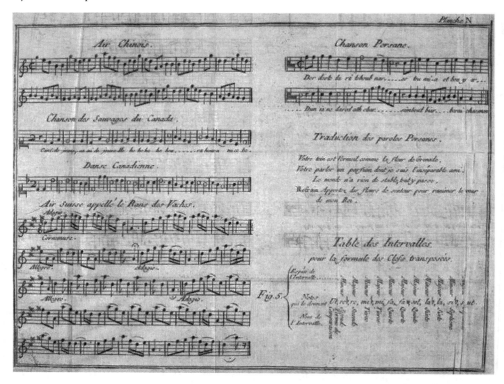

Figure 12.1 Rousseau, *Dictionnaire de Musique*, Plate N

did include bits and snippets of what they deemed to be indigenous musics. However, perhaps the most important attempt at a compendium can be found in Rousseau's *Dictionnaire de Musique*, where there is a plate with tunes ranging from the Chinese melody borrowed directly from Du Halde to a lengthy melody used in Switzerland to call cows home (Figure 12.1).

Throughout the Classical Period, attempts to describe the music of the people, the actual folk music that came from traditional sources, were largely dependent on how this might be used for art music or for exotic comparisons. For example, Charles Burney, in his *History of Music*, made an assertion that Chinese scales and music were similar to Scots tunes, an issue that resonated with his readers.[2] While this comparison seems odd, it was nonetheless accepted as a possibility for many years. On the other hand, actual folk music collections began to appear in earnest about 1730 or so, forming a foundation upon which tunes normally passed on by aural tradition became more widespread.

In 1783, for example, Joseph Ritson published his *A Select Collection of English Songs*, an important three-volume set that included both texts and melodies. Included were selections gathered or composed by playwrights such as Colley Cibber, and a number reflect their usage as tunes for such ballad operas as *The Beggar's Opera*. One of the ironic aftermaths of the Battle of Culloden in 1745 was an interest in Scots songs, although earlier works such as William Thomson's 1733 compendium *Orpheus Caledonius or A collection of Scots songs* had been published previously. A second major collection by David Herd from 1751 (*Ancient and modern Scottish songs, heroic ballads, etc.: collected from memory, tradition and ancient authors*) enhanced interest in England, but the main work published in several volumes between 1787 and 1803 by publisher James Johnson and poet Robert Burns was the *Scots Musical Museum*. In order that these popular songs be adapted, composers of renown were hired to arrange sets of them. One of the earliest was Joseph Haydn, who was commissioned to set a portion of the collection (Figure 12.2), though his

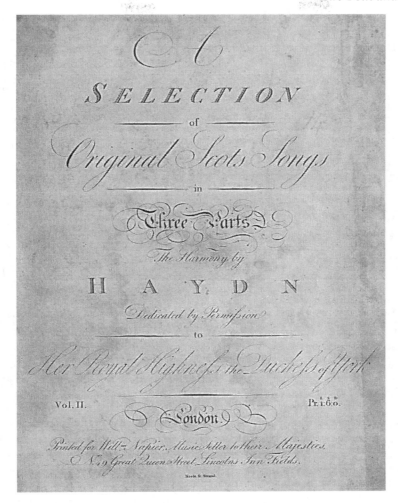

Figure 12.2 Title page of the *Selection of Original Scots Songs in Three Parts, The Harmony by Joseph Haydn*, published by William Napier, 1795

colleague in Vienna, Leopold Kozeluch, also arranged others. The accompaniments are simple; the easy flow of the language enhances the "native" character of the pieces (Example 12.1).

In 1778, the Highland Society of London was established with the sole purpose of preserving what was thought to be traditional instrumental music from Scotland. This included a revival of folk instruments, such as the bagpipe. The history of the society, published in 1813, notes the following:

> The song, or plaintive music of Scotland, does not seem to require any encouragement from public institutions, as it is so generally known, and stands unrivalled for the happiest combination of pleasing melody. The dancing music of Scotland is universally preferred, for quick steps, in almost every part of the world, though the true style of playing it is not generally practised. It might be expedient, therefore, to have an Academy established, for teaching that sort of music that it may be more generally played in the same perfection in which it is now executed.[3]

The popularity of Scots songs in Europe was probably influenced by the literary success of "primitive" bardic poetry attributed to Ossian, but it also had ramifications in the newly independent United States of

280 *Music for the People*

Example 12.1 Joseph Haydn/Traditional, "As I cam down by yon Castle wa'," mm. 1–8 (violin part, ad lib. omitted)

America. British broadside ballads were popular among the colonials, as was dance music done in the same fiddling style as could be found in Great Britain. About 1755 the ubiquitous American folk song "Yankee Doodle" first appeared, and thereafter, much of the folk music published took on political overtones, as will be described in the next section.

For northern and central Europe, traditional music often found its way into art music, with composers making use of rhythmic and melodic material in their conventional works. As we have seen, the German Singspiel of Hiller and others sought to imitate a folk style in the simplicity of the music and the rural settings of the stories. Here one does not speak of a folk tradition, though some of the pieces did eventually become popular enough to make the transition between the classical and traditional. The foremost genre was the Lied, or song, often strophic. Two of these, one by Hiller, "Als ich auf meiner Bleiche" ("As I Was at My Washing") from *Die Jagd* (*The Hunt*) and "Der Mond is aufgegangen" ("The moon has risen") by J. A. P. Schulz (Example 12.2), were immediately seized on by the German public as accessible and in the folk idiom. Indeed, both were to become "legitimate" folk songs beginning in the nineteenth century.

Operas could also incorporate folk music directly, if the dramatic or comic situation allowed for it. The most obvious use of it was in the English ballad opera, but the tunes were often background for new and more appropriate texts, used as **contrafacta**. The audiences of the time would know the tune and would be able to associate the new words with the melody by memory. However, they were also incorporated in an unadulterated manner, generally in those works in peripheral countries where the tunes would resonate with the listeners. In more serious works, it would allow for an element of folksiness, linking the social status of all the characters without obvious parody. For example, in Sweden, the opera *Gustaf Adolph och Ebba Brahe* by Abbé Vogler, the entire second act features the general Swedish folk, characterized by a number

Example 12.2 Johann Abraham Peter Schulz, *Der Mond ist aufgegangen*, 1778 (poem by Matthias Claudius)

Example 12.3 Abbé Georg Vogler, "Hönsgummans Visa" from *Gustaf Adolph och Ebba Brahe* (1787, Stockholm), mm. 1–12

of dances and a popular tune known as the "Hönsgummans visa" ("Poultry Woman's Song"), which had first appeared about 1702 but, by 1780, had achieved the status of historical folk song. Troubadour Carl Michael Bellman noted in his *Fredmans Testament*: "One could not have listened in the smallest corner or alley without being close to a place in the city where some servant was knocking on wagon wheels or some old lady singing the *Hönsgummans visa* from the chimney tops."[4] While there was a political undertone in the opera itself, the use of the folk song, with its simple tune and nostalgic historical text, spoke to the cultural nationalism of the local audiences (Example 12.3).

Vogler was perhaps one of the most public promoters of "folk" material during the Classical Period. His concerts regularly featured "national" music from both European and non-Western cultures. An eclectic composer and performer, Vogler began his career as a touring virtuoso with organ concerts about 1785, opting at first to improvise "impressions" received from paintings. Bach biographer Johann Nicholas Forkel expressed his disgust with this sort of "tone painting," noting that it created disingenuous and "disorderly" music that served no purpose. Thereafter Vogler broadened his work by inserting "national folk" elements into his concerts, eventually becoming known for extemporizations on folk music. The issue of whether Vogler actually collected folk music as the source for his concerts is debatable, but in 1790, the *Musikalische Korrespondenz der teutschen filarmonischen Gesellschaft* noted: "Shortly Herr Abt Vogler will publish with Bossler in Speyer in two parts *Polymelos or Characteristic National Music of Various Peoples*, an original and rare collection of folk songs and dances" (Figure 12.3).[5] This work, which appeared the following year, consisted of a mishmash of pieces, including dances from Sweden, Germany, Russia (a Cossack dance), and Spain, along with "arias" from Switzerland, Germany, France, and Italy. Finally, there was a "Chinese" rondo (*Cheu-Teu*). This collection may have been intended as a byproduct of Vogler's self-promotion, but his interest in folk music was further explored in his theoretical works of the next decade.

Figure 12.3 Title page of Abbé Vogler, *Polymelos* (1790, published by Bossler in Speyer, Germany)

Example 12.4 African Chorus notated by Abbé Vogler, from the *Allgemeine musikalische Zeitung*

By 1800, reviews in the *Allgemeine musikalische Zeitung* began printing the melodies that Vogler produced in his concerts, including a wide variety of "national" or exotic tunes, such as an "African chorus" that was allegedly used to pound chalk (Example 12.4). Within a few years, the first international collections of folk music began to appear, with works supposedly from around the globe. These include the *Lyric Airs* of Welshman Edward Jones and William Crouch's *Specimens of Various Styles of Music* of 1807. The former includes some plates of musicians or dancers in costume (Figure 12.4). Many other collections, unfortunately, have only the texts of the melodies and little or no music.

Other folk music was notated down as dance tunes. While some of these were revised as manuals, compendiums of this type are largely found in manuscript form. These generally give local variations on folk melodies that were suitable for small ensembles or single musicians. Folk music that had been elevated into the social dance world was ubiquitous throughout Europe, but this was a more sophisticated style that had little to do with its more common origins.

The most common use of folk music was as the source of rhythms, melodies, or both for composers of this period. For example, due to their triadic tunes, Bohemian folk songs and dances were used in orchestral and chamber music. One such is the opening of a Symphony in D major by Johann Stamitz, which uses a paraphrase of a Czech Christmas carol as its main theme. Native Russian composers also mined folk music as sources for their popular operas. For example, Dmitri Bortniansky uses one as the main theme of the finale to his Sinfonia concertante of 1790 (Example 12.5).

These examples demonstrate that folk music offered ready-made material that composers could exploit, in terms of both musical substance and accessibility.

Folk music itself, however, also depended upon performers who specialized in the field. Most localities had their own musicians, some of whom were well trained and others less so, but were willing to support the music of the common people. For example, Franz Benda, the noted virtuoso on the violin, spent time

Figure 12.4 Plate from William Crouch and Edward Jones, *Specimens of Various Styles of Music* (1807, London)

Example 12.5 Dmitri Bortniansky, Sinfonia Concertante, Movement III, mm. 1–8

during his youth as an itinerant folk musician, while others, such as Niel Gow of Scotland, achieved renown as a folk fiddler, but he disguised his abilities by playing the Scottish Highlander in public, speaking with a thick dialect and pretending to improvise tunes that he had composed. This crossing of classes was particularly important, and the mythology that developed was often belied by both professional stature and portraiture, as the painting of Gow by artist Henry Raeburn shows (Figure 12.5).

Folk music, however, often had a second side that appealed to the people. This was its ability to be used for political purposes. The political realm of the Classical Period has already been shown to be contentious, ranging from local skirmishes to violent revolutions to expansive wars in which the various realms or countries made alliances that were fluid. The nature of the variable political situation meant that culture had to be enlisted to support whatever governmental decision was made and the popularity of campaigns or alliances would often depend on how the event or ruler was portrayed in art and music. Such needs gave rise to works that were clearly political in nature, sometimes in the form of pseudo-folk tunes and others as larger scale pieces meant to glorify the state or the ruler.

Figure 12.5 Painting of Scots fiddler Niel Gow by Henry Raeburn
Source: Used by permission from the Scottish National Portrait Gallery.

Music in the Service of the State: Politics and Revolution

There was a concerted attempt throughout the Classical Period on the part of the governments to use music as a means of identifying political agendas. Whether it was the absolute monarchies of France or Russia or the newly minted republics as in the United States or France following revolutions, music was seen as a common identifier that was meant to unify people behind the government. In some cases it meant the support of a monarch, and in others it served to begin the identification of a nation or country. As implied earlier, musical centers in the cities and courts had their own musical cultures that were patronized by the nobility and citizens alike, but music in the service of the state was relatively rare, even if celebratory events such as operas marking dynastic marriages or Te Deums celebrating military victories were relatively common. Given the complex boundaries and political alignments of Europe and its colonies, local music that defined these entities beyond the folk elements usually did not occur. For instance, the Electors of Mannheim or Saxony or Prince Esterházy of Hungary did not have any special signature work that identified them with their realms, even though events such as marriages, deaths, and alliances would result in specialized commissions of music. Nonetheless, there were political elements that began to emerge musically during the Classical Period that marked a trend toward political nationalism that developed in the nineteenth century.

Perhaps the oldest of these was the motet *Domine, salvum fac regem*, a short motet that dates from the medieval period in France.[6] This had been performed as a sort of monarchist hymn text for several centuries, and until about 1780 was still done during each Sunday Mass. Although there does exist a monophonic tune for the motet, almost all composers of the Classical Period, such as Louis-Nicholas Clérambault, set it to their own original music (Example 12.6). Another similar royalist anthem was the English "God Save the King," antecedents of which can be traced back to a work for keyboard by John Bull in 1619. In the Classical Period, it first appears in 1745 in the *Gentlemen's Magazine* (Figure 12.6), where it apparently was sung in honor of George II at the theatres in Drury Lane and Covent Garden. Shortly thereafter, it became a popular anthem, being used first in 1763 by Johann Christian Bach as the theme of a set of variations for the final movement of his keyboard concerto Op. 1 No. 6.[7]

Perhaps the most famous of the royalist anthems, however, was Joseph Haydn's iconic *Gott erhalte Franz den Kaiser*, Hob. XXVIa:43. It was composed shortly after his return from London in 1794, based on his being impressed by patriotic music in Britain. This short work, later orchestrated and used as a theme and variations for string quartet (Hob. III:77 or Op. 76 No. 3), became an iconic work that has had a history beyond praising Holy Roman Emperor Franz Josef I.[8]

Anthems during this period, however, were not always connected directly with a ruler, even though they may have been linked to them in one form or another. These pieces were composed largely to celebrate a nation (in the eighteenth-century sense) or realm, focusing on history or ancestry as the patriotic sentiment. The main format for such works was opera, but contained within were pieces that came to symbolize the nation as a whole. The best example of this is Arne's patriotic-historical masque *Alfred*, first produced privately in 1740 at the estate of the Prince of Wales in Cliveden, England. Although originally a small play with music to a text by authors David Mallet and James Thomson, actor-impresario David Garrick produced a large stage version in 1753 that was performed with enormous success at both the Drury Lane and King's theatres. While the main plot of the work is a fictionalized story surrounding Alfred the Great, the key movement was the finale, a vaudeville on the tune "Rule, Britannia!" (Example 12.7). The chorus extolled both the country and liberty ("Britons never, never, never will be slaves"), as well as its position as a maritime power, becoming a symbol of England overall.[9]

Example 12.6 Nicholas Clérembault, *Domine salvum fac Regem*, mm. 1–5

Figure 12.6 Page from the October 1745 *Gentlemen's Magazine* showing the first rendition of "God Save the King"

Example 12.7 Thomas Arne, "Rule Britannia" from *Alfred, King of the Danes* (1753), mm. 21–24

Two national anthems that combine both royalty and country emerged in the 1780s in Denmark and Sweden, both also the result of theatre pieces, as has already been mentioned in Chapter 7. As Denmark struggled to overcome the political nightmare of the Streuensee affair, author Johannes Ewald produced a patriotic play, *Fiskerne* (*The Fishermen*) in 1778 that included the lyrics for "Kong Christian stod ved højen Mast" ("King Christian Stood at the High Mast"), a reference to the 1644 maritime battle of Colberg Heath in which a wounded Christian IV encouraged his sailors to defeat a Swedish force. While the actual composer of the melody is not known, Johann Ernst Hartmann arranged the tune (Example 12.8), and almost immediately thereafter, it became adopted as the Danish national anthem. The same development occurred in Sweden, where in 1786 the opera *Gustaf Wasa* contained a national hymn to freedom sung by the main character on the eve of the battle against a tyrannical Danish king (Christian II). The main melody, to a text originally written by King Gustav III himself and versified by poet Johan Henrik Kellgren, was composed by Johann Gottlieb Naumann, accompanied by reflective woodwinds (Example 12.9). Unlike the bombastic Danish anthem, this movement in E-flat major is reflective and pensive, with the focus on liberty and freedom ("Give us freedom that we require").

Politics in music, however, could also reflect the trends of the day on a much broader level. Two events in particular created music on all levels that reflected the political state of the day: the American War of Independence and the French Revolution. The former was fought between 1776 and 1781 on the North American continent between the English forces and colonials. The colonies were well settled along the Eastern seaboard, but in terms of culture were hardly united, as they contained a blend of religious groups, landowners, and new immigrants from numerous European regions. During the fight for independence, however, unity was achieved musically through the adoption of a popular tune, "Yankee Doodle," the origins of which remain obscure. At first meant as a derisive slur against restive colonials, it took on iconic status as the revolutionaries embraced it. During the political turmoil between 1789 and 1792, it often appeared as the foundation of a new genre, the Federal Overture. The music of this consisted of a series of tunes in imitation of the popular British Medley Overture spread out over one or two movements. The difference lay in that the Federal Overture incorporated patriotic music that referred directly to American

Example 12.8 Johann Ernst Hartmann, "Kong Christian stod ved højen Mast" from *Fiskerne*, mm. 1–12

Example 12.9 Johann Gottlieb Naumann, "Ädla skuggor, vördade fader" from *Gustaf Wasa*, mm. 4–8

politics. Benjamin Carr's work was the first of a number of similarly titled works, coming in 1794 as the epilogue to the play *The Grecian Daughter* in Philadelphia. This work incorporated French Revolutionary music, such as "Le Marseillaise" and "Ça ira," with interludes in stormy minor keys to indicate the divisive positions of the pro-French Republicans and pro-British Federalists. There is even a whimsical rendition of "Oh Dear, What Can the Matter Be?" where the composer, himself an emigrant from England, inserted a comment on the issue. The finale is an arrangement of "Yankee Doodle," thereby putting the musical matter to rest (Example 12.10). The *New York Magazine* lauded this neutral position after a performance in that city: "Let us pay a due tribute of praise to Mr. Carr's overture, which, beside its intrinsic merit, has the advantage of being eminently calculated to attract an universal admiration."[10] Also included in virtually all of works of this special political genre was General Washington's March, originally composed by Philip Phile, which subsequently became a folk song "The Itsy-Bitsy Spider." Although short-lived, this genre was a musical means of representing the popular music of both new immigrants and their national ambitions in a new land.[11]

Music of the French Revolution, however, was more focused on the larger political issues that arose with the storming of the Bastille and rise of state control of music calculated to inflame the political emotions of the populace. Royalist anthems were discouraged, and patriotic songs seemed to spring up from every corner of the country. The Bulletin of the Convention printed a larger number of these in 1793, as delegates to

Example 12.10 Benjamin Carr, *Federal Overture* (1794), mm. 306–313

the convention arrived from throughout France. This caused the revolutionary leader, Danton, to question the practice, but one member of the convention is said to have replied: "Nothing is more suitable than patriotic songs to electrify republican spirits; I have been a witness to the prodigious effect they produce while on my mission to the departments."[12] Regional creation of revolutionary music occurred continuously and was largely localized, but two songs were particularly popular everywhere. Both of these have already been identified earlier, with "Le Marseillaise" being considered the theme song of the Revolution. Allegedly created by army officer Claude Joseph Rouget de Lisle in a fit of patriotic fervor in 1792, it spread beyond its origin in Strasbourg to become designated as the national anthem by the convention the following year.[13] However, more significant was the drafting of popular composers into writing large-scale works for the republic, each extolling patriotic fervor and the egalitarian ideals of the revolution. Cherubini, Gossec, and Grétry all composed patriotic operas, cantatas, and oratorios, some of which were truly massive in scope. They also devoted efforts toward the **Revolutionary hymn**. As these had to appeal to the general populace, the usual operatic devices were suppressed in favor of easy homophonic choruses, glosses on revolutionary propaganda, and powerful orchestration that emphasized the new martial focus of France. Often, these were catchy and immediately popular as symbols of the new France. Examples include Cherubini's *Hymne du Panthéon* of 1794 and Gossec's *Le Triomphe de la Republique*, whose overture begins with a unison C-minor introduction that ends with a brilliant fanfare and cannon shot (Example 12.11). Often these

Example 12.11 François Gossec, Overture to *Le Triomphe de la Republique*, mm. 1–21

Example 12.12 Étienne Méhul, *Le Chant du depart* (1794), mm. 4–10

musical events would attract large audiences out of doors, and in some cases, the numbers of performers would exceed a thousand. In terms of the patriotic hymn, the *Chant du départ* (*Song of Departure*) by Etienne Méhul from 1794 served as a second anthem to "La Marseillaise" (Example 12.12).

A final type of political music can be found in the creation of so-called battle music, in which major military confrontations were outlined, replete with a clash of arms and word painting of the event. The subgenre itself dates from the Renaissance, but in the Classical Period the development of political alignments, revolution, and a clash of nations was a good source of inspiration. The common military music of the time, marches, wind band music (*Feldparthie*), and marching songs, such as the *British Grenadiers*, were common during the period, and parade displays featuring them occurred throughout Europe and the Americas frequently. As the tunes were well known, they found their way into stage works, as did military signals. For example, various battle scenes in operas could portray victory for the state, such as the defeat of the Danes in the Swedish opera *Gutsaf Wasa*. This posed dramaturgical problems for directors, but composers such as Naumann rose to the occasion required by the spectacle. In instrumental music, two works that achieved considerable popularity can be mentioned.

The first is *The Battle of Prague* composed in 1788 by František Kočwara. It depicted a decisive engagement between Prussian and Austrian forces in 1757 and was scored as fortepiano sonata with extra instrumentation (violin, violoncello, and drum) to reinforce the special effects.[14] The second is the *Battle of Trenton*, subtitled "an historic sonata," composed by James Hewitt in 1797 with a dedication to George Washington. Here, the entire battle is followed, with the victory at the end. The work features "Yankee Doodle" in a patriotic conclusion that was popular enough for Hewitt to contemplate a sequel.[15] Such politically charged music forms the background to pieces such as Beethoven's *Wellington's Victory* and the entire nineteenth-century battle symphony as a subgenre.

The issue of political music during the Classical Period is one of extremes, ranging from hymns of national support and identity to songs containing revolutionary fervor. The creation of an anthem, whether in the Holy Roman Empire or Scandinavia, was conceived as uniting a people with its ruler, but popular music could be more plebian in content and purpose. It could also lie at the heart of political propaganda, the purpose of which was to reinforce alignments or enhance a political ideology. It could not, however, have existed without the dissemination of music brought about by the creation of the business of popular music.

The Rise of the Popular Music Business

Many courts and salons during the Classical Period were venues in which politics, literature, art, and music were discussed on a daily basis. The social interactions between the classes were limited, but both nobility and the upper classes of the citizenry indulged in pastimes whenever their obligations or duties permitted. These often took the form of amateur gatherings, but there were also social organizations that served this function as well. These existed in practically every court, town, and city during the eighteenth century, and often they have been overlooked as a source of musical creativity. A few examples can show how they functioned and integrated themselves into both local and broader social culture.

Perhaps the most prominent of these was the so-called Berlin *Liederschule*, which began about 1750 as an adjunct to the better-known Berlin School that gathered around Frederick the Great (see Chapter 5 for a discussion of the Lied itself as a chamber genre). The term itself dates only from 1909, but there can be no doubt that the group of composers gathered around Christian Gottfried Krause, who in 1752 published a critical work on music and poetry at the request of the king titled *Von der musikalischen Poesie* (*Concerning Musical Poetry*). Members included other composers of the Berlin court, including Carl Philipp Emanuel Bach, and their meetings were intended to promote the development of the parlor song, though the treatise deals with all other forms of vocal music. The naiveté with which this work and the music it engendered was roundly criticized by Schubart, who noted,

> For this reason, his Berlin *Liedersammlung*, Songs of the Germans in four parts, wherein the greatest masters worked, has been approved by few people, even though the composition is correct, the songs well chosen, and even the tunes are often not considered too poor. But there is nothing less borne within the musical song than faults and stiffness.[16]

Krause's circle, however, influenced poet Carl Wilhelm Ramler and Justus Friedrich Zachariä to expand their song texts so that composers of the circle, especially Bach and Carl Heinrich Graun could set works in a more naturalistic manner. The group met weekly and by 1760 included a wide selection of Berlin's intelligentsia; it was renamed the Monday Club in 1765. Members also include Julianne Benda, who wrote songs "in the folk idiom," (*im Volkston*) for performance in the salon. Her husband, Kapellmeister Reichardt, as noted in Chapter 5, eventually composed over 1,500 songs, many of which were published in journals such as the *Göttinger Musenalmanach*. This group was also associated with Goethe and Herder, both of whose texts were distributed to the composers for setting. The Berlin *Liederschule* thus contributed to the development of the popular German Lied on into the Romantic Period, as exemplified in the famed Singakademie established by Carl Friedrich Fasch in 1791.

Another example of a popular type of club is the catch and glee societies of eighteenth-century London. The catch, a simple *a cappella* tune done in unison or in canon, dates from the middle of the Baroque Period, when it was used to avoid the censorship of the Commonwealth and Restoration governments. It was based upon the medieval *rota* but, by 1700, had become widely popular and published in large collections. In 1761, the Gentlemen's Catch Club was founded to promote both these canons and a new genre, the glee, which was a sort of part song. Within a few years, this club and the imitators it spawned were offering prizes for newly written works. The glee was often found to be more pastoral and laudatory than the catch, which often includes bawdy or obscene lyrics. For example, Dutch composer Pieter Hellendaal chose to parody the rivalry between Handel and Bononcini with a four-part catch *Tweedledum and Tweedledee*, published around 1750. The text, possibly by John Byron, reads: "Some say, compar'd to Bononcini / That Mynheer Handel's but a Ninny / Others aver, that he to Handel / Is scarcely fit to hold a Candle. / Strange all this Difference should be / Twixt Tweedle-dum and Tweedle-dee!" Perhaps the most lasting work, however, was the theme song of the Anacreontic Society, "To Anacreon in Heav'n," composed by Sir John Stafford Smith around 1774 (Figure 12.7). This work forms the foundation for the later American anthem "The Star-Spangled Banner."

Publishers were keen to cash in on this sort of society, and while full scores of major works in Paris, London, and Vienna for the beneficial or public concert societies were often too expensive to print, collections that emerged from the smaller private intellectual groups made for a tailor-made customer. Most popular were medleys or collections of the main popular pieces of the day. In Paris, for example, the *Recueil en musique* was a means of putting theatrical works into the hands of the salon societies so that they could continue to perform in private what they enjoyed on stage.[17] These were often collections of songs drawn from the opéra comique, arranged either for voices and accompaniment or for chamber ensembles, very

Figure 12.7 Original print of Sir John Stafford's "Anacreon in Heav'n," precursor to "The Star-Spangled Banner" (1774, London)

much like today's medleys or potpourris of the nineteenth century. But they could also include various other smaller works, such as minuets, short keyboard works, and ballet movements (Figure 12.8). This example shows the prelude of a suite by Michel Blavet meant for private performance in Parisian homes and salons.

Elsewhere in Europe, collections of the same sort included a wide variety of works, ranging from keyboard transcriptions of larger pieces such as opera overtures to simple songs and canons. In places which may not have had permanent or publicly accessible ensembles, these publications were an affordable substitute for the average household or salon. They could also allow for music that appeared on the public concerts to be reproduced in more intimate settings. They were usually obtained by subscription or at

Figure 12.8 (a) Title page of the *Recueils de Musique* published for the Duc de Clérmont; (b) Excerpt from the *Recueils* of a Suite by Michel Blavet

booksellers, where copies were generally advertised as for sale in the local newspapers. The contents were a compilation of various pieces in settings that ranged from vocal music (songs, popular arias from operas, the occasional paean to rulers, and even some simpler sacred music) to chamber works (solo piano pieces, sonatas, duos or trios generally incorporating a melody instrument such as a flute or violin) to keyboard arrangements of larger works (overtures, symphonies).

An example of this form of popular compendium is the *Musikalisches Kunstmagazin* published by Berlin composer Johann Friedrich Reichardt in one volume of four issues in 1782 (see Document 2).[18] The third issue includes fifteen complete compositions, including a duet ("Andate, andate o mio sospiri") by Neapolitan composer Francesco Durante, a ballet from Rameau's *Castor et Pollux*, a small essay on musical performance, and in each issue a listing of the latest publications, including sets of symphonies and string quartets by Haydn. Such musical magazines could be found even on the periphery of Europe during the Classical Period. In Sweden, publisher Olof Åhlström began a magazine titled *Musikaliskt tidsfördrif*

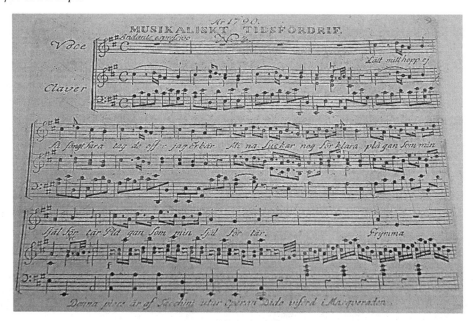

Figure 12.9 First page of music of the 1790 issue of *Musikaliskt tidsfördrif*, published by Olof Åhlström in Stockholm; piece is the aria "Lätt min hopp" by Antonio Sacchini from the pasticcio *Masqueraden* (*The Masquerade*)

(*Musical Pastimes*) in 1789 that appeared annually until 1834 (Figure 12.9). The music likewise consists of a potpourri of works that were well known to the citizens of Stockholm at the time through either the theatre or public concerts. For example, in the first issue they included both vocal and instrumental works, including a G minor violin sonata by the concertmaster, Christian Friedrich Müller, an overture by Abbé Vogler, songs and opera arias by Joseph Martin Kraus, Sacchini, Sarti, Monsigny, and even Åhlström himself, as well as an assortment of individual pieces (several without authorship, but including a theme and variations by Mozart, KV 552, as well as by music amateurs such as Count Nils Barck). With such a variety, amateur musicians in the various salon societies were able to perform at will all of the popular pieces of the day, as well as explore repertory that was broad from throughout the continent. Publishers tapped this market, noting that the purchases for polite society might eventually lead to other more substantial works.

Epilogue

As one might note from the kaleidoscopic contents of this text, the Classical Period was not just either a waystation moving from the Baroque to the Romantic, or a short interim when the music of Mozart, Haydn, or Beethoven dominated the development of classical music. It was, instead, a vibrant period of change, some reactive, some evolutionary, and some even revolutionary. Our modern concept of society was fundamentally formed during the eighteenth century, along with it the reception of music as an integral part of civilization. It was an age where the modern orchestra, modern genres, and the modern place of the musician in society were developed. The period also led to the creation of the nation as a repository of national culture, as well as the use of music as a political mechanism.

To give more than a fleeting glimpse into the musical and historical developments would be encyclopedic, but it is the intent of this book at least to demonstrate the multitude of avenues that both musicians and historians can travel in order to unravel the many streams of the period. In this way, we can grasp the diversity of our own age and those in between.

Documents

Document 1. From Christian Friedrich Daniel Schubart, *Ideen zu einer Ästhetik der Tonkust* (Vienna, 1806), p. 354.

One can also add the *popular style*, among which one can consider social songs and folk songs. It is actually uncommonly difficult to set a good folk song. No imitation will do, but rather the national character must be so engrained that it resounds in throughout the song thus set. The apprentice, the farmer, all of the young girls will find none of the ornamented songs to their taste; they wish to hear *naturally occurring sounds*. Therefore, we study our magnificent folk melodies, whose effects have been widespread well over a century. Only then can one set a song that the people will accept.

Document 2. From the Preface to Johann Friedrich Reichardt, *Musikalisches Kunstmagazin* (Berlin, 1782).

Moreover, in this work I have endeavored to awaken the highest sense of art and inspiration in artists, making them aware of the high value and enlightening power of sacred music, of the dedicated, accessible musical poetry, of noble, great vocal music, of the edification and education through music, of effusive noble feelings that dramas with music have on a sense of the art and good taste, of the greater truth, empathy, and dissemination of vocal music in the lesser plays with music, of the noble elevation and truth of the happy songs and dances of the people, of the betterment of the song mainly through schools of singing, of the special meaning of instrumental music, of the importance as well as difficulty of good, more noble accomplishments, of the purposeful use of instruments, of the perfection of the instruments themselves, of effective construction, and, finally, something that concerns almost everything else, of the better and more purposeful noble upbringing of the artist. Through examples drawn from the works of the greatest German, Italian, and French composers, I have attempted to enlighten the spirit of my contemporaries who have been consumed by lesser standards. I have presented entire works and some individual large excerpts of Couperin, Durante, Gluck, Handel, Kaiser, Kirnberger, Leo, Lully, Rameau, Schulz, and those of my own not yet recognized works of principal worth. I have included the preselected works of these masters, as well as critically illuminating the latest of our works by C. P. E. Bach, Georg Benda, Fasch, Haydn, Rolle, Wolff, etc. I have made our composers aware of the most noble and, to them, important German authors, and presented my own best ideas as I see fit.

Notes

1 For a good discussion of the concept of folk music, see Matthew Gelbart, *The Invention of Folk Music and Art Music: From Ossian to Wagner* (Cambridge: Cambridge University Press, 2007). The Kircher comments on music of the people appears in context with his concept of the Doctrine of Affections as presented in in *Musurgia universalis* of 1650.
2 Burney, *A General History of Music* (London, 1789), I: 47.
3 John Sinclair, *A History of the Highland Society of London* (London, 1813), 13.
4 Carl Michael Bellman, *Fredmans Testamente* (Stockholm, 1780), 66.
5 *Musikalische Korrespondenz der teutschen filarmonischen Gesellschaft* No. 23 (December 1790).
6 The text for the motet was taken from the last verses of Psalm 19 and the doxology and originally was performed following Communion beginning in 1245. It was meant to celebrate the recovery of Louis IX. Originally monophonic, by the Renaissance it was turned into a motet by Jean Mouton; Lully later set a more standardized version for Louis XIV. The text is "*Domine salvum fac regem / et exaudi nos in die qua invocaverimus te*" (Lord, save our King / and hear us in that day that we call upon you).
7 Other used was made of the tune by Thomas Arne (1745), Ludwig van Beethoven (Theme and Variations, WoO 78), and Muzio Clementi (Symphony No. 3, WoO 34).

8 Today it is better known as the national anthem of Germany during the Second World War, *Deutschland über alles*.
9 It was so popular that it was quoted by Handel in his *Occasional Oratorio* and by Beethoven in *Wellington's Victory*, where it symbolized the British troops.
10 See Bertil van Boer, "Federalists, Immigrants and Wild Irish Savages," in *Haydn and His Contemporaries* (Ann Arbor: Steglein, 2011), 198.
11 This genre is discussed in more detail in A. Peter Brown, *The Symphonic Repertoire: The Eighteenth-Century Symphony* (Bloomington, IN: Indiana University Press, 2012), 714–718.
12 Quoted in Charles Hughes, "Music of the French Revolution," *Science and Society* 4 (1940): 198. The deputy who made the statement is not known.
13 Claude Joseph Rouget de Lisle (1760–1836) was at the time imprisoned for antirevolutionary activities. The song gained its title after it was sung by a regiment arriving in Paris.
14 Kočwara was string player in London at the time, whose greater claim to notoriety was in the manner of his rather gruesome death in 1791. The *Battle of Prague*, probably originally written for orchestra, was a popular model for other pieces, such as Beethoven's *Wellington's Victory*, retaining its popularity on into the nineteenth century, when it was cited by Mark Twain.
15 It is, however, not known if Hewitt did an orchestration of this work, but a later sequel entitled *The Battle of Tripoli* has cues for instrumentation in the keyboard score.
16 Schubart, *Ästhetik der Tonkunst*, 85.
17 The *Recueil* was not only used for music, but various excerpts from philosophy, poetry, political broadsides, and so on were also published in this collected form for reading and discussion in private abodes.
18 A second volume was published a decade later in 1792.

Register of Names

Abel, Carl Friedrich (1723–1787), German-English composer and gambist
Abella, José (*ca*1740-*ca*1803), Mexican composer
Adelcrantz, Carl Fredrik (1716–1796), Swedish architect
Adlgasser, Cajetan (1729–1777), Austrian composer
Agrell, Johan (1701–1765), Swedish composer active in Nuremburg
Åhlström, Olof (1756–1835), Swedish composer, keyboardist, and publisher
Albrechtsberger, Johann Georg (1736–1809), Austrian composer and keyboardist
Allegri, Gregorio (*ca*1582–1652), Italian composer
Altenbuurg, Johann Ernst (1734–1801), German trumpet player, composer, and theorist
Anfossi, Pasquale (1727–1797), Italian composer
Anna Amalia, Princess of Prussia (1723–1787), German aristocrat and composer
Araja, Francesco (1709–*ca*. 1770), Italian composer active in Russia
Arenzana, Manuel (*ca*. 1762–1821), Mexican composer
Arne, Thomas Augustine (1710–1778), English composer and organist
Attwood, Thomas (1765–1838), English composer
Azzopardi, Francesco (1748–1809), Maltese composer
Bach, Carl Philipp Emanuel (1714–1788), German composer and theorist
Bach, Johann Christian (1735–1782), German-English composer
Bach, Johann Christoph Friedrich (1732–1795), German composer
Bach, Johann Sebastian (1685–1750), German composer and keyboardist
Bach, Wilhelm Friedemann (1710–1784), German keyboardist and composer
Baguer, Carles (1768–1808), Catalan composer
Ballière, Denis (1729–1800), French theorist
Barck, Nils von (1760–1822), Swedish diplomat and amateur composer
Baurans, Pierre (1710–1764), French composer
Beaumarchais, Pierre Auguste Caron de (1732–1799), French playwright
Beck, Franz (1734–1809), German composer
Beethoven, Ludwig van (1770–1827), German-Austrian composer
Bellman, Carl Michael (1740–1795), Swedish troubadour and playwright
Benda, Franz (1709–1786), Bohemian-German violinist and composer
Benda, Georg Anton (1722–1795), Bohemian-German composer
Benda, Julianne (1752–1783), German singer
Berezovsky, Maxim (1745–1777), Russian composer
Berlin, Johan Daniel (1714–1787), German-Norwegian polymath and composer
Bernasconi, Andrea (1706–1784), Italian composer
Bertie, Willoughby, Lord Abington (1740–1799), English aristocrat and patron of the arts
Bertoni, Ferdinando (1725–1813), Italian composer and pedagogue
Bickerstaff, Isaac (1733–*ca*. 1800), English librettist

Biehl, Dorothea (1731–1788), Danish librettist
Billings, William (1746–1800), American composer
Billoni, Santiago (*ca.* 1700–*ca.* 1763), Mexican composer
Bishop, Henry (1786–1855), English Romantic composer
Bisséry (*fl.* 1777–1782), Haitian composer
Blavet, Michel (1700–1768), French composer
Blainville, Charles-Henri de (1711–1769), French historian
Boccherini, Luigi (1743–1805), Italian composer active in Spain
Bondini, Pasquale (*d.* 1789), Italian singer and impresario
Bononcini, Giovanni (1670–1747), Italian-English composer
Bontempi, Giovanni (1624–1725), Italian Baroque composer and encyclopedist
Bordoni, Faustina (1697–1781), Italian soprano active in Dresden
Bortniansky, Dmitri (1752–1825), Russian composer
Bouganville, Louis Antoine de (1729–1811), French explorer and man of letters
Bournonville, Anton (1760–1843), French-Danish choreographer and dancer
Boyce, William (1711–1779), English composer
Bredal, Niels Krog (1733–1778), Danish-Norwegian politician and librettist
Bretzner, Christoph Friedrich (1748–1807), German librettist and playwright
Brixi, Franz Xaver (1732–1771), Bohemian composer and organist
Broadwood, John (1732–1812), English keyboard maker
Brunetti, Gaetano (1744–1798), Italian composer active in Spain
Bull, John (1562–1628), English Renaissance and early Baroque composer
Burney, Charles (1726–1814), English historian and musical patron
Burney, Francis (1752–1840), patroness of the arts
Burns, Robert (1759–1796), Scottish poet
Caffarelli (Gaetano Morjano) (1710–1783), Italian castrato
Caldara, Antonio (1670–1736), Italian Baroque composer active in Vienna
Cambini, Giuseppe (1746–*ca.* 1819), Italian composer active in Paris
Campdérros, José de (1742–1811), Spanish-Chilean composer
Canaletto (Canal, Giovanni Antonio) (1697–1768), Italian painter
Cannabich, Christian (1731–1798), German composer
Caro de Boesi, José (*ca.* 1740–1814), Venezuelan composer
Carr, Benjamin (1768–1831), English-American composer and publisher
Castellanos, Rafael (*d.* 1791), Guatemalan composer and organist
Casti, Abbé Giovanni Battista (1724–1803), Italian librettist
Ceruti, Roque (*ca.* 1683–1760), Peruvian composer
Chardin, Jean (1643–1713), French polymath
Chelleri, Fortunato (1690–1757), Italian composer active in Germany
Cherubini, Luigi (1760–1842), French-Italian composer
Cibber, Colley (1671–1757), English playwright and author of *The Beggar's Opera*
Cimarosa, Domenico (1749–1801), Italian composer
Clementi, Muzio (1752–1832), Italian composer and keyboardist
Clérambault, Louis-Nicholas (1676–1749), French organist and composer
Coffey, Charles (*ca.* 1690–1745), Irish playwright active in London
Colloredo, Hieronymus (1732–1812), Archbishop of Salzburg
Corelli, Archangelo (1753–1713), Italian Baroque violinist and composer
Corrette, Michel (1707–1795), French composer, flautist, and theorist
Cramer, Johann Baptist (1771–1858), German-English composer
Cramer, Johann Wilhelm (1746–1799), German-English violinist and impresario
Crouch, William Robert (1775–1847), English organist and folk song collector

Crusell, Bernhard (1775–1838), Swedish-Finnish clarinetist and composer
Cuivilliés, François de (1695–1767), French architect
Cupis, François (1732–1808), French cellist and composer
Dalayrac, François (1753–1809), French composer
Dalin, Olof (1708–1763), Swedish man of letters and aristocrat
Danzi, Franz (1763–1826), German composer
D'Aquin de Châteaulyon, Pierre-Louis (1720–1796), French author
Dauvergne, Antoine (1713–1797), French composer
De Fesch, Willem (1687–1761), Dutch violinist and composer
De Lisle, Claude Joseph Rouget (1760–1836), French military man and amateur composer
Della Pietà, Agata (*ca.* 1720–*ca.* 1780), Italian convent composer and teacher
Della Pietà, Samaritana (*ca.* 1715–*ca.* 1754), Italian convent composer and teacher
Dell'Croubelis, Simon (1727–1790), Dutch-Danish composer
Devienne, François (1759–1803), French composer
Diderot, Denis (1713–1784), French encyclopedist
Dias de Oliveira, Manoel (*ca.* 1734–1814), Brazilian composer
Dittersdorf, Carl Ditters von (1739–1799), Austrian composer
Druschetzky, Georg (1745–1819), Austrian-Bohemian composer and percussionist
Dufresne (*fk.* 1775), Haitian composer
Du Halde, Jean Baptiste (1674–1743), French historian and polymath
Duni, Egidio (1708–1775), Italian composer active in France
Duport, Jean-Pierre (1741–1818), French cellist active in Berlin
Dupuy, Eduoard (1770–1822), Swiss-Swedish composer
Durante, Francesco (1684–1755), Italian composer and pedagogue
Du Roullet, François-Louis Gand Le Bland (1716–1786), French librettist
Dušek, František (1731–1799), Bohemian composer
Dušek, Josepha (1754–1824), German soprano
Dussek, Jan Ladislav (1760–1812), Bohemian keyboardist and composer
Eberlin, Johann Ernst (1702–1762), Austrian composer and organist
Endler, Johann Samuel (1694–1762), German composer
Erskine, Thomas, Earl of Kelly (1750–1823), Scottish composer
Esteve, Benet (1702–1772), Catalan composer
Ewald, Johannes (1743–1781), Danish plawright
Farinelli (Carlo Broschi) (1705–1782), Italian castrato and composer
Fasch, Carl Friedrich (1736–1800), German composer and keyboardist
Favart, Charles Simon (1710–1792), French impresario and playwright
Federico, Gennaro Antonia (*d.* 1744), Italian librettist
Felsted, Samuel (1743–1802), English-Jamaican composer
Fiala, Joseph (1748–1816), Bohemian-German oboist and composer
Fils, Anton (1733–1760), German composer and cellist
Fleischer, Friedrich Gottlob (1722–1806), German composer
Fomin, Yevstigney (1761–1800), Russian composer
Forkel, Johann Nicholas (1749–1818), German composer, theorist, and biographer
Fränzl, Ignaz (1736–1811), German violinist and composer
Fuseli (Füselli), Henry (1741–1825), Swiss-English painter
Fux, Johann Joseph (*ca.* 1660–1741), Austrian composer and *Kapellmeister*
Galeazzi, Francesco (1758–1819), Italian composer and theorist
Galitzin, Dmitri (1728–1803), Russian diplomat and music patron
Galuppi, Baldassare (1706–1785), Italian composer
Garcia, José Mauricio Nunes (1767–1830), Brazilian composer

Garrick, David (1717–1779), English actor and playwright
Gaßmann, Florian (1729–1774), Austrian composer
Gaveaux, Pierre (1761–1825), French composer
Gay, John (1685–1732), English actor and playwright
Gehot, Joseph (1756–1820), Belgian-American composer
Gerber, Ernst Ludwig (1746–1819), German lexicographer
Gibert, Paul (1717–1787), French composer
Ginguené, Pierre-Louis (1748–1816), French encyclopedist
Glackmeyer, Joseph (1759–1836), German-Canadian composer
Gluck, Christoph Willibald von (1714–1787), German-Austrian composer
Goethe, Johann Wolfgang von (1749–1832), German playwright and author
Goldoni, Carlo (1707–1793), Italian playwright
Gomes, André da Silva (1752–1844), Brazilian composer
Gossec, François-Joseph (1734–1829), French composer
Gottsched, Johann Christoph (1700–1766), German playwright and academic
Gow, Niel (1727–1807), Scottish folk musician and arranger
Graaf, Christian Ernst (1723–1804), German-Dutch composer and *Kapellmeister*
Graun, Carl Heinrich (1704–1759), German composer
Graun, Johann Gottlieb (1703–1771), German violinist and composer
Graupner, Christoph (1683–1760), German composer and *Kapellmeister*
Greene, Maurice (1696–1755), English organist and composer
Grenser, Johann Friedrich (1758–1794), German-Swedish woodwind player and composer
Grétry, André Ernest Modest (1741–1813), French-Belgian composer
Grua, Carlo (*ca.* 1700–1773), Italian composer active in Munich
Guardasoni, Domenico (*ca.* 1731–1806), Italian impresario active in Prague
Guldberg, Ove (1731–1808), Danish politician
Haeffner, Johann Christian Friedrich (1759–1833), German-Swedish composer
Halle, Carolina (Müller) (1755–1826), Danish-Swedish soprano
Hampel, Anton (1710–1771), German-Bohemian horn player
Handel (Händel), George Frédéric (Georg Friedrich) (1685–1759), German-English composer
Hartmann, Johann Ernst (1726–1793), German-Danish composer
Hasse, Johann Adolph (1699–1783), German composer and *Kapellmeister*
Hässler, Johann Wilhelm (1747–1822), German composer and keyboardist
Haydn, Joseph (1732–1809), Austrian composer and *Kapellmeister*
Haydn, Michael (1737–1806), Austrian composer and organist
Heinichen, Johann David (1683–1729), German violinist and composer
Hellendaal, Pieter (1721–1799), Dutch-English violinist and composer
Herd, David (1732–1810), English collector of folk songs
Herder, Johann Gottfried (1744–1803), German philosopher and author
Herschel, Frederick William (1738–1822), German-English composer and astronomer
Hewitt, James (1770–1827), English-American composer and publisher
Hierrezuelo, Francisco (1763–1824). Cuban composer
Hiller, Johann Adam (1754–1819), German theorist, pedagogue, and composer
Hoffstetter, Pater Romanus (1742–1815), German monastic composer
Hölty, Ludwig (1748–1776), German author
Holý, Ondřej (1747–1783), Bohemian composer
Holzbauer, Ignaz (1711–1783), German-Austrian composer
Homilius, Gottfried August (1714–1785), German Protestant composer
Höpken, Arvid Niklas von (1710–1778), Swedish composer and military administrator
Hopkinson, Francis (1737–1791), American composer

Hotteterre, Jean-Jacques (1674–1763), French flautist and composer
Hummel, Johann Nepomuk (1778–1837), Austrian composer and keyboardist
Hupfeld, Bernhard (1717–1796), German composer
Janitsch, Johann Gottlieb (1708–1763), German composer
Jarnovic, Ivan (1747–1804), Croatian violinist and composer
Jefferson, Thomas (1743–1826), American politician and amateur musician
Jenner, Edward (1749–1823), English physician
Jerusalem, Ignacio de (1707–1769), Italian-Mexican composer
Johnsen, Hinrich Philipp (ca. 1717–1779), German-Swedish composer
Johnson, James (ca. 1753–1811), Scottish engraver and folk song arranger
Jommelli, Niccolò (1714–1774), Italian composer active in Germany
Jones, Edward (1752–1824), Welsh poet, harpist, and arranger
Julià, Benet (1726–1787), Catalan composer
Kelly, Michael (1762–1826), Irish tenor
Kerner, Anton (1726–1806), Austrian horn maker
Kerzelli, Franz (ca. 1730–ca. 1794), Russian composer
Kerzelli, Ivan (ca. 1760–1820), Russian composer
Kerzelli, Josef (ca. 1710–ca. 1775), Austrian-Russian composer
Khandoshkin, Ivan (1747–1804), Russian violinist and composer
Kirnberger, Johann (1721–1783), German Protestant composer
Kittel, Johann Christian (1732–1809), German Protestant organist and composer
Klein, Pater Anton (1746–1810), German Jesuit academic and librettist
Klinger, Maximilian (1752–1831), German playwright
Klopstock, Friedrich Gottlieb (1724–1803), German poet
Knecht, Heinrich Justus (1752–1817), German composer
Knipper, Karl (1739–1820), German impresario
Koch, Heinrich Christoph (1749–1816), German composer and theorist
Kočwara, František (1730–1791), Bohemian composer and keyboardist
Königsperger, Pater Marianus (1708–1769), German Benedictine composer
Kotzebue, August von (1761–1819), German playwright
Kozeluch, Leopold (1747–1818), Austrian composer and *Kapellmeister*
Kraus, Joseph Martin (1756–1792), German-Swedish composer and *Kapellmeister*
Krause, Christian Gottfried (1717–1770), German poet and composer
Krebs, Johann Ludwig (1713–1780), German composer and organist
Kreutzer, Rudolphe (1766–1831), German-French violinist and composer
Kunzen, Friedrich Ludwig Æmelius (1761–1817) German-Danish composer
La Borde, Jean-Benjamin (1734–1794), French composer and theorist
Lacépède, Bernard Germain de (1756–1825), French naturalist and freemason
Lamas, José Angel (1775–1810), Venezuelan composer
Leclair, Jean-Marie (1697–1764), French violinist and composer
Le Gros, Joseph (1739–1793), French composer and impresario
Lenz, Jakob Reinhold (1751–1792), German playwright
Leo, Leonardo (1694–1744), Italian composer
Le Seur, Jean François (1760–1837), French composer
Lessing, Gotthold Ephraim (1729–1781), German poet and playwright
Linley, Thomas Jr. (1756–1778), English composer
Linley, Thomas Sr. (1733–1795), English singer and composer
Litares, Antonio (1673–1747), Spanish composer
Lobo de Mesquita, José (1746–1805), Brazilian composer
Locatelli, Pietro (1695–1764), Italian violinist and composer active in the Netherlands

Lolli, Giuseppe (1701–1778), Italian composer active in Salzburg
Lully, Jean Baptiste (1632–1687), Italian-French Baroque composer
Lyon, James (1735–1794), American composer
Mallet, David *ca*1705–1765), English playwright
Manzuoli, Giovanni (1720–1782), Italian castrato
Mara, Gertrude Elisabeth (1749–1833), German soprano
Marpurg, Friedrich Wilhelm (1718–1795), German historian and theorist
Marsh, John (1752–1828), English composer and theorist
Martín y Soler, Vincente (1754–1806), Spanish-Italian composer active in Russia
Martini, Padre Giovanni Battista (1706–1784), Italian composer and academic
Mattheson, Johann (1681–1764), German Baroque composer and theorist
Méhul, Étienne (1763–1817), French composer
Merckl, Lorenz (*ca*. 1754–1800), Swedish trumpet player
Mersenne, Marin (1588–1648), French polymath and encyclopedist
Mesplès, François (*fl*. 1780), Haitian-French architect
Metastasio, Pietro (Pietro Antonio Domenico Trapassi) (1698–1782), Italian librettist
Milton, John (1608–1674), English author and playwright
Mingotti, Pietro (1702–1759), Italian actor, singer, and impresario
Misón, Luis de (1727–1776), Spanish composer
Molter, Johann Melchior (1696–1765), German composer
Monn, Georg Matthias (1717–1750), Austrian composer
Monnet, Jean (1703–1785), French impresario
Monsigny, Pierre-Alexandre (1729–1817), French composer
Montgolfiére, Jacques-Étienne (1745–1799), French paper manufacturer and aeronaut
Montgolfiére, Joseph-Michel (1740–1810), French paper manufacturer and aeronaut
Morlacchi, Francesco (1784–1841), Italian composer
Mozart, Leopold (1719–1787), German-Austrian violinist and composer
Mozart, Wolfgang Amadeus (1756–1791), Austrian composer and musical icon
Müller, Christian Friedrich (1752–1827), German-Swedish violinist and composer
Müller, Wenzel (1767–1835), Austrian composer
Mysliviček, Josef (1737–1781), Bohemian composer
Naudot, Jacques-Christoph (*ca*. 1690–1762), French flautist
Naumann, Johann Gottlieb (1741–1801), German composer and *Kapellmeister*
Nebra, José de (1702–1768), Spanish composer
Ness, Abbot Rupert (*abbot* 1710–1740), German Benedictine administrator
Nichelmann, Christoph (1717–1762), German composer
Noverre, Jean-Georges (1727–1810), French choreographer
Olivares, Juan Manuel (1760–1797), Venezuelan composer
Ordonez, Carl von (1734–1786), Austrian composer
Orejón y Aparicio, José (1706–1765), Peruvian composer
Ossian (Macpherson, James) (1736–1796), Scottish poet allegedly a Celtic bard
Ozi, Étienne (1754–1813), French bassoonist and composer
Pagainin, Nicolo (1782–1840), Italian violinist of the Romantic Period
Paisiello, Giovanni (1740–1816), Italian composer
Palacios y Sojo, Padre Pedro (1739–1799), Venezuelan composer
Palmstedt, Erik 1741–1803), Swedish architect
Palmstedt, Gustava 1759–1812), Swedish patroness of the arts
París, Juan (1759–1845), Cuban composer
Paskevich, Vasily (1742–1797), Russian composer
Pausch, Pater Eugen (1758–1838), Benedictine monk and composer

Pepusch, Johann Christoph (1667–1752), German-English violinist and composer
Perez, David (1711–1778), Italian-Spanish composer active in Portugal
Pergolesi, Giovanni Battista (1710–1736), Italian composer
Persico, Pietro Anello (1565–1644), Italian Renaissance theologian
Petrosellini, Giuseppe (1727–1799), Italian librettist
Phile, Philip (ca1734–1793), American composer
Philidor, François-André Danican (1726–1795), French composer and chessmaster
Philidor, Anne-Danican (1681–1728), French composer and impresario
Piccinni, Niccolò (1728–1800), Italian composer active in Paris
Pinto, João de Santa Clara (1735–1825), Brazilian composer
Piranesi, Giovanni Battista (1720–1778), Italian architect
Pisendel, Johann (1688–1755), German violinist and composer
Pleyel, Ignaz (1757–1831), Austrian composer active in Paris and Alsace
Pokorny, Franz (1729–1794), Bohemian-German composer
Popov, Mikhail (1742–1790), Russian librettist
Porpora, Nicola (1686–1768), Italian composer
Portugal, Marcos Antonio (1762–1830), Portuguese composer
Pouplinière, Alexandre de la (1693–1762), French patron and man of letters
Puppo, Giuseppte (1749–1827), Italian violinist
Quaglio, Lorenzo (1730–1804), Italian stage designer active in Mannheim
Quantz, Johann Joachim (1697–1773), German flautist, theorist, and composer
Quesnel, Louis-Joseph (1746–1809), French-Canadian composer
Quincy, Antoine-Chrysostome Quatremère de (1755–1849), French architecture historian
Racine, Jean (1639–1699), French Baroque playwright
Raeburn, Henry (1756–1823), Scottish-English painter
Rameau, Jean-Philippe (1683–1764), French composer, keyboardist, and theorist
Ramler, Carl Wilhelm (1725–1798), German poet and academic
Rauzzini, Venanzio (1746–1810), Italian castrato and composer
Regnard, Jean François (1655–1709), French Baroque playwright
Reichardt, Johann Friedrich 1752–1814), German composer and *Kapellmeister*
Reicha, Joseph (1752–1795), German-Bohemian composer
Reiche, Gottfried (1667–1734), German Stadtpfeifer associated with Johann Sebastian Bach
Reinagle, Alexander (1756–1809), Scottish-American composer
Reutter, Johann Georg von (1708–1772), Austrian composer and *Kapellmeister*
Reynolds, Joshua (1723–1792), English painter
Richter, Franz Xaver (1709–1789), German-Bohemian composer active in Alsace
Riepel, Joseph (1709–1782), German theorist and composer
Ritson, Joseph (1752–1803), English publisher and arranger
Rode, Pierre (1774–1830), French violinist and composer
Rodriguez de Hita, Antonio (1722–1787), Spanish composer
Roeser, Valentin (1735–1832), French-German composer and pedagogue
Roman, Johan Helmich (1694–1758), Swedish composer
Rosetti, Antonio (1750–1792), Italian-Bohemian composer active in Germany
Rossini, Giaocchino (1792–1868), Italian opera composer of the Romantic Period
Rousseau, Jean-Jacques (1712–1778), French theorist, encyclopedist, writer, and composer
Ryba, Jan Jakub (1765–1815), Bohemian-Moravian composer
Sacchini, Antonio (1730–1786), Italian composer active in Paris
Saint-Georges, Joseph Boulogne, le Chevalier de (1745–1799), French-Caribbean violinist, composer, and swordsman
Salas y Castro, Esteban (1725–1803), Cuban composer

Salazar y Mendoza, José Francisco Xavier de (*ca.* 1750–1802), Spanish-American artist
Salieri, Antonio (1750–1825), Italian composer active in Vienna
Salomon, Johann Peter (1745–1815), German-English violinist, impresario, and composer
Sammartini, Giovanni Batista (1700–1775), Italian composer
Sammartini, Giuseppe (*ca.* 1695–1750), Italian-English oboist and composer
Sammartini, Giuseppe (*ca.* 1700–1765), Italian composer active in Malta
Sarette, Bernard (1765–1858), French pedagogue
Sarti, Giuseppe (1729–1802), Italian composer active in Denmark and Russia
Scalabrini, Paolo (1713–1803), Italian composer and singer, active in Denmark
Scarlatti, Alessandro (1660–1725), Italian Baroque composer
Scarlatti, Domenico (1685–1757), Italian keyboardist and composer active in Spain
Schacht, Baron Theodor von (1748–1823), German aristocrat and composer
Schaffroth, Christoph (1709–1763), German composer and keyboardist
Scheibe, Johann Adolf (1708–1776), German-Danish composer and theorist
Schickaneder, Emauel (1751–1812), Austrian actor, composer, and librettist
Schiller, Friedrich von (1759–1805), German playwright
Schobert, Johann (*ca.* 1720–1765), German keyboardist active in Paris
Schröter, Corona (1751–1802), German soprano
Schubart, Christian Daniel Friedrich (1739–1791), German composer and theorist
Schubert, Franz Peter (1797–1828), Austrian composer of the Romantic Period
Schulz, Johann Abraham Peter (1747–1800), German-Danish composer
Schweitzer, Anton (1735–1807), German composer
Senesino (Francesco Bernardi) (1686–1758), Italian castrato (see also Tenducci, Giusto)
Seyler, Abel (1730–1800), German actor and impresario
Shakespeare, William (1564–1616), English Renaissance playwright
Silva, António José da (1705–1739), Portuguese composer
Skjöldebrand, Anders Fredrik (1757–1834), Swedish diplomat, administrator, and composer
Smith, John Stafford (1750–1836), English composer
Sodi, Carlo (1715–1788), Italian composer
Sokolovsky, Mikhail (1756–*ca.* 1795), Russian composer
Soler, Padre Antonio (1729–1783), Catalan-Spanish composer
Solimena, Francesco (1657–1747), Italian artist
Sousa Carvalho, João de (1745–*ca.* 1798), Portuguese composer
Stadler, Anton (1752–1812), Austrian clarinetist
Stadler, Maximilian (1748–1833), Austrian composer
Stamitz, Anton (1750–*ca.* 1809), German composer
Stamitz, Carl (1745–1801), German composer and violist
Stamitz, Johann (1717–1757), Bohemian-German violinist and composer
Standfuß, Johann Georg (*ca.* 1720–*ca.* 1759), German composer
Stein, Johann Andreas (1728–1792), Austrian keyboard maker
Stenborg, Carl (1752–1813), Swedish tenor, impresario, and composer
Stenborg, Petter (1719–1781), Swedish impresario and actor
Stephanie, Gottlob Jr. (1741–1800), Austrian librettist
Storace, Stephen (1762–1796), Italian-English composer
Streuensee, Johann Friedrich von (1737–1772), German physician and politician in Denmark
Sulzer, Johann Georg (1720–1779), German music theorist
Süßmayer, Franz Xaver (1766–1803), Austrian composer
Swift, Jonathan (1667–1745), English satirist and author
Tartini, Giuseppe (1692–1770), Italian violinist and composer
Taylor, Raynor (1747–1825), English-American composer

Teixeira, Antonio (1707–1769), Portuguese composer
Telemann, Georg Philipp (1681–1767), German composer
Temanza, Andrea (*fl.* 1730–1740), Italian composer
Tenducci, Giusto Fernando (1730–1790), Italian-English castrato and composer
Thielo, Carl August (1702–1763), Danish composer
Thomson, William (*ca.* 1695–1753), English singer and collector of folk songs
Tillière, Joseph (1750–1790), French cellist and composer
Toeschi, Carl (1731–1788), German composer
Touchmoulin, Joseph (1727–1801), French violinist active in Germany
Townsend, Joseph (1739–1816), English traveler and man of letters
Traetta, Tommaso (1727–1779), Italian composer
Trediakovsky, Vasily (1703–1769), Russian author
Tuček, Jan (1743–1783), Bohemian composer
Tůma, František (1704–1774), Bohemian composer
Türk, Daniel Gottlob (1750–1813), German theorist and composer
Umlauf, Ignaz (1746–1796), Austrian composer
Uttini, Francesco Antonio Baldassare (1723–1795), Italian-Swedish composer
Vanbrugh, Edward (1722–1802), English impresario
Vanhal, Johann Baptist (1739–1813), Bohemian-Austrian composer and cellist
Van Swieten, Baron Gottfried (1733–1803), German-Austrian librarian, amateur composer, patron of the arts
Ville-Issey, Jean Nicholas Jadot de (1710–1761), French architect
Vinci, Leonardo da (1452–1519), Italian Renaissance polymath
Viola, Anselm (1738–1798), Catalan composer
Viotti, Giovanni Battista (1755–1824), Italian violinist and composer
Vivaldi, Antonio (1678–1741), Italian violinist and composer
Vogler, Abbé Georg Joseph (1749–1814), German composer, keyboardist, and theorist
Voltaire (Arouet, François-Marie) (1694–1778), French philosopher
Wagenseil, Georg Christoph (1715–1777), Austrian composer
Walsh, John (1666–1736), English publisher
Walter, Anton (1752–1826), Austrian keyboard maker
Walther, Thomas Christian (1749–1788), Danish composer and administrator
Wanzura, Arnošt (1750–1802), Polish-Russian composer
Watt, James (1736–1819), Scottish engineer and inventor
Watteau, Jean-Antoine (1684–1721), French painter
Weber, Carl Maria von (1786–1826), German composer and conductor
Weidinger, Anton 1766–1852), Austrian trumpet player
Werner, Georg (1749–1813), German horn maker
Werner, Gregor Joseph (1693–1766), Austrian composer and *Kapellmeister*
Wesley, Charles Junior (1757–1834), English organist and composer
Wesley, Charles Senior (1707–1788), English organist and composer
Wesley, Samuel (1766–1837), English organist and composer
Weyse, Christian Felix (1774–1842), German-Danish composer
Wieland, Christoph Martin (1733–1813), German playwright
Winter, Peter von (1754–1825), German composer
Wrantizky, Paul (1756–1808), Bohemian-Austrian composer
Zachariä, Justus Friedrich (1726–1777), German poet and academic
Zander, Johan David (1752–1796), Swedish violinist and composer
Zani, Andrea (1696–1767), Italian composer
Zappa, Francesco (1717–1803), Italian composer active in the Netherlands

Zarafa, Benigno (1726–1804), Maltese composer
Zedler, Johann Heinrich (1706–1751), German author
Zelenka, Jan Dismas (1679–1745), German-Bohemian composer
Zelter, Carl Friedrich (1758–1832), German conductor and composer
Zielche, Hans (1741–1802), German-Danish flautist and composer
Zingarelli, Niccolò (1752–1837), Italian composer
Zinzendorf, Count Nicholas (1700–1760), Moravian-German aristocrat

Selected Reading

Scholarship on music of the Classical Period is vast and often kaleidoscopic in nature, especially if one includes the extensive research in other languages. For example, the literature on both Haydn and Mozart is vast and exhaustive in itself, with more appearing annually that explores intimate facets of their life, works, and legacy. In order not to overwhelm the reader, here are a few suggestions of main sources, from which one can branch out into numerous avenues of interest. It should be noted that this list does not include articles or websites, as these may be found through search engines such as JSTOR, RILM, or web search engines. The few suggestions here are to gain a basic acquaintance with the literature; other readings can be found on www.routledge.com/cw/vanboer

Chapter 1

Blanning, Tim. *The Pursuit of Glory: Europe 1648–1815* (New York: Viking/Penguin, 2007).
Cobban, Alfred, ed. *The Eighteenth Century: Europe in the Age of the Enlightenment* (New York: McGraw-Hill, 1969).
Keefe, Simon, ed. *The Cambridge History of Eighteenth-Century Music* (Cambridge: Cambridge University Press, 2009).
Pauly, Reinhard. *Music in the Classical Period* (Englewood Cliffs, NJ: Prentice Hall, 1988 [3rd Edition]).
Taruskin, Richard. *The Oxford History of Western Music II: The Seventeenth and Eighteenth Centuries* (New York: Oxford University Press, 2005).
van Boer, Bertil. *Historical Dictionary of Music in the Classical Period* (Lanham, MD: Scarecrow Press, 2012).
Zaslaw, Neal, ed. *The Classical Era: From the 1740s to the End of the 18th Century* (Englewood Cliffs, NJ: Prentice Hall, 1989).

Chapter 2

Gjerdingen, Robert. *Music in the Galant Style* (New York: Oxford University Press, 2007).
McClelland, Clive. *Tempesta: Stormy Music in the Eighteenth Century* (Lanham, MD: Lexington Books, 2017).
Ratner, Leonard. *Classic Music: Expression, Form, and Style* (New York: Schirmer, 1980).
Rosen, Charles. *The Classical Style: Haydn, Mozart, Beethoven* (New York: Norton, 1972).

Chapter 3

Carse, Adam. *The Orchestra in the XVIIIth Century* (Cambridge: W. Heffer and Sons, 1950).
Donnington, Robert. *The Interpretation of Early Music* (New York: Norton, 1992 [Revised Edition]).
Spitzer, John and Neal Zaslaw. *The Birth of the Orchestra: History of an Institution 1650–1815* (Oxford: Oxford University Press, 2004).

Chapter 4

Brown, A. Peter, Mary Sue Morrow, and Bathia Churgin. *The Symphonic Repertoire: The Eighteenth Century* (Bloomington, IN: Indiana University Press, 2012).

Drummond, Pippa. *The German Concerto: Five Eighteenth-Century Studies* (Oxford: Clarendon Press, 1980).
Riley, Matthew. *The Viennese Minor Key Symphony in the Age of Haydn and Mozart* (New York: Oxford University Press, 2014).
Will, Richard. *The Characteristic Symphony in the Age of Haydn and Beethoven* (Cambridge: Cambridge University Press, 2002).
Wolf, Eugene K. *The Symphonies of Johann Stamitz: A Study in the Formation of the Classic Style* (Utrecht: Bohn, 1981).

Chapter 5

Hepokoski, James and Warren Darcy. *Elements of Sonata Theory: Norms, Types, and Deformations in the Late Eighteenth-Century Sonata* (New York: Oxford University Press, 2006).
Marshall, Robert. *Eighteenth Century Keyboard Music* (New York: Schirmer, 1994).
Kirkendale, Warren. *Fugue and Fugato in Rococo and Classical Chamber Music* (Durham, NC: Duke University Press, 1979).
Newman, William S. *The Sonata in the Classical Era* (New York: Norton, 1972).

Chapter 6

Feldman, Martha. *Opera and Sovereignty: Transforming Myths in Eighteenth-Century Italy* (Chicago: Chicago University Press, 2007).
Hunter, Mary. *The Culture of Opera Buffa in Mozart's Vienna: A Poetics of Entertainment* (Princeton, NJ: Princeton University Press, 1999).
Robinson, Michael. *Naples and Neapolitan Opera* (Oxford: Clarendon Press, 1972).
Strohm, Reinhard. *Dramma per musica: Italian Opera Seria of the Eighteenth Century* (New Haven: Yale University Press, 1997).

Chapter 7

Baumann, Thomas. *North German Opera in the Age of Goethe* (Cambridge: Cambridge University Press, 1985).
Brown, Bruce Alan. *Gluck and the French Theatre in Vienna* (Oxford: Clarendon Press, 1991).
Flaherty, Gloria. *Opera in the Development of German Critical Thought* (Princeton, NJ: Princeton University Press, 1978).
Mattson, Inger, ed. *The Gustavian Opera: Swedish Opera, Dance and Theatre 1771–1809* (Stockholm: Royal Academy of Music, 1991).
Ritzarev, Marina. *Eighteenth-Century Russian Music* (Aldershot: Ashgate, 2006).

Chapter 8

Knouse, Nola, ed. *The Music of the Moravian Church in America* (Rochester: University of Rochester Press, 2008).
Smither, Howard. *A History of the Oratorio III: The Oratorio in the Classical Era* (Chapel Hill: University of North Carolina Press, 1987).

Chapter 9

Heartz, Daniel. *Music in the European Capitals: The Galant Style 1720–1780* (New York: Norton, 2003).
Helm, Eugene. *Music at the Court of Frederick the Great* (Norman: Oklahoma University Press, 1960).
Jones, David Wyn. *Music in Eighteeth Century Austria* (Aldershot: Ashgate, 1996).
Jones, David Wyn. *Music in Eighteenth Century Britain* (Aldershot: Ashgate, 2000).
McVeigh, Simon. *Concert Life in London from Mozart to Haydn* (Cambridge: Cambridge University Press, 1993).

Chapter 10

Baker, Geoffrey and Tess Knighton, eds. *Music and Urban Society in Colonial Latin America* (Cambridge: Cambridge University Press, 2011).

Boyd, Malcolm. *Music in Spain during the Eighteenth Century* (Cambridge: Cambridge University Press, 1998).
Cripe, Helen. *Thomas Jefferson and Music* (Charlottesville: University Press of Virginia, 1979).
Findeizen, Nikolai. *History of Music in Russia from Antiquity to 1800* (Bloomington, IN: Indiana University Press, 2008).
Murray, Sterling. *The Career of an Eighteenth-Century Kapellmeister: The Life and Music of Antonio Rosetti* (Rochester: University of Rochester Press, 2014).
Russell, Craig. *From Serra to Sancho: Music and Pageantry in the California Missions* (New York: Oxford University Press, 2009).

Chapter 11

Clark, Caryl, ed. *The Cambridge Haydn Companion* (Cambridge: Cambridge University Press, 2011).
Geiringer, Karl. *Haydn: A Creative Life in Music* (Berkeley: University of California Press, 1982 [Revised Edition]).
Heartz, Daniel. *Haydn, Mozart and the Viennese School 1740–1780* (New York: Norton, 1995).
Heartz, Daniel. *Mozart, Haydn and Early Beethoven 1781–1802* (New York: Norton, 2009).
Jones, David Wyn. *The Life of Haydn* (Cambridge: Cambridge University Press, 2009).
Landon, H. C. Robbins. *Haydn Chronicle and Works*. 5 volumes (Bloomington, IN: Indiana University Press, 1976–1980).
Landon, H. C. Robbins. *The Mozart Compendium* (London: Thames and Hudson, 1991).
Wolff, Christoph. *Mozart at the Gateway to His Fortune: Serving the Emperor 1788–1791* (New York: Norton, 2012).

Chapter 12

Boyd, Malcolm, ed. *Music and the French Revolution* (Cambridge: Cambridge University Press, 1992).

Glossary

A cappella   music solely for voices
Accademia filarmonia   organization in Bologna, Italy for composers, many of whom were honorary members
Accompagnato   a recitative that is more thickly accompanied by instruments.
Ancien régime   a reference to the French court during the reigns of Louis XIV and XV.
Anthem   an English choral work equivalent to the motet but used both in sacred and secular functions
Aria   setting for voice and accompaniment to a poetic text, used in operas, cantatas, oratorios, or as concert pieces; see Concert Aria
Ballad opera   a type of theatre work originating in England that incorporates spoken dialogue, popular tunes, and low-brow comedy
Binary form   a two-part formal structure, with repetitions for each part; may be simple or complex, with a return (rounded binary, such as the sonata principle)
Cadenza   occurs most often at the end of an aria or concerto in order to allow for the performer to improvise in a virtuoso manner, expanding on themes of the main work while the accompaniment pauses on a fermata
Cantata   a vocal work accompanied by instruments, which can be either sacred or secular and consisting of several movements that include arias, recitatives, ensemble numbers, and choruses
Canzonetta   a vocal genre usually with a poetic text for several singers, sometimes with instrumental accompaniment
Cassation   alternative name for a Divertimento, comes from the Viennese word for street (*Gasse*)
Castrato   a male singer castrated prior to puberty to preserve his soprano or alto vocal range; mature voices achieved power and depth of the adult voice and were often used in leading roles, achieving superstar status for their virtuoso display; castratos became less common during the Classical Period as more conventional voice ranges predominated
Chiaroscuro   Italian contraction meaning light and dark, used to denote distinctive contrasts in the arts during the Baroque and Classical Periods
Chiasm   also known as an arch form in which the first section returns following an expanded second section; see sonata principle or rondo
Clavichord   smaller chamber keyboard instrument of limited range and projection ability
Coloratura   virtuoso musical display with heavy ornamentation and melismatic passages
Comédie mêlée d'ariettes   a French comedy with musical insertions similar to modern musicals
Concert Aria   a vocal work similar to an instrumental concerto, but often in only a single extended movement; see Rondò
Concerto   a work for solo instrument and orchestra, generally in three movements
Continuo   (also **basso continuo**) the bass line in music performed generally in the Classical Period by a keyboard instrument and a bass melodic instrument (contrabass, cello, or bassoon) with figures indicating the harmony realized by the keyboard; declines in use during the period
Crise romantique   term coined by musicologist H. C. Robbins Landon to describe the *Sturm und Drang* movement in music
Da Capo aria   an aria, generally in an opera, oratorio, or cantata, in which the first section is repeated, often with more elaborate ornamentation; the **dal segno aria** repeats the first section only partially.
Development   (also in German, *thematische Arbeit* or thematic working out) the second section of the sonata principle where the themes of the first section are varied
Divertimento   a shorter instrumental work of several movements meant primarily for entertainment

Divertissement a series of dances that were often incorporated into the opéra Lyrique at the conclusion
Duo/Duo sonata a sonata for two instruments; a melody and generally a keyboard; could also refer to any chamber music for two instruments
Embellishments ornaments, often improvised in solo vocal and instrumental music
Empfindsamkeit (also *empfindsamer Stil*) German word meaning roughly "sensitivity" or "sensitive style" referring to a period in German literature and the arts, as well as a style of inserting emotion or expression into a work
Enlightenment a general term describing the eighteenth century as a period of secular humanistic thought opposed to religious or feudal thought
Entrée French operatic term equivalent to a scene
Exposition the first section of a work, mainly in the sonata principle or concerto in which the main themes, often contrasting, are played
Fantasy or Fantasia a work that was originally improvisatory in nature with a fluid sense of rhythm, tempo, and ornamentation; usually the provenance of keyboard instruments
Figured bass the numerical notation of the chords above or below a bass line indicating the harmonies to be played by the continuo instrument
Galant French term for social behavior used in music to describe a style different from the Baroque. Used in the eighteenth century as a general term for the modern style.
Genre the type of musical composition; that is, sonata, symphony, string quartet, and so on
Grand Tour an educational journey through foreign lands undertaken to enhance a student's intellectual experience and knowledge beyond their studies
Harmoniemusik music written for wind bands or ensembles, often used for the ensembles themselves
Historically Informed Performance (HIP) using documents from the eighteenth century to inform how music was performed; see Performance practice
Impresario the organizer and administrator of an opera company
Incidental music music meant to accompany a play or drama, often performed in between the acts
Intendant the official administrator, often a nobleman, of court opera during the Classical Period
Intermezzo a comic interlude originally in two acts to be performed in between the acts of the opera seria; later in the Classical Period a short, one-act satirical work
Kapelle generally refers to the instrumental ensemble of a court or church
Kapellmeister (Italian *maestro di cappella*; French *maître de chapelle*) title given to the principal musical administrator or resident composer
Kenner und Liebhaber German terms used to distinguish professionals and those knowledgeable about music from amateurs and dilettantes
Keyboard in the eighteenth century, a generic term indicating any instrument with keys (German *Klavier*), but mainly harpsichord, clavichord, or fortepiano
Kleinmeister a pejorative comparative German term used to compare iconic composers with the myriad of other professionals working in the discipline of music during the Classical Period
Konzertmeister the concertmaster who generally conducted the ensembles with gestures and his bow from the principal violin stand during the Classical Period
Learned Style used by eighteenth-century theorists to describe Baroque counterpoint
Libretto text used for an opera, oratorio, or cantata, or other musical composition
Lied German word for song denoting one voice and accompaniment
Liturgy the main organization of a worship service
Masque a term from the English Renaissance which had evolved into a sort of modern opera, often with political or pastoral plots
Mass Roman Catholic worship service in which there are unchangeable (Ordinary) and changeable (Proper) portions throughout the year; often the former is set as a series of movements in sequence while the latter is composed individually
Medley a series of well-known tunes strung together in series, sometimes with political or folk musical content (Medley Overture)
Melodrama/Duodrama a stage work in which the libretto is entirely spoken while the instruments provide a musical backdrop or punctuation; originates in Germany
Menuet/Minuet a triple meter binary form dance that is often used as the third or final movement of a symphony; it may have a contrasting Trio section, after which the main dance is repeated

Motet in the Classical Period a catch-all term indicating a sacred work used for special occasions or regular worship services, generally performed by voices and instruments

Musica da camera/Chamber music music meant to be performed in intimate settings by individual musicians

Notturno a work intended for voices or instruments similar to a divertimento

Ode A work similar to a motet or anthem but of substantially greater length used to honor a specific event or patron

OOAP or one on a part, reduced ensemble music to chamber stature

Opera buffa Italian comic opera, one of the more popular genres of the Classical Period

Opéra comique French comic opera, sometimes with spoken dialogue and accessible memorable music

Opéra Lyrique (also **tragédie Lyrique**) a French opera genre descended from the Baroque Period in which the music and text are often exotic, but which uses choruses and static action

Opera seria Italian dramatic opera with plots generally drawn from Classical subjects and featuring the castrato and prima donna as the chief characters; plots are often convoluted and unrealistic

Oratorio a genre mainly intended for Lent consisting in Italy of biblical stories and elsewhere on topics ranging from nature to didactic dramas; oratorios were rarely if ever staged, though they mimic the format of operas

Ospedale originally orphanages in Venice where young women were trained in music

Overture often used interchangeably with *Symphony/Sinfonia* during the Classical Period; can be used both to open an opera or theatrical work or as an independent instrumental genre

Parthie also Feldparthie, generally a short occasional work for wind instruments

Partimento a bass line either figured bass or unfigured used principally as pedagogical aids for the teaching of harmony, counterpoint, and improvisation during the Classical Period

Performance practice the study of how music was performed during the Classical Period

Quartet a chamber music genre intended for four instruments, generally of a similar type (i.e., string quartet, woodwind quartet, etc.)

Quintet a chamber music genre intended for five instruments, generally of a similar type

Quodlibet meaning "whatever you'd like," a multimovement occasional work meant as an arrangement of popular tunes strung together

Recitative the main dialogue portion of an opera in which the characters converse or declaim against simple continuo chords

Rescue opera a type of French opera in which the main characters are involved in rescuing someone from an untenable situation

Ripieno the main group of instruments of an ensemble

Rococo from the French term for the shape of a shell describing extreme ornamentation in the arts.

Rondo a form used often for final movements of instrumental works in which a main theme reappears several times in the original key

Rondò French term used mainly for large vocal works, such as concert arias, consisting of a slow section followed by a faster one

Scordatura retuning string instruments to increase the harmonic breadth

Serenade a multimovement instrumental work meant for entertainment, usually beginning with a march and ending with a large-scale rondo or sonata principle movement; sometimes incorporates a two-movement concerto or concertante

Serenata an Italian opera similar to the opera seria but with a pastoral plot, generally used for special celebratory occasions

Service a series of intonations and anthems in Anglican worship set as a sequence of a cappella pieces

Servizio di Tavola a divertimento-like instrumental musical work meant to accompany presentation of the various courses at Imperial dinners in Vienna and elsewhere

Sinfonia an Italian term originally meant to describe a three-movement overture to an opera, later used interchangeably with *symphony*

Sinfonia concertante a genre that combines both the symphony and concerto, but generally means a concerto for two or more instruments

Sinfonia da chiesa or Church Symphony, generally follows the pattern of a slow introduction (sometimes with pompous dotted rhythms) followed by a faster portion in a single movement

Singspiel a German opera with memorable music and simple, often pastoral plots, and spoken dialogue

Sonata a chamber music work, generally in three movements, intended for one or more instruments

Sonata principle or sonata form one of the complex binary forms developed that consist of three sections: exposition, development, and recapitulations; used in virtually every genre

Stretto part of an opera finale in which the tempos increase section by section

Sturm und Drang German literary movement translated as "Storm and Stress," from 1770–1790, during which extreme emotions are depicted, occasionally in a sociopathic manner

Style a term that has numerous implications, but generally refers to a specific sound, manner of composition, or musical idiom

Style brisé French for "broken style," consisting of irregular rhythmic patterns

Symphony an instrumental work in several movements, mainly three or four, intended as the principal music for public or private concerts

Te Deum a hymn of praise from the twelfth century used for celebrations and often set with brilliant orchestration

Tonadilla a Spanish brief operatic form that is often satirical

Treatise a theoretical or aesthetical work by an author on some aspect or pedagogical matter in music.

Trio a chamber music genre intended for a trio of instruments, usually of various sorts (e.g. string trio, piano trio with violin, cello, and piano, etc.)

Troupe a traveling group of performers, often including actors, instrumentalists, and vocalists

Turkish opera a work that is set in an exotic location, generally Asia, Turkey, or Arabia and that uses a variety of percussion instruments for color

Verso an instrumental transition between Psalms or parts of the worship service; popular in New Spain

Vespers a series of Psalm text settings meant for part of the Catholic evening worship service

Viennese Classical Style a term that refers to the music of the Classical Period in Vienna, mainly Haydn and Mozart, but used generally to describe all late eighteenth-century musical style

Villancico a short cantata-like work popular in Iberia and New Spain, strophic with refrain, for voices and instruments, most often performed at holidays such as Christmas

Zarzuela Spanish opera form similar to the opera buffa.

Index

Abel, Karl Friedrich 80, 210, 297
Abella, José 242
Académie de Musique 146
Accademia Filarmonica 125, 164, 263
Adelcrantz, Carl Fredrik 162, 297
Adlgasser, Cajetan 98n17, 180, 237, 297
Adolf Fredrik, King of Sweden 230
Agata della Pietà 215
Agrell, Johan 87, 297
Åhlström, Olof 162, 293–4, *294*, 297
Alabado 241
Alaska 115, 240
Albrechtsberger, Johann Georg 76, 111, 297
Aldana, José 94
Algarotti, Francesco *135*, 137, 143nn14–15
Allegri, Gregorio 182, 263, 297
Allgemeine musikalische Zeitung 92, 248, 282
Altenburg, Johann Ernst 17, 23n15, 62, 72n14; *Versuch einer Anleitung zur heroisch-musikalischen Trompeter- und Paukerkunst* 23n15, 62, 72n14
Amicis, Anna de 131
Amsterdam: Schouwburg Theatre 87, 227, *227*
André, Johann 154
Anfossi, Pasquale 139, 214, 297
Angiolini, Gasparo 41, 137
Anna Amalia of Prussia 154, 207, 297
Annibali, Domenico 131
Araja, Francesco 162, 232, 297
Archduke Ferdinand 132, 264–5
Arenzana, Manuel 242, 297
aria cantabile 134
aria d'affetto 134
aria di furore 134
aria di mezzo carattere 134
Arne, Thomas 119, 158–60, 209–10, 285, 295n7, 297
Attwood, Thomas 160, 297
Augsburg 121n1, 186, *187*, 197n12, 221
August the Strong of Saxony 192
Australia: Botany Bay 115, 240
Austria 12–13, 16–17, 66, 76, 89, 93, 110, 113, 132, 174, 183, 196n8, 201–2, 209, 234, 236, 249, 251, 269, 277, 290, 297
Avison, Charles 68, 72n26
Azzopardi, Francesco 240, 297

Bach, Carl Philipp Emanuel 6, 17, 23n14, 31, 35–6, 38, *39*, 42, 62, *63*, 72n15, 103, 105, 188–9, 207–8, 250, 269, 291, 295, 297
Bach, Johann Christian 28, 42, 77, 79–80, 91, 119, 210, 227, 261, 285, 297
Bach, Johann Sebastian 10–11, 16–17, 171, 179, 186, 269, 297, 303
Bach, Wilhelm Friedemann 187, 218, 297
Bach, Wilhelm Friedrich Ernst 107
Bach-Abel concerts 28, 210
Baguer, Carles 239, 297
ballad opera 14, 148, 153, 158–60, 167, 244, 278, 280
Ballière, Denis 29, 297
Barcelona 239
Barck, Count Nils 294
Barton, Andrew 167
Basso continuo 54, 97, 120, 175
Beaumarchais, Pierre Augstin Caron de 5, 297
Beethoven, Ludwig van 11, 16, 64, 92, 156, 248, 258, 295n7, 297
Beggar's Opera 13–14, *14*, 158, 209, 278, 298
Belgium 201
Bellman, Carl Michael 231, *231*, 281, 295n4, 297; Order of Bacchus 231
Benda, Franz 38, 40, 53, 71, 72n1, 76, 207, 282, 297
Benda, Georg Anton 156, 295, 297
Benda, Julianne 291, 297
Berezovsky, Maksim 164, 297
Berlin 21, 24, 37, 62, 65–7, 71, 72n1, 72n15, *81*, 89, 91, 104, 117, 126, 128, 137, 141, 153–4, 195, 201, 207–9, *208*, 217, 221, 269, 272n1, 291, 293, 295, 299; *Singakademie* 291
Berlin, Johan Daniel 66–7, 297
Berlin School 89, 117, 291
Bertoni, Ferdinando 214, 297
Besozzi, Carlo 57
Bethlehem 188–9, 193
Bianchi, Francesco 139
Bibiena, Giovanni 166
Bickerstaff, Isaac 158, 297
Billings, William 192, 244, 298
Billoni, Santiago 241, 298
Bissèry 167, 298
Blainville, Charles-Henri de 19, 298
Blavet, Michel 57, 121n30, 292, 293, 298

Boccherini, Luigi 25, 113, 115, 225, 238, 298
Boesi, José Caro de 242, 298
Bohemia 21, 36, 182–3, 196n8, 202, 218, 235, 252
Böhm, Johann Heinrich 268
Boieldieu, François-Adrien 151
Bolivia 241, 245
Bologna 71, 97n9, 125, 164, 263–4; *Accademia Filarmonia* 21
Bondini, Pasquale 218, 269, 298
Bono, Giuseppe 251
Bononcini, Giovanni 97n9, 133, 291, 298
Bontempi, Giovanni 218, 298
Bordoni, Faustina 128, 133, 152, *152*, 217, 298
Bortniansky, Dmitri 169n11, 190, 282–3, 298
Boston 167, 244–5
Bouganville, Louis Antoine de 240, 298
Bournonville, Antoine 229, 298
Boyce, William 190–1, 209, 298
Brazil 167, 239, 241, 245
Bredal, Niels 160, 298
Breitkopf 82
Brioschi, Antonio 36, 87–8
Brixi, František 218
Broadwood, John 63, 298
Broschi, Carlo 64, 125, 209
Broschi, Carlo (Farinelli) 64, 125, 299
Brunetti, Gaetano 225, 238, 298
Brunswic (Braunschweig) 25
Burney, Charles 16, 18, 23n12, 25, 34, 37, 47n15, 57, 64, 71, 72nn17–18, 98n22, 102–3, 119, 121n7, 125, 203–4, 207, 223, 223n1, 226, 246, 257, 261, 264, 278, 298
Burney, Fanny 119
Burney, Francis 210, 298
Burns, Robert 278, 298

Cádiz 94, 238, 256
Cambini, Giuseppe 79, 273n21, 298
Campderrós, José de 81, 238, 242, 298
Campra, André 268
Canada: Québec 166, 241, 244
Canal (Canaletto), Giovanni Antonio 4, *5*
Cannabich, Christian 89, 156, 219, 266, 298
canzonetta 119
Cap Hatiën (Cap François) 167
Carlos II of Spain 3
Carlos III of Spain 165, 238–9
Carl Theodor 88–9, 219–20, 222
Carl XII of Sweden 229
Carr, Benjamin 167, 244, 288, 298
cassation 92–3
Castellanos, Rafael 183–4, 298
Catherine II (Catherine the Great) of Russia 28, 162, 190, 226, 232, 277
Ceruti, Roque 242, 298
Charles VI of Naples 12
Charles VII, King of Naples and the Two Sicilies 212
Charleston: St. Cecilia Society 244
Châteaulyon, Pierre-Louis D'Aquin de 145, 169n1

Chelleri, Fortunato 87, 298
Cherubini, Luigi 151, 207, 289, 298
chiaroscuro 3
Christian II of Denmark 287
Christian IV of Denmark 287
Christian VII of Denmark 160
Chronique de Paris 19
Cimarosa, Domenico 139, 142n3, 162, 213, 298
Clavier 62, 118
Clérambault, Louis-Nicholas 285
Coffey, Charles 153, 298
Colleredo, Heironymus von 173
Colombia: Bogotá 242
comédie-ballet 150
Conservatoire 18, 58, 65, 151, 207
Copenhagen 65, 132, 160, 227–9, *228*; *Det Danske Skueplats* 228; *Det harmoniske Selskab* 229; *Nye Musikalske Selskab* 229
Corelli, Archangelo 82, 101, 298
Corette, Michel 55–6, *56*, 72n5
Cornelys, Teresa 210
Couperin, François 17
Cramer, Johann Baptist 225, 298
Cramer, Johann Wilhelm 210–11, 272, 298
Crouch, William 282, *283*
Crusell, Bernhard 232, 299
Cuba: Havana 242; San Basilia a Magro 242
Cupis, François 55, 299
Cuvilliés, François de 220

d Capua, Rinaldo 138
Dalberg, Baron Herbert von 268
d'Alembert, Jean 29
Dalin, Olof 231, 299
Danzi, Franz 113, 220, 299
Da Ponte, Lorenzo 269
Darmstadt 89, 219
Dauvergne, Antoine 148, 205, 299
da Vinci, Leonardo 7
dell'Croubelis, Simon 229, 299
Denmark 13, 160, 162, 169n9, 225–6, 228–9, 246, 247n3, 287, 304
Diderot, Denis 19, *20*, 299
Dies, Albert 272n5
Dittersdorf, Carl Ditters von 79, *85*, 110, 121n24, *155*, 203, 299
divertimento 83, 92–3, 95, 101, 108, 110–12, 203–4
Divertissement 92, 144, 146
Doctrine of affections 51
dramma per musica 133
Dresden 15, 21, 59, 70, 89, 128, 152, 162, 171, 214, 217–18, 269, 298
Drottningholm 128, *130*, 161, 230, *230*
Druschetzky, Georg 66, 93, 299
Dufresne 167, 299
Du Halde, Jean Baptiste 277–8, 299
Duni, Egidio 149, 299
Duport, Jean-Pierre 209, 299
Durante, Francesco 16, 87, 213, 293, 299

316 Index

Du Roullet, François-Louis Gand Le Bland 145, 299
Dušek, František 218, 299
Dussek, Jan Ladislav 63, 299
Du Valgay, Anne-Pierre-Jacques de Vismes 266

Eberlin, Johann Ernst 176, 237, 299
École Royale du Chant 65, 206
Edouard 120
Eisenstadt 234, 252, 254, 256, 259
Elisabetta, Queen of Spain 238
Elizabeth I of Russia 13, 226
Empfindsamkeit 5–7, 10, 17, 24, 34–8, 41–2, 53, 58, 75, 89, 153, 188, 207, 230, 250
Empress Anna of Russia 162, 232
Endler, Johann Samuel 89, 299
England 3, 8, 12, 21, 28, 58, 66, 80, 101, 119, 138, 158, 167, 170, 192, 209, 225, 246, 248, 256, 261, 272, 277–8, 285, 288
Enlightenment (*Aufklärung*) 35
Envalsson, Carl 162
Ernst Ludwig, Landgrave of Darmstadt 89
Erskine, Thomas, Earl of Kelly 222, 299
Esterháza 74, *127*, 234
Esteve, Benet 239, 299
Ewald, Johannes 161, 287, 299

Fasch, Carl Friedrich 291
Favart, Charles Simon 148, *148*, 299
Federico, Gennaro Antonio 27, 299
Felsted, Samuel 191, 299
Ferdinand IV of Naples 202, 213, 257
Fesch, Willem de 87, 227, 299
festa teatrale 132
Fiala, Josef 58, 93, 299
Fils, Anton 89–90, 299
Firmian, Count Karl Joseph 132
Fischer, Johann Christian 57, 72n8, 247n5
Fleischer, Friedrich Gottlob 25, 299
Fomin, Yevstigney 164–5, 299
Fontenelle, Bernard le Bovier de 103, 120
Forcroy 120
Forkel, Johann Nikolas 19, 104, 281, 299
Forrest, Thomas 167
France 3, 5, 9–10, 12, 15, 17, 19, 21, 28–9, 31, 37, 46, 71, 72n13, 72nn17–18, 79, 82, 87, 89, 94, 101, 112–13, 120, 143nn11–12, 144–5, 151, 157–8, 161, 166–8, 201–2, 205, 213, 223n3, 223n9, 223n11, 224n14, 240, 244, 248, 273n15, 277, 281, 284–5, 289, 299
Frankh, Johann Matthias 249
Franz I of Austria 13
Franz Josef I of Austria 285
Fränzl, Ignaz 219, 299
Frederick the Great 19, 37, 53, 76, 77, 89, 104, 117, 126, 153, 161, 201–2, 207, *208*, 291
Fredrik V of Denmark 160, 228
French Revolution 3, 11, 137, 151–2, 167, 205, 273n19, 287–8
Friedrich I of Hesse-Kassel 87

fuging tunes 192
Fürnberg, Count Carl Joseph von 251
Fuseli, Henry 4, 7
Fux, Johann Joseph: *Gradus ad Parnassum* 16, *16*, 23n11, 202, 250

Gainsborough, Thomas 4
galant 10, 15, 22–4, 34–5, 53, 63, 101, 107, 157, 188, 204, 207, 230, 242
Galeazzi, Francesco 17, 68, 299
Galitzin, Dmitri 204, 299
gallichone 76
Galuppi, Baldassare 16, 134, 138, 162, 176, 214, 299
Garrick, David 285, 300
Gay, John 14, 158, 300
Gazzaniga, Giuseppe 139
Gebler, Thomas von 156, 268
Gehot, Joseph 244, 300
George I of England 12, 209
George III of England 209, 261
Gerber, Ernst Ludwig 20, 300
Germany 10, 17, 19, 21, 27, 29, 31, 34, 36, 46, 58, 61, 65, *68*, 89, 101, 110, 112, 121n13, 125, 144, 152, 154, 156, 158, 182, 201, 217, 223, 223nn1–3, 223n5, 235–6, 246, 246n1, 247n2, 247n11, 281, *282*, 296n8
Ghezzi, Pier Leone *126*, *140*
Ginguené, Pierre Louis 65, 71, 72n21, 300
Gjerdingen, Robert 34
Glackemeyer, Joseph 244
Gluck, Christoph Willibald von 11, 25, 41, 58, 103, *104*, 128, 142, 145, 147, 251, 300
Goethe, Johann Wolfgang von 6, 8, 41, 118, 156, 300; *Die Leiden des jungen Werthers* 6, 8, 41
Goldoni, Carlo 5, 138, 300
Gomes, André da Silva 243, 300
Gossec, François 85, 205, 289
Göttingen 41
Gottsched, Johann Christoph 5, 47n17, 116, 121n25, 155, 168, 300
Gow, Niel 283, 300
Graaf, Christian Ernst 227, 300
Gräfe, Johann Friedrich 116
Grand Tour 20–1, 213, 263
Graun, Carl Heinrich 37–8, 126, 128, 134, 153, 188, 207, 291, 300; *Adriano in␣Sciro* 37–8
Graupner, Christoph 58, 89, 171, 219, 300
Greene, Maurice 190, 209, 300
Grenser, Johann Friedrich 231
Grétry, André-Ernest-Modest 29–30, 149, *150*, 300; *Zémire et Azor* 29–30, 150, *150*
Griesinger, Georg August 98n25, 110, 121n23, 249, 272n4
Grimm, Baron Friedrich Melchior von 266
Grua, Carl 220, 300
Guardasoni, Domenico 218, 270, 300
Guglielmi, Pietro 139
Guignon 120
Guldberg, Ove 160, 226, 300

Gustav III of Sweden 161, 162, *163*, 164, 226, 231, 272n2, 277, 287
Gustavian opera 162

Haeffner, Johann Christian Friedrich 153, 300
Hague, The 226–7, 246, 261
Haiti 240
Halifax 166, 244
Halle, Carolina (Müller) 160, 162, 300
Hamburg 5–6, 47n7, 91, 96, 97n10, 120, 125, 153, 188, 269
Hampel, Anton 59, 300
Handel, George Frédéric (Frederick) 11, 28, 101, *102*, 125, 300
Harmonie 58, 92–3, 113, 203
Hartmann, Johann Ernst 161, *161*, 229, 287, 300
Hasse, Johann Adolph 27–8, 70, 128, 152, *152*, 217, 300
Hässler, Johann Wilhelm 106, 300
Haydn, Joseph 10, 16, 25, 47n3, 58, 66, 72n25, 76, 80, 83, 91, 107, 109–10, 112, 121nn23–4, 126, *127*, 143n16, 154, 174, 183, 211, 213, 223n3, 225, 234, 248–9, 251, *253*, 254, *258*, 272, 272nn4–5, 278, *279*, 280, 285, 300
Haydn, Michael 91, 93, 98n17, 175, 178, 180, 186, 237, 300
Heartz, Daniel 34, 77, 308–9
Heidelberg 219
Heinichen, Johann David 15, 217, 300
Hellendaal, Pieter 227, 291, 300
Henry VIII 189
Herd, David 278
Herder, Johann Gottfried 4, 189
Herrenhut 192
Herschel, Sir Fredrick William 8, 258
Hewitt, James 167, 244–5, 290, 300
Hierrezuelo, Francisco 242, 300
Hiller, Johann Adam 19, 65, 72n19, 118, 153, 188, 300; *Wöchentliche Nachrichten* 19
Hispaniola 167
Historically Informed Performance 67
Hita, Antonio Rodriguez de 166, 303
Hoffmeister, Franz Anton 268
Hoffstetter, Pater Roman 72n25, 110, 121n22, 174–5, 223n3, 272n9, 300
Hölty, Ludwig 118, 300
Holý, Ondřej 218
Holy Roman Empire 3, 12, 65, 89, 92, 132, 152, 177, 180, 201, 217–18, 234–6, 269–70, 290
Holzbauer, Ignaz 80, 156, 220, 266, 300
Homilius, Gottfried August 187, 218, 300
Höpken, Arvid Niklas von 87, 231, 300
Hopkinson, Francis 245, 300
Hopkinson, John 167
Hotteterre, Jean-Jacques 57, 301
House of Orange 3, 12
Hummel, Johann Nepomuk *81*, 106, 301
Hungary 12, 201–2, 234, 285
Hupfeld, Bernhard 87, 301

India 115, 161
intermèdes 168
intermezzo 27, 136, 138, 140, 147, 158
Italy 3, 10, 13, 15–16, 18, 21, 27–8, 31, 34, 36, 46, 64, 71, 72nn17–18, 78, 82, 87, 95, 101, 112, 125–6, 128–9, 132, 136–9, 142n3, 143nn11–12, 144, 152–3, 160–1, 164–5, 174, 180, 182, 201, 208, 210, 212–13, 217–20, 223, 223nn9–11, 224n14, 225, 228, 230, 233, 240–2, 247n12, 263–4, 273n15, 277, 281
Ivan V of Russia 13
Iversen, Johan Erasmus 228

Jamaica 160, 191
Janitsch, Johann Gottlieb 89, 208, 301
Jarnovic, Ivan 209, 301
Jefferson, Thomas 244, 301
Jenner, Edward 8, 301
Jerusalem, Ignacio de 28, 167, 238, 241–2, *242*
João V of Portugal 166, 239
Johnsen, Hinrich Philipp 230, 301
Johnson, James 278
Jommelli, Niccolò 16, 58, 153, 184, 301
Jones, Edward 282
Joseph II of Austria 154, 173–4, 196n3, 201, 269
Julià, Benet 239, 301

Kant, Immanuel 3
Kellgren, Johan Henrik 287
Kelly, Michael 112–13, *113*, 121n24, 160, 272, 273n24, 301
Kempten 36
Kerner, Anton 59, 301
Kerzelli, Ivan 164, 301
Khandoshkin, Ivan 233
Kirnberger, Johann 187, 208, 301
Kittel, Johann Christian 187, 301
Klein, Pater Anton 156, 301
Klinger, Maximilian: *Sturm und Drang* 6, 41
Klopstock, Friedrich Gottlieb: *Messias* 5
Knecht, Heinrich Justus 84, 301
Koch, Heinrich Christoph 10, 19, 22, 47n22, 68, 96–7, 97n2, 99, 119–20, 153, 301
Kočwara, František 290
Königsperger, Pater Marianus 186, 301
Kotzebue, August von 162, 301
Kozeluch, Leopold 62, 272n2, 279, 301
Kraft Ernst, Prince of Oettingen-Wallerstein 236
Kraus, Joseph Martin 19, 25, 58, 72n25, 86, 121n5, 136, 143n13, 156, 162, 195, 216, 224n15, 247n4, 272n2, 272n9, 294, 301
Kraus, Pater Lambert 107, 109, 196n11
Krause, Christian Gottfried 117, 208, 291, 301
Krebs, Ludwig 186, *188*, 301
Kunzen, Friedrich 161, 229, 301

Laborde, Jean Benjamin de 17
Lamas, José Angel 242
Latilla, Gaetano 138
Lavater, Johann Caspar 256

Le Brun, Élisabeth Vigée 4
Leclair, Jean-Marie 10
Le Gros, Joseph 205, 256, 266, 301
Leipzig 21, 46, 47n17, 65, 72n19, 82, 96–7, 97n8, 118, 120, 121n3, 121n8, 121n11, 121n25, 153, 168, 169n3, 187, 195, 269, 272n4
Lenz, Jakob Reinhold 41, 301
Leopold II of Austria 21, 137, 270
Lessing, Gotthold Ephraim 5, 47n17, 153, 220, 301; Miss Sara Sampson 5
Lichnowsky, Prince Karl 269
Liederschule 117, 208, 291
lira organizzata 76, 213, 259
Lisbon 165–6, 238–9; Teatro da Rua dos Condes 166; Teatro do Ajuda 166; Teatro do Salitre 166; Teatro do Salvaterra 166; Teatro do Tejo 166; Teatro San Carlo 136, 213
Litares, Antonio 166, 301
Locatelli, Pietro 75, 87, 227, 301
Logroscino, Nicola 139
London 13–14, 23n12, 42, 45–7, 47n15, 63–4, 69, 71, 72n2, 72n17, 72n20, 72n26, 74–5, 79–81, 92, 98n22, 119, 121n7, 121n13, 121n24, 125–6, 128, 153, 158–60, 167, 169n12, 201, 209–11, *211–12*, 223, 223n1, 225, 244, 246, 248, 256–9, 264, 272, 272nn2–3, 272n7, 279, 285, 291, 295nn2–3, 296n14, 298, 308–9; Anacreontic Society 291; Drury Lane Theatre 160, 285; Gentlemen's Catch Club 291; Highland Society of London 279, 295n3; Lincoln's Fields 158; Royal Academy of Music 14, 209, 231, 261; Vauxhall Gardens 69, 80, *210*; Westminster Abbey 211
Louis Joseph de Bourbon, Prince of Condé 206
Louis XIV 3, 12, 29, 144, 202, 204–5, 207, 295n6
Louis XV 10, 29, 144, 169n1, 201, 204–5, 261
Louis XVI 10, 151, 202
Louis-Philippe-Joseph, Duc d'Orleans 206
Lovisa Ulrika, Queen of Sweden 161
Ludwig VIII, Landgrave of Darmstadt-Hesse 89
Lully, Jean Baptiste 46, 144, 295, 302
Lyon, James 192, 302

Madame de Pompadour 144
Madrid 5, 113, 165–6, 238–9; El Escorial 238; Teatro Buen Retiro 165; Teatro del la Cruz 166; Teatro de los Caños del Peral 165, *165*; Teatro del Principe 166
Mallet, David 285
Malta 16, 126, 213, 238–40, *240*, 247n12, 304; Mdina 240; Rabat 240; Teatro Manoel 240; Valetta 240; Żebbug 240
Mannheim 21, 31, 37, 58, 60, 66–7, 74, 80, 82–3, 88–90, 94, 98n22, 111–12, 156, 174, 217–22, *220*, 235–6, 261, 266, 268, 285, 303; Jesuit Gymnasium and Music Seminar 219–20
Mara, Gertrude Elisabeth 65, *65*, 153, 302
Marcello, Benedetto 133, *134*, 142nn7–8; *Il teatro alla moda* 133, 142nn7–8
Maria Theresia, Empress of Austria 12, 125, 128, 173, 201–3, 234, 256, 265
Marie Antoinette, Queen of France 145–6, 202

Marmontel, Jean-François 146, 168
Marpurg, Friedrich Wilhelm 17, 65, 302
Martines, Marianna 250–1
Martini, Padre Giovanni Battista 19, 302
Mattheson, Johann 17, *18*, 25, 51, 79, 96, 97n10, 120, 250, 302
Maximilian Franz, Elector of Cologne and Bonn 236
Medley 94, 287
Méhul, Etienne 151, 290, 302
melodrama (duodrama) 156, 222, 268–9
Mercier, Philip 104
Merckl, Lorenz 62, 302
Mércure de France 19, 31, 205, 223n4
Mersenne, Marin 241, 277
Mesplès, François 167, 302
Mesquita, José Lobo de 243
Metastasio, Pietro (Pietro Trapassi) 133, 202, 302
Mexico 28, 94, 126, 158, 167, 241, 247n13; Teatro Coliseo Nuevo 167
Milton, John: *Paradise Lost* 5, 259
Minas Gerais 243; Belo Horizonte 243; irmandades 243; Ouro Preto 243; Tiradentes 243
Mingotti, Pietro 28, 128, 153, 302
Misón, Luis de 166, 302
Molter, Johann Melchior 58, 80, 302
Monn, Georg Matthias 89, 203, 302
Monserrat 239; Escolania 239
Monsigny, Pierre Alexandre 94, 149, 302
Moravians 192–3, 217, 244–5
Morzin, Count Karl Joseph 252
Moscow 164, 232–3
Mozart, Leopold 17, 38, 54, *54–5*, 66, 72n2, 83–4, 176, 237–8, 261, *264*, 266, 268, 273n18, 301
Mozart, Maria Anna (Nannerl) 261
Mozart, Wolfgang Amadeus 5, 42, 79, 91, 93, 114, 121n24, 132, 139, 181, 184, 236, 248–9, 261–2, 302
Müller, Christian Friedrich 294
Müller, Wenzel 154, 302
Munich: Cuvilliés Theatre 220, *221*; Mariankirche 221; Salvator Theatre 220
musica concreta 38
Muzykalye useveniya (*Musical Amusements*) 233
Myslivicek, Josef 119

Naples 16, 64, 71, 136, 138–9, 165, 171, 202, 212–14, 216, 223n10, 238–9, 247n12, 257, 263–4, 308; Accademia de'Cavalieri 213; Teatro dei Fiorentini 138; Teatro San Carlo 136, 213
Napoleon Bonaparte 3
Naudot, Jacques-Christoph 57, 302
Naumann, Johann Gottlieb 162, 184, 217, 269, 287–8, 302
Nebra, José de 166, 302
Neefe, Christian Gottlob 248, 272n2
Neuss, Abbot Rupert 185
New Orleans 116, *117*, 167, 242
New Spain 28, 94, 167, 183, 238, 241–2, 247n13
New York 22, 167, 192–3, 245–6, 288

Niemetschek, Franz 266
Nostitz-Rieneck, Count Franz Anton 218
notturno 119
Noverre, Jean-Georges 149, 266, 302
Nunes Garcia, José Mauricío 243

Oettingen-Wallerstein 74, 233, 235, *236*, 256, 266, 272n2
Olivares, Juan Manuel 242
Oliveira, Manoel Dias de 242
Orejón y Aparicio, José de 242
Ossian (James MacPherson) 6, 23n4, 41, 279, 295n1, 302
Ozi, Étienne 58, 302

Paisiello, Giovanni 5, 121n24, 131, 143n16, 162, 213, 302
Palacios y Sojo, Padre Pedro 242, 302
Palma, John vi
Palmstedt, Erik 231, 302
Paraguay 243
Paris 7, 17–19, 21, 23n13, 23n15, 28–9, 31, 37, 55, 57–8, 63, 65–7, 71, 72n5, 72n21, 73n31, 74, 79–81, 85, 88–91, 97, 101, 120, 121n9, 121n15, 138, 141, 146–7, 151, 153, 157, 162, 167–8, 169nn1–2, 170, 201, 203–7, *205*, 221, 223n4, 224n13, 225, 228, 236, 241–2, 256, 261, 266–8, 273nn18–20, 291, 296n13, 298, 303–4; Comédie-Italienne 149, 151; *Concerts des Amateurs* 80, 205; *Concerts Spirituels* 66, 73n31, 77, 80, 88, 90, 170, 205–6, 228, 256, 266, 268; *École gratuité de la garde nationale* 207; *Institut National de Musique* 207; Loge Olympique 80, 205; Opéra-Comique 148–9, 151; St. Germain 148–9, 151; St. Laurent 148, *148*; Théâtre Feydeau 151, *151*; Théâtre Italien 149
París, Juan 242
parthie 92
partimento 16
Pashkevich, Vasily 164
Paul Anton, Prince Esterházy 234, 252
Pausch, Pater Eugen 186, 197n12, 302
Pepusch, Johann 14, 158
Perez, David 166, 239, 303
Pergolesi, Giovanni 10, 27, 179–80, 303; *Il prigionier superbo* 27; *La serva padrona* 27, 136, 138, 147
Peru 242, 247n13; Lima 167, 241–2
Peter I (The Great) of Russia 13, 162, 233
Petronsellini, Giuseppe 220
Philadelphia 167, 221, 244, *244*, 288; Chestnut Street Theatre 244, *244*; City Tavern 244
Phile, Philip 245, 303
Philidor, François-André Danican 149, 205, 303
Philippe Duc d'Orleans 12
Philippe of Anjou 3
Piccinni, Niccolò 65, 139, 146, 303
Pinto, Fra João de Santa Clara 243
Piranesi, Giovanni Battista 4, 6
Pleyel, Ignaz 63, 79, 107, 109, 205, 211, 272n2, 272n9, 303

Pokorny, Franz 235
Pope Benedict XIV 171, 196n2, 216; *Annus qui hunc* 171, 173, 216
Popov, Mikhail 164, 303
Porpora, Nicola 16, 250, 303
Port au Prince (Sainte-Domingue) 167
Portugal 166, 223, 238–9, 243, 303
Portugal, Marcos Antonio 239
Pouplinière, Alexandre de la 89, 303
Prague 128, 137, 217–18, *219*, 269–70, 300; Kotce Theatre 218
Pre-Classical 10
Prince Anton Esterházy 234, 257
Prince Karl Anselm of Thurn und Taxis 235
Prince Nicholas II Esterházy 91, 235
Puppo, Giuseppe 25, 303

Quaglio, Lorenzo 137, 220, 303
Quantz, Johann Joachim 15, 22, 23n9, *26*, *57*, 141, 195, 207, 303
Queen Anne of Great Britain 12
Querelle des Bouffons 138, 148, 152
Quesnel, Joseph 166, 244, 303
Quincy, Antoine-Chrysostome Quatremère de 28

Raeburn, Henry 283
Rameau, Jean-Philippe 17, 30, *52*, 144, *146*, 303; *Les Indies galantes* 29, 157
Ramler, Carl 188, 291, 303
Ratner, Leonard 11, 31, 47n13, 307
Rauzzini, Venanzio 64, 303
Recueils 94, 116, *293*
Regensburg 90, 186, 233, 235, 247n10
Reicha, Anton 113
Reicha, Joseph 236
Reichardt, Johann Friedrich 118–19, *118*, 154, 184, 209, 293, 295, 303
Reiche, Gottfried 51, 303
Reinagle, Alexander 94, 167, 244, 303
Reutter, Johann Georg von 175, 202, 249, 303
Reval (Tallin, Estonia) 154
Reynolds, Sir Joshua 4
Rheinsberg 89, 207
Richter, Franz Xaver 36–7, 75–6, 111, 182, 219, 266, 303; *Six Grands Simphonies* 37
Riepel, Joseph 235
Rio de Janeiro 167, 243
Ritson, Joseph 278
Rococo 9, 12, 185, 308
Rodolphe, Jean-Josephe 268
Roeser, Valentin 17, 23n15, 58, *59*, 303
Roman, Johan Helmich 34, 87, 229
Rome 4, 6, 7, 21, 25, 71, 125, 133–4, 136, 138, 173, 211–12, 216–17, 228, 239, 263–4; Arcadian Academy 133, 216; *Cancelleria Apostolica* 216; Oratorio di San Fillipi Neri 216; Pantheon 4, 6, 80, 211; Teatro Argentina 216; Teatro Capranica 216; Teatro Valle 216
rondò 77

320   Index

Rosen, Charles 11, 24, 47n1, 307
Rosetti, Antonio 91, 225, 236, *236*, 256, 272n2, 303, 309
Rouget, Claude Joseph 289
Rousseau, Jean Jacques 3, 19, 46, 97, 97n1, 120, 141, 169n2, 303
Russia 13, 28, 115, 138–9, 151, 162, 164, 189–90, 204, 225–6, 232–3, 240, 243, 246, 247n7, 248, 256, 277, 281–2, 284, 297, 302, 304, 309
Ryba, Jan 218, 303

Sacchini, Antonio 147, *294*, 303
Saint Georges, Joseph Boulogne de 77
Salas y Castro, Esteban 242
Salazar y Mendoza, José Francisco Xavier de 116
Salieri, Antonio 47n3, 137, 143n18, 147, 154, 184, 269, 304
Salomon, Johann Peter 67, 80, 210, 257, 304
Salzburg 38, 91, 98n17, 155, 171, 173, 176–7, *178*, 181, 186, 233, 236–7, 261, 264–6, 268–70, 298, 302
Samaritana della Pietà 215
Sammartini, Giovanni Battista 34–5, 87, 304
Sammartini, Giuseppe (Malta) 240
Santiago de Chile 81, 242
São Paulo: *Societas Ordem Terceira do Carmo* 243, *243*
Sarette, Bernard 18, 207, 304
Sarti, Giuseppe 28, 128, 160, 162, 190, 225, 228, 232, 304
Savioli, Count Louis Aurel von 266
Scalabrini, Paolo 65, 228, 304
Scarlatti, Alessandro 133, 202, 237, 304
Scarlatti, Domenico 34, 143n18, 225, 238, 304
Schacht, Baron Theodor von 235, 304
Schaffroth, Christoph 207, 304
Scheibe, Johann Adolf 15, 25, 47n7, 195, 227–9, 304
Schickaneder, Emanuel 154, 273n22, 304
Schiller, Friedrich von 6, 41; *Die Räuber* (*The Robbers*) 6, 41
Schobert, Johann 105–6, 261, 304
Schrattenbach, Archbishop Sigismund von 261
Schröfl, Patr Andreas 186
Schröter, Corona 65, 304
Schubart, Christian Daniel 89, 98n22, 117, 121n28, 238, 295, 304
Schubert, Franz 10, 118, 304
Schulz, Johann Abraham Peter 79, 96, 121n11, 161, 229, 280, 304
Scotland 279, 283
sepolcro 184
Seville 5, 238
Seyler, Abel 153, 304
Shakespeare, William 5, 6, 29, 41, 304; *Tempest* 29
Silva, António José da 166
sinfonia characteristica 83
Singspiel 143n18, 153–6, 169, 169n5, 203, 208, 218, 250, 261, 263, 269, 280
Singstunde (or Singing Time) 193
Skjöldebrand, Anders Fredrik 231
Smith, Sir John Stafford 291

Sodi, Carlo 184, 304
Sokolovsky, Mikhail 164, 304
Soler, Padre Antonio 238, 304
Soler, Vincent Martin y 162, 238, 302
sonata principle 82, 85, 92–3, 104
Sophie Magdalene, Queen of Denmark 227
Sousa, João de 239
Spain 16, 28, 34, 94, 113, 125, 128, 139, 160, 165–7, 169n12, 183, 212, 223, 225, 238–9, 241–2, 247n13, 256, 277, 281, 298, 304, 309
Spangler, Johann Michael 250
Spieß, Pater Meinrad 99, 121n1, 196n11
Sporck, Count Anton 218
Stadler, Anton 58, 304
Stadtpfeifer 61, 303
Stamitz, Anton 73n32, 219
Stamitz, Carl 219
Stamitz, Jan (Johann) 31, 33, 58, 66, 73n32, 83, 88–90, 94, 174, 177, 205, 218–19, 282, 308; *La melodia Germanica* (Op. 11) 31, *32*, 33
Standfuß, Johann Georg 153, 304
Stenborg, Carl 162, 304
Stenborg, Petter 161, 304
Stephanie Jr, Gottlob 154, 269, 304
stile antico 171, 216
Stockholm 23n17, 47n3, 62, 74, 88, *130*, 132, 161–2, *163*, 167, 169, 221, 229, 230–1, 231–2, 246, 247nn5–6, 256, 281, 294, *294*, 295n4, 308; *Musikaliskt tidsfördrif* 231, 293, *294*; *Nytta och Enighet* 232; *Nytta och Nöje* 231; Riddarhus 229–31, *230*; *Utile dulci* 231
Storace, Stephen 160, 304
St. Petersburg 128, 162, 164, 190, 232–3, *232*; Kamenny (Bolshoi) Theatre 164; Petrovsky Theatre 164
Strasbourg 37, 168, 182, 266, 289
Streuensee, Johann Friedrich von 160, 247n3, 304
Sturm und Drang 6, 7, 10, 24, 38, 41–2, 85, 156
Stuttgart 84, 153, 220, 261
style brisé 29
Süßmayr, Franz Xaver 270
Sulzer, Johann Georg 19, 96, 97n8, 304
Sweden 13, 34, 87, 128, *130*, 151, 160–2, *163*, 164, 226, 232, 246, 272n2, 277, 280–1, 287, 293
Swieten, Baron Gottfried van 204, 259, 269, 305
Swift, Jonathan: *A Modest Proposal* 5; *Gulliver's Travels* 5
Switzerland 171, *172*, 261, 278, 281
Symphonie en quatour 110
Symphonie périodique 84

Tahiti 240–1
Tartini, Giuseppe 75, 304
Taylor, Raynor 167, 304
Teixeira, Antonio 166
Telemann, Georg Philipp 11, 75, 101, 120, 171, 305
Temanza, Andrea 87, 305
Tenducci, Giusto Fernando (Senesino) 28, 64, 77, 305
Thielo, Carl August 160, 305
Thomson, James 285

Thomson, William 278
Toeschi, Carl 219, 305
Tomasini, Luigi 257
tonadilla 166
Tonkünstlersozietät 204, 211
Touchmoulin, Joseph 235, 305
Traeg, Johann (publisher) 268
Tragédie lyrique: opera lyrique 144
Treaty of Utrecht 214
trio sonata 34, 87, 100, *100*, 107–8
Tuček, Jan 218, 305
Tůma, Antonín 218
Türk, Daniel Gottlob 31, 121n8, 305

Ulhoorn, Jan 87
Umlauf, Ignaz 154, 269, 305
United Kingdom 3, 8, 189, 201, 209
United States of America 189, 240, 244; California 241, 272n6, 309; Louisiana 241; War for Independence 167
Uttini, Francesco Antonio Baldassare 28, 128, 161, 230, 305

Vanbrugh, Edward 209, 305
Vanhal, Johann Baptist 42, 91, 121n24, 305
Varesco, Abbé Gianbattista 268
Venezuela 242; Caracas 242; Chacao School 242
Venice 4, 16, 71, 75, 128, *131*, 133–4, *134*, 136, 138, 142n7, 171, 212–14, *214–15*, 216, 220, 238; La Fenice 129, *131*, 214; *ospedale* 16
Versailles 3–4, 12, 205, 261, 267
Vienna 10, 16, 19, 24–5, 34, 36, 41, 63, 67, 74, 82–3, 85, 88, 91–4, 98n22, 110, 112, 125, 128, 134, 137, 142, 145, 152, 154, 160, 171, 173, 175, 184, 196n3, 201–4, *202–3*, 206–7, 211, 214, 217–18, 221, 223, 225, 234, 248–52, *250*, 256–9, *260*, 261, 265–6, 268–70, 272n2, 272n5, 279, 291, 295, 298, 304, 308; Burgtheater 137, *203*, 269; *Gesellschaft der Associierten* 269; Hofoper 154, 217; Kärntnertor 154, 202–3, *202*, 269; Leopoldstadt theatre 155; St. Stephen's 128, 175, 223, 249–50, 270; Theater auf der Wieden 270
Viennese Classicism 10
villancico 183, 241

Ville-Issey, Jean Nicholas Jadot de 203
Viola, Anselm 239
Viotti, GIovanni Battista 206, 305
Vivaldi, Antonio 11, 16, 34, 75, 202, 214, 305
Vogler, Abbé Georg Joseph 17, 162, 219–20, 231, 280–2, 294, 305
Voltaire 3, 5, 10, 204, 305

Wagenseil, Christoph 89, 110, 251, 305
Walther, Thomas Christian 229, 305
Wanzura, Arnošt 233
War of the Austrian Succession 13, 201, 209
Washington, George 245, 290
Watt, James 7–8, 305
Watteau, Jean-Antoine 4, *4*
Weber, Aloysia 266
Weber, Carl Maria von 11, 156
Weber, Constanze 269
Weidinger, Anton 62, 305
Weisse, Christian Felix 147, 153, 169n3
Werner, Gregor Joseph 234, 252
Wesley, Charles Sr. 190, 305
Weyse, Christian Felix 229
Wiener Diarium 19, 87
Winston-Salem 193
Wrantizky, Paul 154, 305
Würzburg 219

Zander, Johan David 231
Zappa, Francesco 227
Zarafa, Benigno 240
zarzuela 166
Zaslaw, Neal 11, 23n6, 24, 47n2, 68, 72n27, 82, 225, 249, 307
Zedler, Johann Heinrich 100, 121n3, 306
Zelenka, Jan Dismas 11
Zelter, Carl Friedrich 71, 209, 306
Zeno, Apostolo 133
Zielche, Hans 229
Zingarelli, Niccolò 95, 306
Zinzendorf, Count Nicholas von 192, *193*, 217, 306
Zweibrücken 219

Taylor & Francis eBooks

www.taylorfrancis.com

A single destination for eBooks from Taylor & Francis with increased functionality and an improved user experience to meet the needs of our customers.

90,000+ eBooks of award-winning academic content in Humanities, Social Science, Science, Technology, Engineering, and Medical written by a global network of editors and authors.

TAYLOR & FRANCIS EBOOKS OFFERS:

- A streamlined experience for our library customers
- A single point of discovery for all of our eBook content
- Improved search and discovery of content at both book and chapter level

REQUEST A FREE TRIAL
support@taylorfrancis.com